LERT! EMERGE LERT! EMEF

YOU'RE READING THE WRONG WAY!

1
1
2
2
3
4
3
5
6
4
7
8
5
9
142

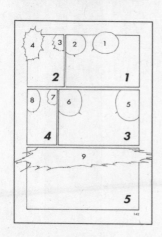

For your own protection, the last page of the book has been sealed off to prevent the ending from being spoiled. To safely consume the contents of *Kaiju No. 8* in their intended order, please flip the book over and start again.

Kaiju No. 8 reads from right to left, starting in the upper-right corner, to preserve the original Japanese orientation of the work. That means that the action, sound effects, and word balloons are completely reversed from English order.

ENTER! DO NOT ENTER! DO NO

A FUTURISTIC TALE OF SAMURAI ADVENTURE FROM THE CREATOR OF *NARUTO*!

SAMURAI 8
THE TALE OF HACHIMARU

Story by Masashi Kishimoto Art by Akira Okubo

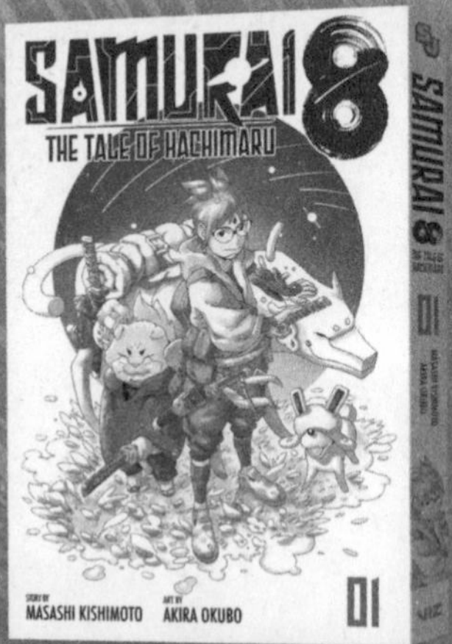
SAMURAI 8
THE TALE OF HACHIMARU
STORY BY MASASHI KISHIMOTO
ART BY AKIRA OKUBO
01
SAMURAI 8 THE TALE OF HACHIMARU
01
VIZ

Becoming a samurai seems like an impossible dream for Hachimaru, a boy who can't even survive without the help of his father. But when a samurai cat appears before him, his whole life changes! The legendary creator of *Naruto* and a rising manga star come together to bring you this science fiction samurai epic!

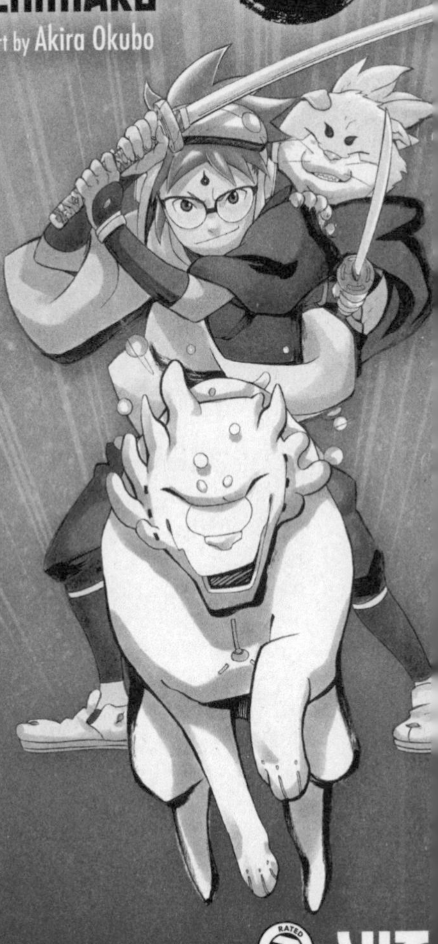

RATED T TEEN

VIZ

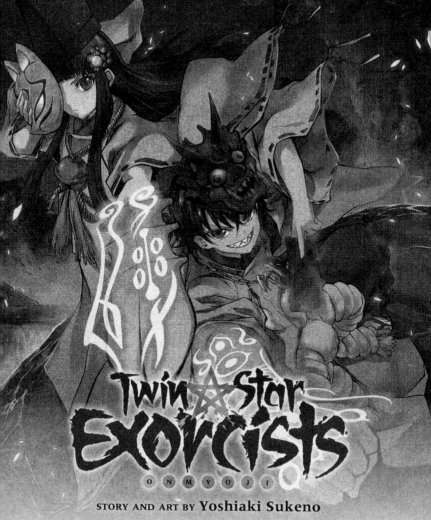

STORY AND ART BY Yoshiaki Sukeno

The action-packed romantic comedy from the creator of *Good Luck Girl!*

Rokuro dreams of becoming *anything* but an exorcist! Then mysterious Benio turns up. The pair are dubbed the "Twin Star Exorcists" and learn they are fated to marry...

Can Rokuro escape both fates?

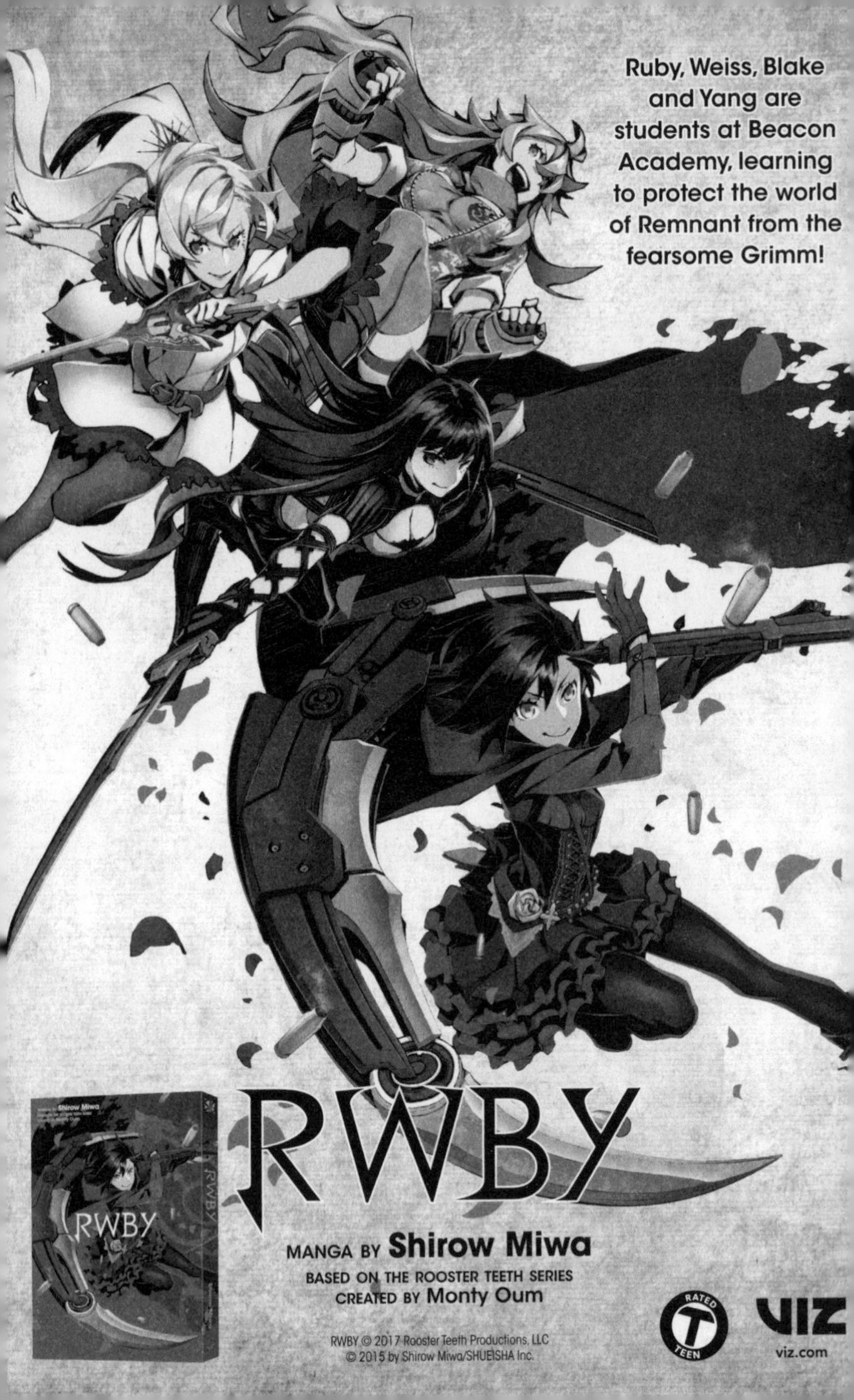
Ruby, Weiss, Blake and Yang are students at Beacon Academy, learning to protect the world of Remnant from the fearsome Grimm!
RWBY
MANGA BY Shirow Miwa
BASED ON THE ROOSTER TEETH SERIES
CREATED BY Monty Oum
RWBY © 2017 Rooster Teeth Productions, LLC
© 2015 by Shirow Miwa/SHUEISHA Inc.
RATED T TEEN
VIZ
viz.com

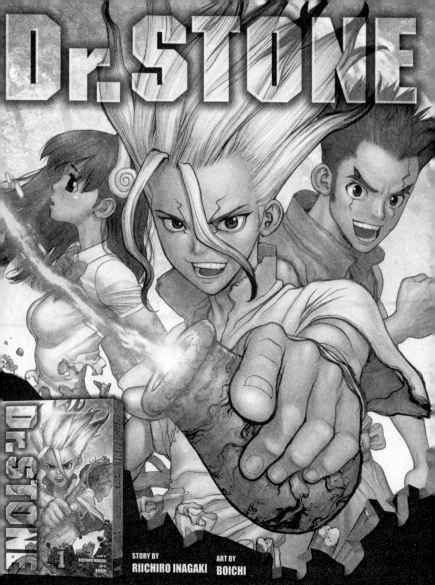

Dr.STONE

STORY BY
RIICHIRO INAGAKI

ART BY
BOICHI

One fateful day, all of humanity turned to stone. Many millennia later, Taiju frees himself from petrification and finds himself surrounded by statues. The situation looks grim—until he runs into his science-loving friend Senku! Together they plan to restart

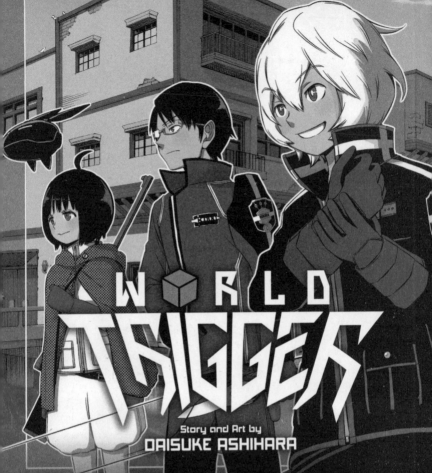

WORLD TRIGGER

Story and Art by
DAISUKE ASHIHARA

DESTROY THY NEIGHBOR!

A gate to another dimension has burst open, and invincible monsters called Neighbors invade Earth. Osamu Mikumo may not be the best among the elite warriors who co-opt other-dimensional technology to fight back, but along with his Neighbor friend Yuma, he'll do whatever it takes to defend life on Earth as we know it

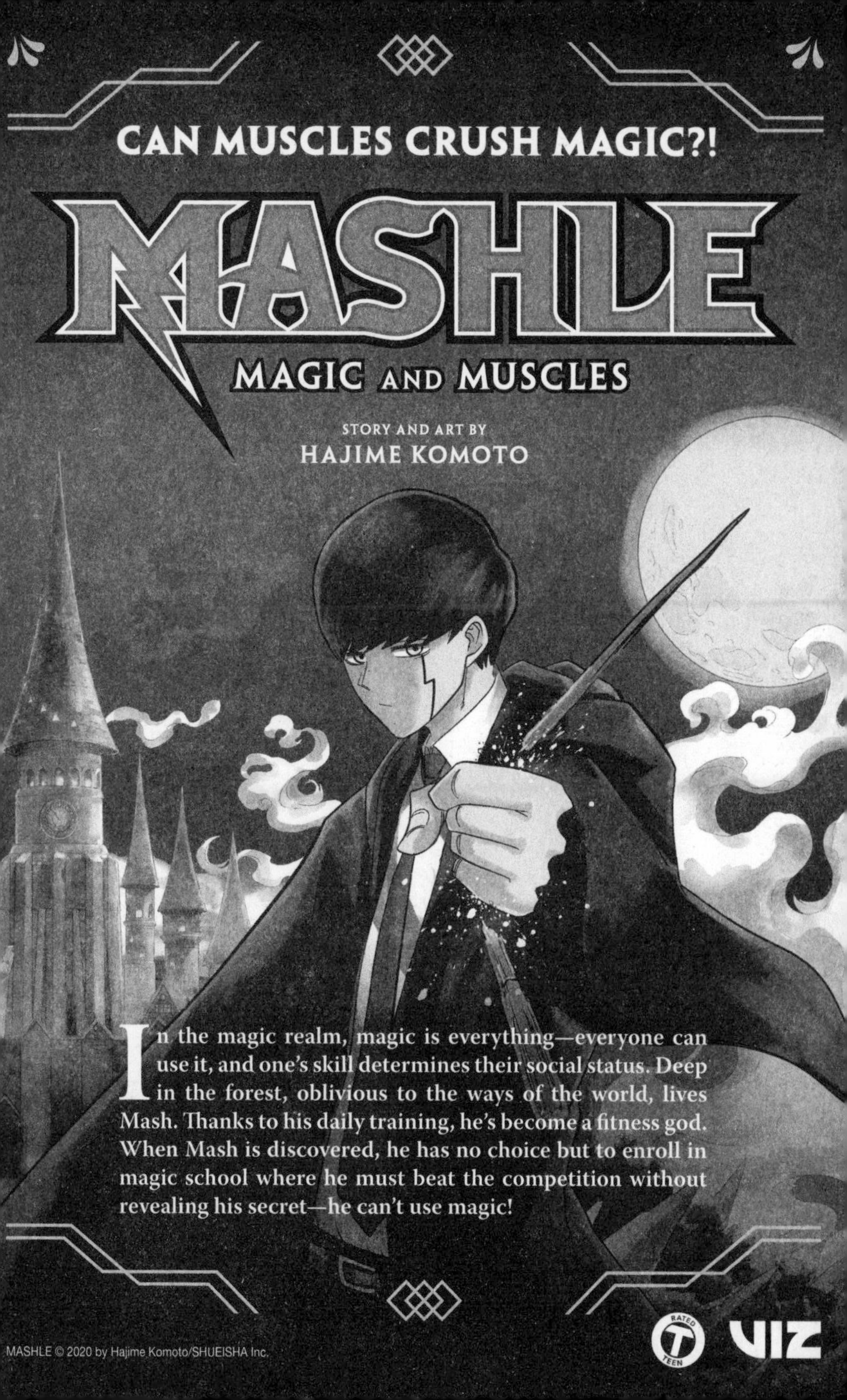

CAN MUSCLES CRUSH MAGIC?!

MASHLE

MAGIC AND MUSCLES

STORY AND ART BY
HAJIME KOMOTO

In the magic realm, magic is everything—everyone can use it, and one's skill determines their social status. Deep in the forest, oblivious to the ways of the world, lives Mash. Thanks to his daily training, he's become a fitness god. When Mash is discovered, he has no choice but to enroll in magic school where he must beat the competition without revealing his secret—he can't use magic!

KAIJU NO. 8 5

SHONEN JUMP EDITION

STORY AND ART BY
NAOYA MATSUMOTO

TRANSLATION
DAVID EVELYN

TOUCH-UP ART & LETTERING
BRANDON BOVIA

DESIGN
JIMMY PRESLER

EDITOR
KARLA CLARK

Printed in the U.S.A.

Published by VIZ Media, LLC
P.O. Box 77010
San Francisco, CA 94107

10 9 8 7 6 5 4 3 2 1
First printing, January 2023

ratings.viz.com RATED T TEEN

PARENTAL ADVISORY
KAIJU NO. 8 is rated T for Teen and is recommended for ages 13 and up. This volume contains crude humor and depictions of violence.

VIZ MEDIA
viz.com

SHONEN JUMP

NAOYA MATSUMOTO

We're finally at volume 5! I wouldn't have made it this far without all of you readers out there. Thank you so much!! It's a long ways off, but my next goal is to make it to volume 10!

Naoya Matsumoto published his first serialized series, *Neko Wappa!*, in *Weekly Shonen Jump* in 2009. His next series, *Pochi Kuro*, began serialization in *Shonen Jump+* in 2014. *Kaiju No. 8* is his follow-up series.

KAIJU NO. 8 ASSISTANTS

BACKGROUND ART **OSAMU KOIWAI (OSA PROD.)**

FINISHING WORK **JIRO SAKURA**

WEAPON DESIGN **MANTOHIHI BINTA**

KAIJU NO. 8 MINI BACKGROUND INFORMATION

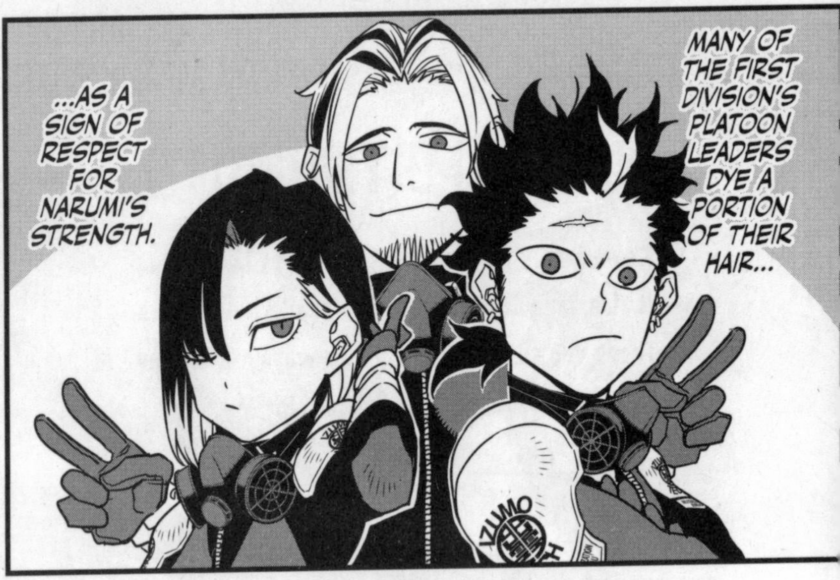
MANY OF THE FIRST DIVISION'S PLATOON LEADERS DYE A PORTION OF THEIR HAIR...
...AS A SIGN OF RESPECT FOR NARUMI'S STRENGTH.

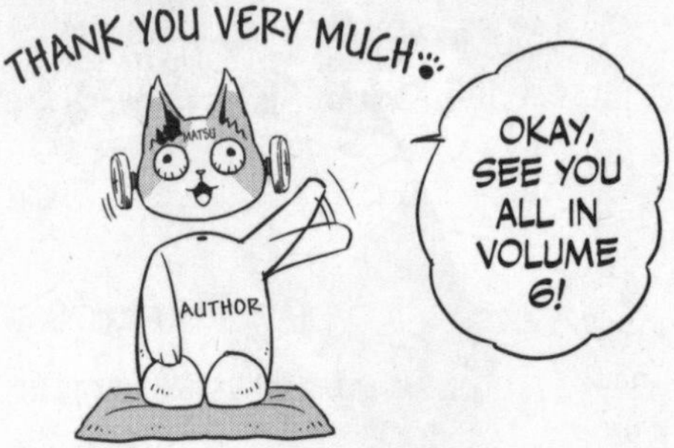
THANK YOU VERY MUCH
OKAY, SEE YOU ALL IN VOLUME 6!
MATSU
AUTHOR

KAIJU NO. 8

5

STORY AND ART BY
NAOYA MATSUMOTO

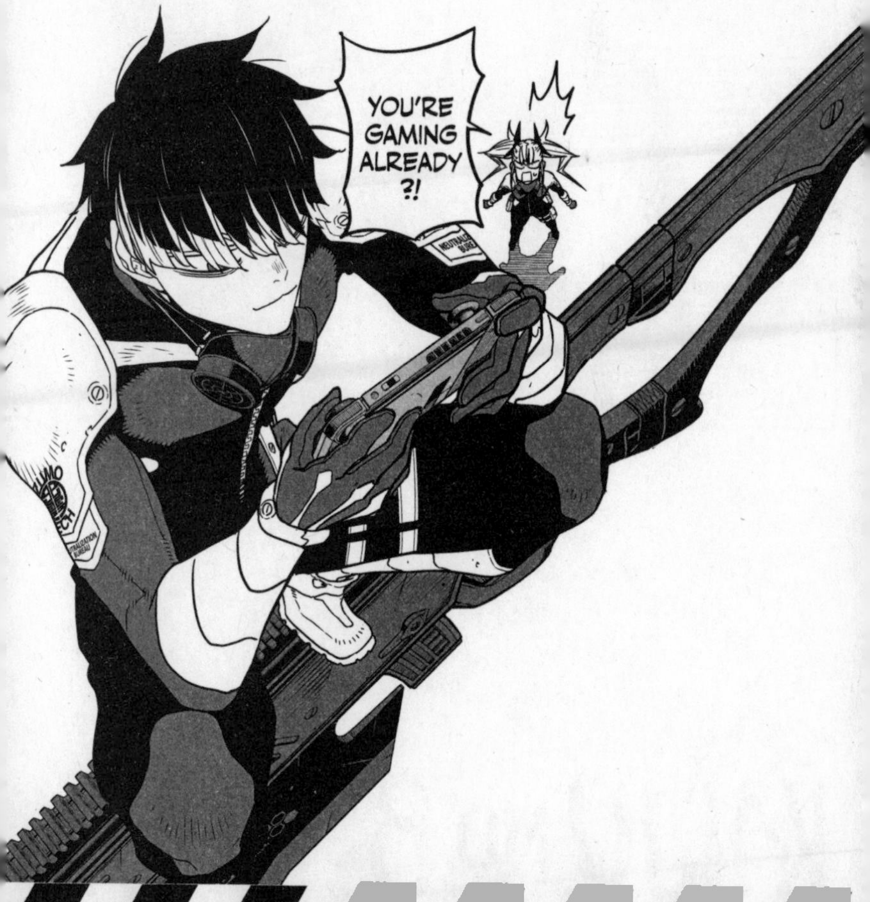
YOU'RE GAMING ALREADY ?!

KAIJU NO.8

KAIJU NO. 8 BACKGROUND INFORMATION

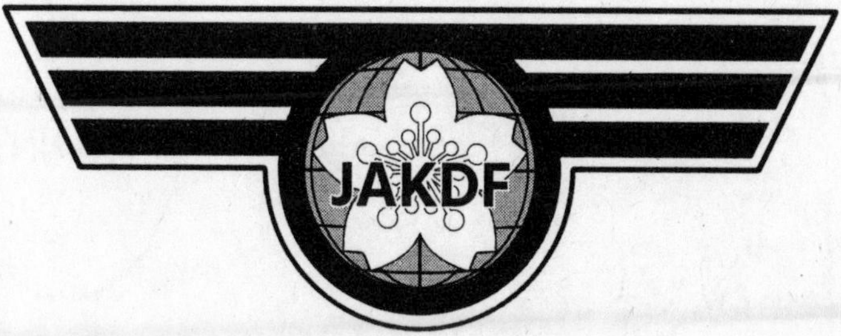
JAKDF

Defense Force Emblem
Japan Anti-Kaiju Defense Force

I wanted to accentuate the Defense Force vibe with some homages to Japan, so I incorporated a torii gate and a cherry blossom.

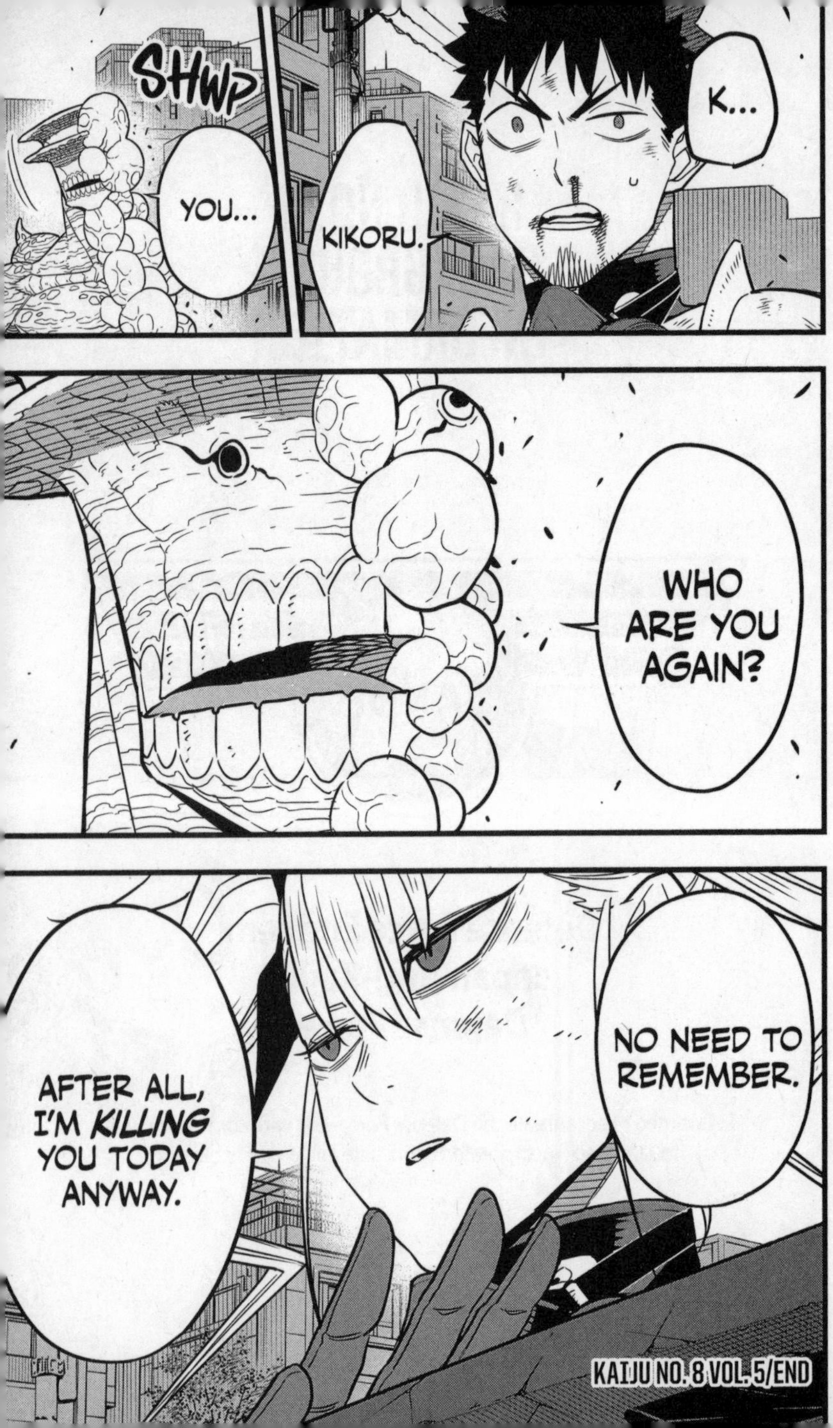
K...
KIKORU.
SHWP
YOU...
WHO ARE YOU AGAIN?
NO NEED TO REMEMBER.
AFTER ALL, I'M *KILLING* YOU TODAY ANYWAY.
KAIJU NO. 8 VOL. 5/END

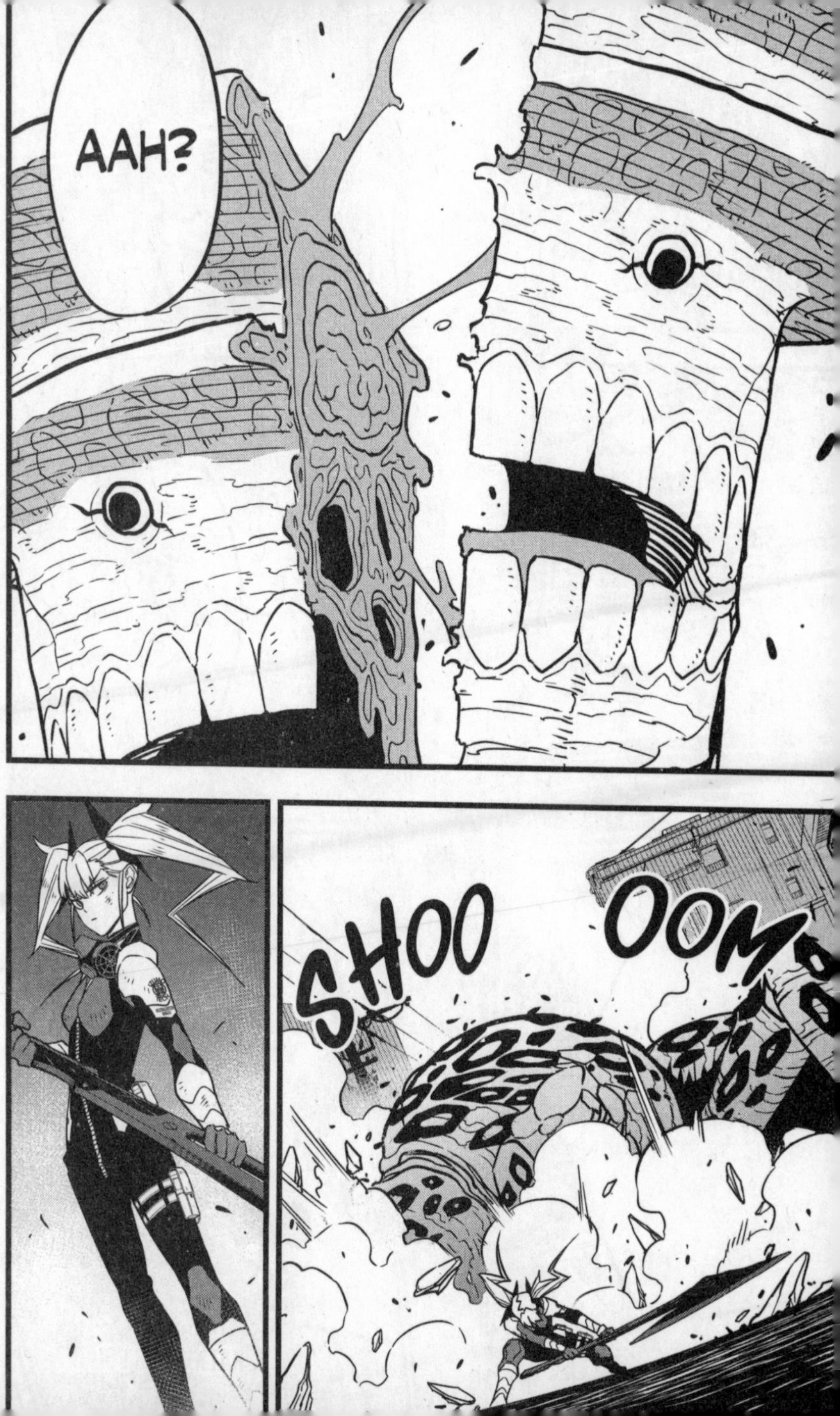
AAH?
SHOO OOM

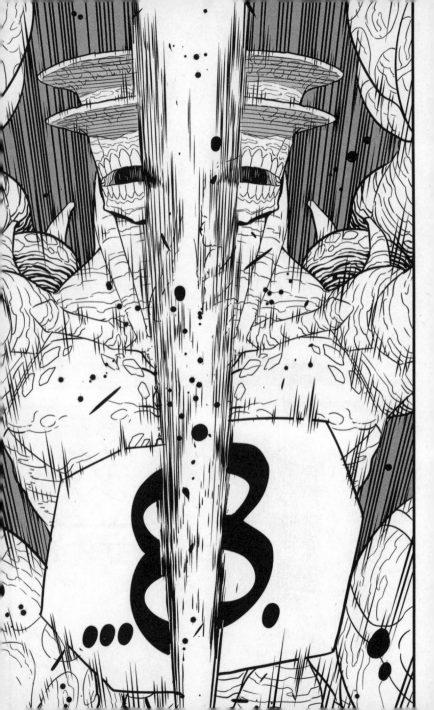

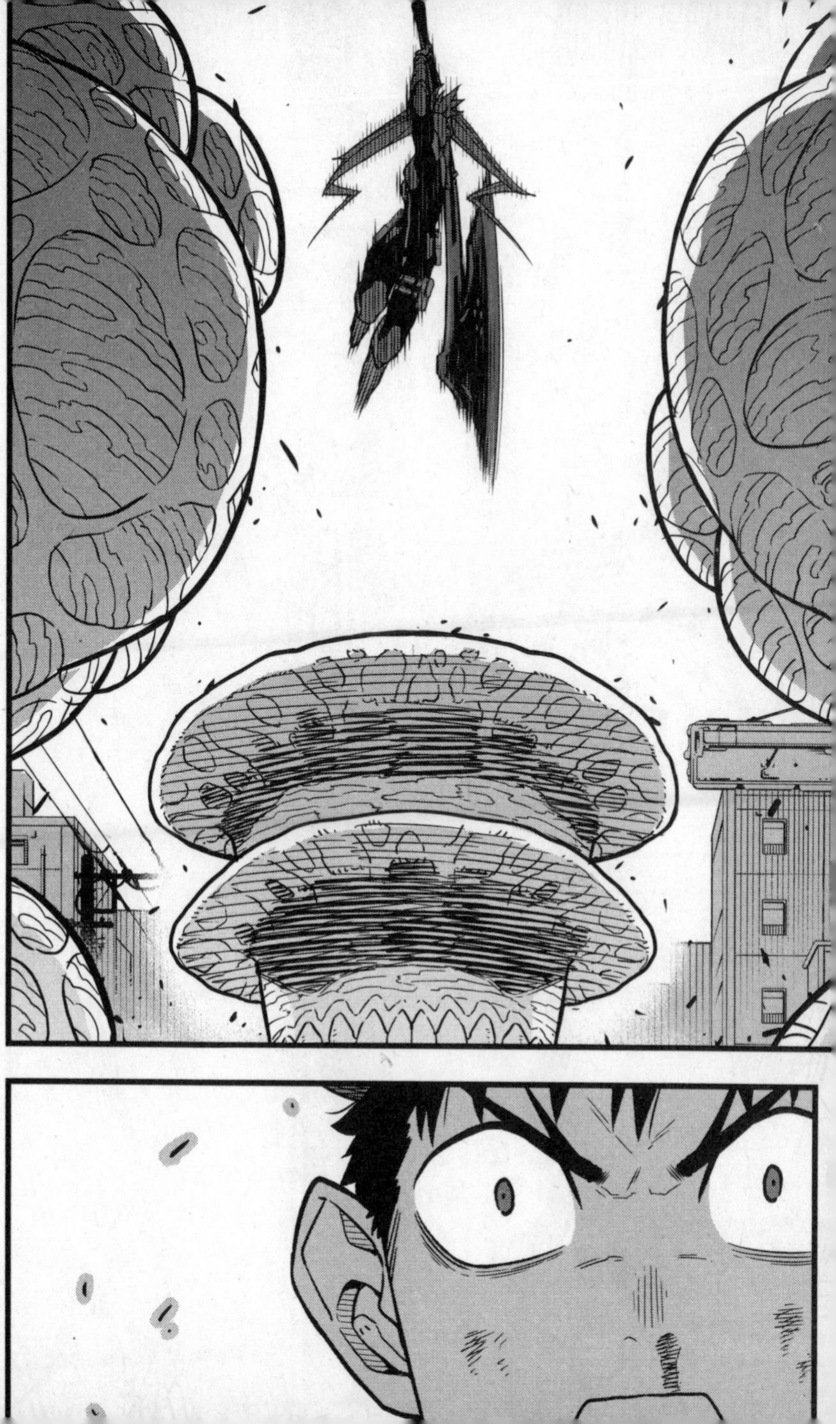

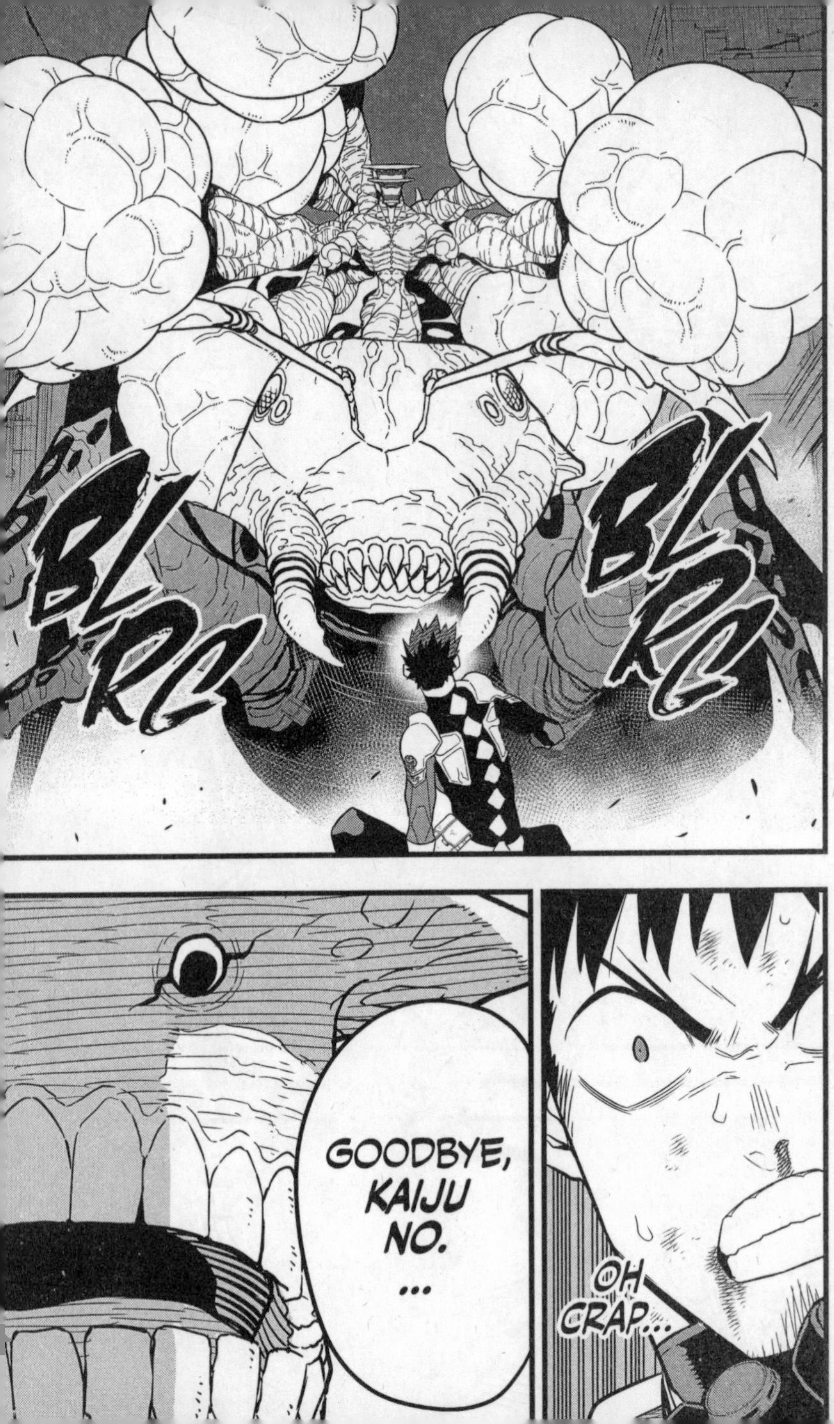
OH CRAP...
GOODBYE, KAIJU NO. ...

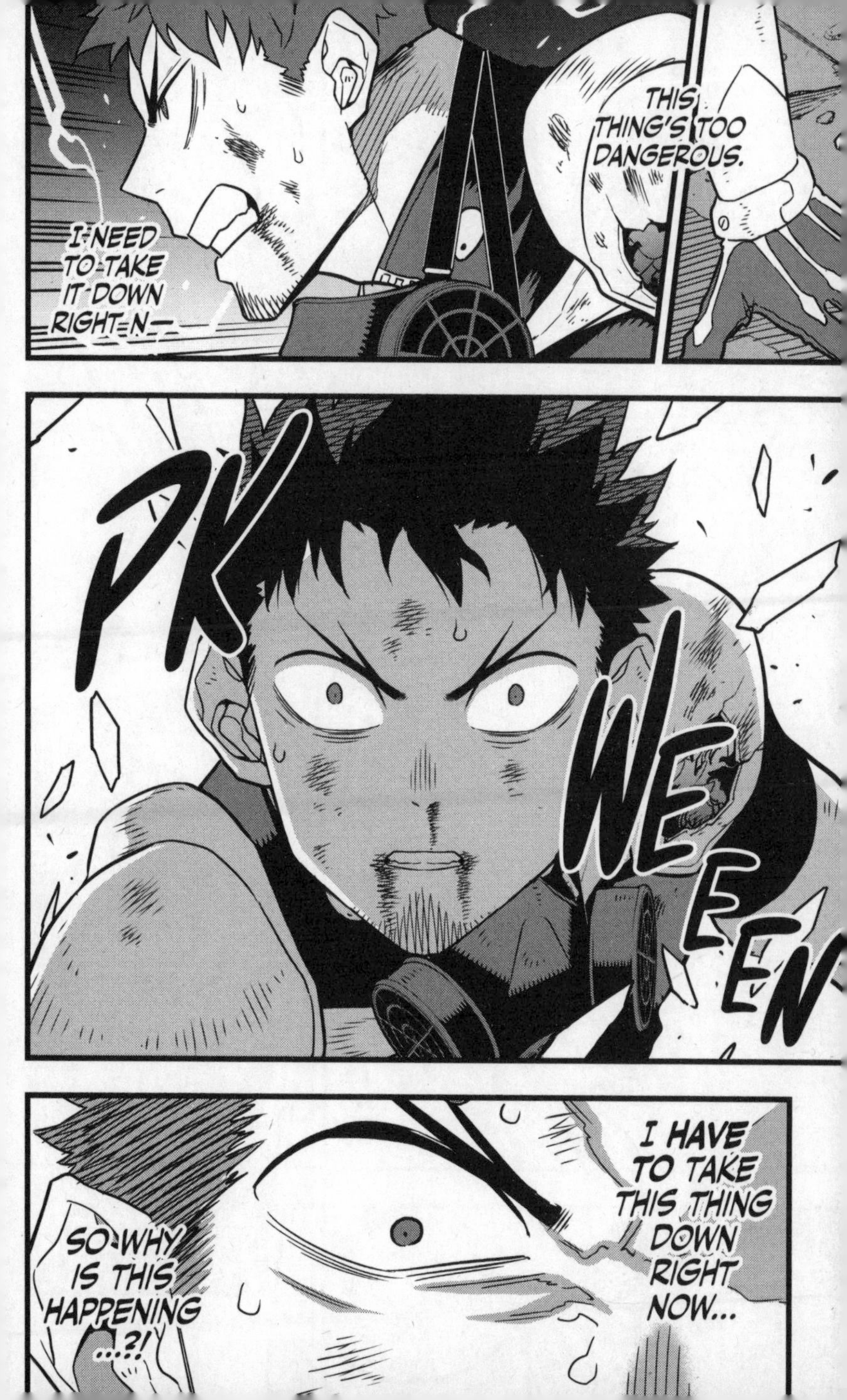
THIS THING'S TOO DANGEROUS.
I NEED TO TAKE IT DOWN RIGHT N—
PKWEEEEN
I HAVE TO TAKE THIS THING DOWN RIGHT NOW...
SO WHY IS THIS HAPPENING ...?!

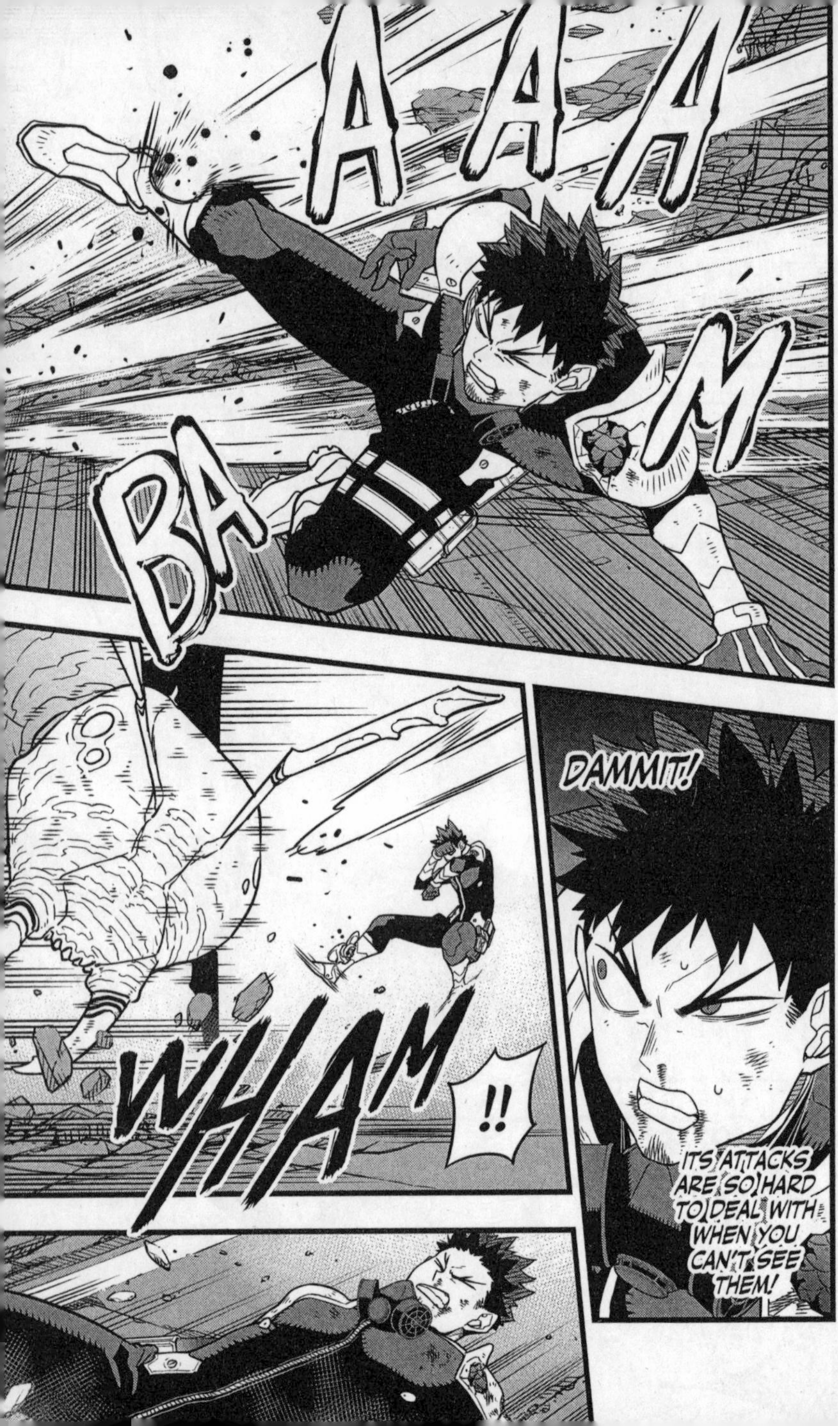
BAAAAM
DAMMIT!
ITS ATTACKS ARE SO HARD TO DEAL WITH WHEN YOU CAN'T SEE THEM!
WHAM
!!

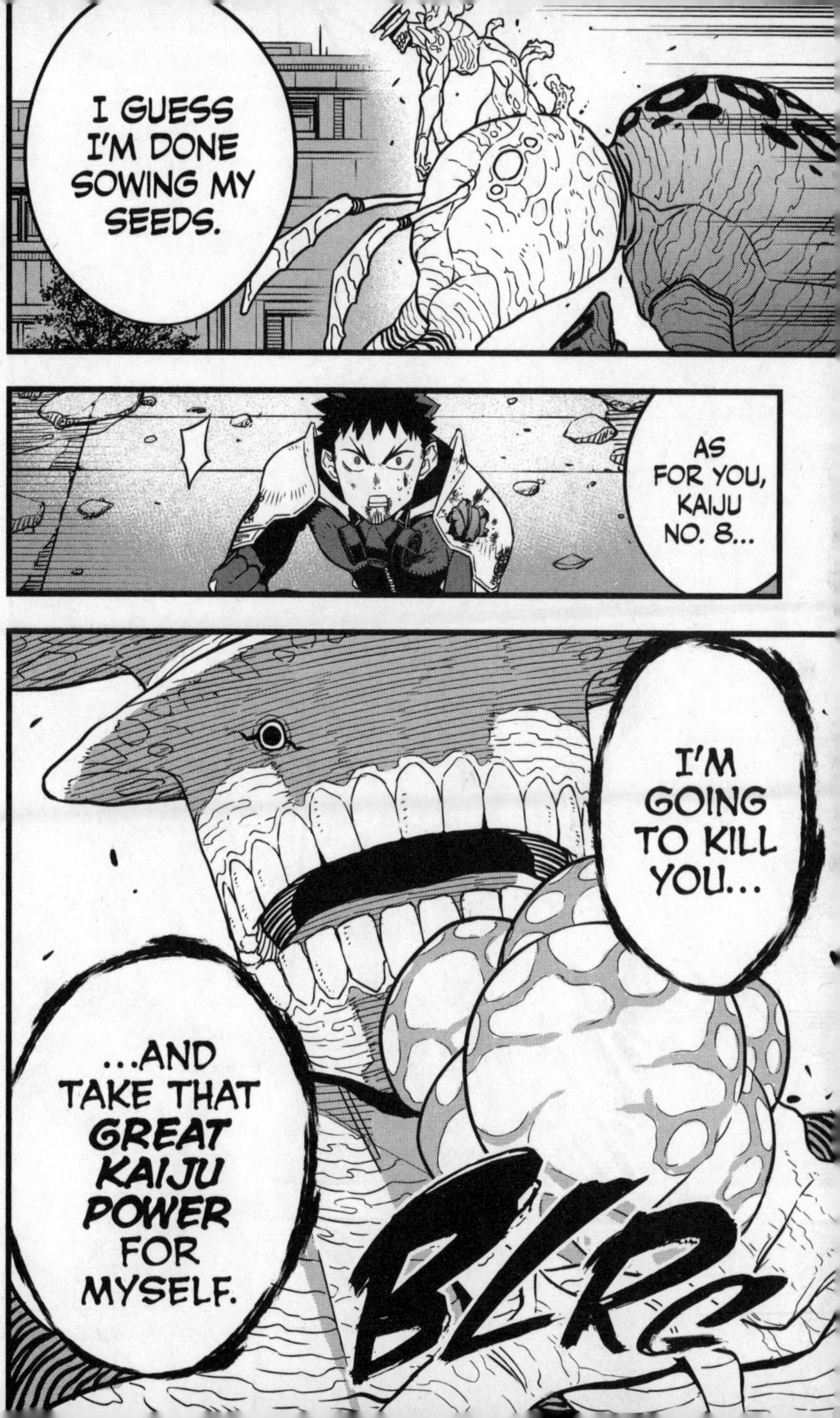
I GUESS I'M DONE SOWING MY SEEDS.
AS FOR YOU, KAIJU NO. 8...
I'M GOING TO KILL YOU...
...AND TAKE THAT *GREAT KAIJU POWER* FOR MYSELF.
BLRG

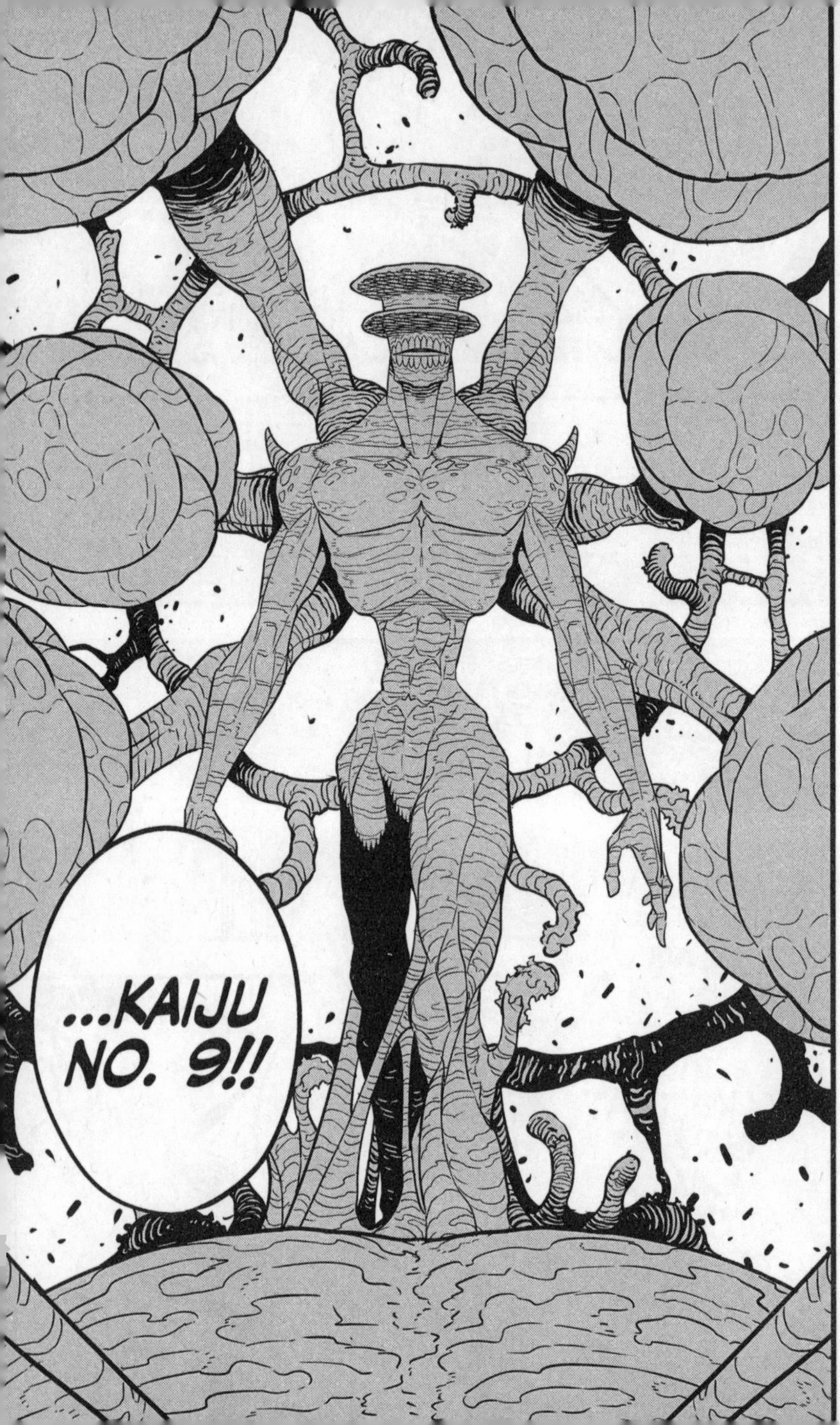
...KAIJU NO. 9!!

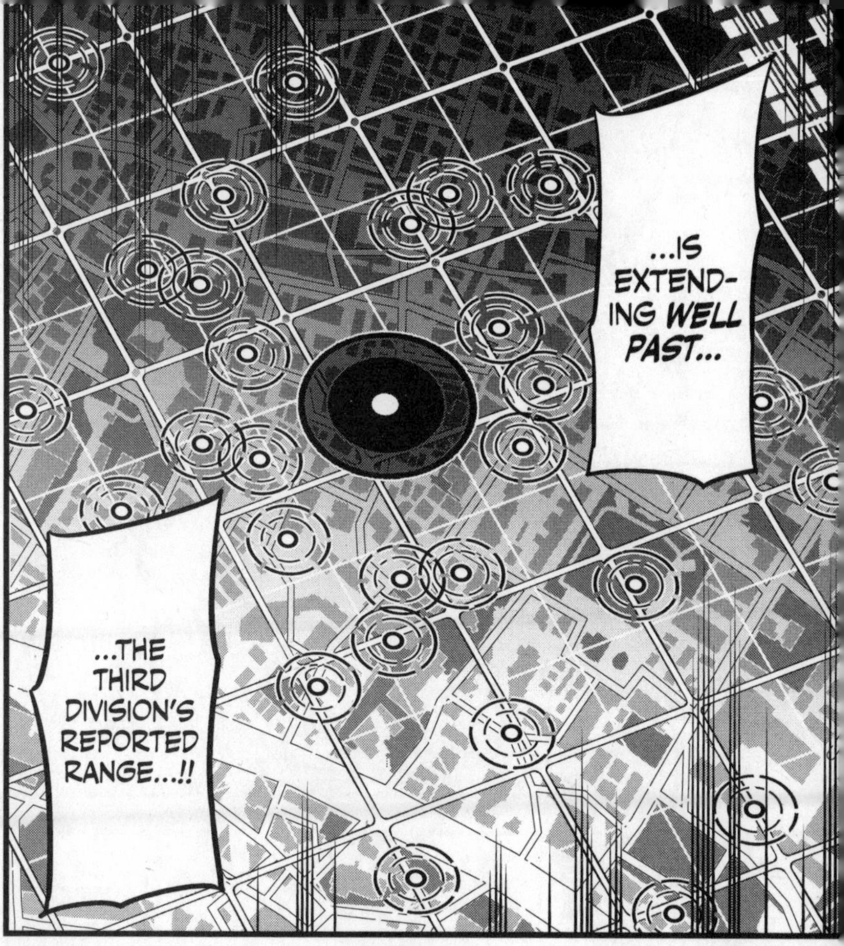
...IS EXTEND-ING *WELL PAST*...
...THE THIRD DIVISION'S REPORTED RANGE...!!
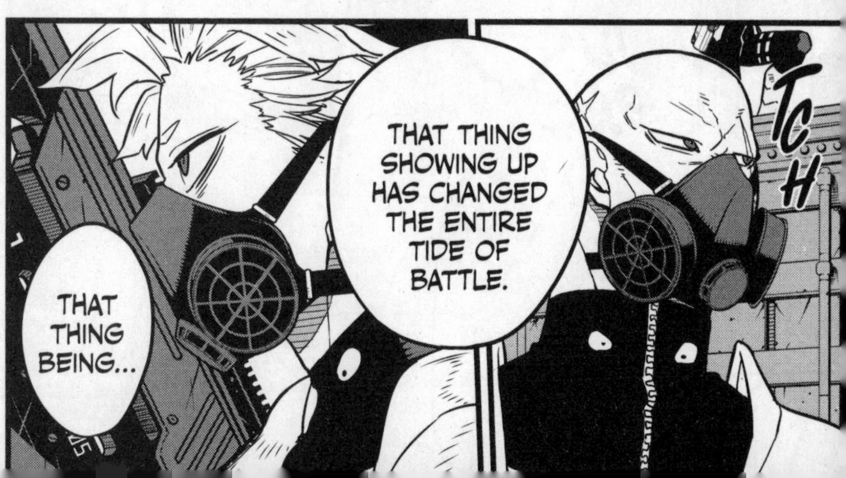
TCH
THAT THING SHOWING UP HAS CHANGED THE ENTIRE TIDE OF BATTLE.
THAT THING BEING...

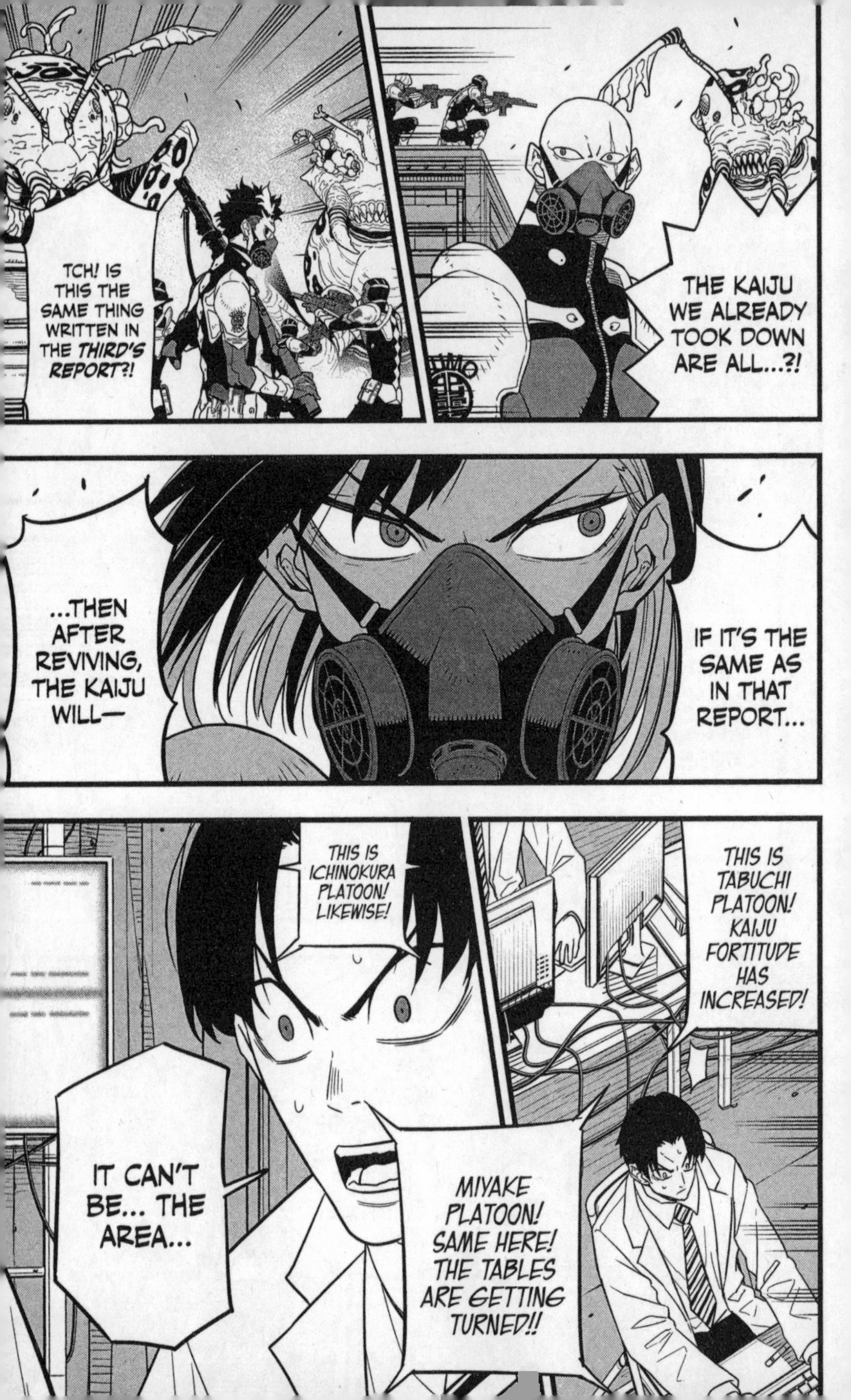
THE KAIJU WE ALREADY TOOK DOWN ARE ALL...?!
TCH! IS THIS THE SAME THING WRITTEN IN THE *THIRD'S REPORT*?!
IF IT'S THE SAME AS IN THAT REPORT...
...THEN AFTER REVIVING, THE KAIJU WILL—
THIS IS TABUCHI PLATOON! KAIJU FORTITUDE HAS INCREASED!
THIS IS ICHINOKURA PLATOON! LIKEWISE!
MIYAKE PLATOON! SAME HERE! THE TABLES ARE GETTING TURNED!!
IT CAN'T BE... THE AREA...

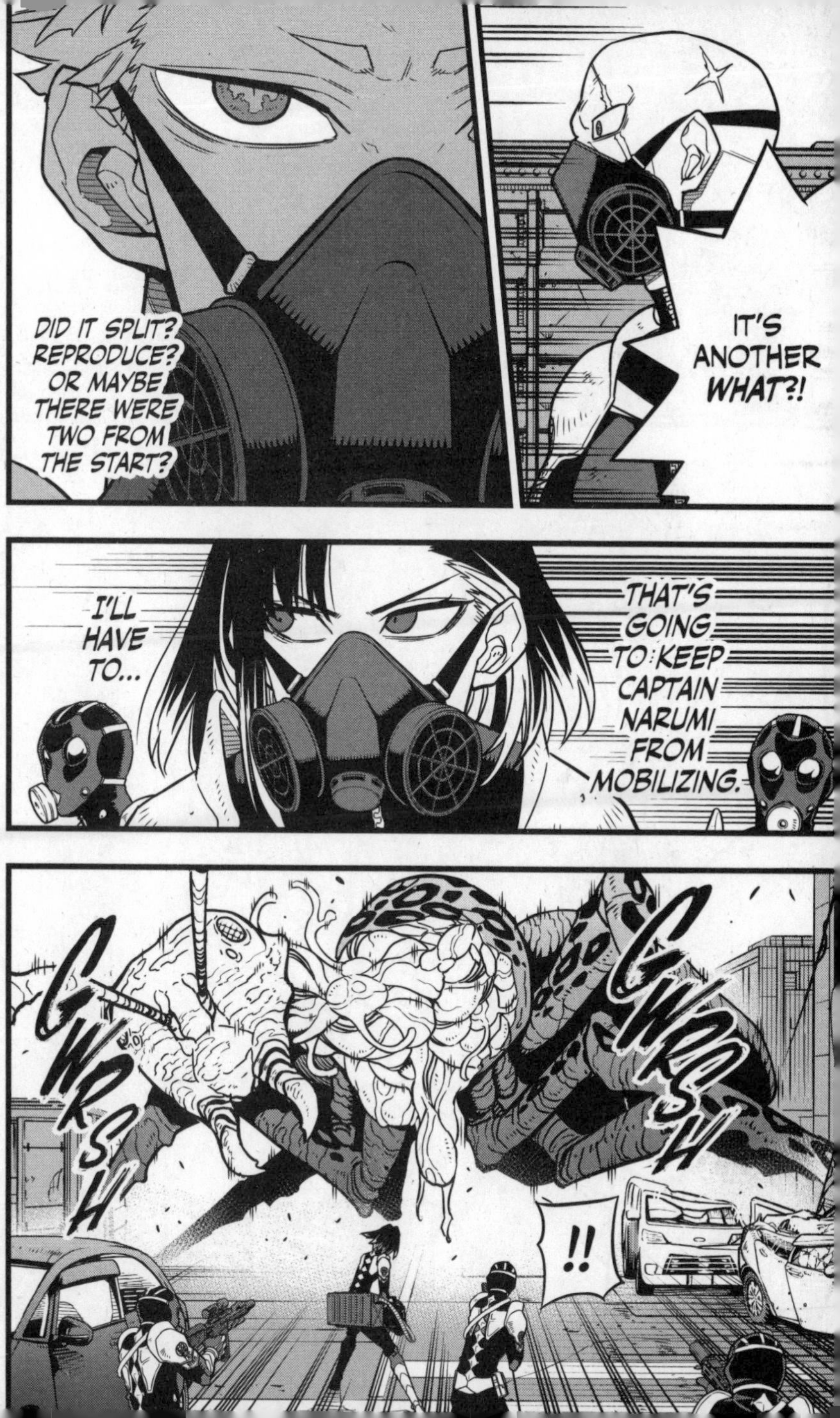
IT'S ANOTHER WHAT?!
DID IT SPLIT? REPRODUCE? OR MAYBE THERE WERE TWO FROM THE START?
THAT'S GOING TO KEEP CAPTAIN NARUMI FROM MOBILIZING.
I'LL HAVE TO...
!!

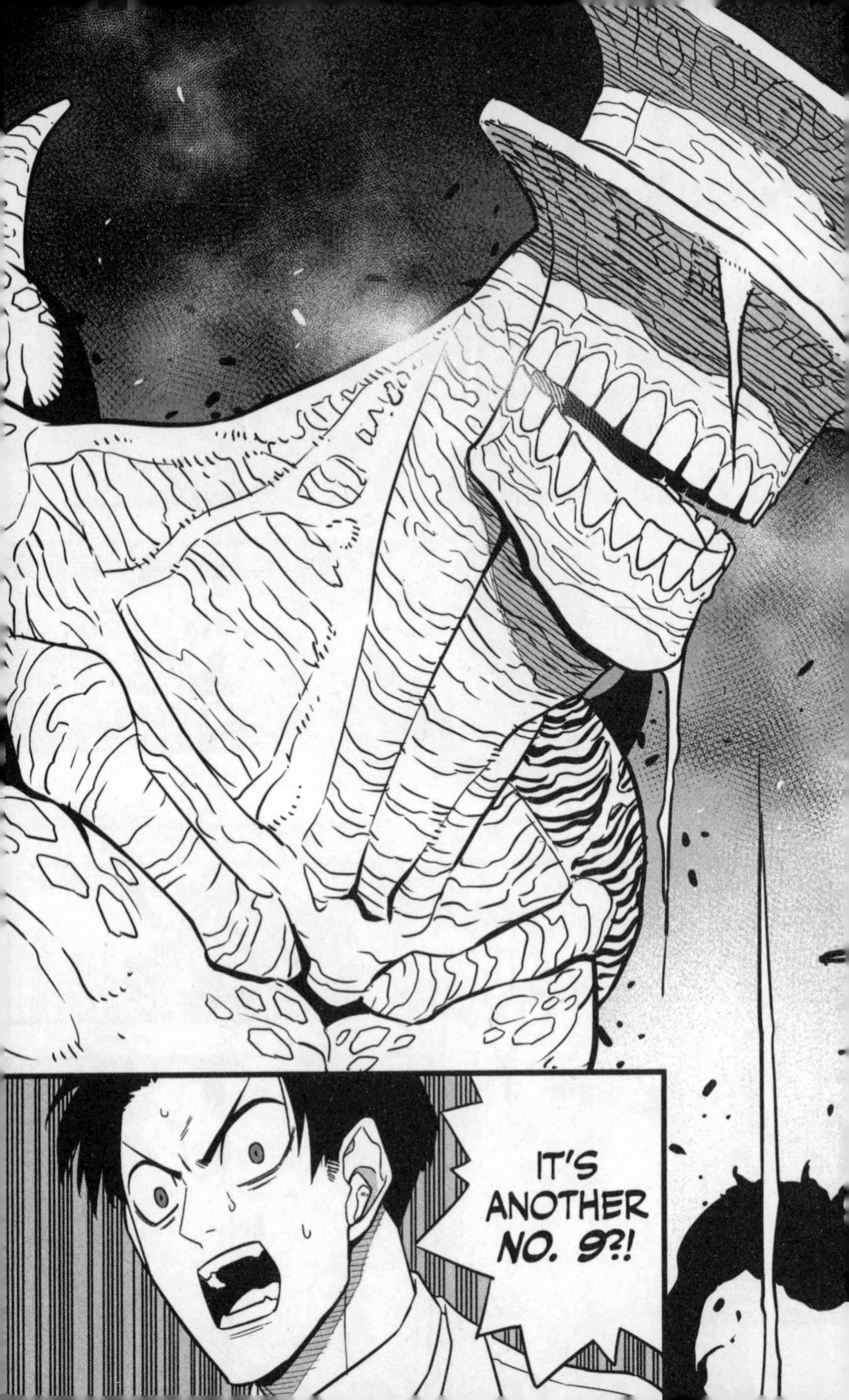
IT'S ANOTHER NO. 9?!

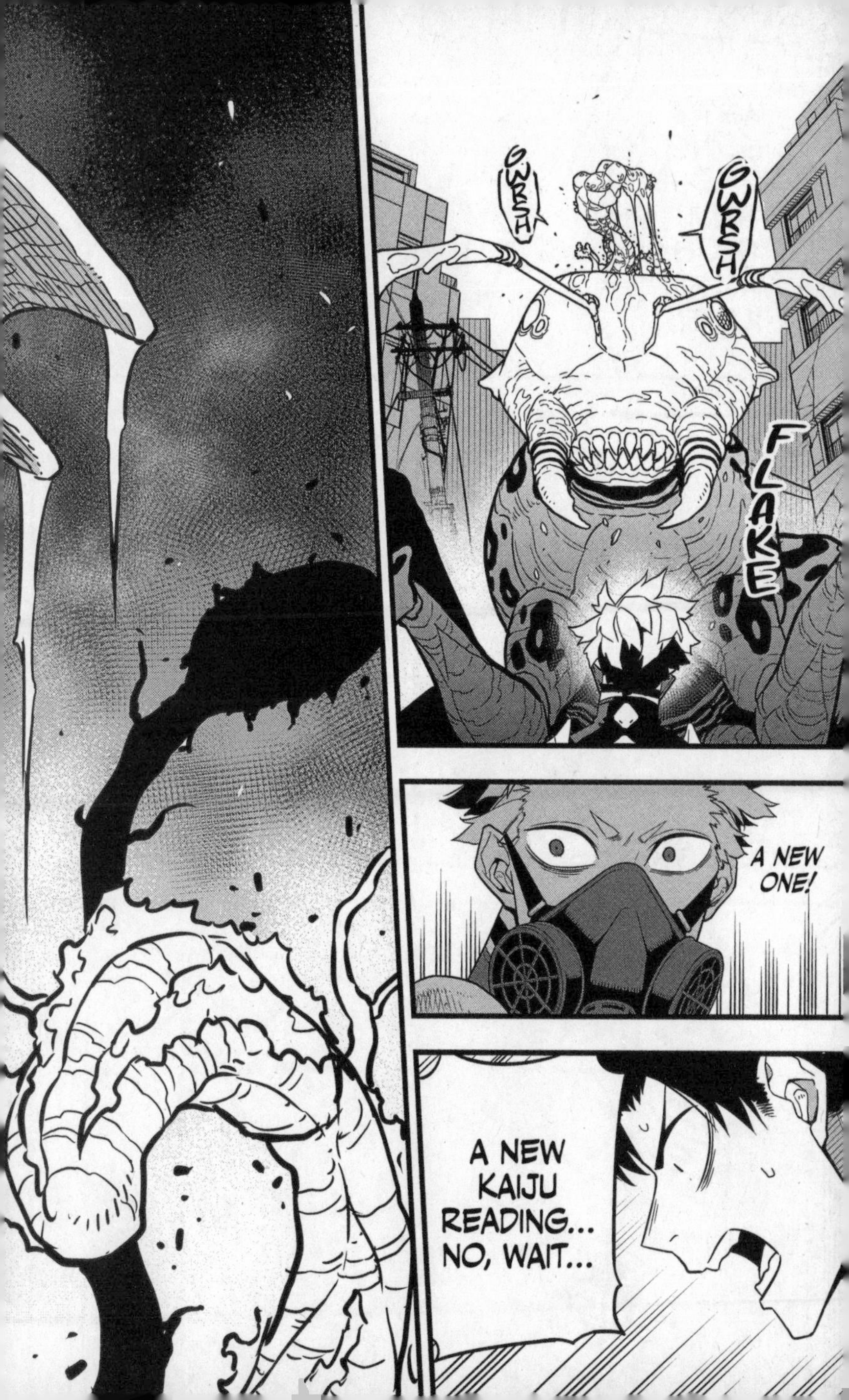
GWRSH
GWRSH
FLAKE
A NEW ONE!
A NEW KAIJU READING... NO, WAIT...

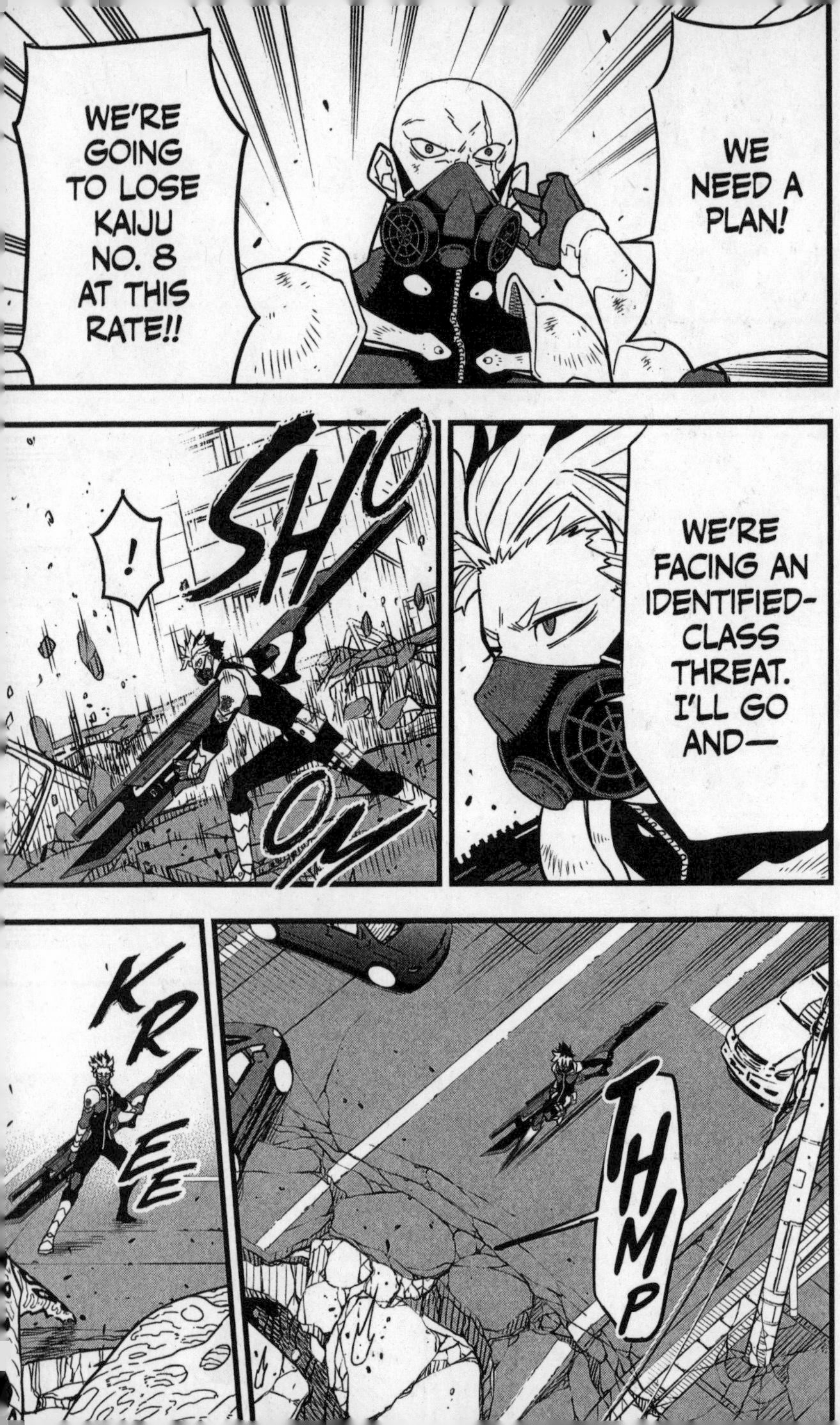

WE NEED A PLAN!
WE'RE GOING TO LOSE KAIJU NO. 8 AT THIS RATE!!
WE'RE FACING AN IDENTIFIED-CLASS THREAT. I'LL GO AND—
SHOOM
!
THMP
KRIEEE

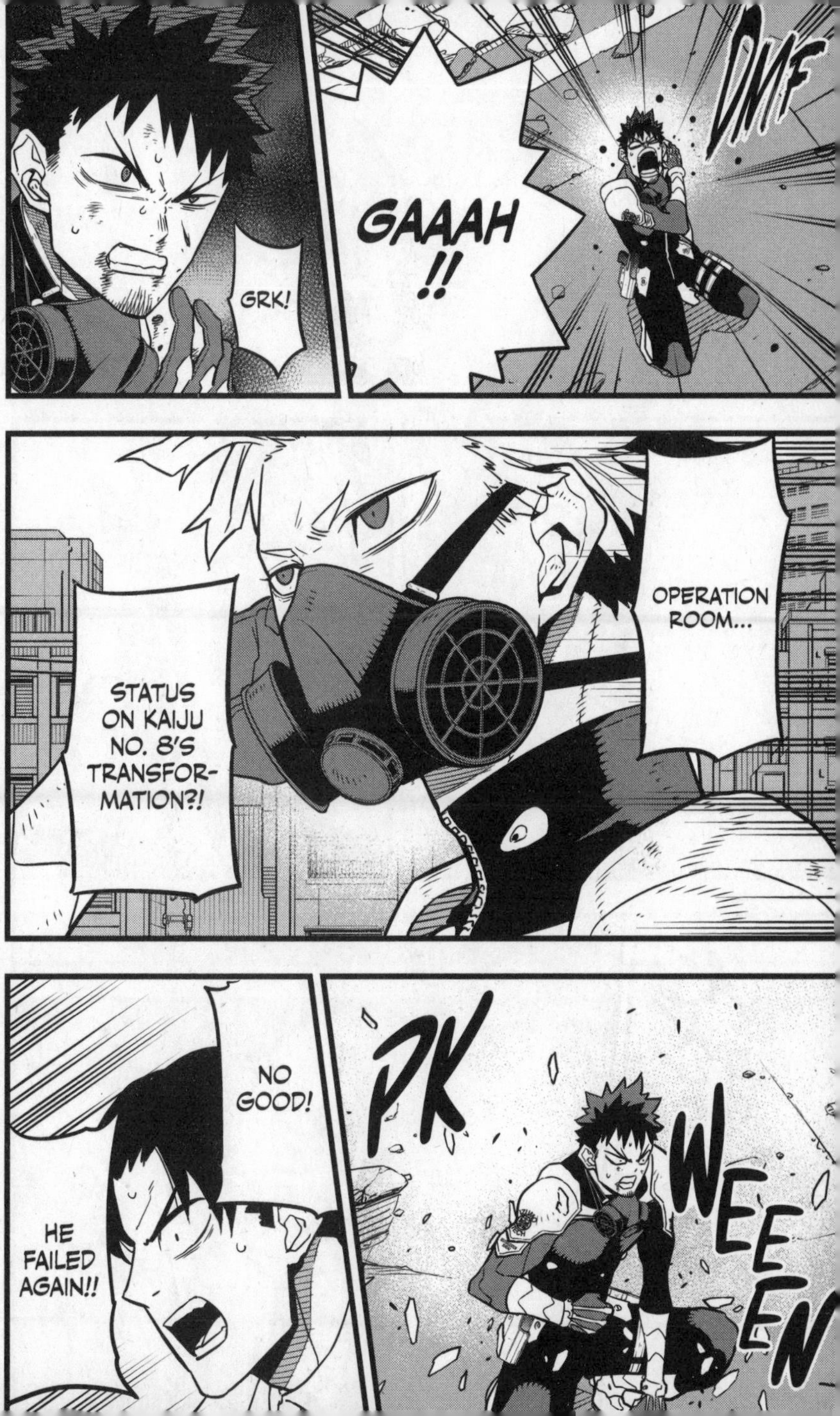
DNF
GAAAH!!
GRK!
OPERATION ROOM...
STATUS ON KAIJU NO. 8'S TRANSFOR-MATION?!
PK
WEEEN
NO GOOD!
HE FAILED AGAIN!!

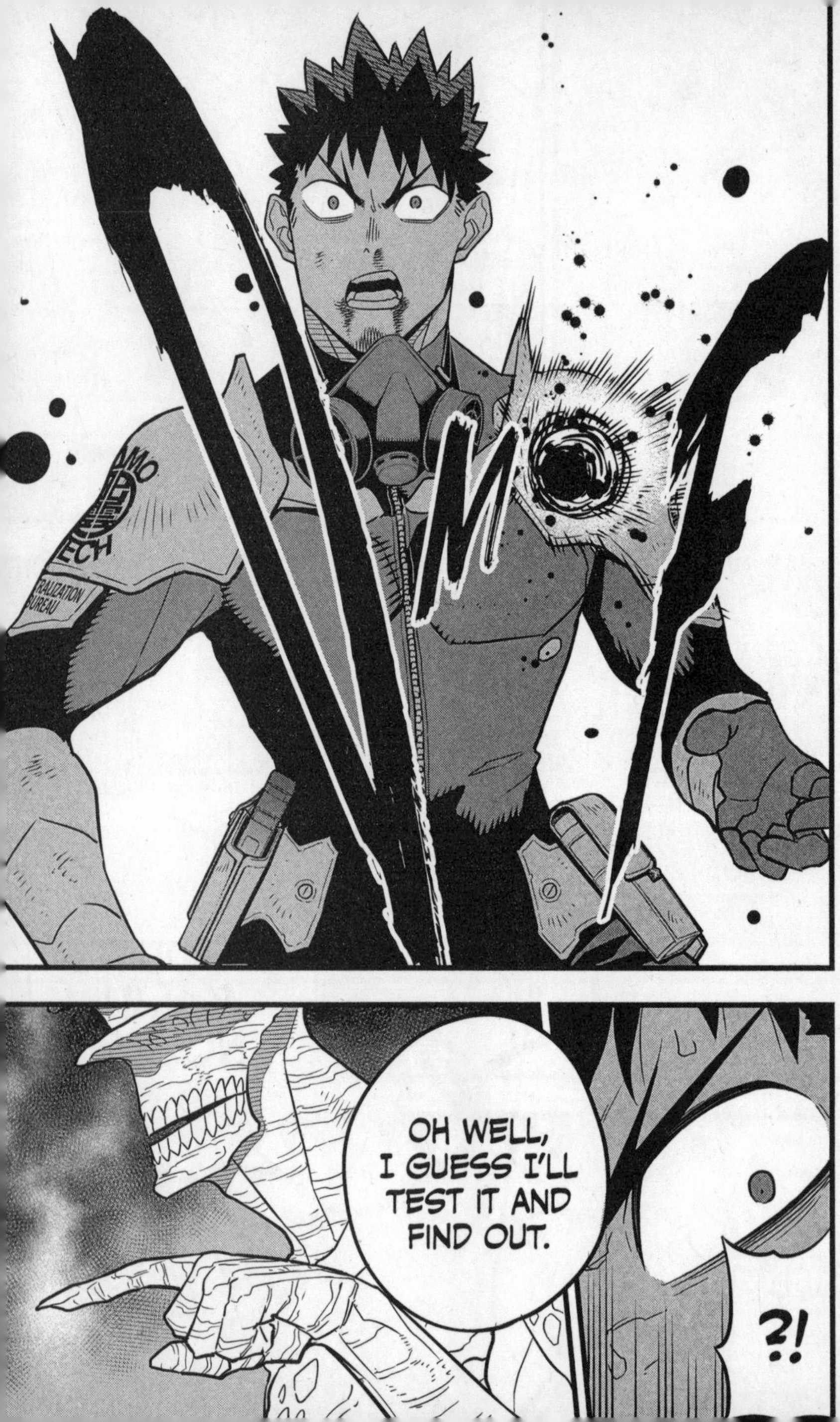
OH WELL, I GUESS I'LL TEST IT AND FIND OUT.
?!

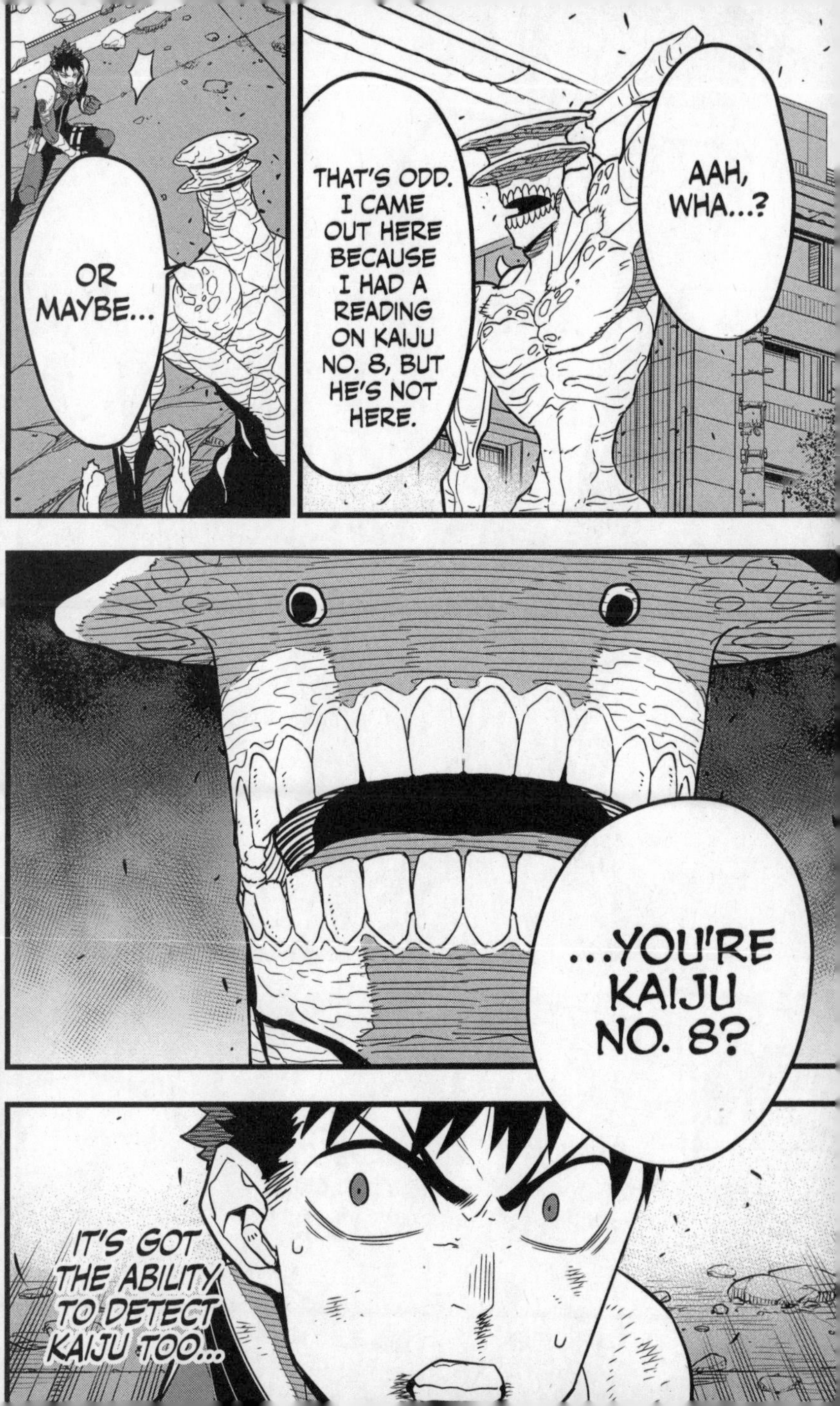
AAH, WHA...?
THAT'S ODD. I CAME OUT HERE BECAUSE I HAD A READING ON KAIJU NO. 8, BUT HE'S NOT HERE.
OR MAYBE...
...YOU'RE KAIJU NO. 8?
IT'S GOT THE ABILITY TO DETECT KAIJU TOO...

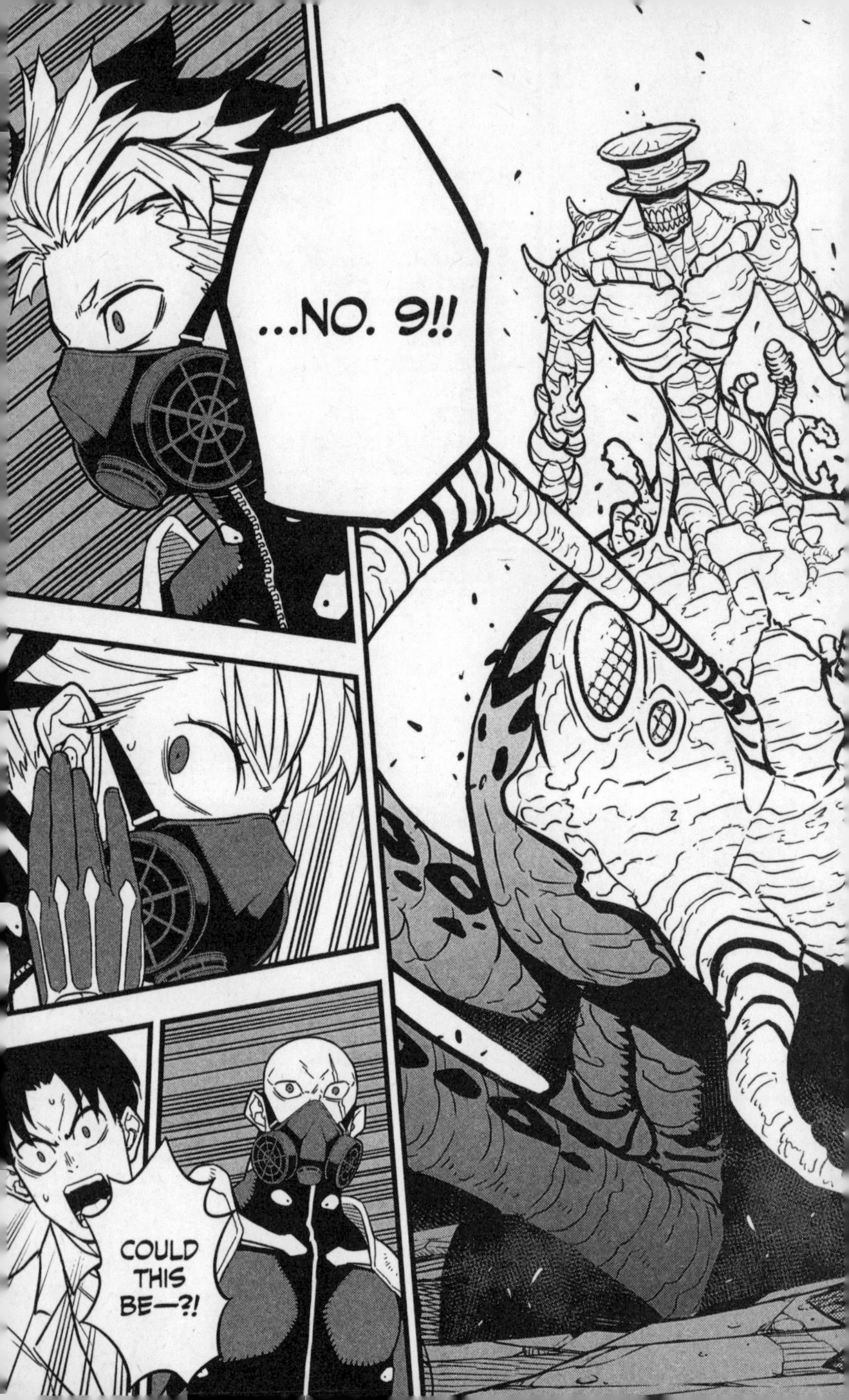
...NO. 9!!
COULD THIS BE—?!

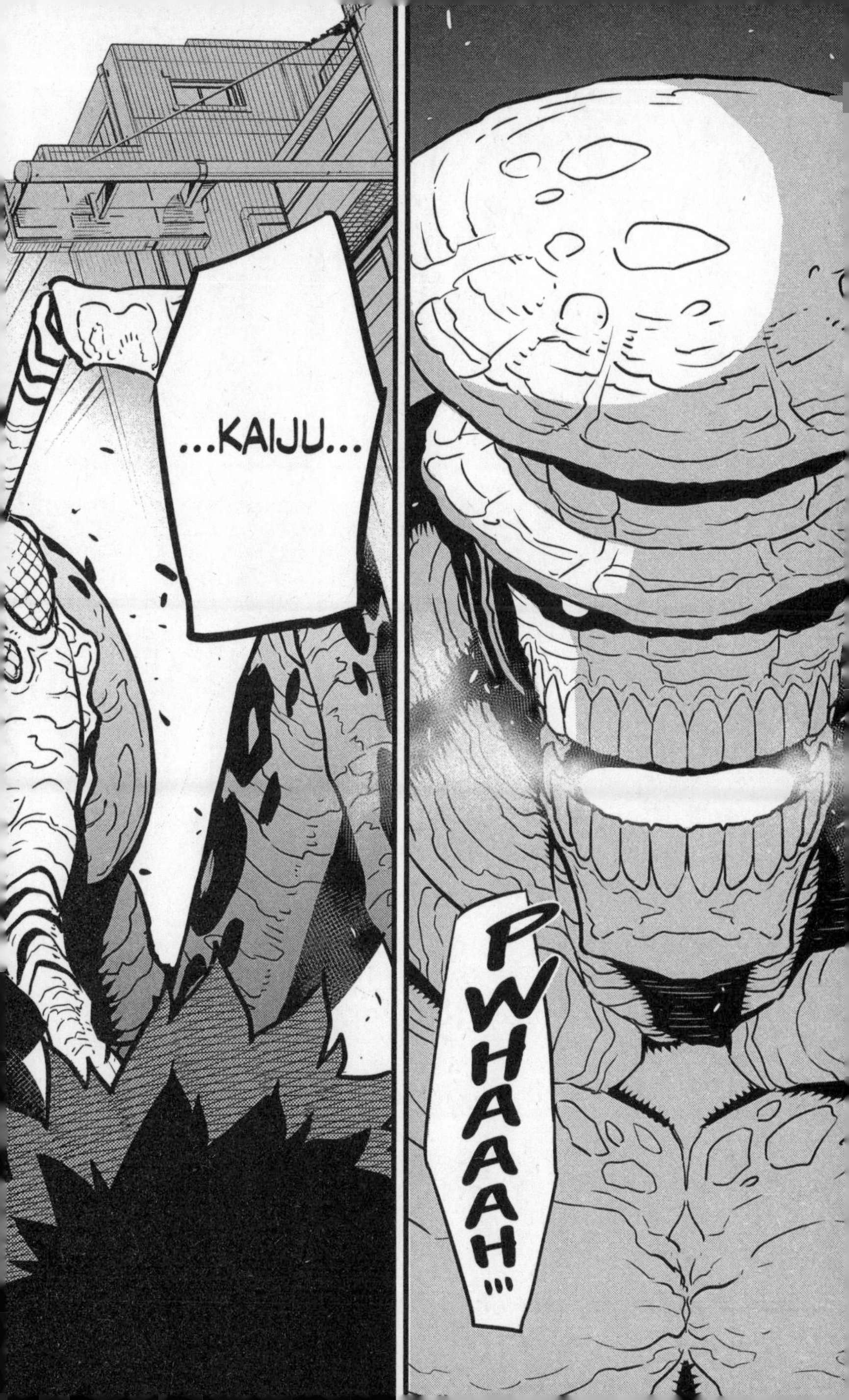
PWHAAAAH!!
...KAIJU...

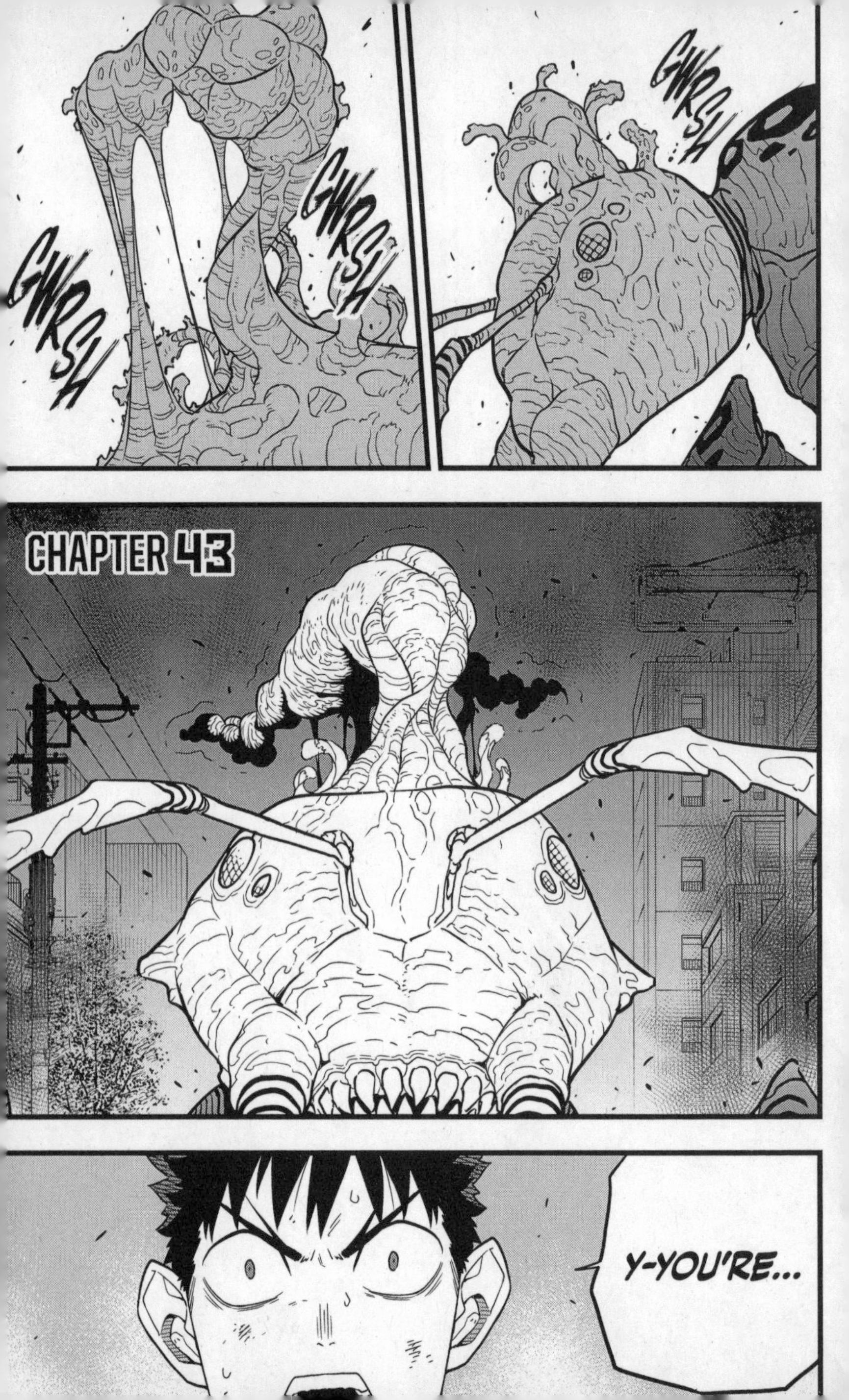
GWRSH
GWRSH
GWRSH
CHAPTER 43
Y-YOU'RE...

KAIJU NO. 8
BACKGROUND
INFORMATION

Narumi's Custom Weapon
GS-3305

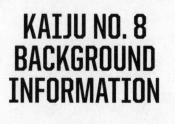

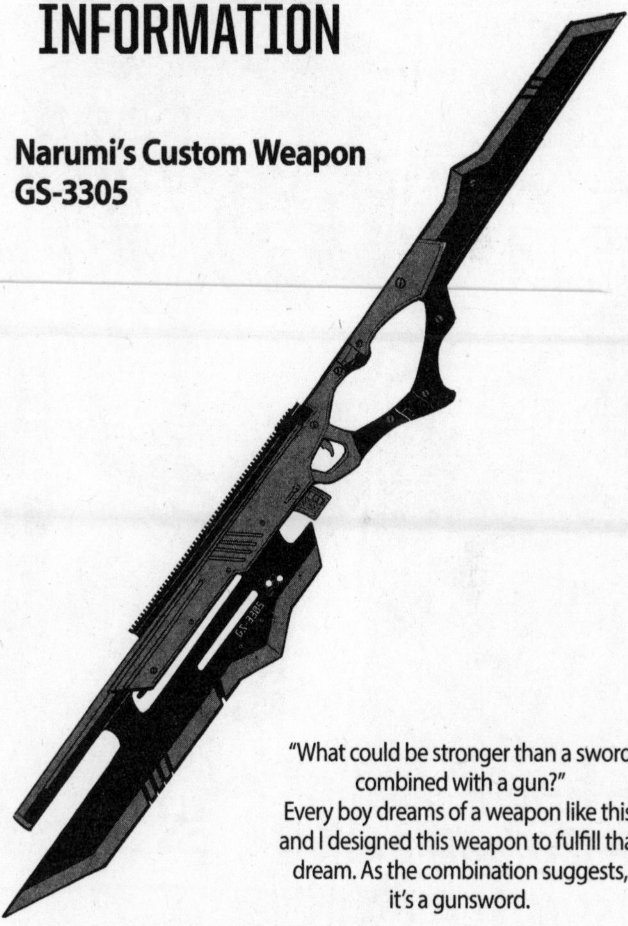

"What could be stronger than a sword combined with a gun?"
Every boy dreams of a weapon like this, and I designed this weapon to fulfill that dream. As the combination suggests, it's a gunsword.

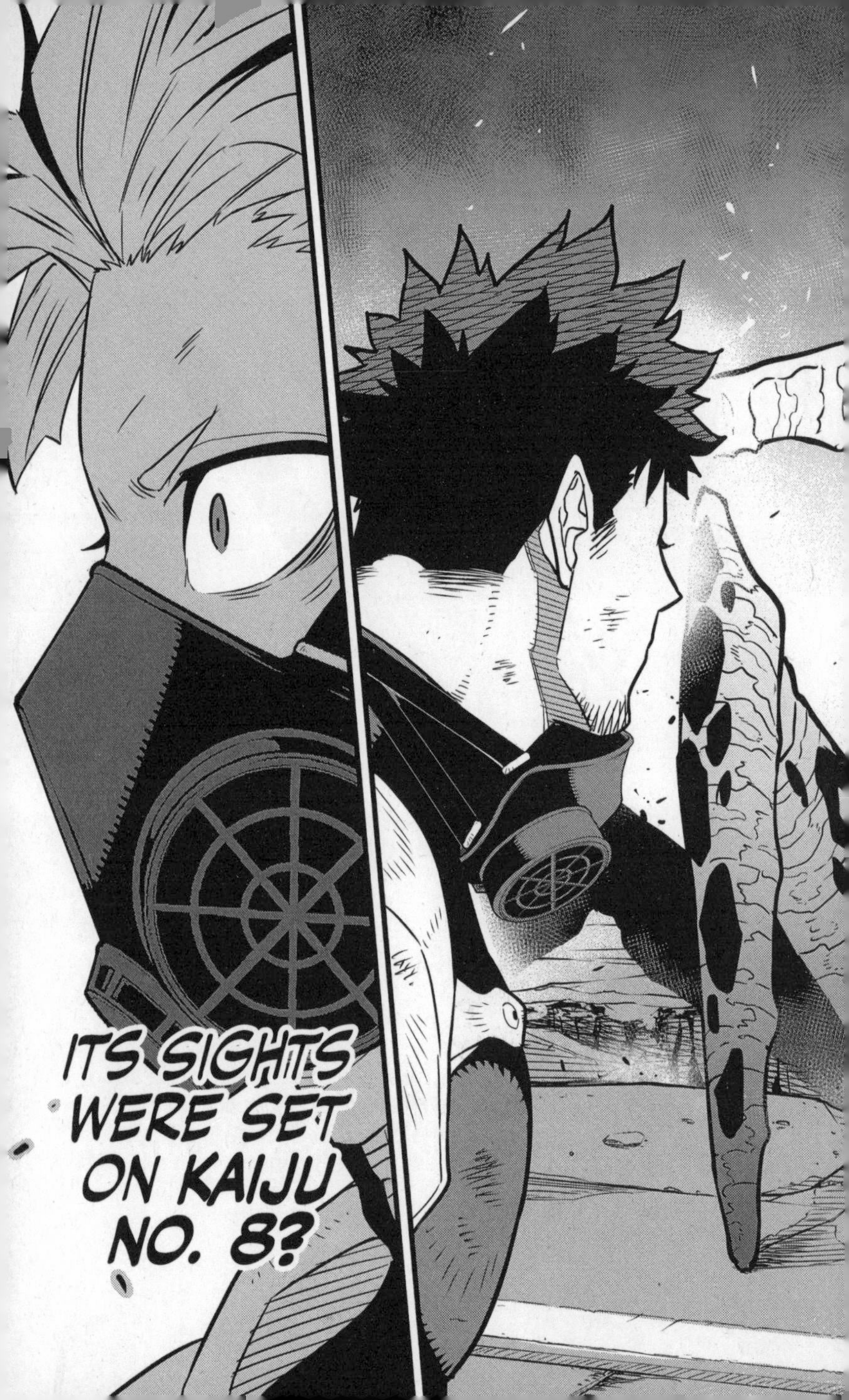
ITS SIGHTS WERE SET ON KAIJU NO. 8?

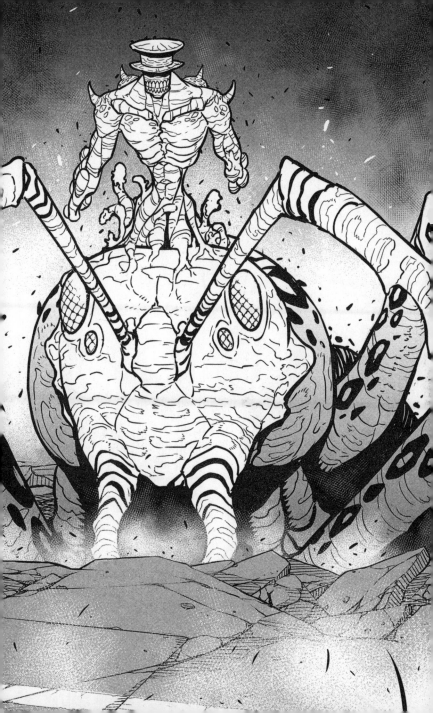

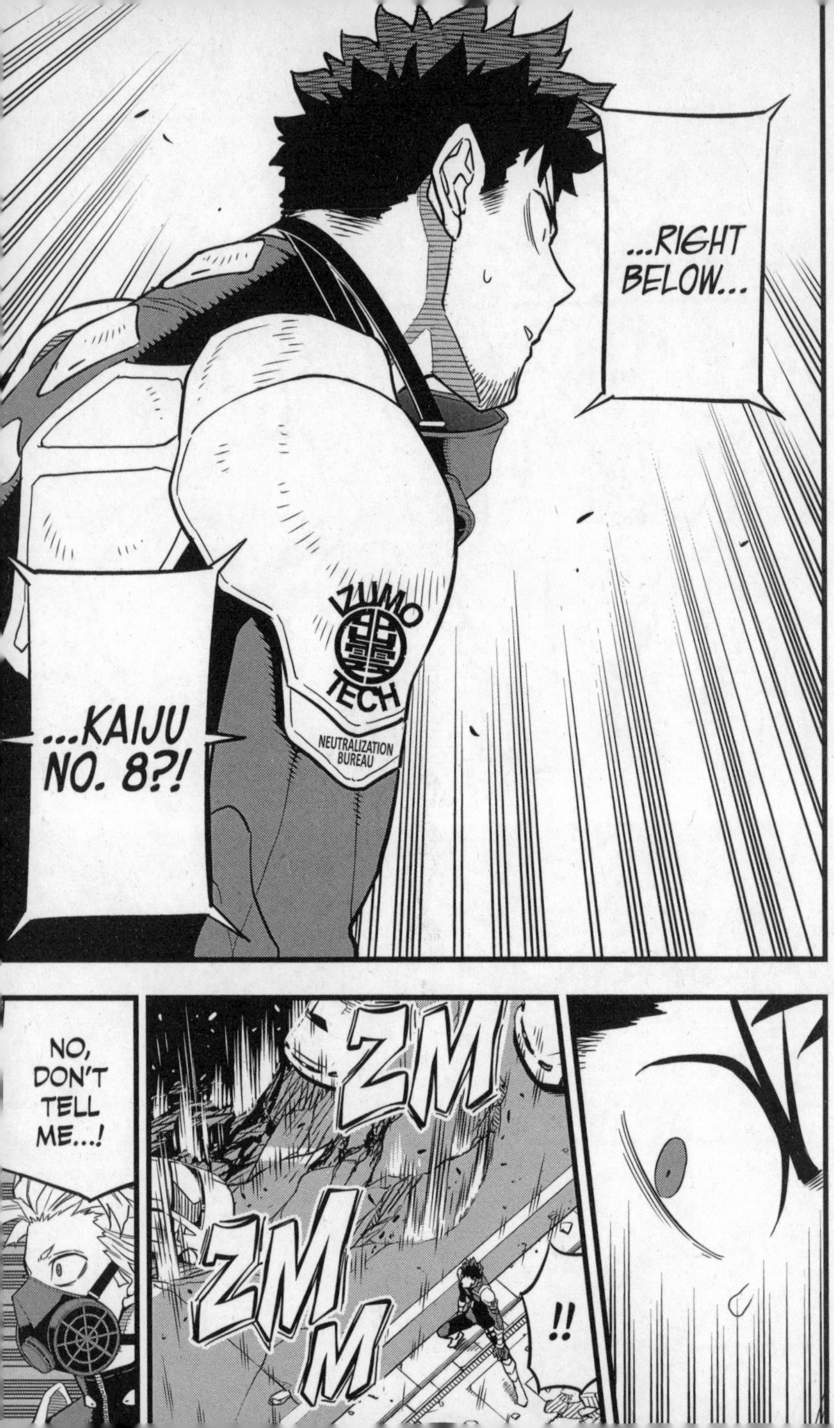
...RIGHT BELOW...
...KAIJU NO. 8?!
IZUMO TECH
NEUTRALIZATION BUREAU
ZM
ZM
M
!!
NO, DON'T TELL ME...!

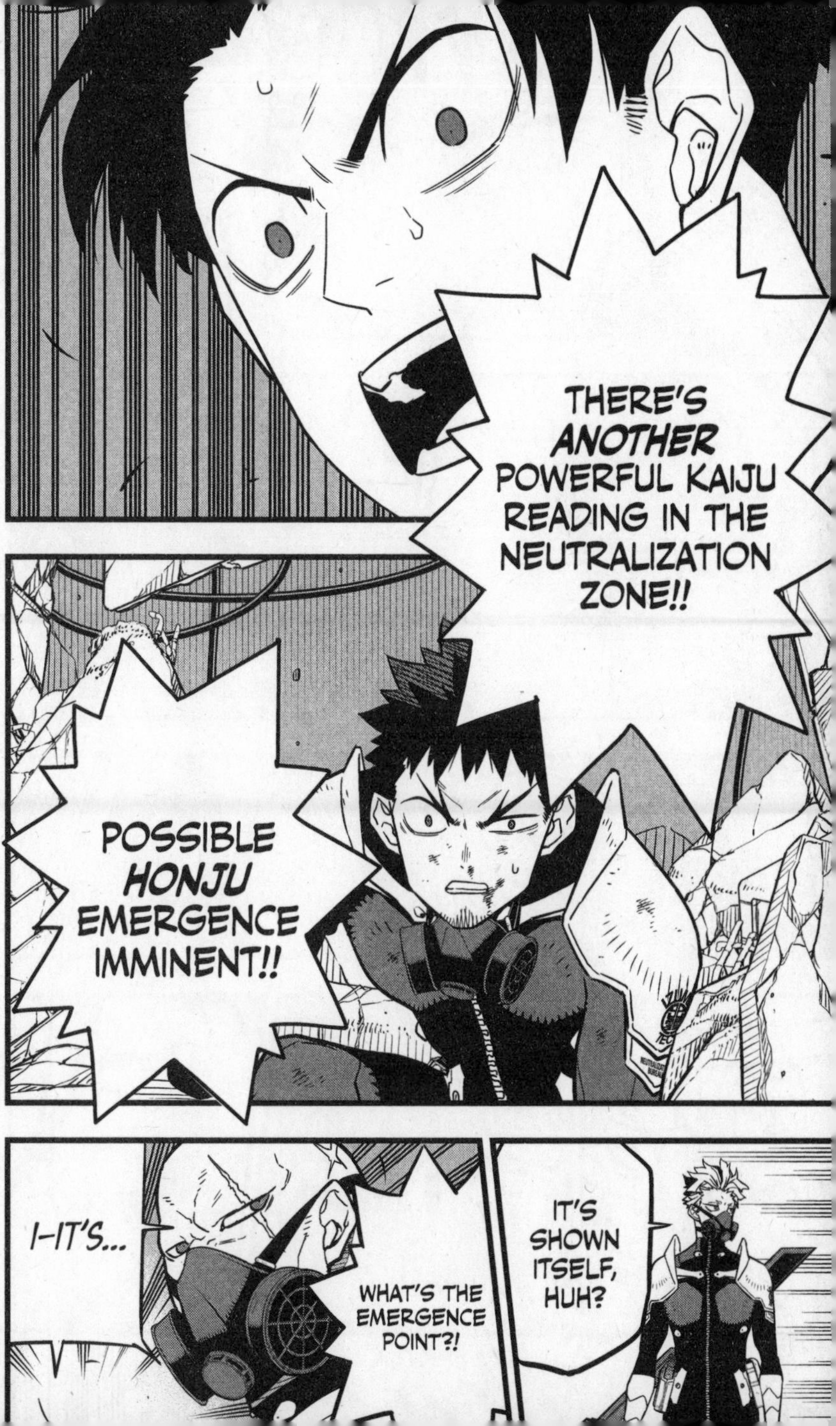
THERE'S *ANOTHER* POWERFUL KAIJU READING IN THE NEUTRALIZATION ZONE!!
POSSIBLE *HONJU* EMERGENCE IMMINENT!!
IT'S SHOWN ITSELF, HUH?
WHAT'S THE EMERGENCE POINT?!
I-IT'S...

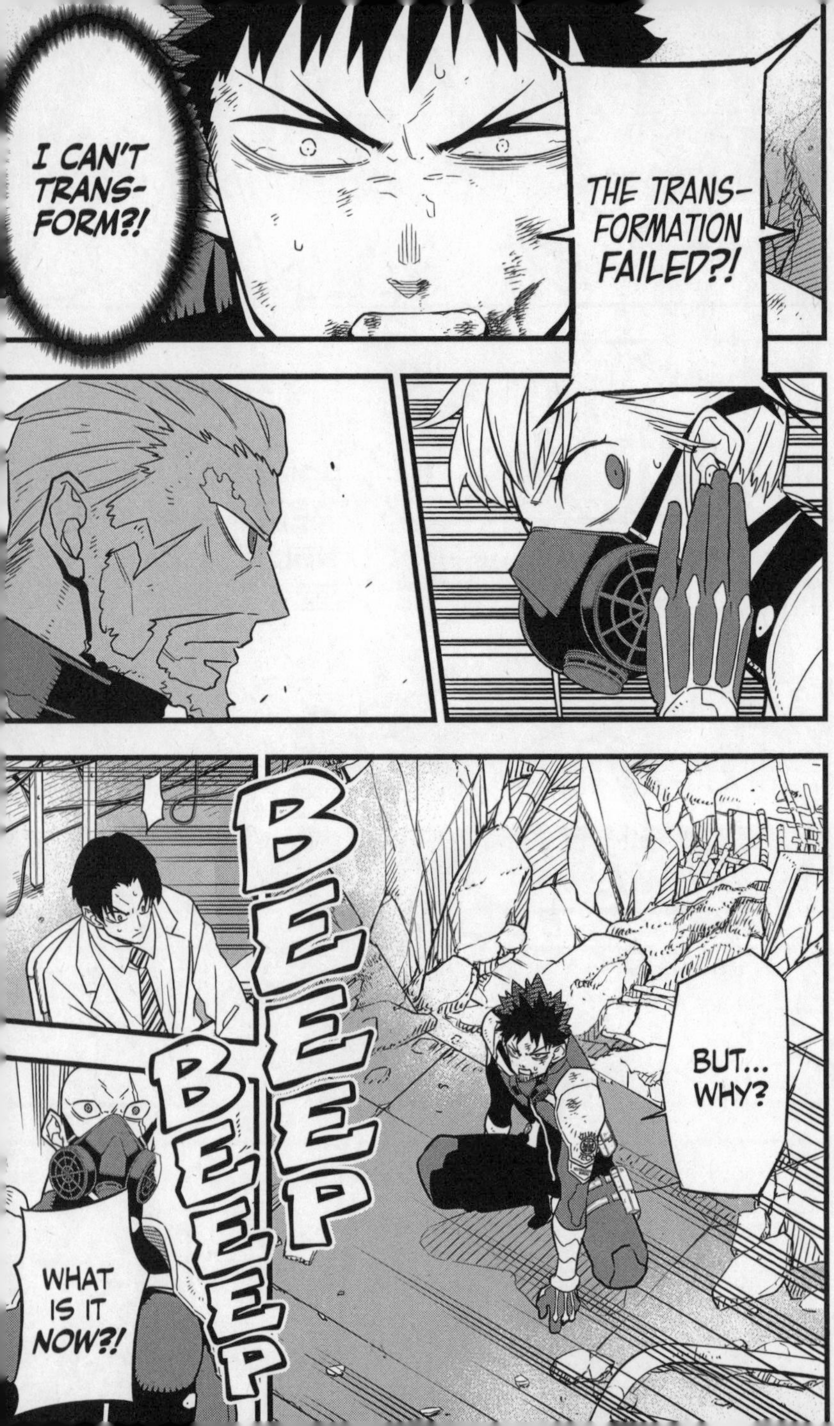
I CAN'T TRANS-FORM?!
THE TRANS-FORMATION FAILED?!
BUT... WHY?
BEEEP
BEEEEP
WHAT IS IT NOW?!

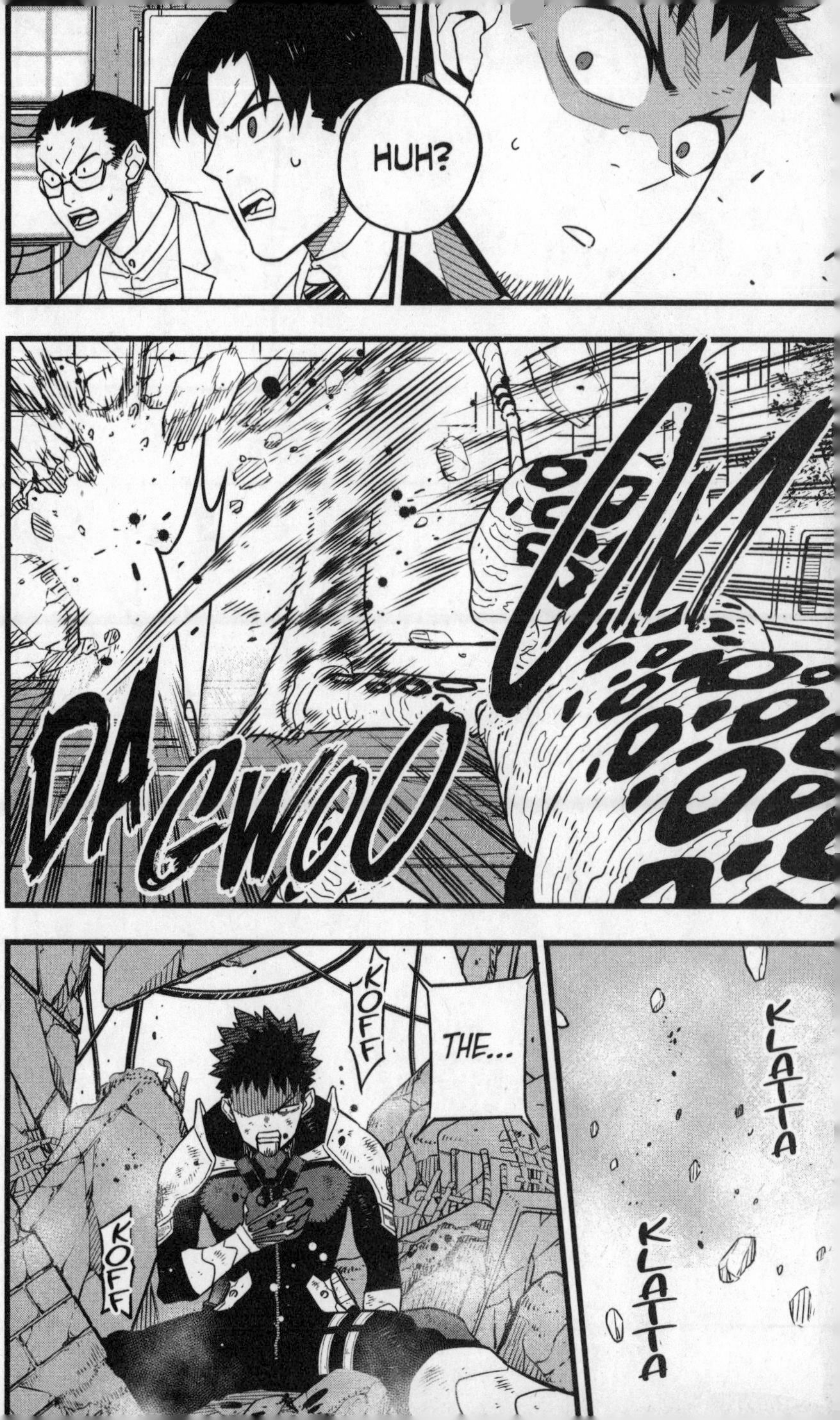
HUH?
DOOM
DAGWOO
KLATTA KLATTA
THE...
KOFF
KOFF

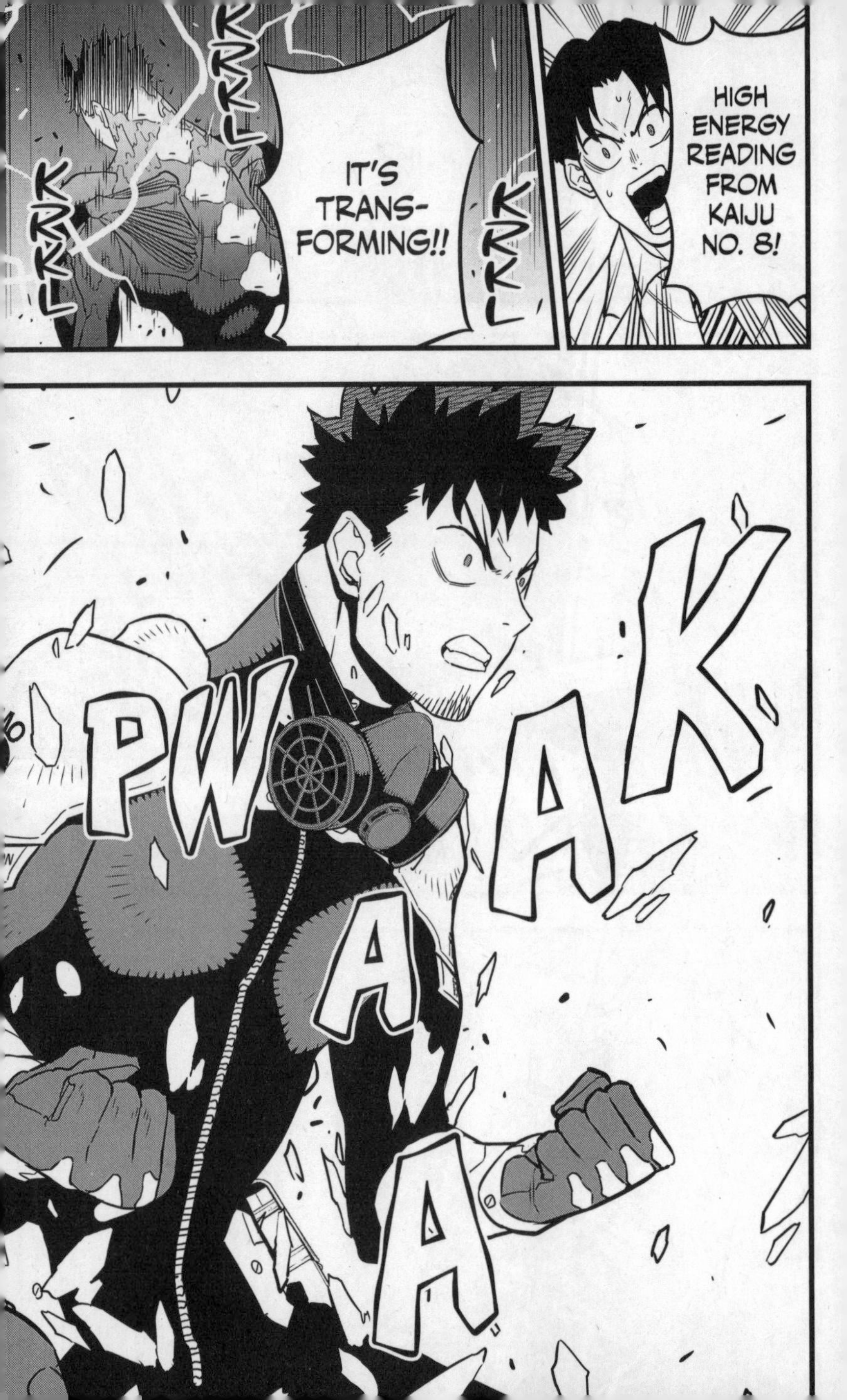
HIGH ENERGY READING FROM KAIJU NO. 8!
IT'S TRANS-FORMING!!
PWAAAK

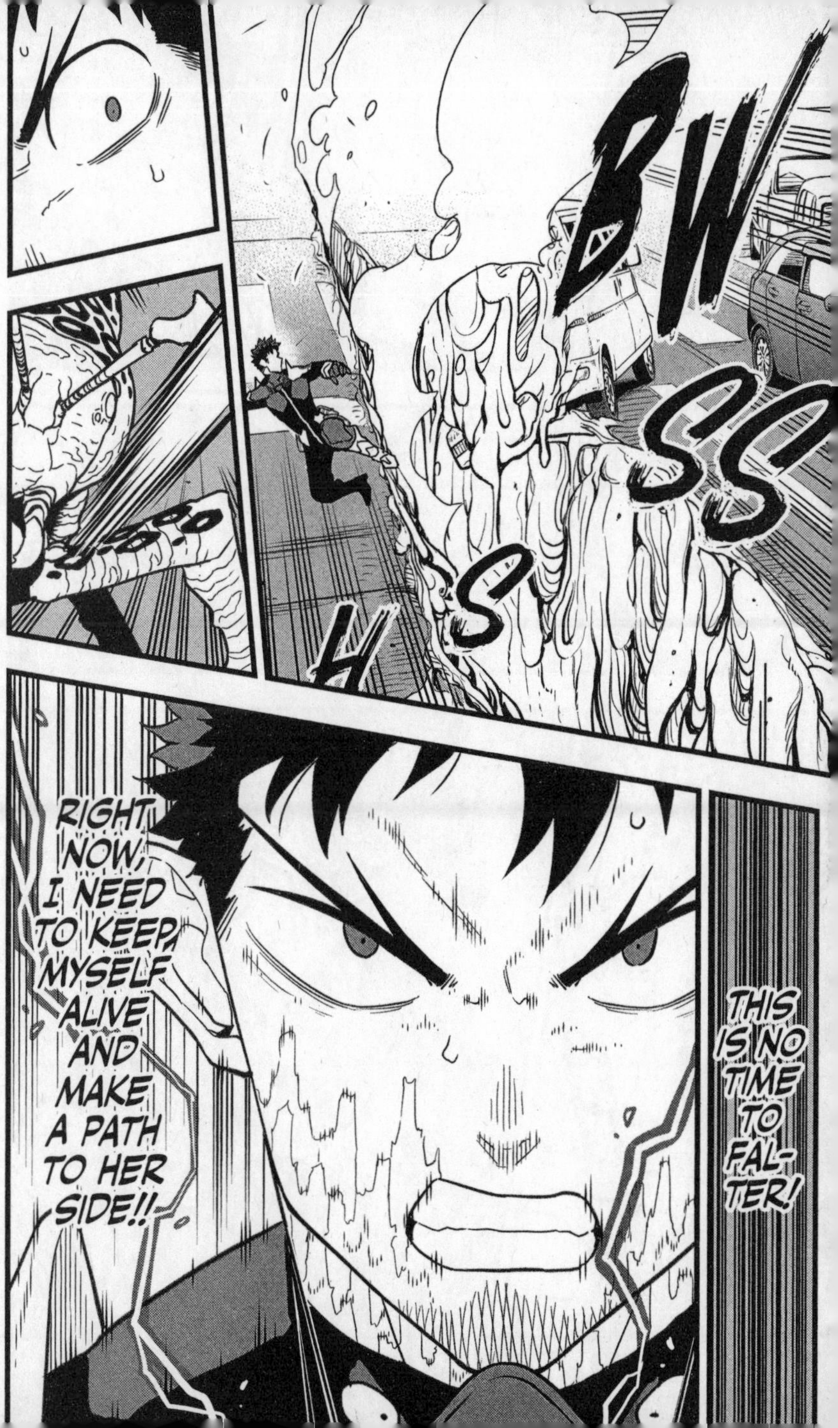
BWSSSH
THIS IS NO TIME TO FAL-TER!
RIGHT NOW, I NEED TO KEEP MYSELF ALIVE AND MAKE A PATH TO HER SIDE!!

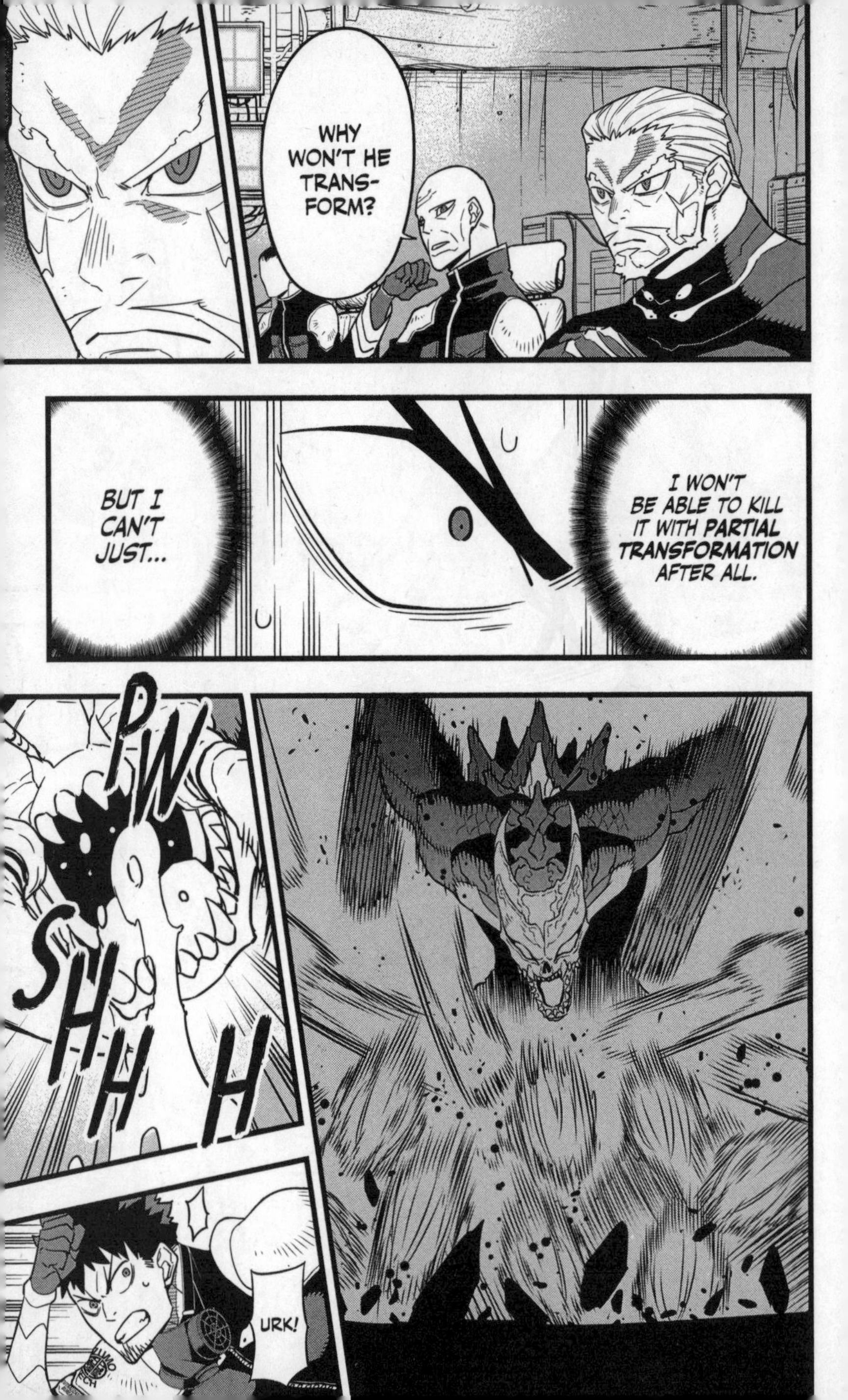
WHY WON'T HE TRANS-FORM?
I WON'T BE ABLE TO KILL IT WITH PARTIAL TRANSFORMATION AFTER ALL.
BUT I CAN'T JUST...
PWSHHH
URK!

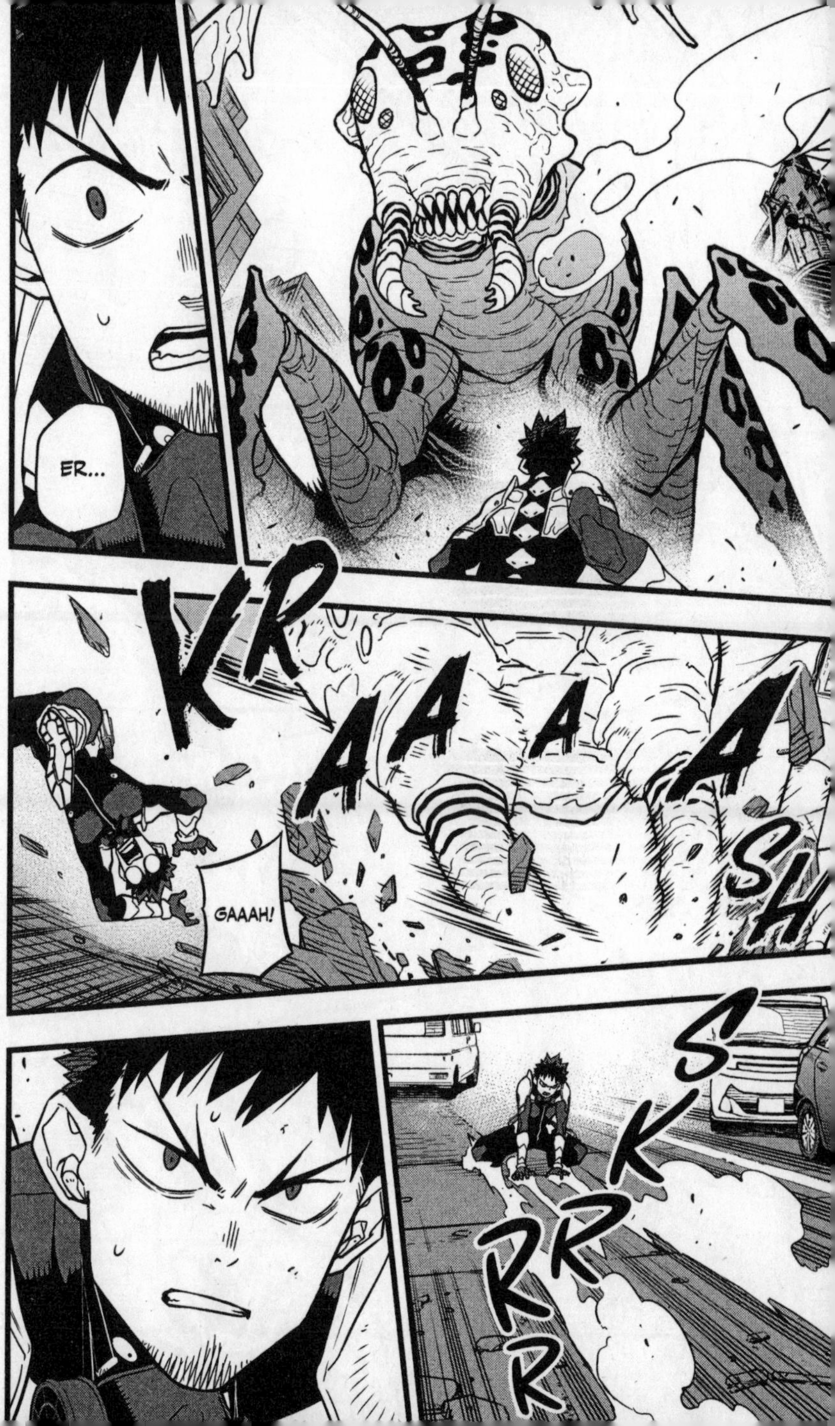
ER...
KRAAAA
SH
GAAAH!
SKRRRK

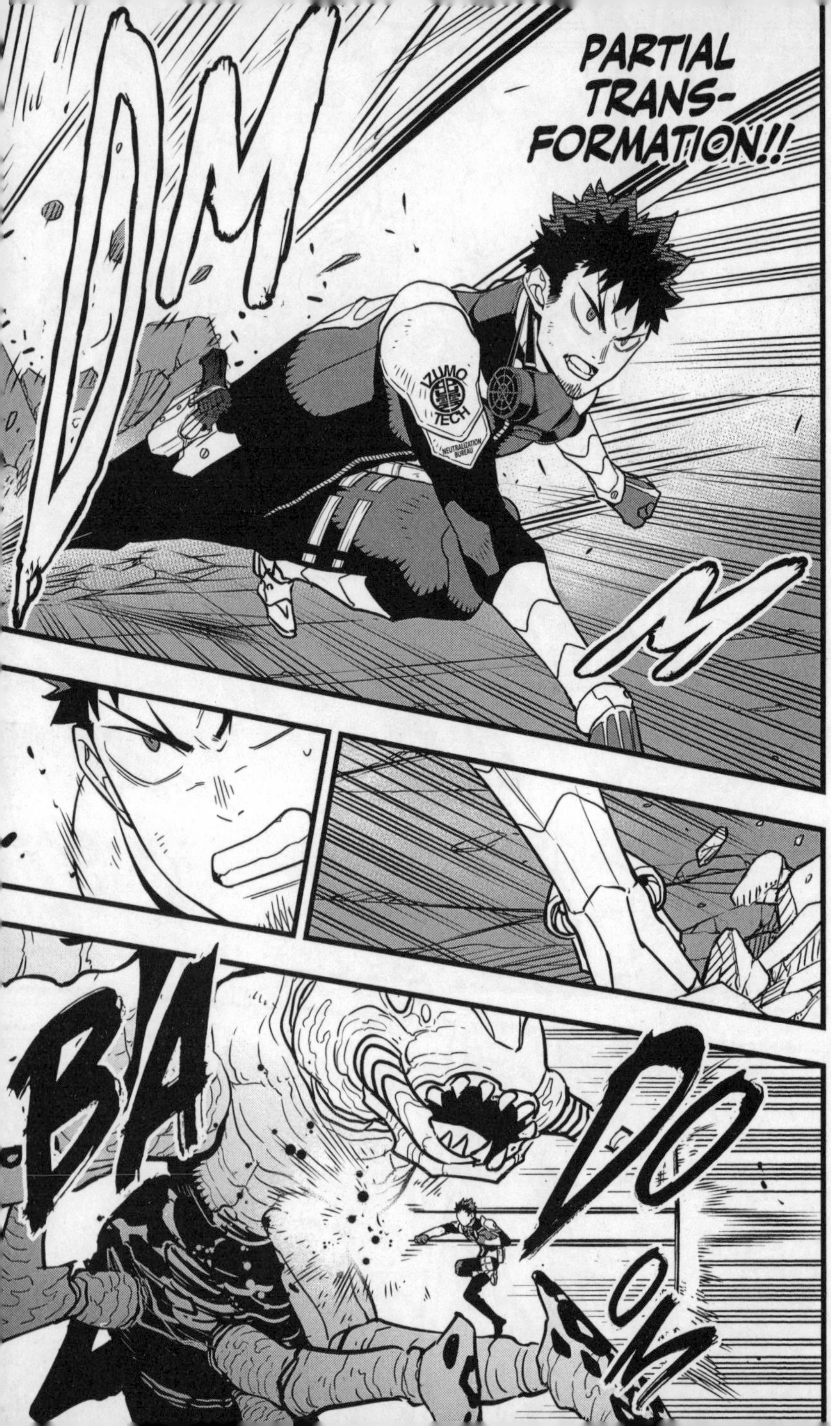
PARTIAL TRANS-
FORMATION!!
DOM
M
IZUMO TECH
NEUTRALIZATION BUREAU
BA

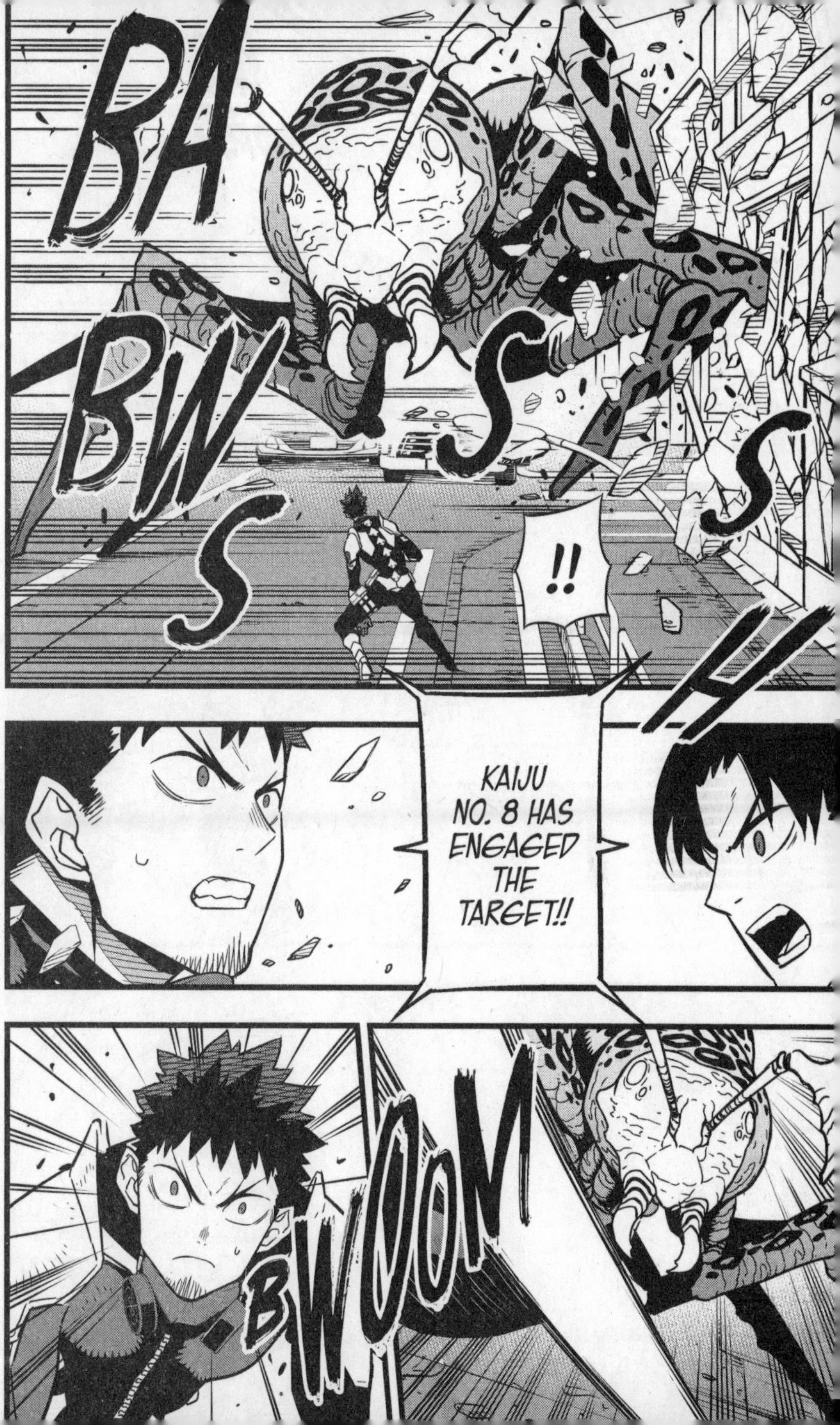
BABWSSSH
!!
KAIJU NO. 8 HAS ENGAGED THE TARGET!!
BWOOOM

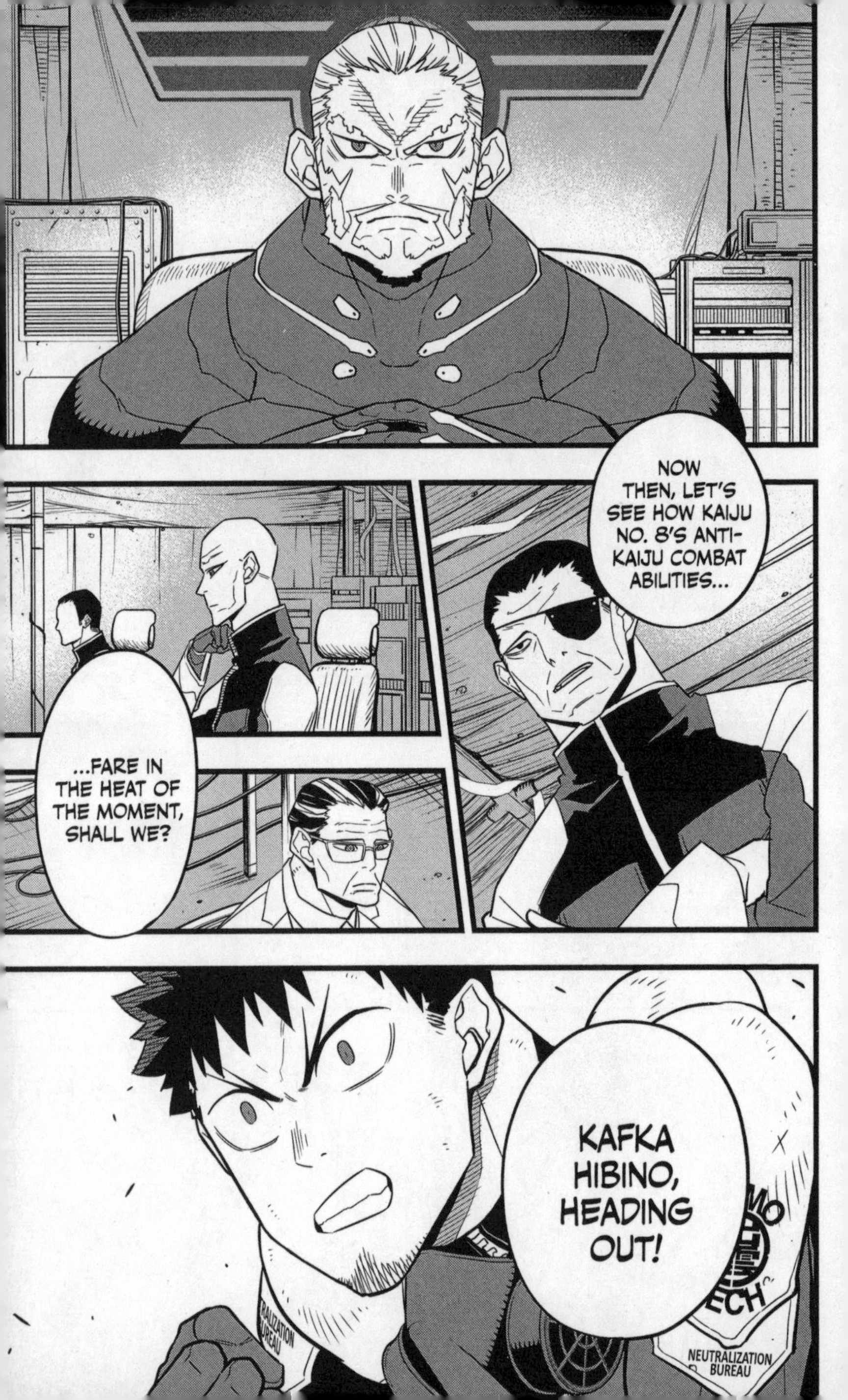
NOW THEN, LET'S SEE HOW KAIJU NO. 8'S ANTI-KAIJU COMBAT ABILITIES...
...FARE IN THE HEAT OF THE MOMENT, SHALL WE?
KAFKA HIBINO, HEADING OUT!
NEUTRALIZATION BUREAU

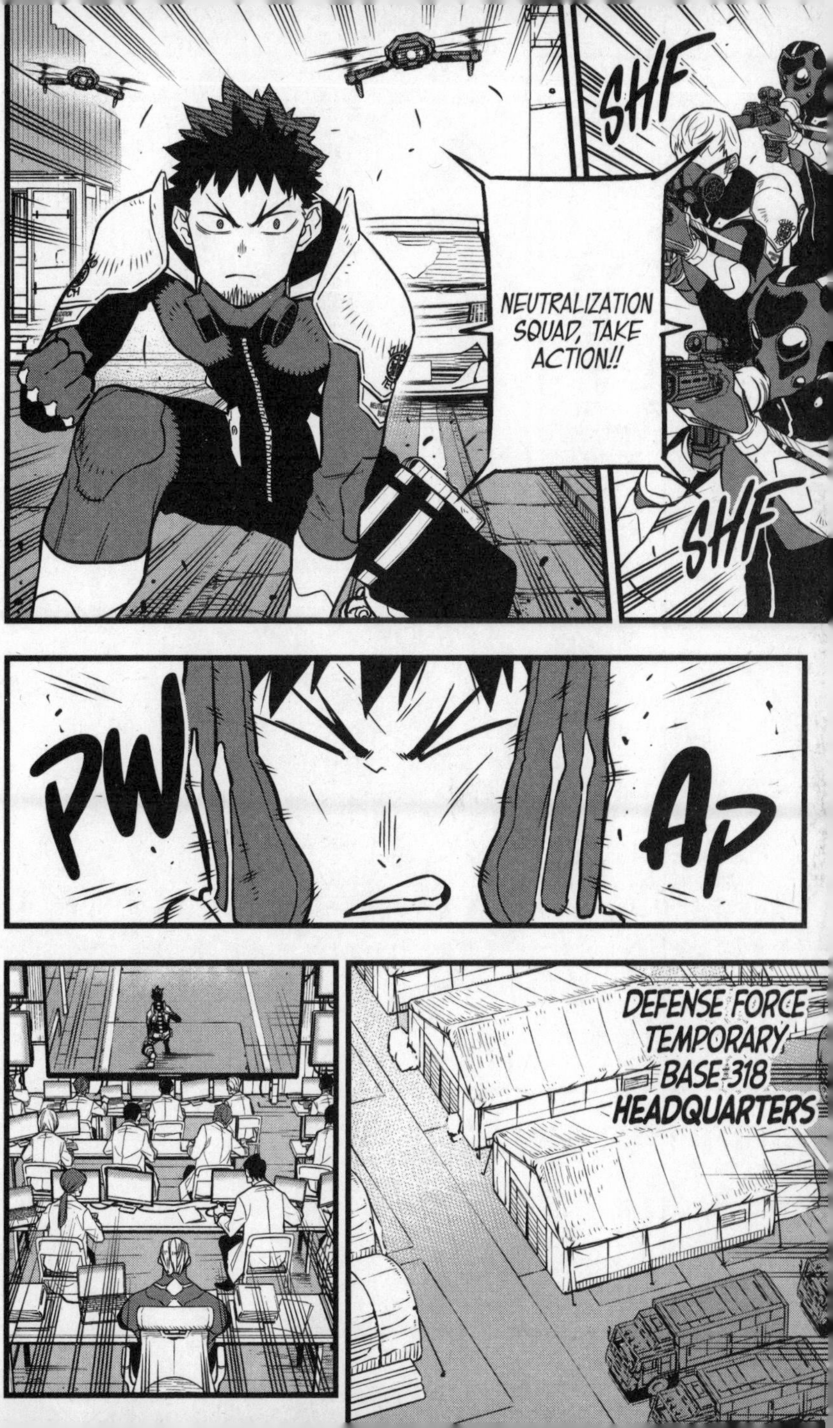
SHF
NEUTRALIZATION SQUAD, TAKE ACTION!!
SHF
PW
AP
DEFENSE FORCE TEMPORARY BASE 318 HEADQUARTERS

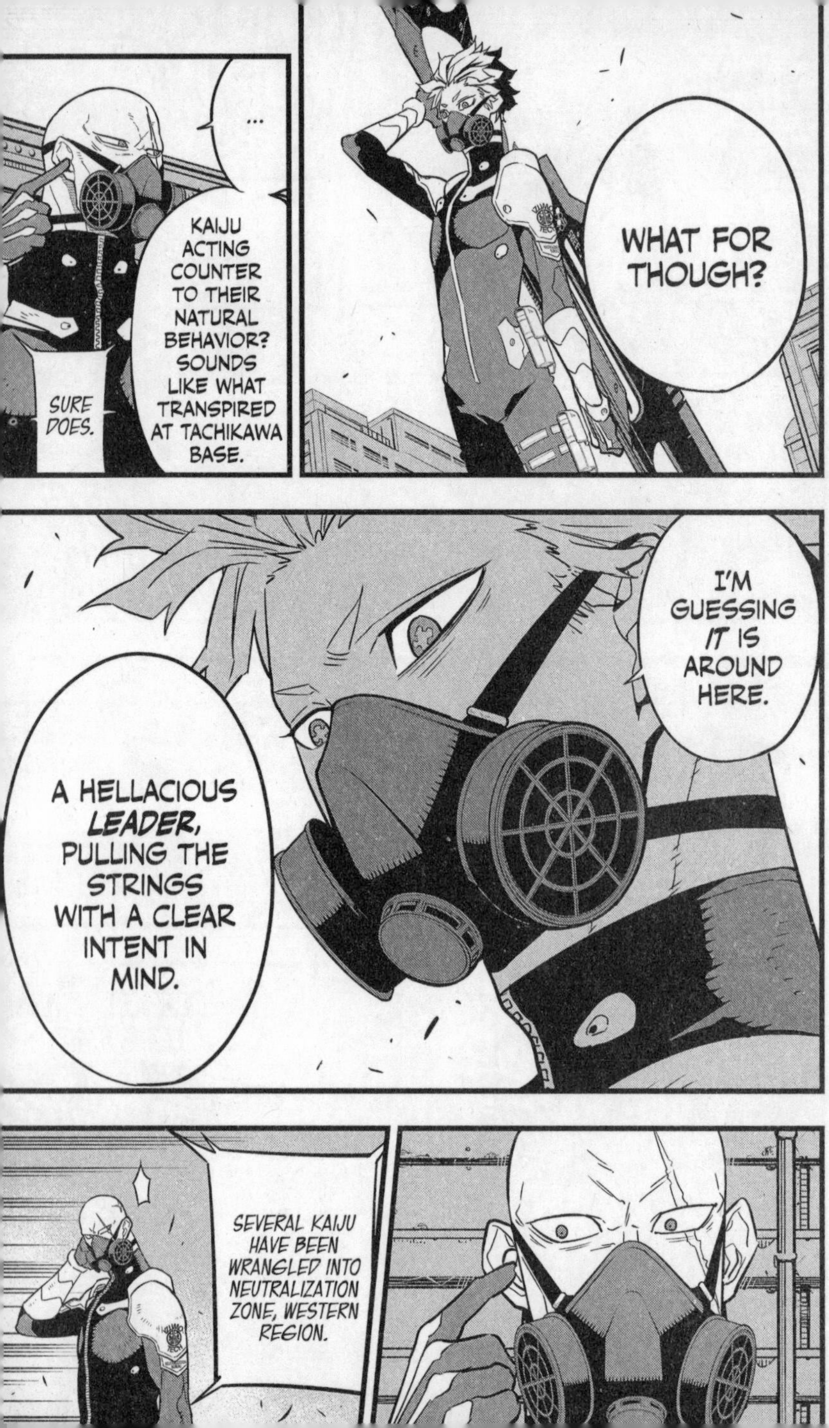
WHAT FOR THOUGH?
...
KAIJU ACTING COUNTER TO THEIR NATURAL BEHAVIOR? SOUNDS LIKE WHAT TRANSPIRED AT TACHIKAWA BASE.
SURE DOES.
I'M GUESSING *IT* IS AROUND HERE.
A HELLACIOUS *LEADER*, PULLING THE STRINGS WITH A CLEAR INTENT IN MIND.
SEVERAL KAIJU HAVE BEEN WRANGLED INTO NEUTRALIZATION ZONE, WESTERN REGION.

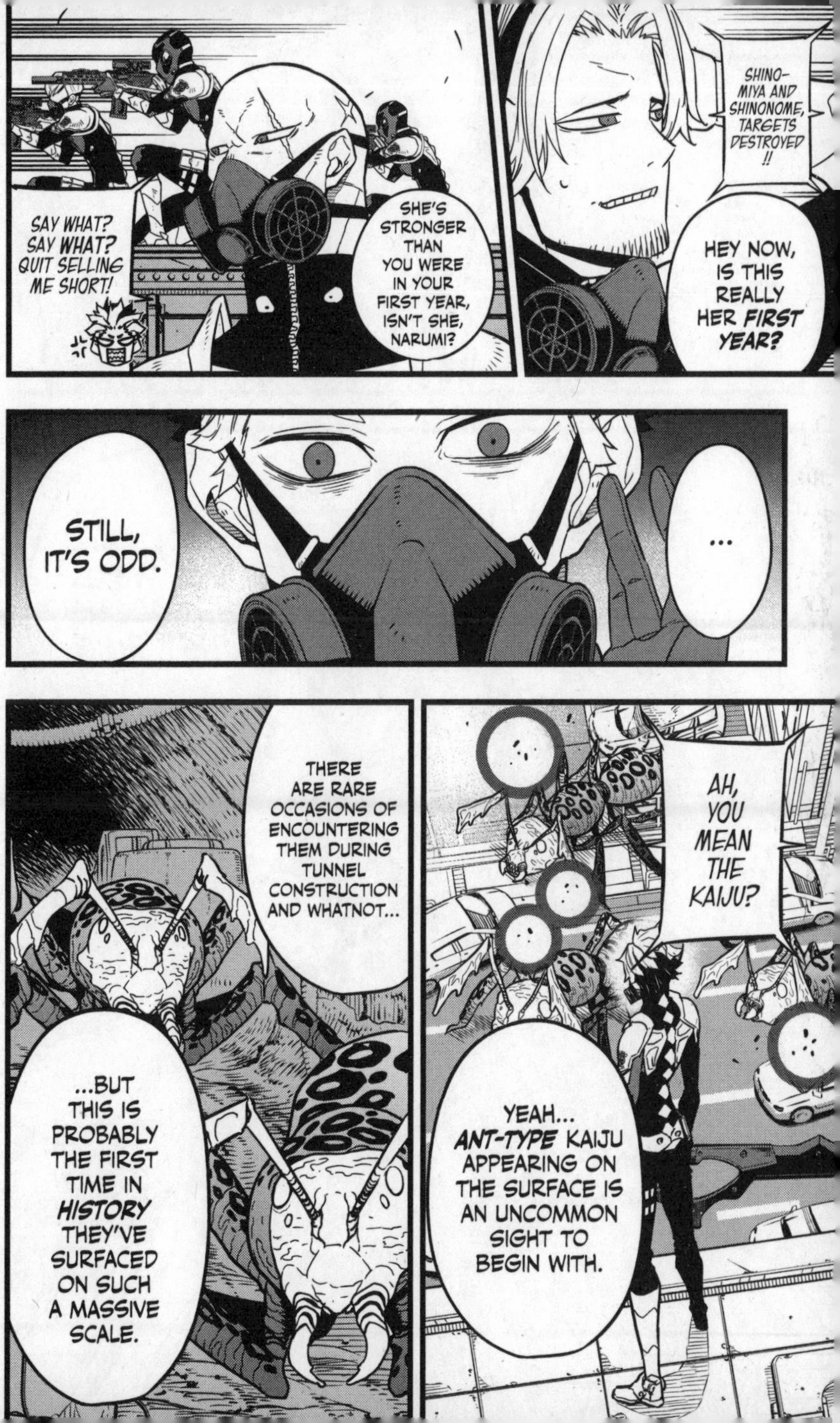
SHINOMIYA AND SHINONOME, TARGETS DESTROYED!!
HEY NOW, IS THIS REALLY HER *FIRST YEAR?*
SHE'S STRONGER THAN YOU WERE IN YOUR FIRST YEAR, ISN'T SHE, NARUMI?
SAY WHAT? SAY *WHAT?* QUIT SELLING ME SHORT!
...
STILL, IT'S ODD.
AH, YOU MEAN THE KAIJU?
YEAH... *ANT-TYPE* KAIJU APPEARING ON THE SURFACE IS AN UNCOMMON SIGHT TO BEGIN WITH.
THERE ARE RARE OCCASIONS OF ENCOUNTERING THEM DURING TUNNEL CONSTRUCTION AND WHATNOT...
...BUT THIS IS PROBABLY THE FIRST TIME IN *HISTORY* THEY'VE SURFACED ON SUCH A MASSIVE SCALE.

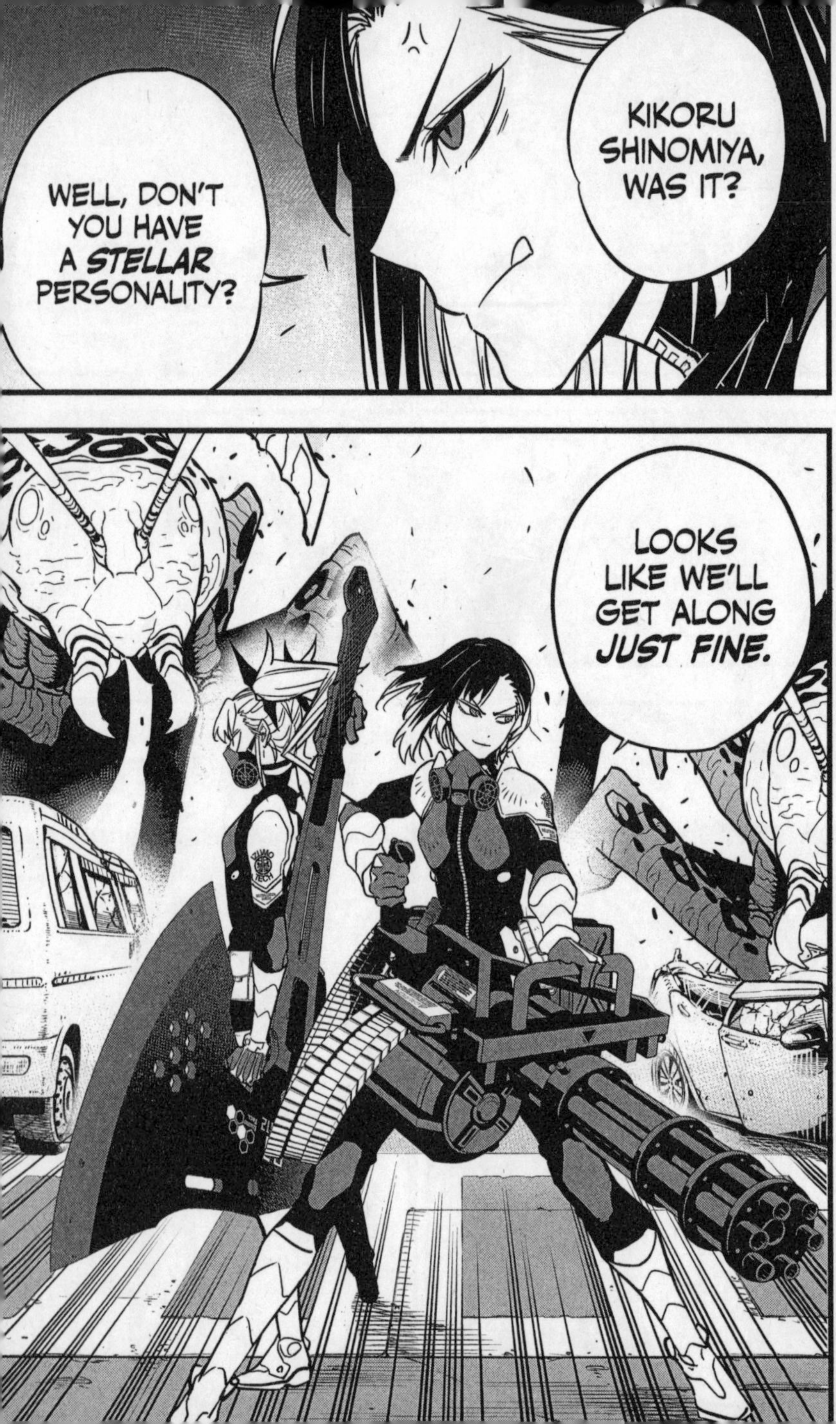
KIKORU SHINOMIYA, WAS IT?
WELL, DON'T YOU HAVE A STELLAR PERSONALITY?
LOOKS LIKE WE'LL GET ALONG JUST FINE.

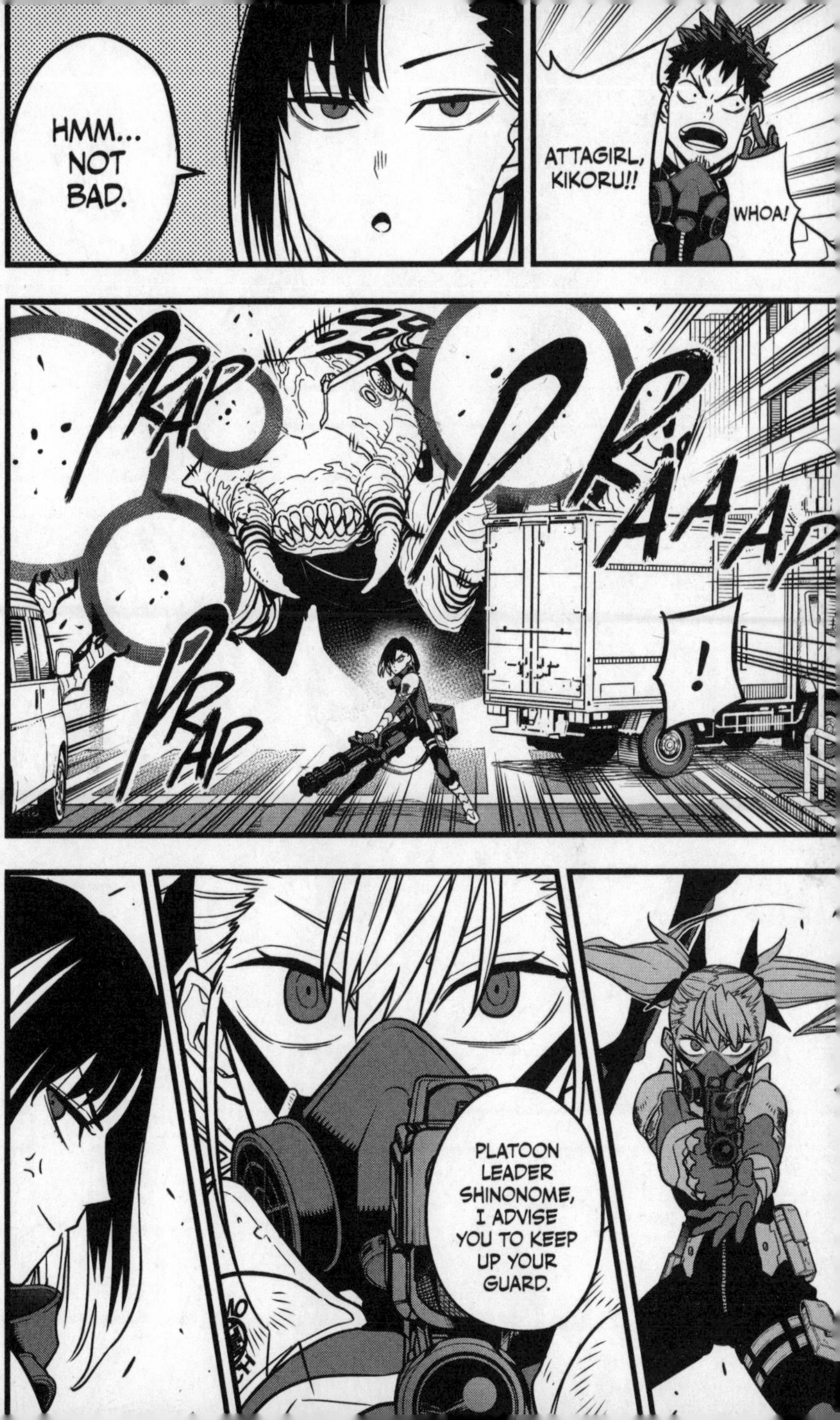
ATTAGIRL, KIKORU!!
WHOA!
HMM... NOT BAD.
PRAAAP
PRAP
!
PRAP
PLATOON LEADER SHINONOME, I ADVISE YOU TO KEEP UP YOUR GUARD.

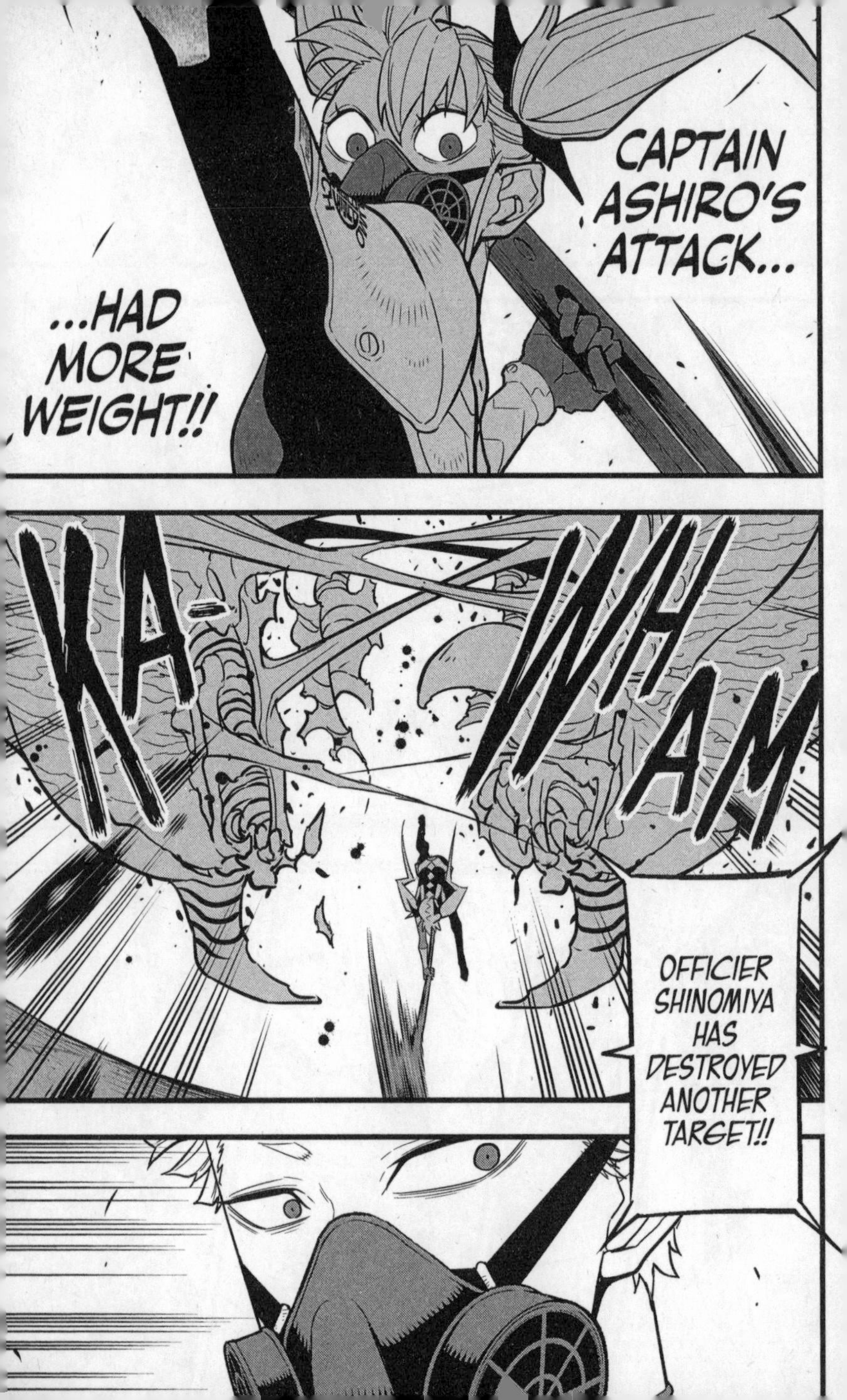
CAPTAIN ASHIRO'S ATTACK...
...HAD MORE WEIGHT!!
KA-
WHAM
OFFICIER SHINOMIYA HAS DESTROYED ANOTHER TARGET!!

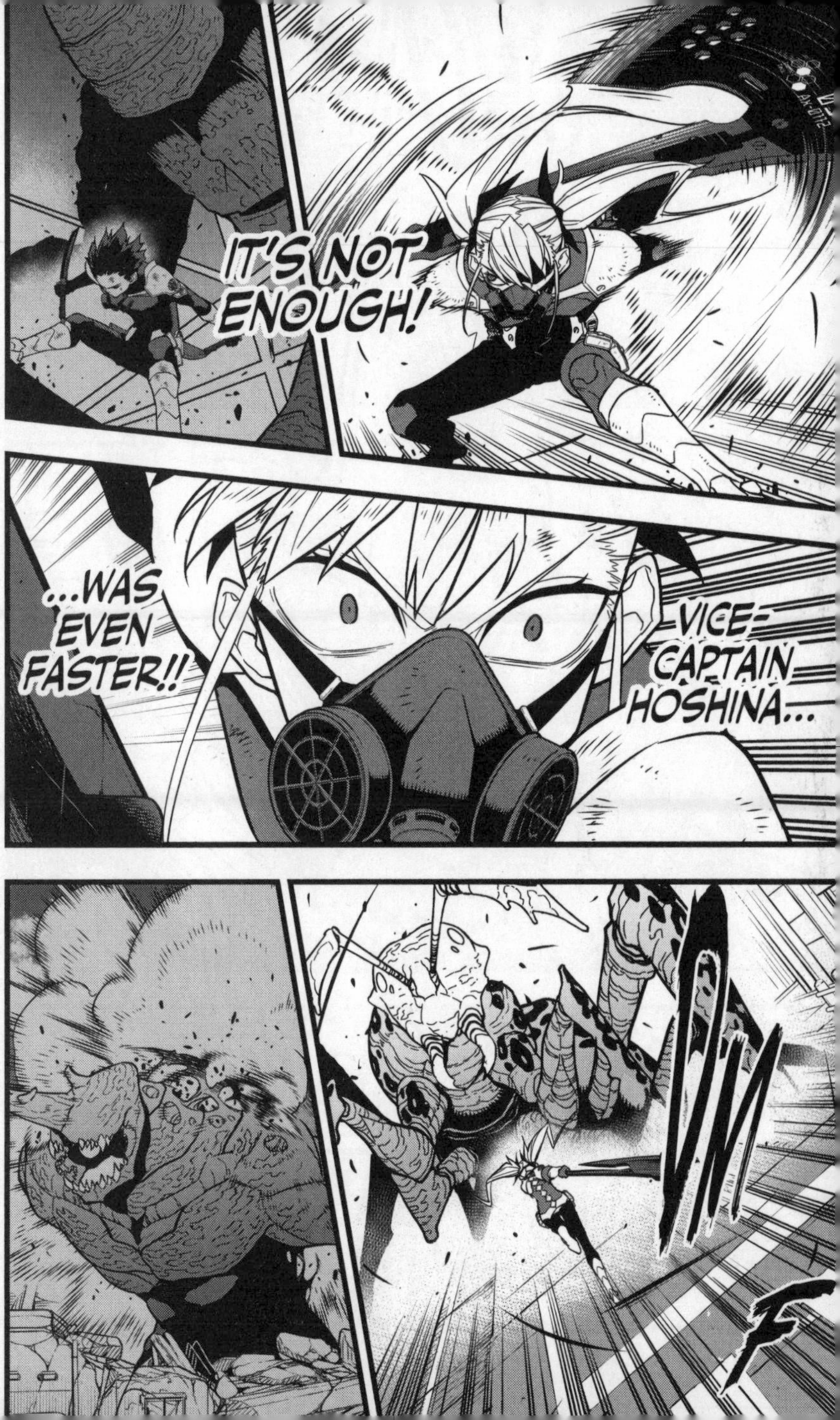
IT'S NOT ENOUGH!
VICE-CAPTAIN HOSHINA...
...WAS EVEN FASTER!!

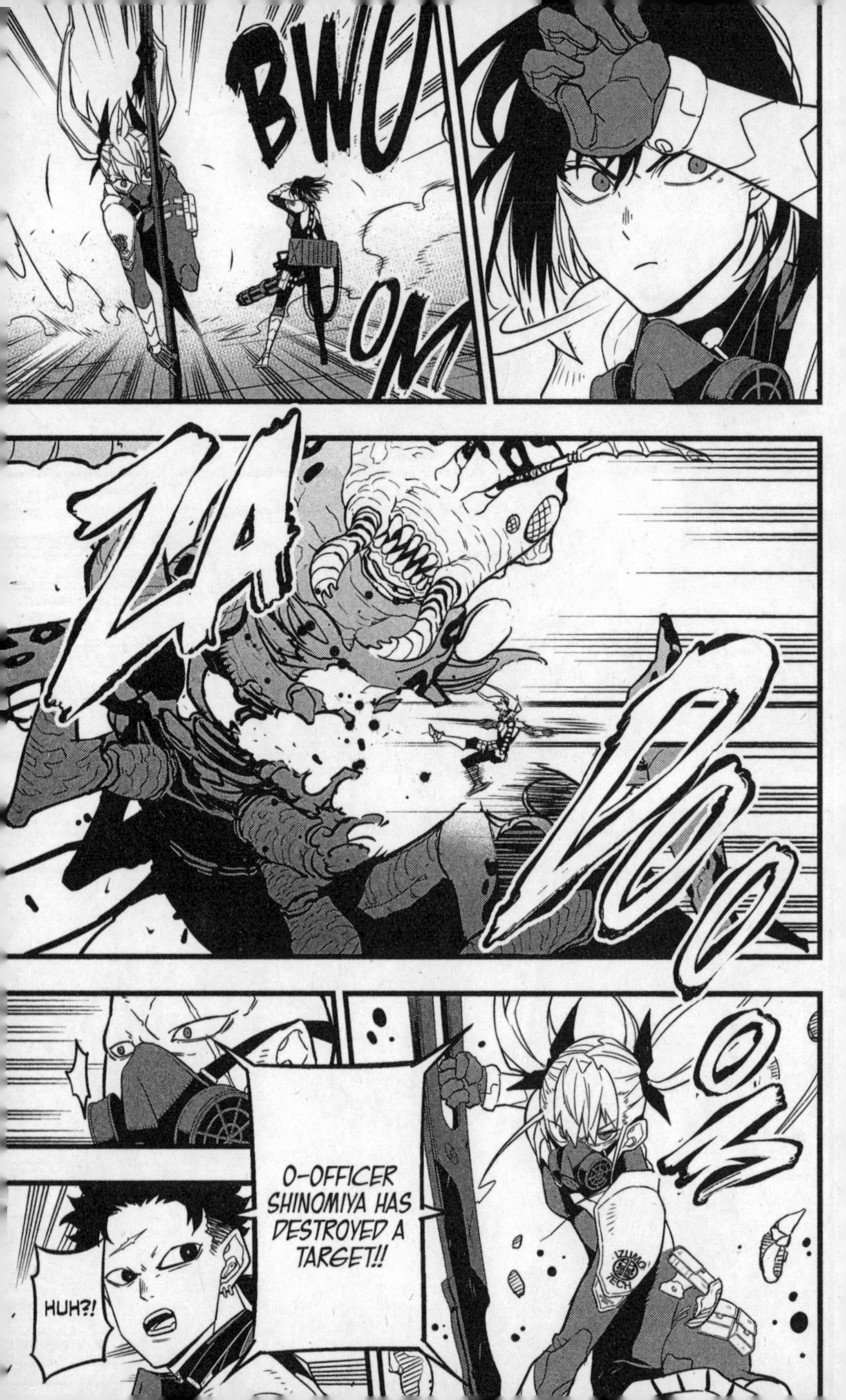

BWUOM
ZAVOOOOM
O-OFFICER SHINOMIYA HAS DESTROYED A TARGET!!
HUH?!

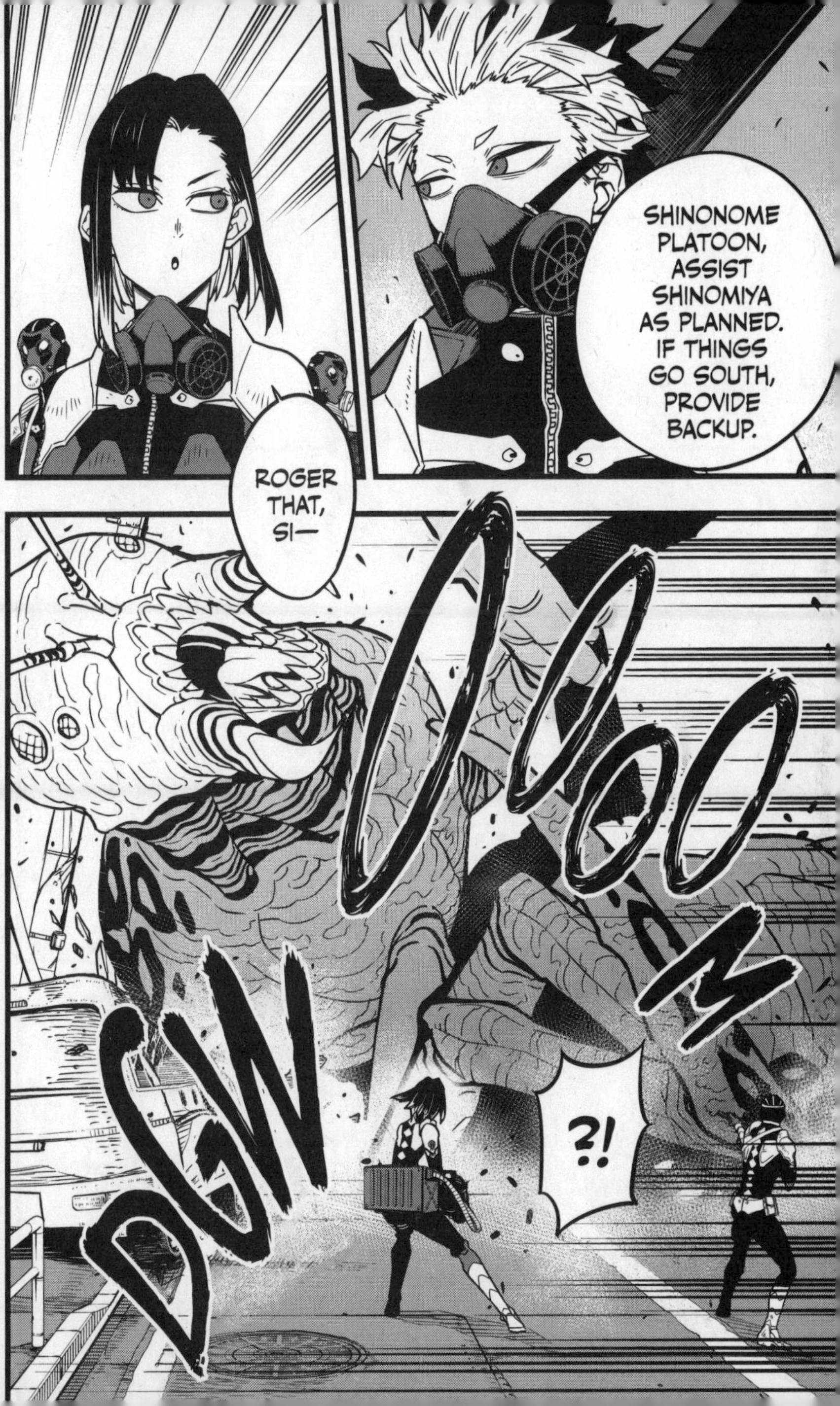
SHINONOME PLATOON, ASSIST SHINOMIYA AS PLANNED. IF THINGS GO SOUTH, PROVIDE BACKUP.
ROGER THAT, SI—
DOOOOOM
?!

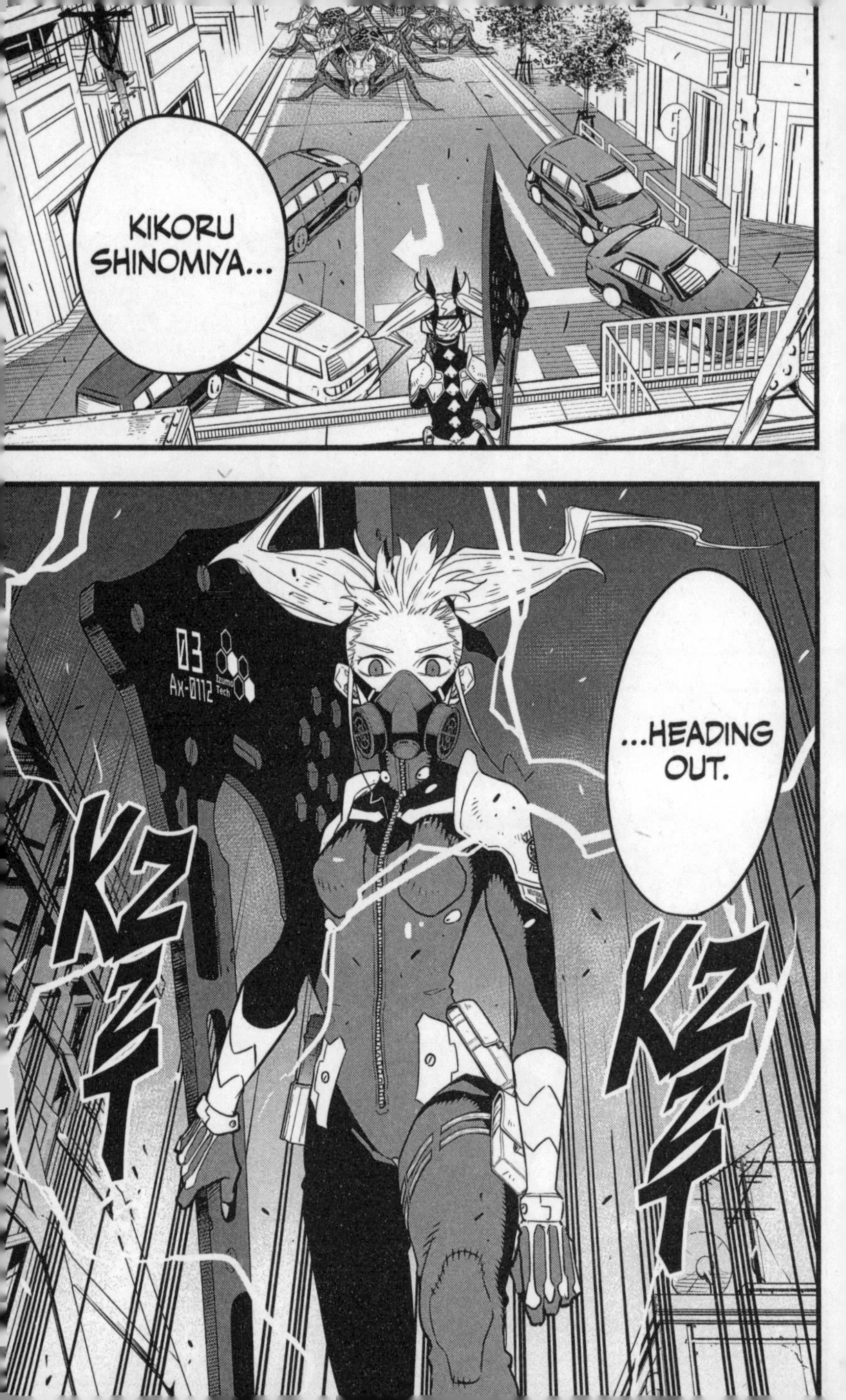
KIKORU SHINOMIYA...
03
Ax-0112
Izumo Tech
...HEADING OUT.
KZZT
KZZT

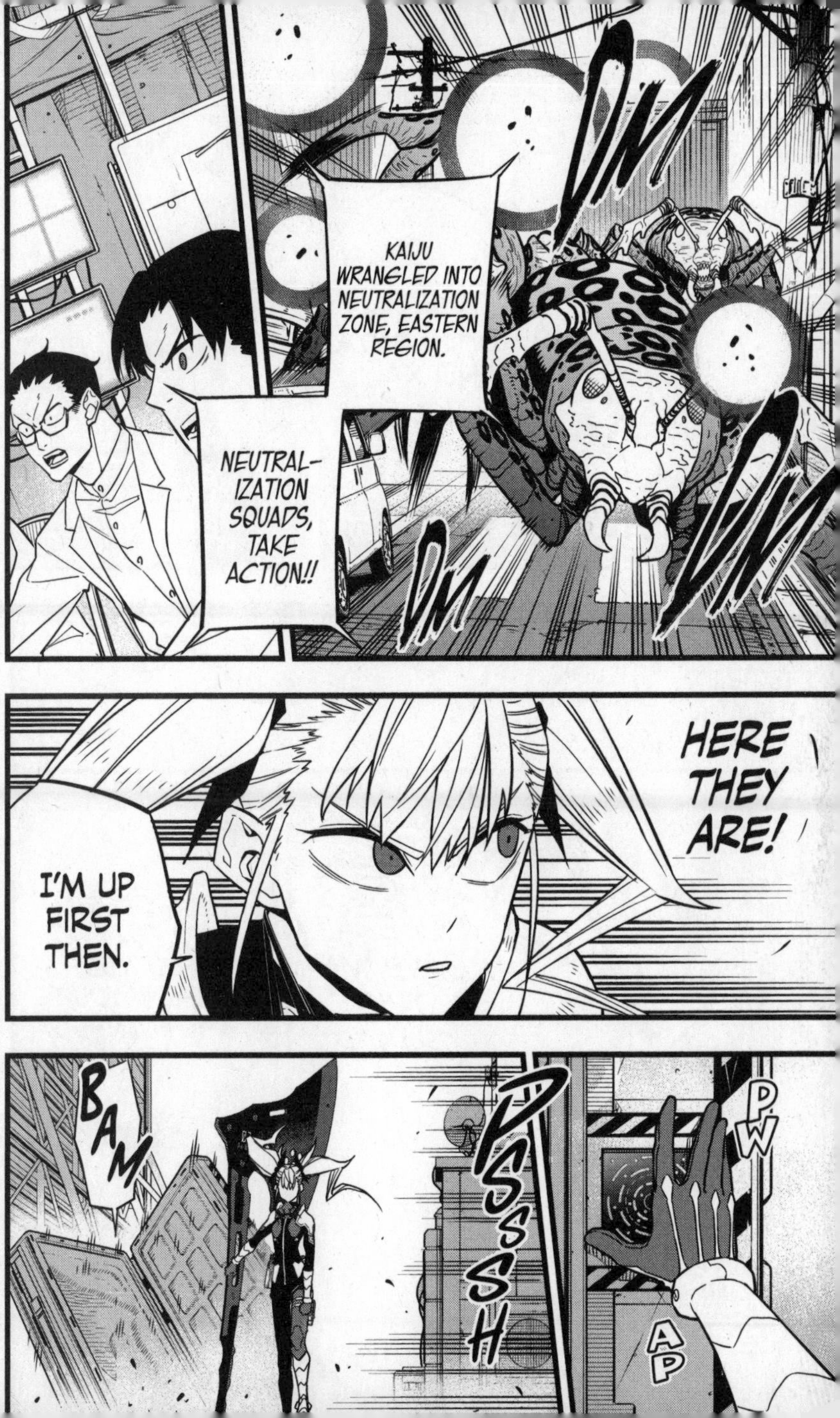
KAIJU WRANGLED INTO NEUTRALIZATION ZONE, EASTERN REGION.
NEUTRAL-IZATION SQUADS, TAKE ACTION!!
DM
HERE THEY ARE!
I'M UP FIRST THEN.
PW
AP
PSSSH
BAM

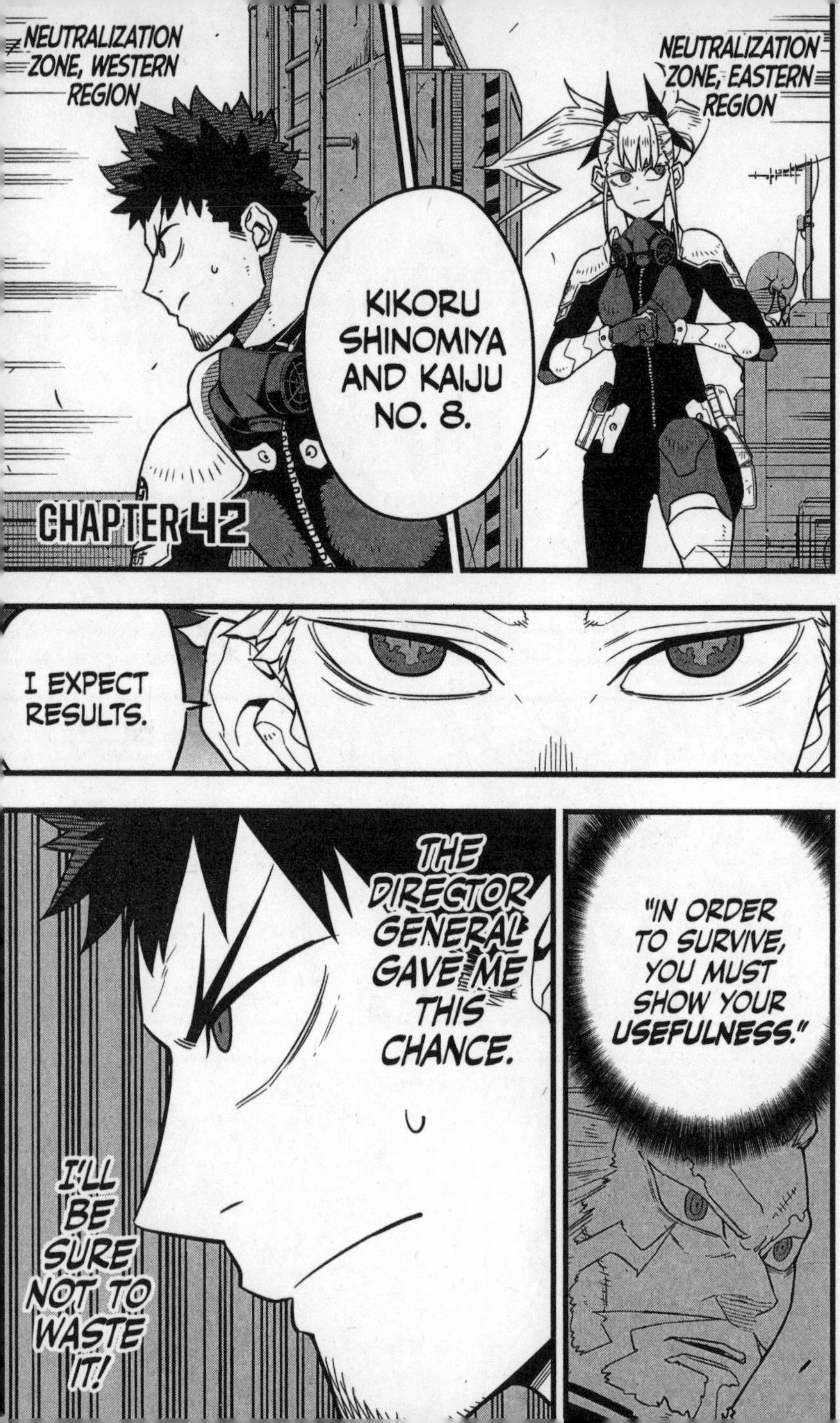
NEUTRALIZATION ZONE, EASTERN REGION
NEUTRALIZATION ZONE, WESTERN REGION
KIKORU SHINOMIYA AND KAIJU NO. 8.
CHAPTER 42
I EXPECT RESULTS.
"IN ORDER TO SURVIVE, YOU MUST SHOW YOUR USEFULNESS."
THE DIRECTOR GENERAL GAVE ME THIS CHANCE.
I'LL BE SURE NOT TO WASTE IT!

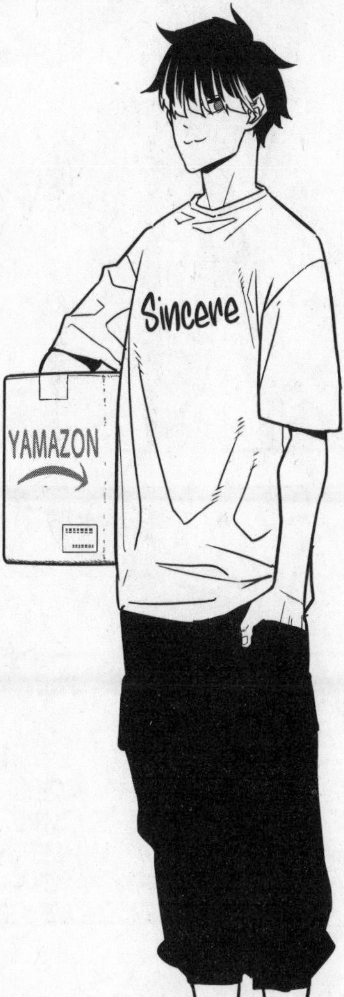
Sincere
YAMAZON

GEN NARUMI

Birthday:
December 28

Height:
175 cm

Likes:
Video games, online shopping, egosurfing, freedom, narrow spaces

Author Comment:
I tried to create a character that fit my vision of "the strongest around" and wound up with this pain in the neck. A single display of his skills overshadows his faults—that's what gives him his cool factor as the strongest soldier around.

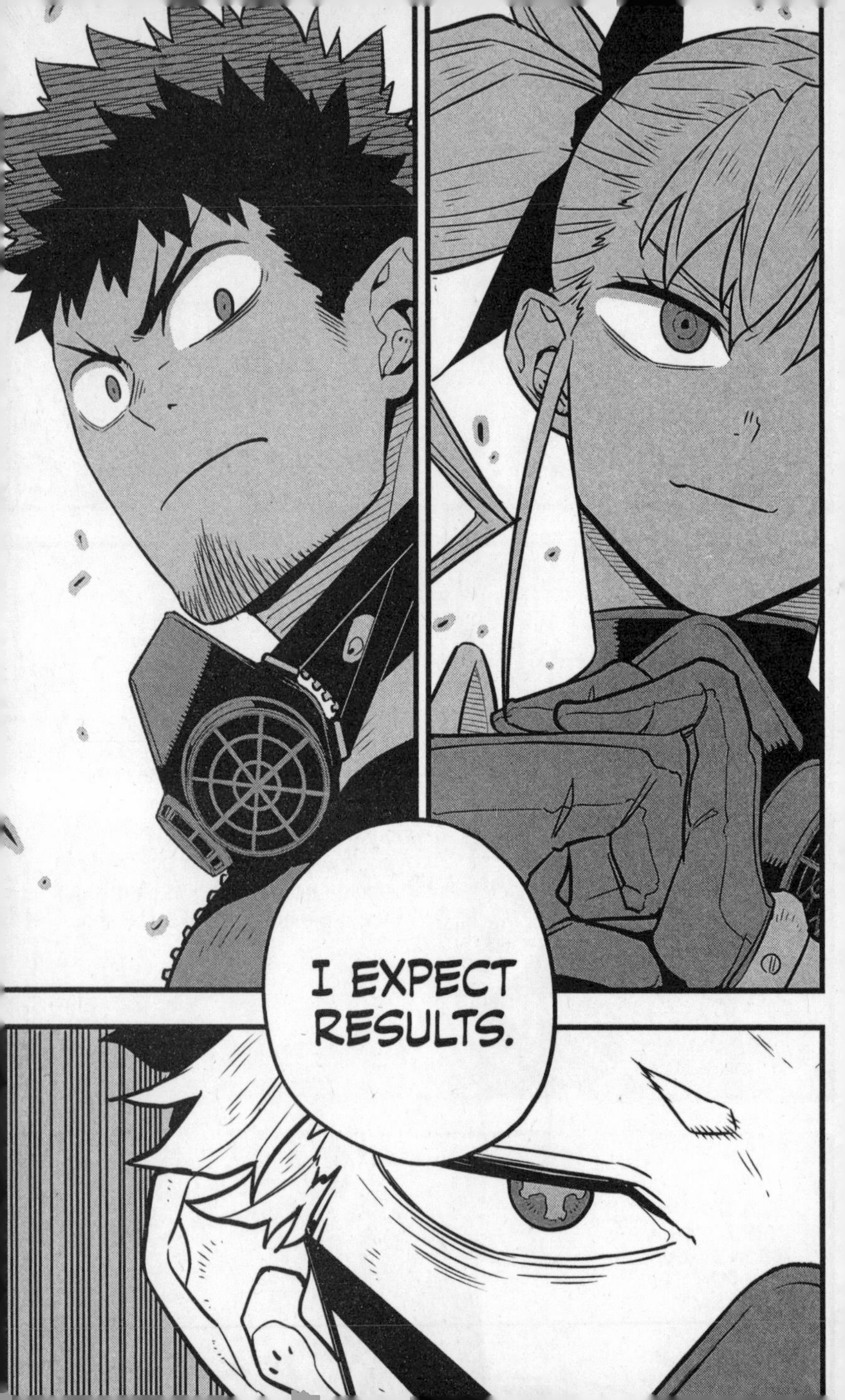
I EXPECT RESULTS.

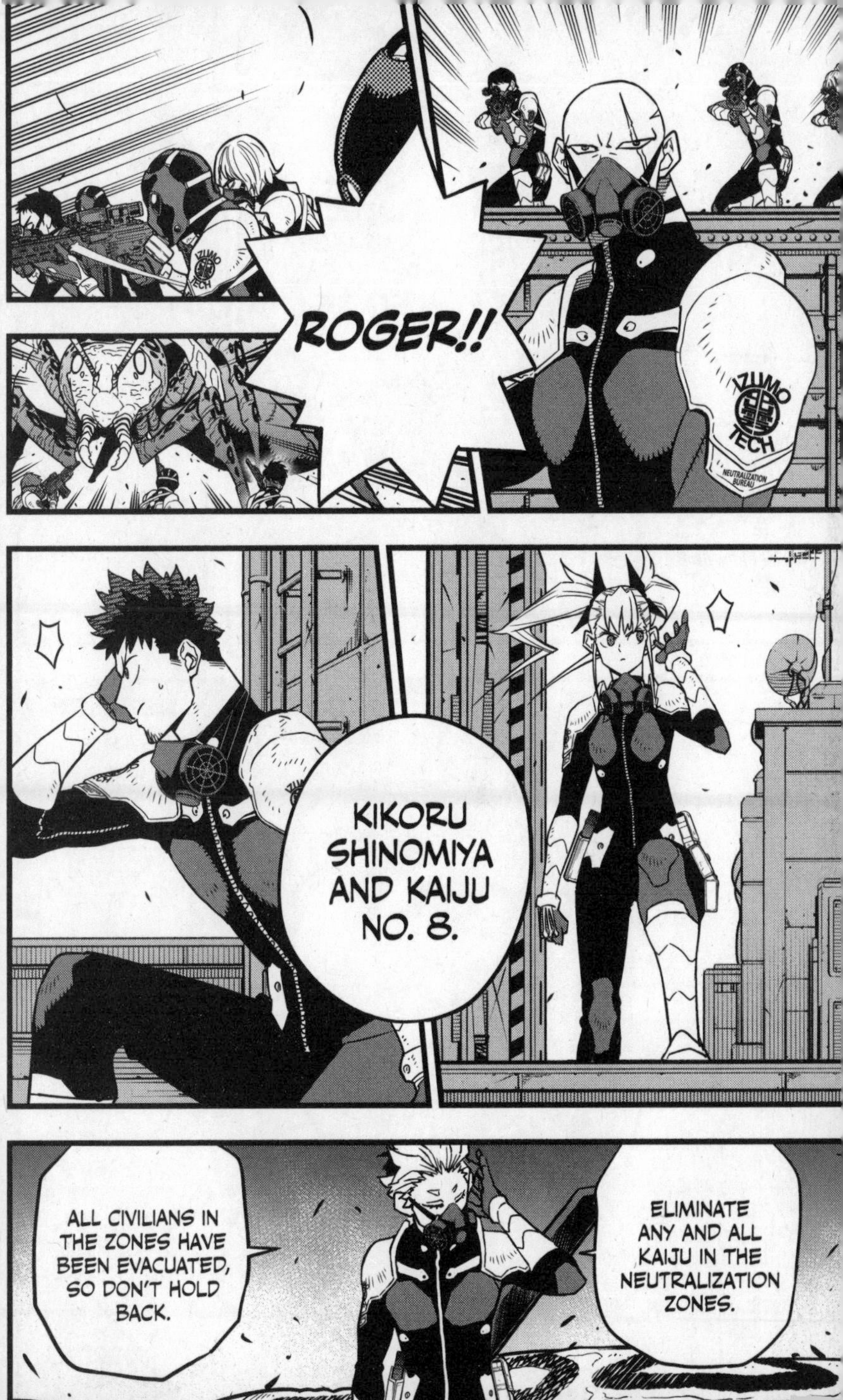
IZUMO TECH
NEUTRALIZATION BUREAU
ROGER!!
IZUMO TECH
KIKORU SHINOMIYA AND KAIJU NO. 8.
ELIMINATE ANY AND ALL KAIJU IN THE NEUTRALIZATION ZONES.
ALL CIVILIANS IN THE ZONES HAVE BEEN EVACUATED, SO DON'T HOLD BACK.

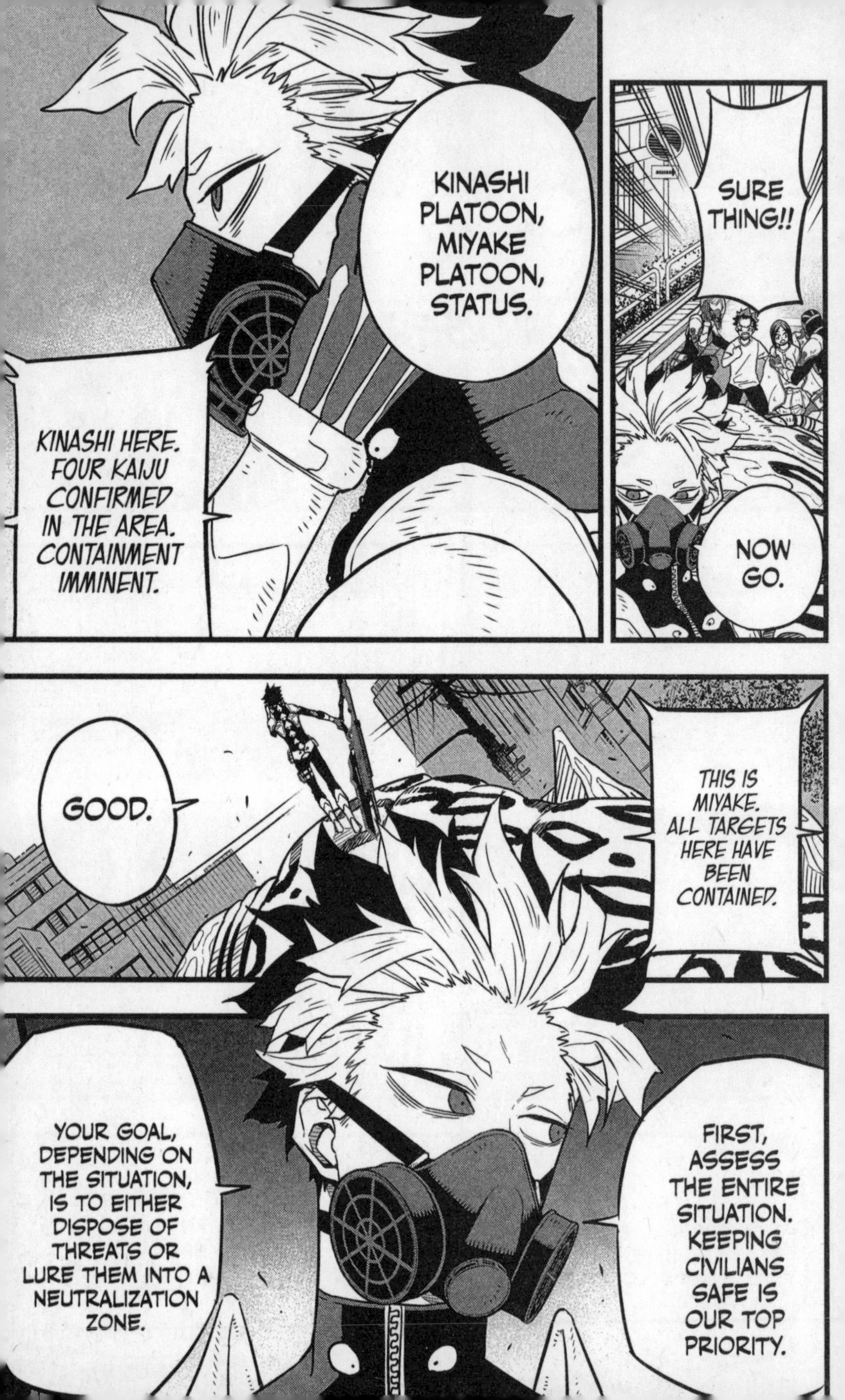
SURE THING!!
NOW GO.
KINASHI PLATOON, MIYAKE PLATOON, STATUS.
KINASHI HERE. FOUR KAIJU CONFIRMED IN THE AREA. CONTAINMENT IMMINENT.
THIS IS MIYAKE. ALL TARGETS HERE HAVE BEEN CONTAINED.
GOOD.
FIRST, ASSESS THE ENTIRE SITUATION. KEEPING CIVILIANS SAFE IS OUR TOP PRIORITY.
YOUR GOAL, DEPENDING ON THE SITUATION, IS TO EITHER DISPOSE OF THREATS OR LURE THEM INTO A NEUTRALIZATION ZONE.

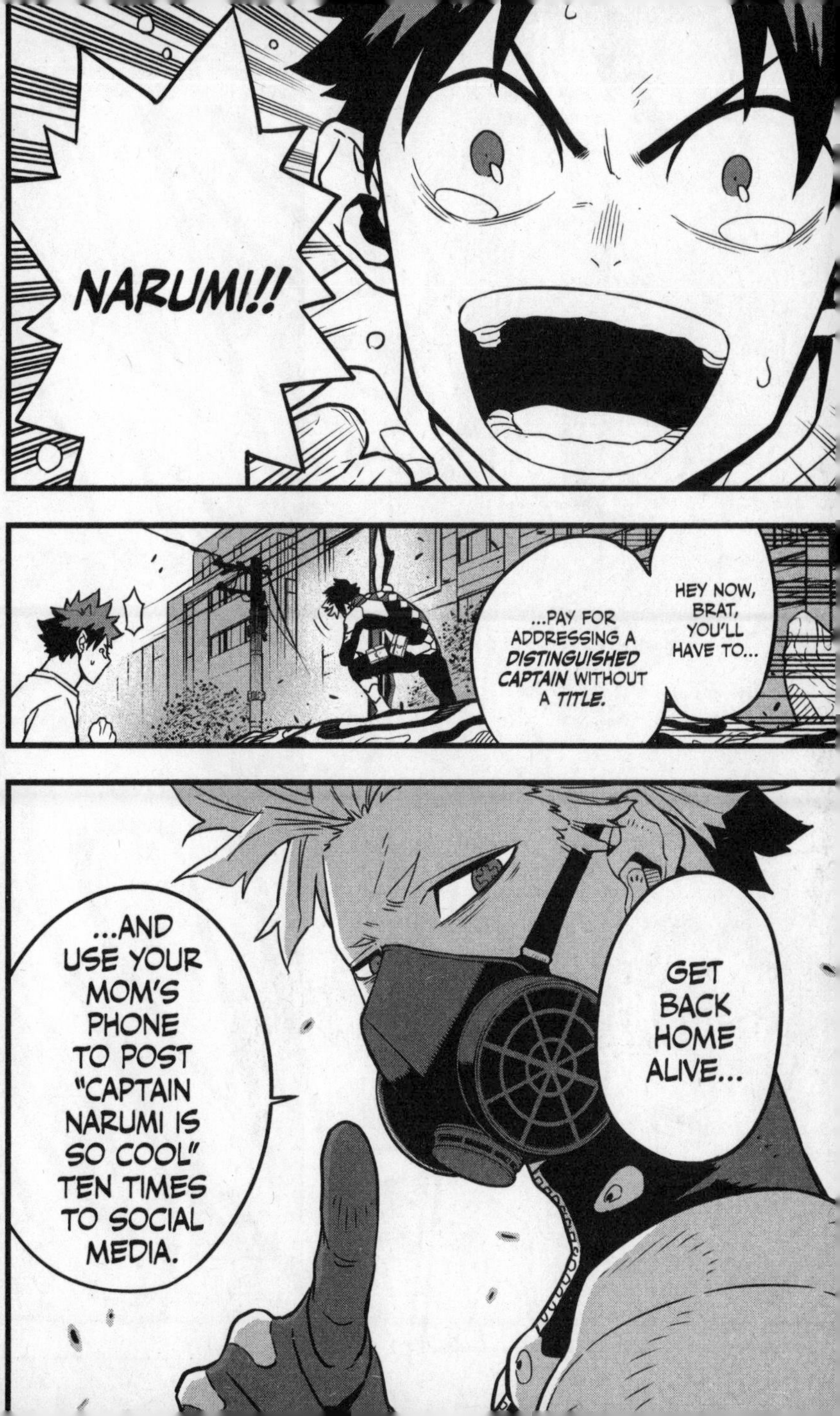
NARUMI!!
HEY NOW, BRAT, YOU'LL HAVE TO...
...PAY FOR ADDRESSING A *DISTINGUISHED CAPTAIN* WITHOUT A *TITLE*.
GET BACK HOME ALIVE...
...AND USE YOUR MOM'S PHONE TO POST "CAPTAIN NARUMI IS SO COOL" TEN TIMES TO SOCIAL MEDIA.

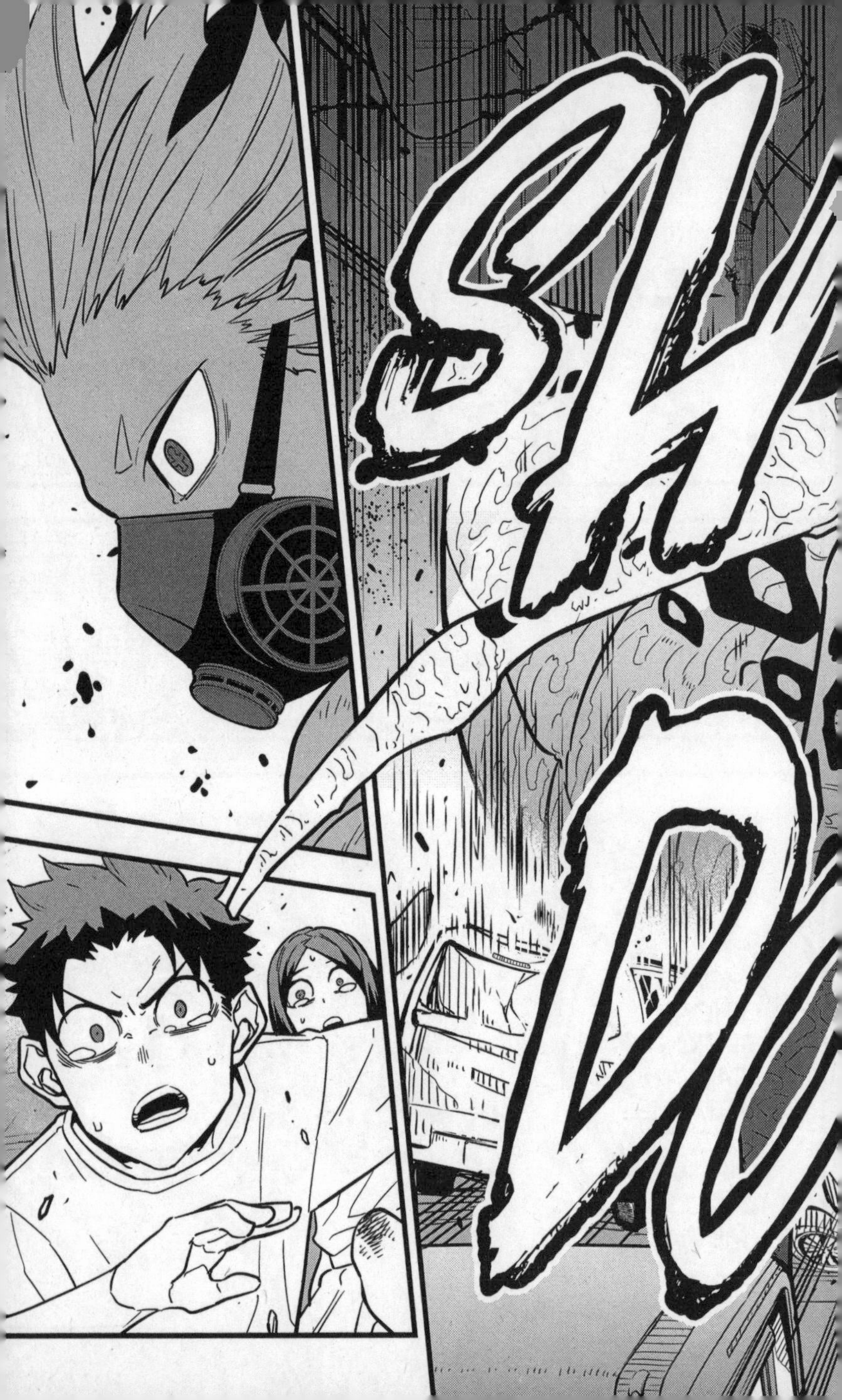

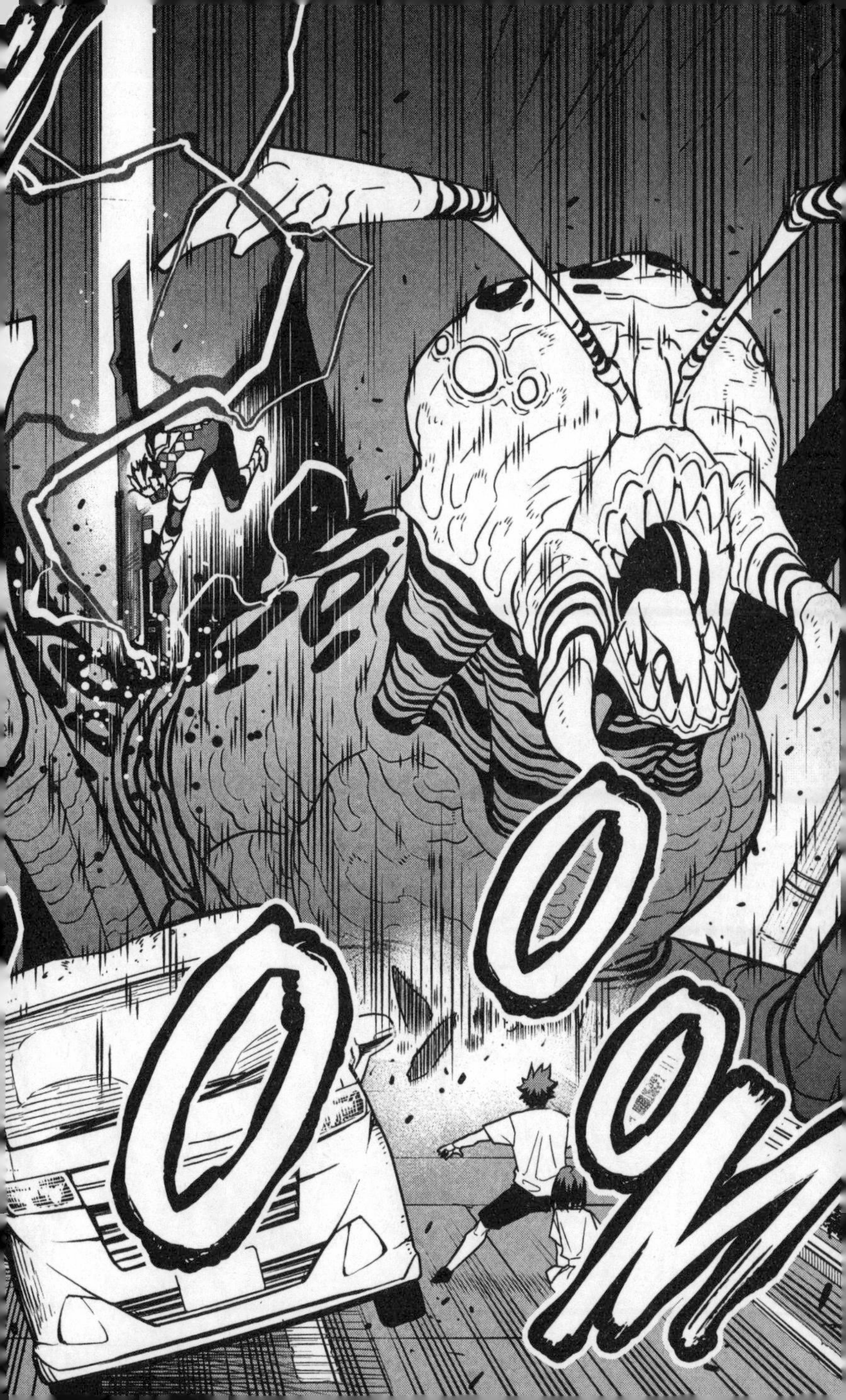
OOOM

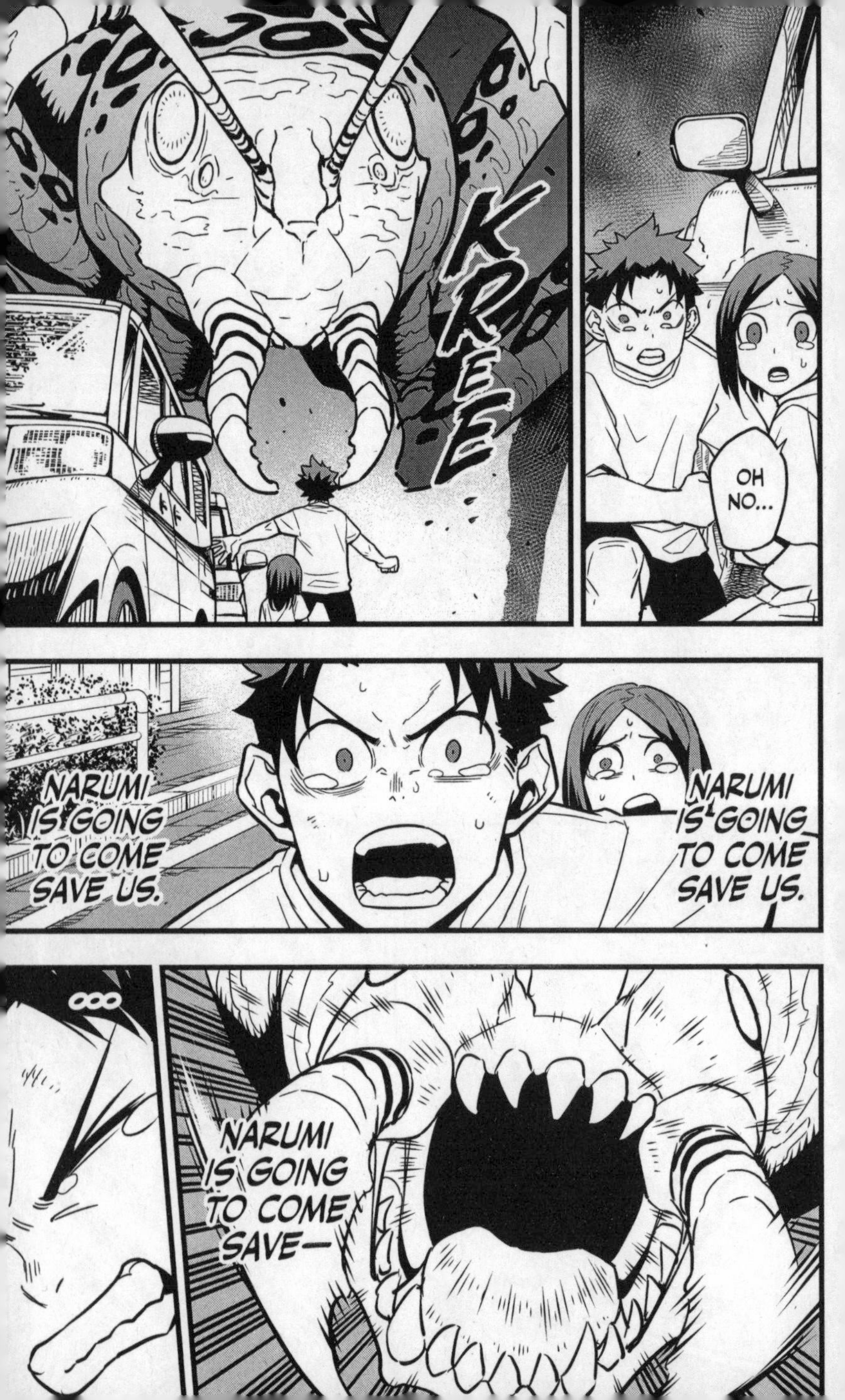
OH NO...
KREE
NARUMI IS GOING TO COME SAVE US.
NARUMI IS GOING TO COME SAVE US.
NARUMI IS GOING TO COME SAVE—
...

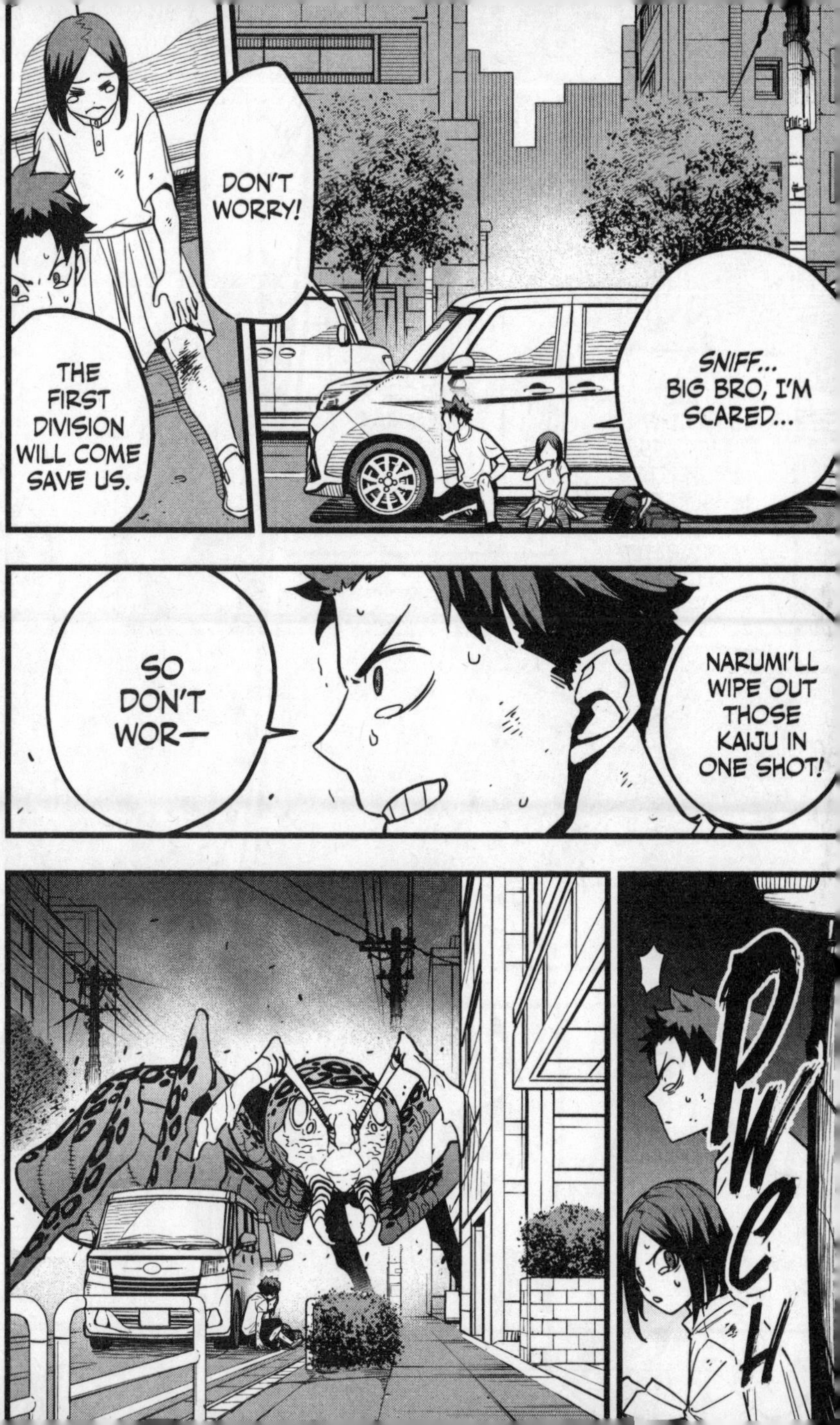
SNIFF... BIG BRO, I'M SCARED...
DON'T WORRY!
THE FIRST DIVISION WILL COME SAVE US.
NARUMI'LL WIPE OUT THOSE KAIJU IN ONE SHOT!
SO DON'T WOR—
PWCH

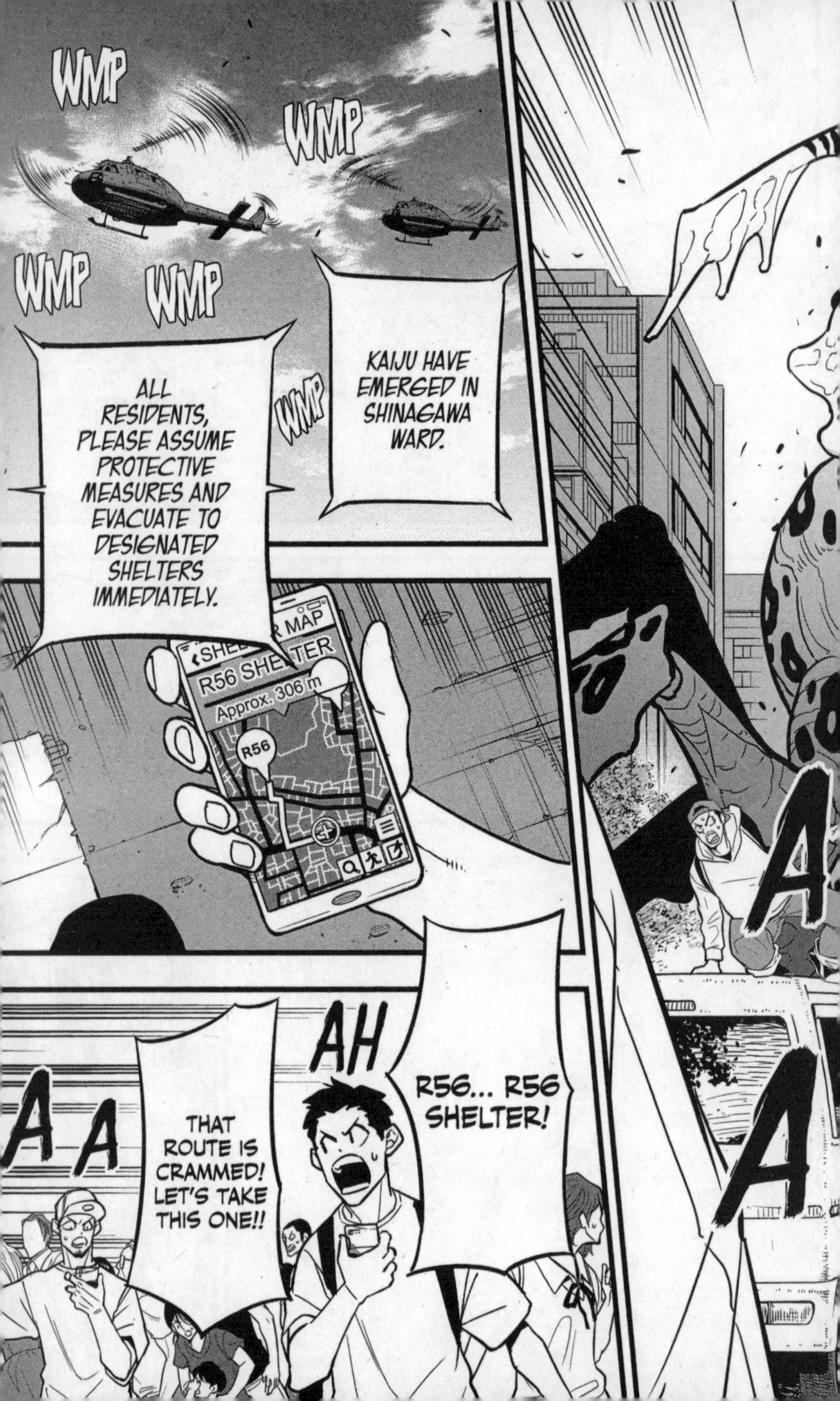
A
A
A
WMP
WMP
WMP
WMP
WMP
KAIJU HAVE EMERGED IN SHINAGAWA WARD.
ALL RESIDENTS, PLEASE ASSUME PROTECTIVE MEASURES AND EVACUATE TO DESIGNATED SHELTERS IMMEDIATELY.
R56 SHELTER
Approx. 306 m
R56
R56... R56 SHELTER!
AH
THAT ROUTE IS CRAMMED! LET'S TAKE THIS ONE!!
A
A

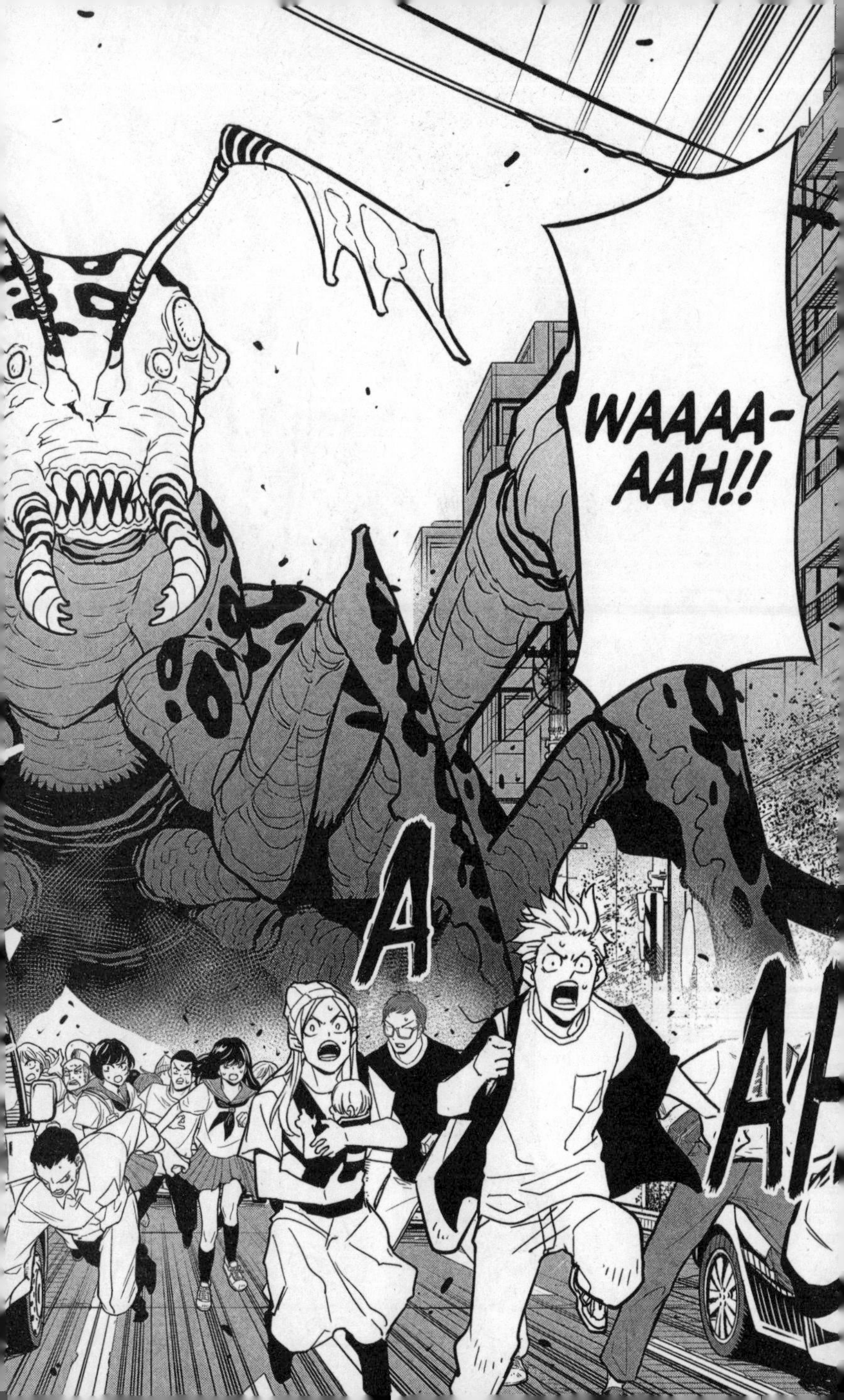
WAAAA-
AAH!!
A
AH

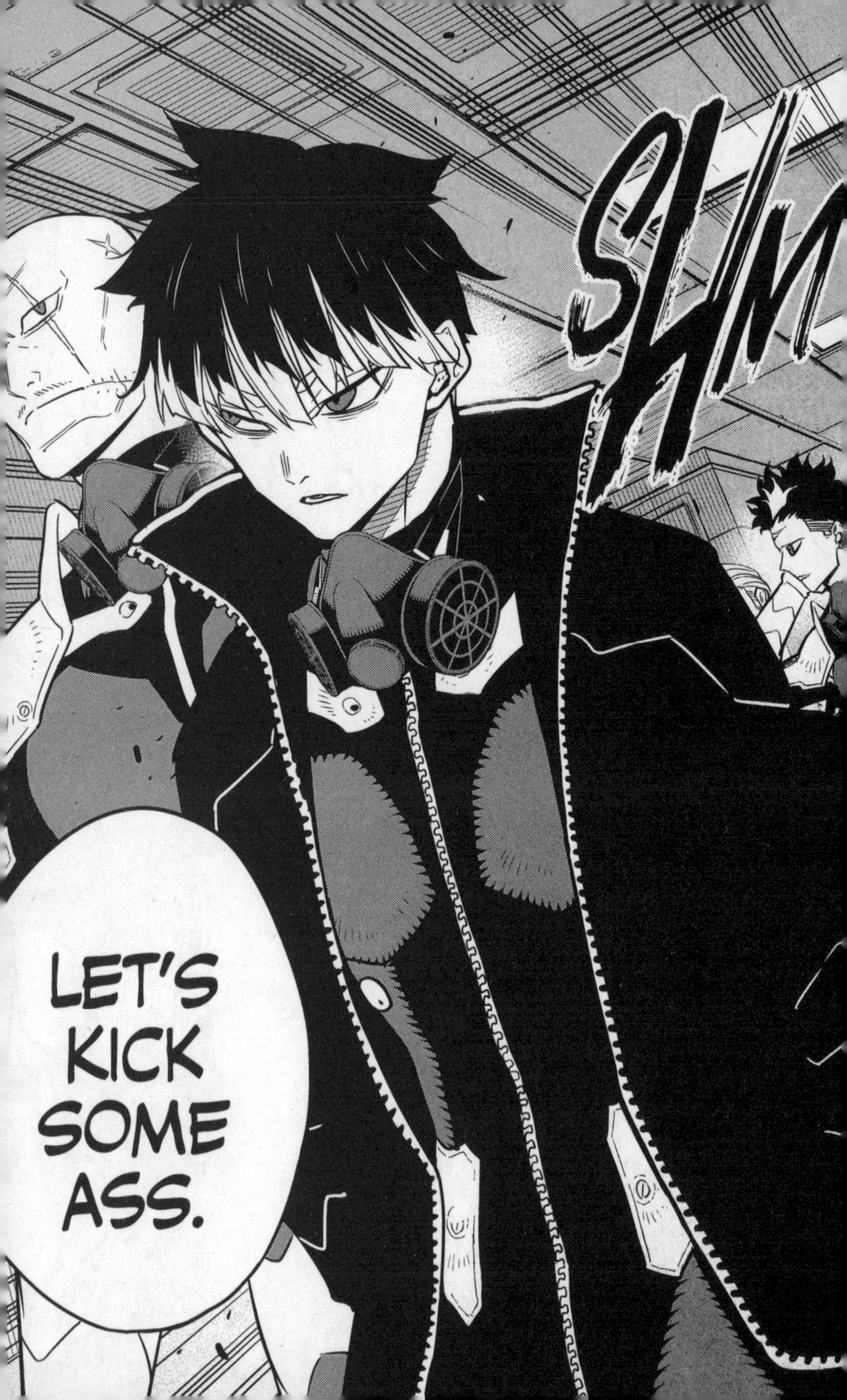
SHM
LET'S KICK SOME ASS.

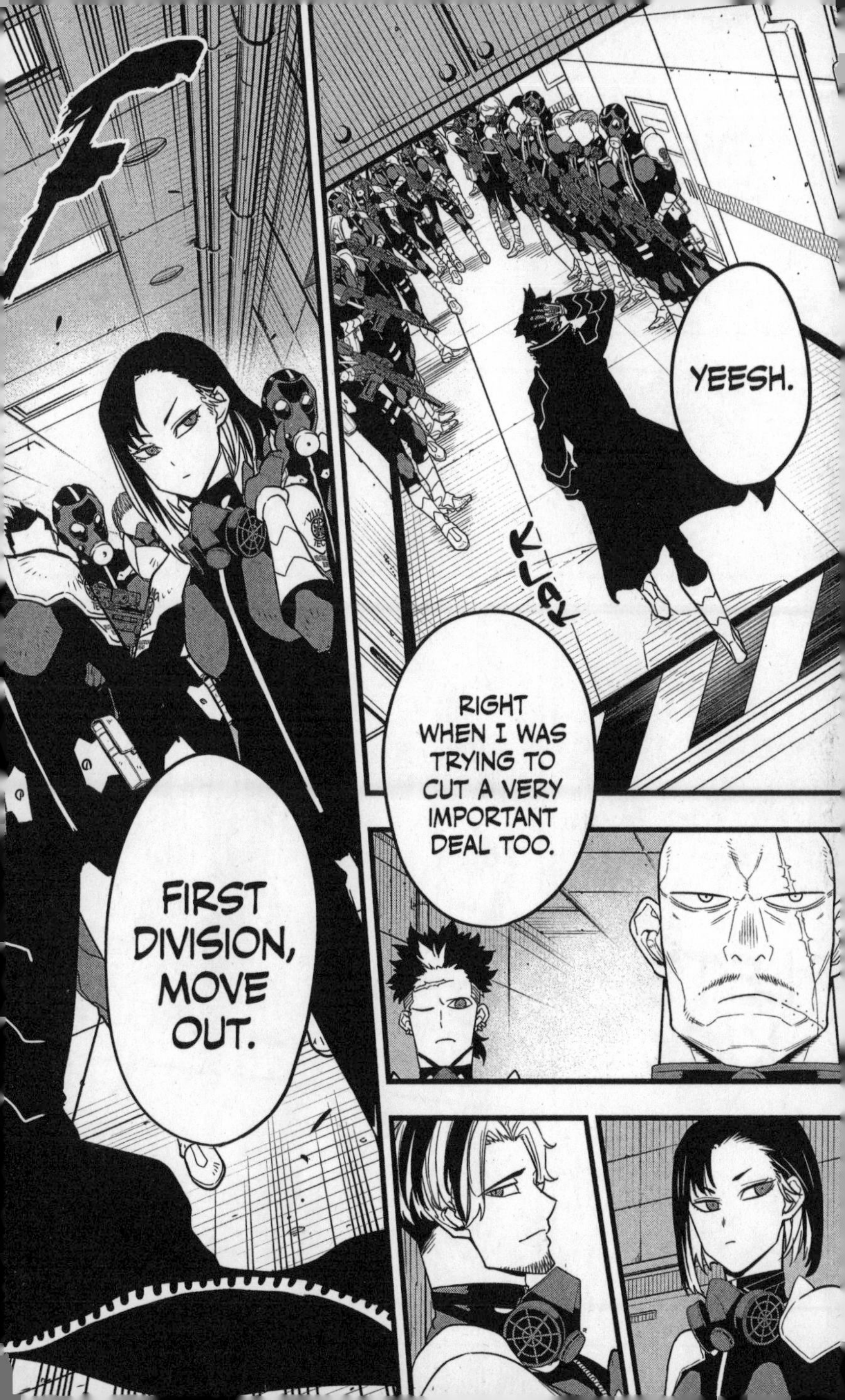
YEESH.
KLAK
RIGHT WHEN I WAS TRYING TO CUT A VERY IMPORTANT DEAL TOO.
FIRST DIVISION, MOVE OUT.

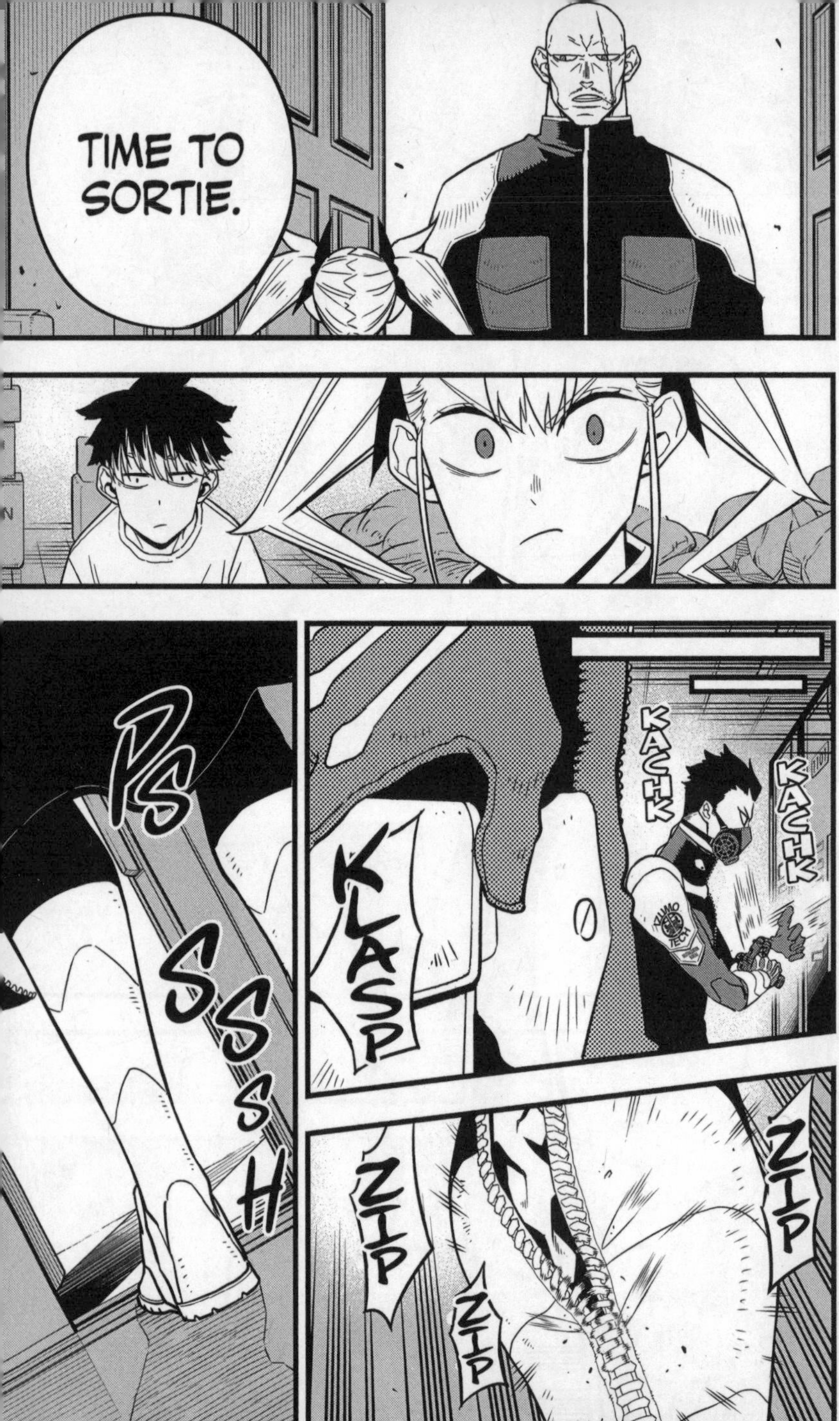
TIME TO SORTIE.
KACHK
KACHK
KLASP
ZIP
ZIP
ZIP
PSSSSH

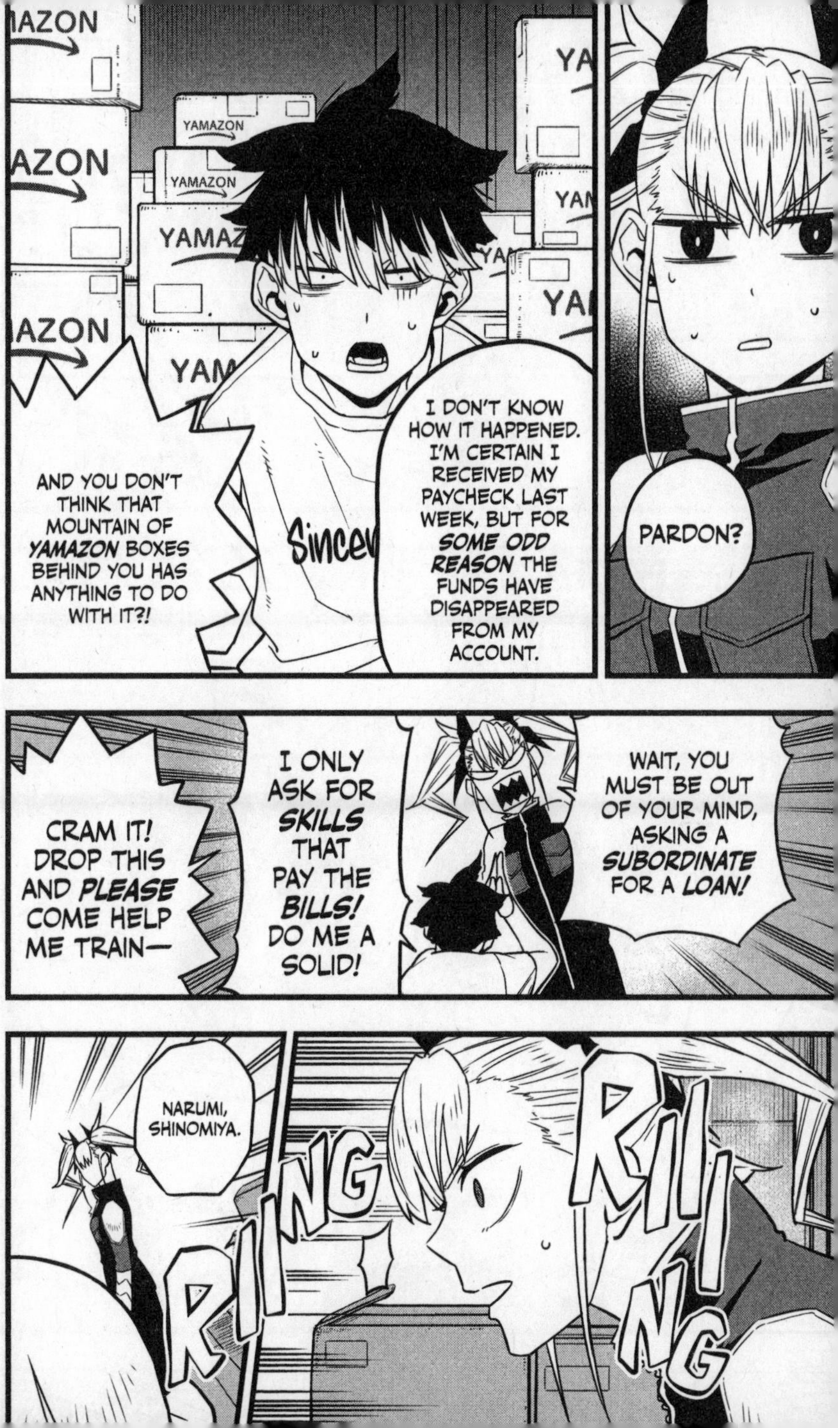
PARDON?
I DON'T KNOW HOW IT HAPPENED. I'M CERTAIN I RECEIVED MY PAYCHECK LAST WEEK, BUT FOR SOME ODD REASON THE FUNDS HAVE DISAPPEARED FROM MY ACCOUNT.
AND YOU DON'T THINK THAT MOUNTAIN OF YAMAZON BOXES BEHIND YOU HAS ANYTHING TO DO WITH IT?!
WAIT, YOU MUST BE OUT OF YOUR MIND, ASKING A SUBORDINATE FOR A LOAN!
I ONLY ASK FOR SKILLS THAT PAY THE BILLS! DO ME A SOLID!
CRAM IT! DROP THIS AND PLEASE COME HELP ME TRAIN—
RIIING
NARUMI, SHINOMIYA.
RIIING

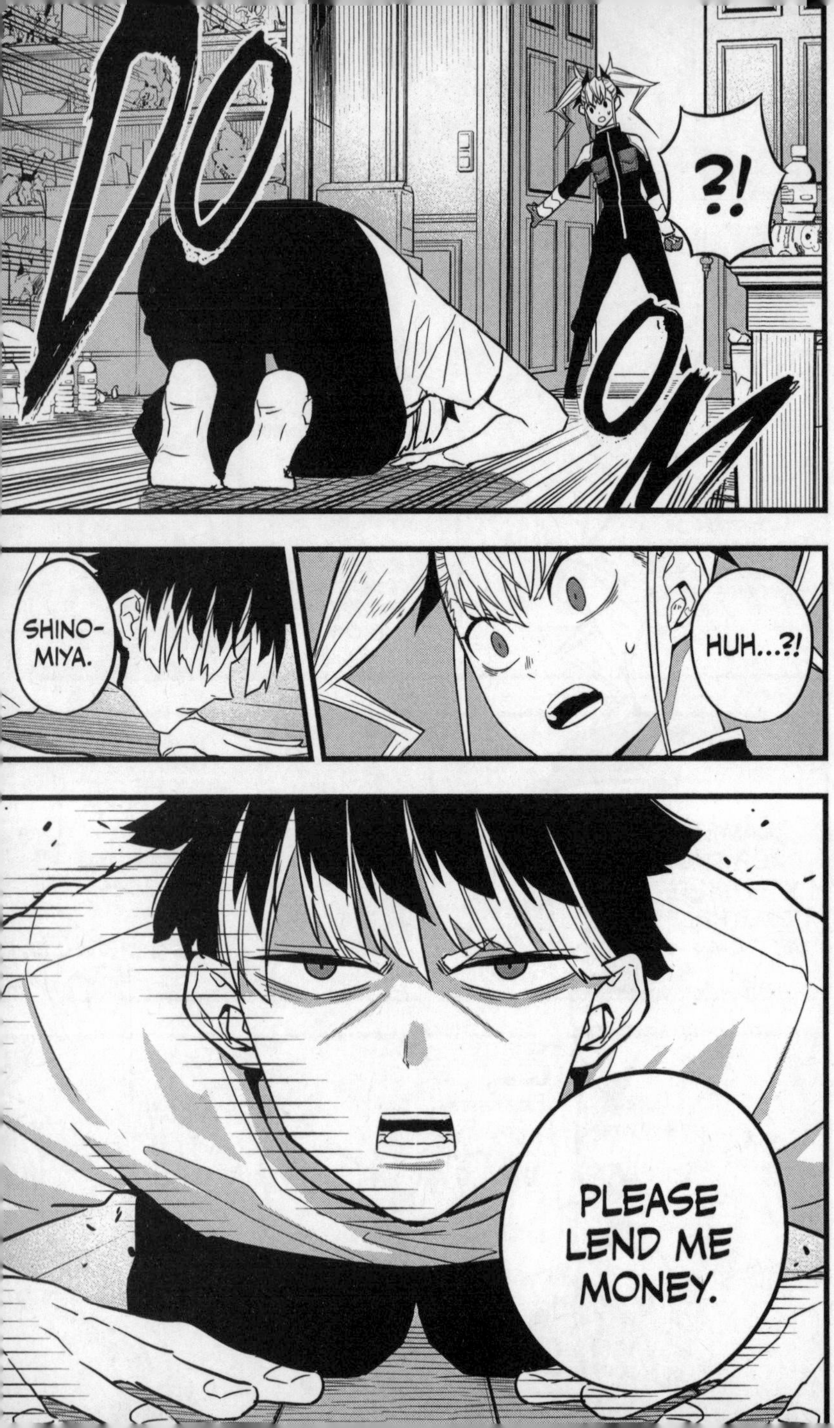
DOOM
?!
HUH...?!
SHINO-MIYA.
PLEASE LEND ME MONEY.

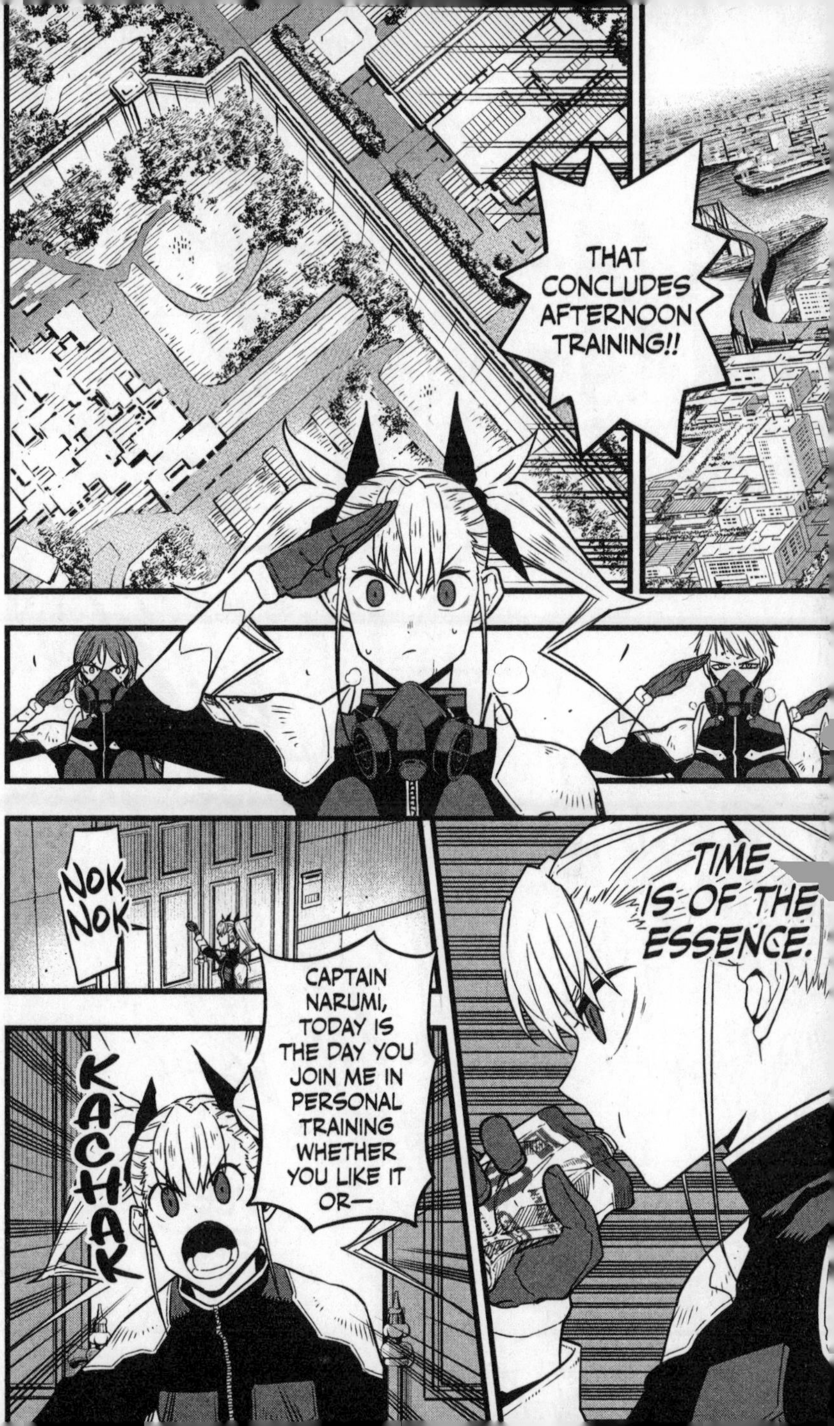
THAT CONCLUDES AFTERNOON TRAINING!!
TIME IS OF THE ESSENCE.
NOK NOK
CAPTAIN NARUMI, TODAY IS THE DAY YOU JOIN ME IN PERSONAL TRAINING WHETHER YOU LIKE IT OR—
KACHAK

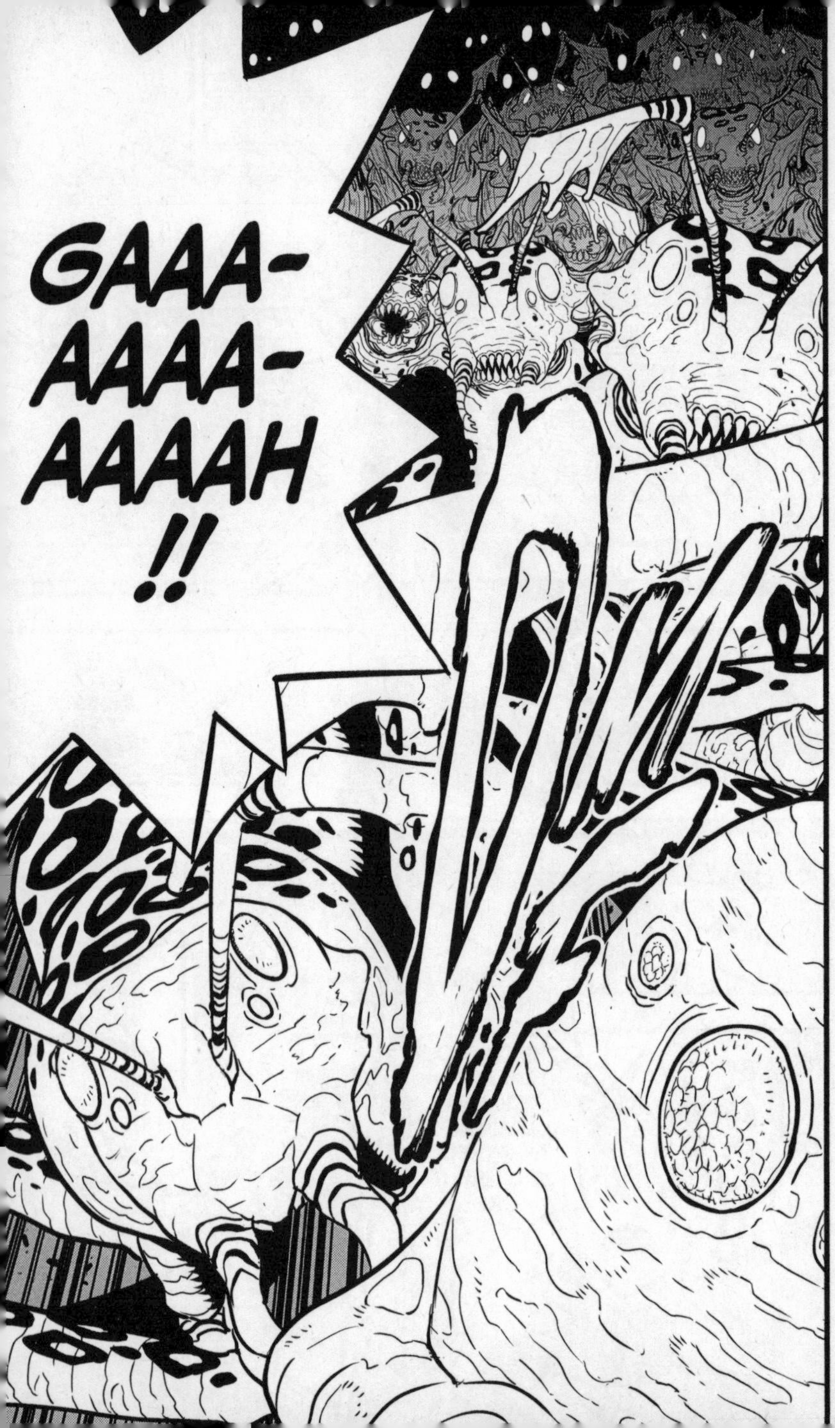
GAAA-AAAA-AAAAH!!

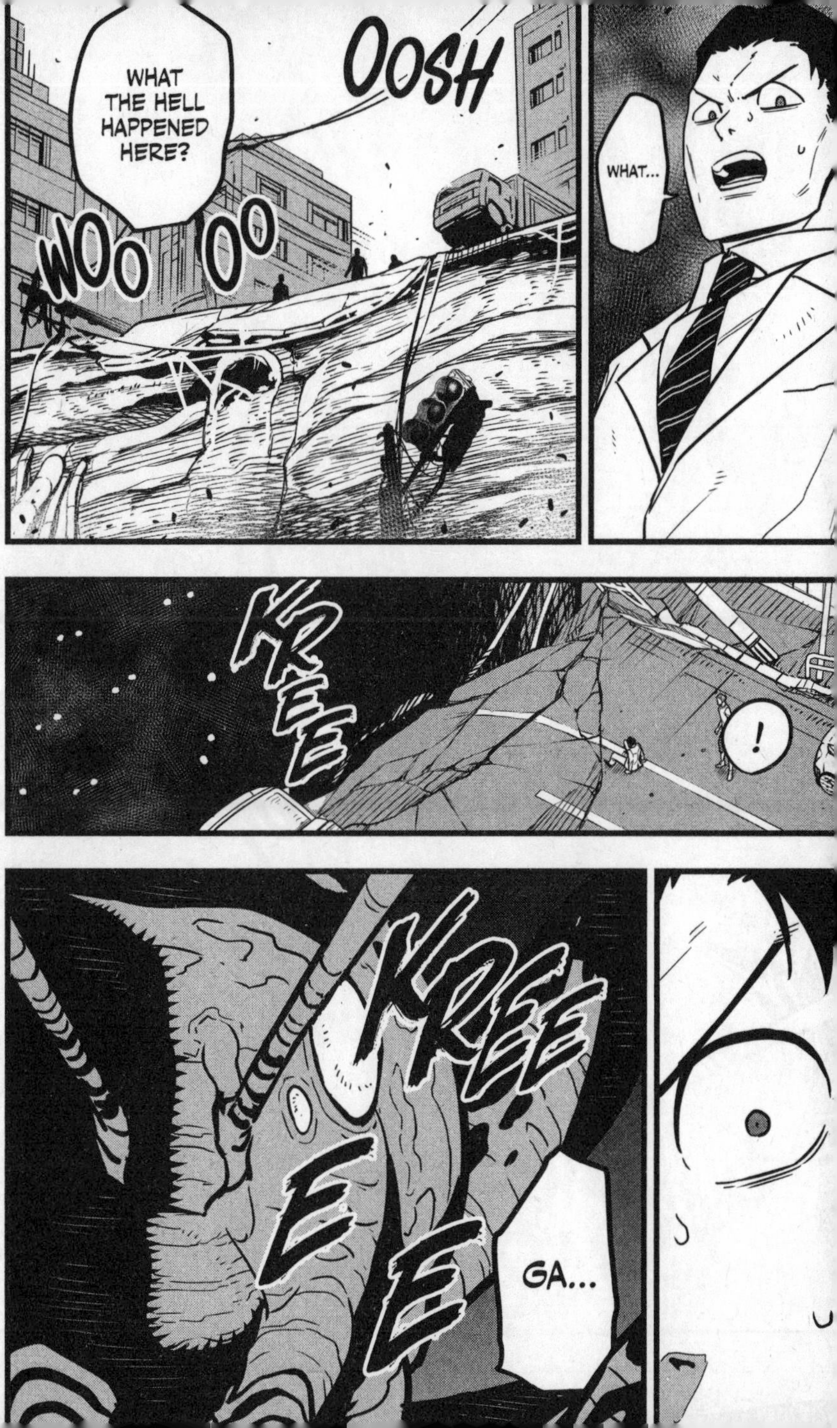
WHAT...
WHAT THE HELL HAPPENED HERE?
OOSH
WOO OO
!
KREE
GA...
KREEEE

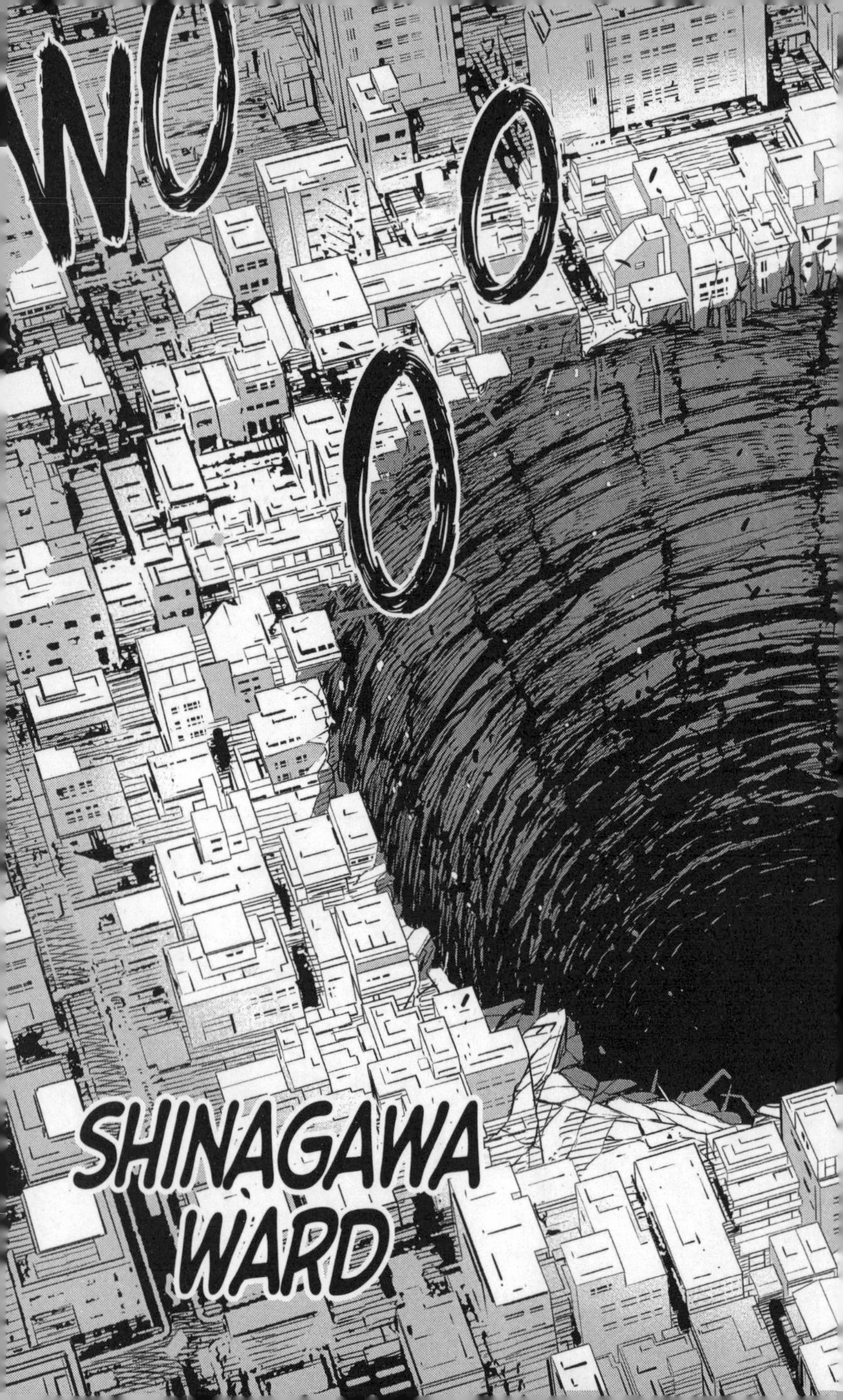
WOOOO
SHINAGAWA WARD

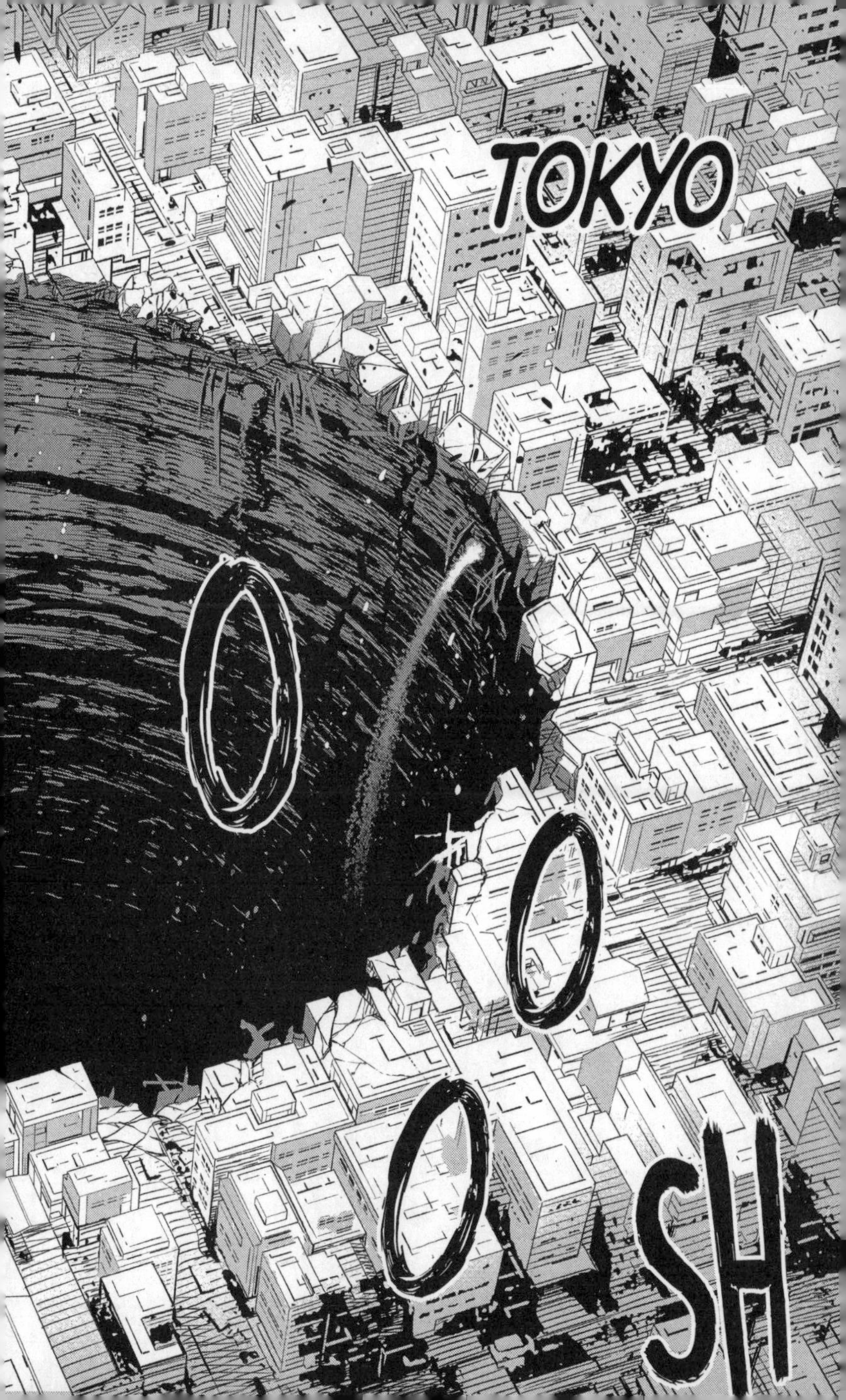
TOKYO
OOOSH

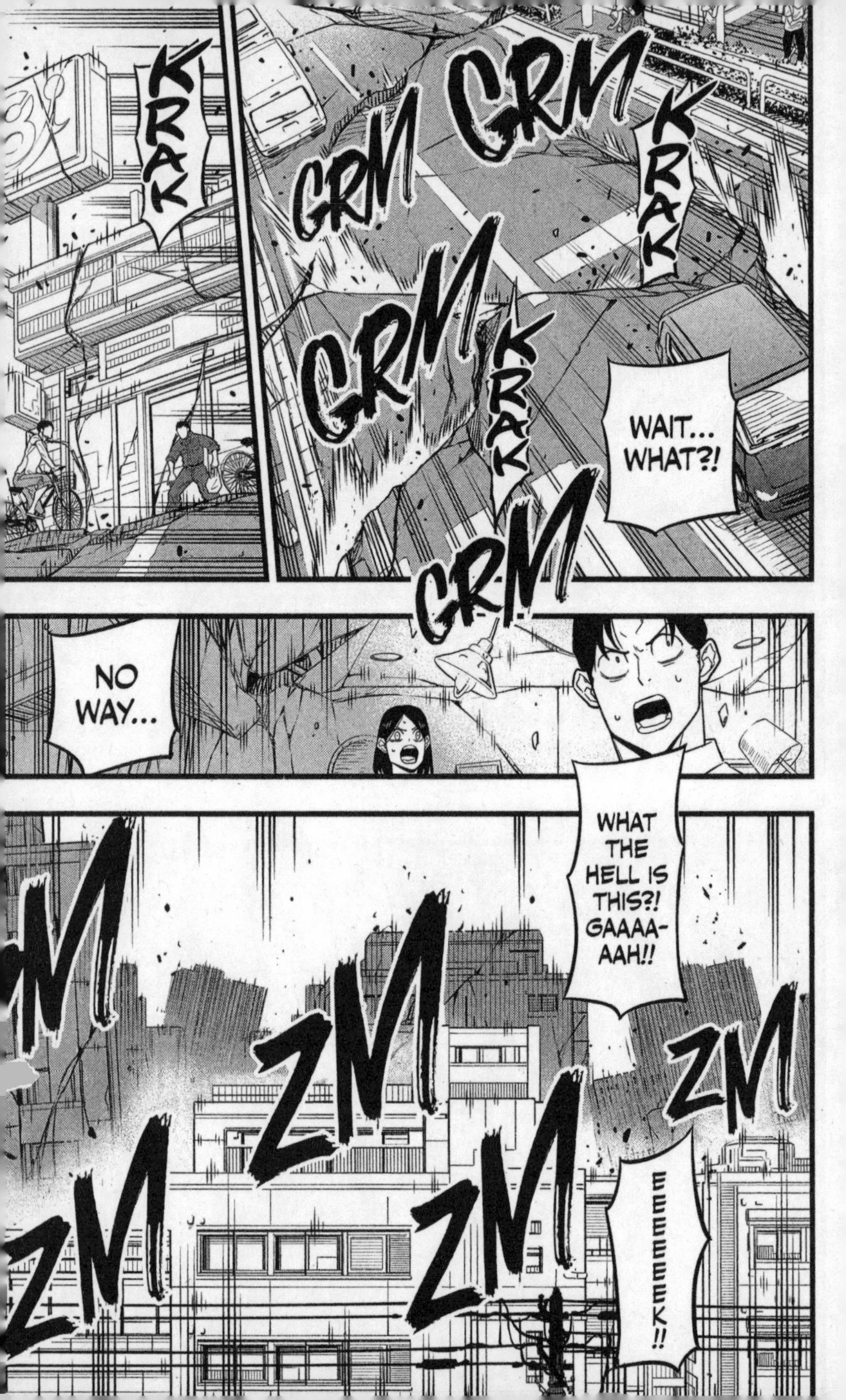
KRAK
GRM GRM
WAIT... WHAT?!
GRM
KRAK
GRM
KRAK
WHAT THE HELL IS THIS?! GAAAA-AAH!!
NO WAY...
ZM
ZM
EEEEEEEK!!
ZM
ZM
ZM
ZM

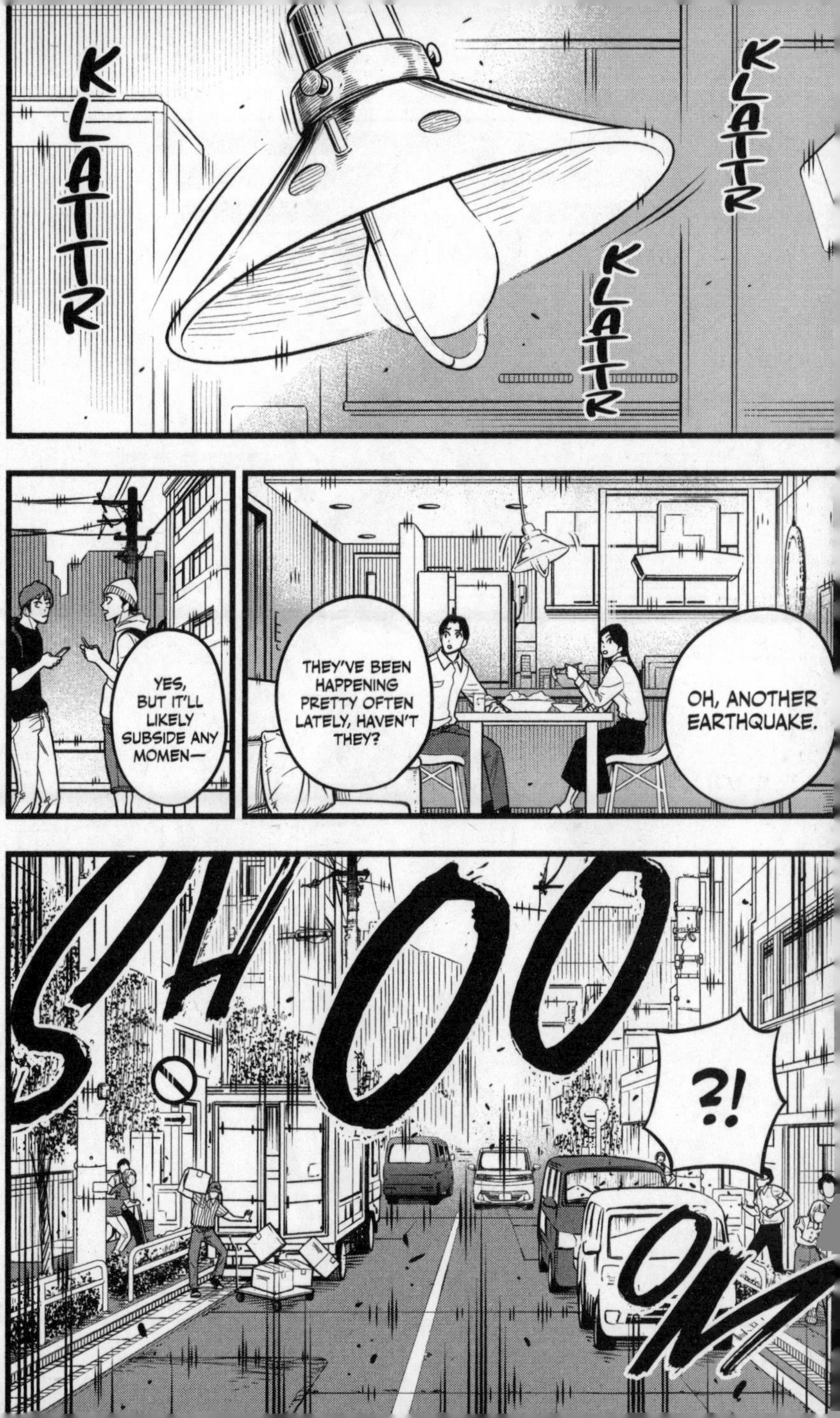
KLATTR
KLATTR
KLATTR
OH, ANOTHER EARTHQUAKE.
THEY'VE BEEN HAPPENING PRETTY OFTEN LATELY, HAVEN'T THEY?
YES, BUT IT'LL LIKELY SUBSIDE ANY MOMEN—
?!
SHOOOM

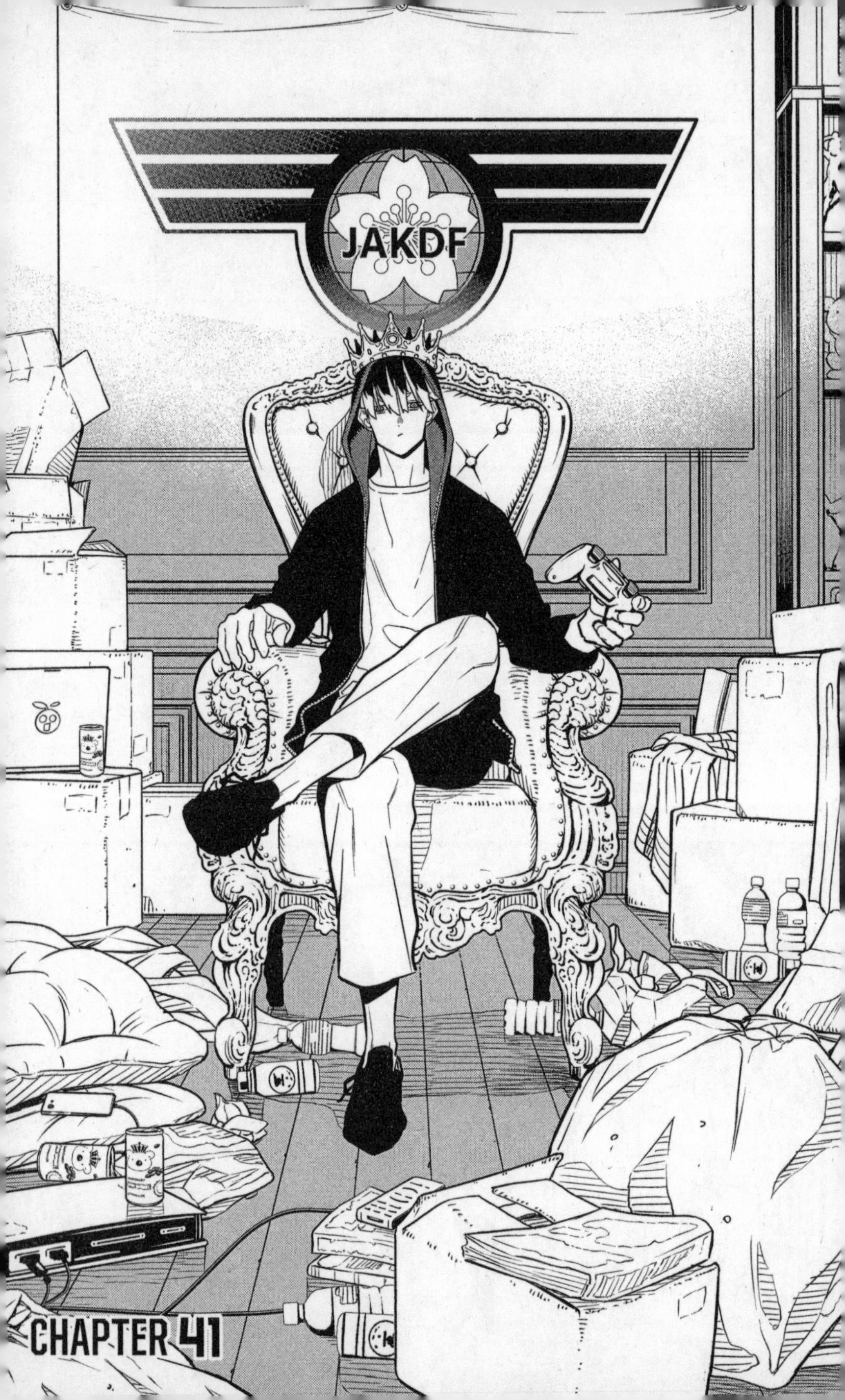
JAKDF
CHAPTER 41

KAIJU NO. 8

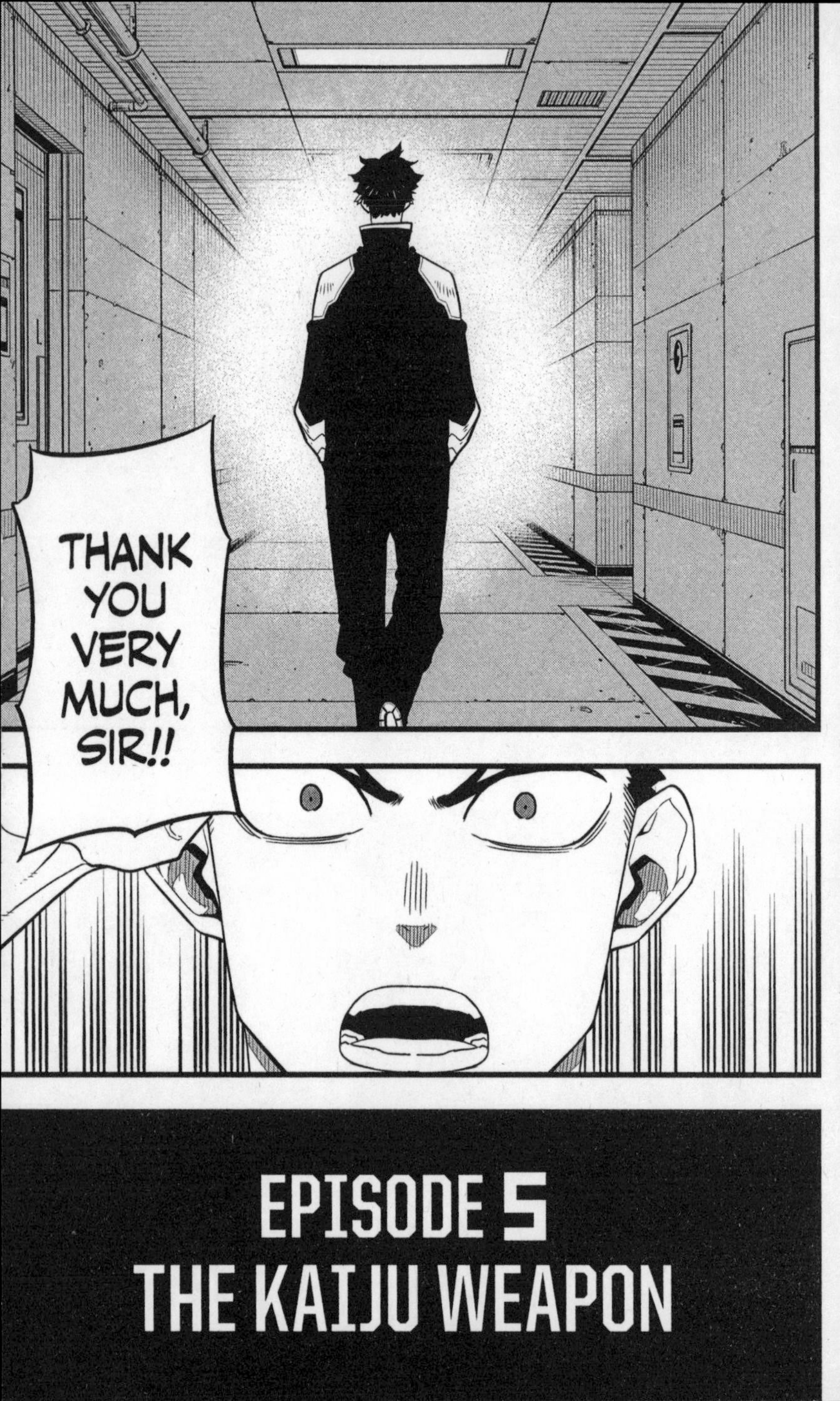
THANK YOU VERY MUCH, SIR!!

EPISODE 5
THE KAIJU WEAPON

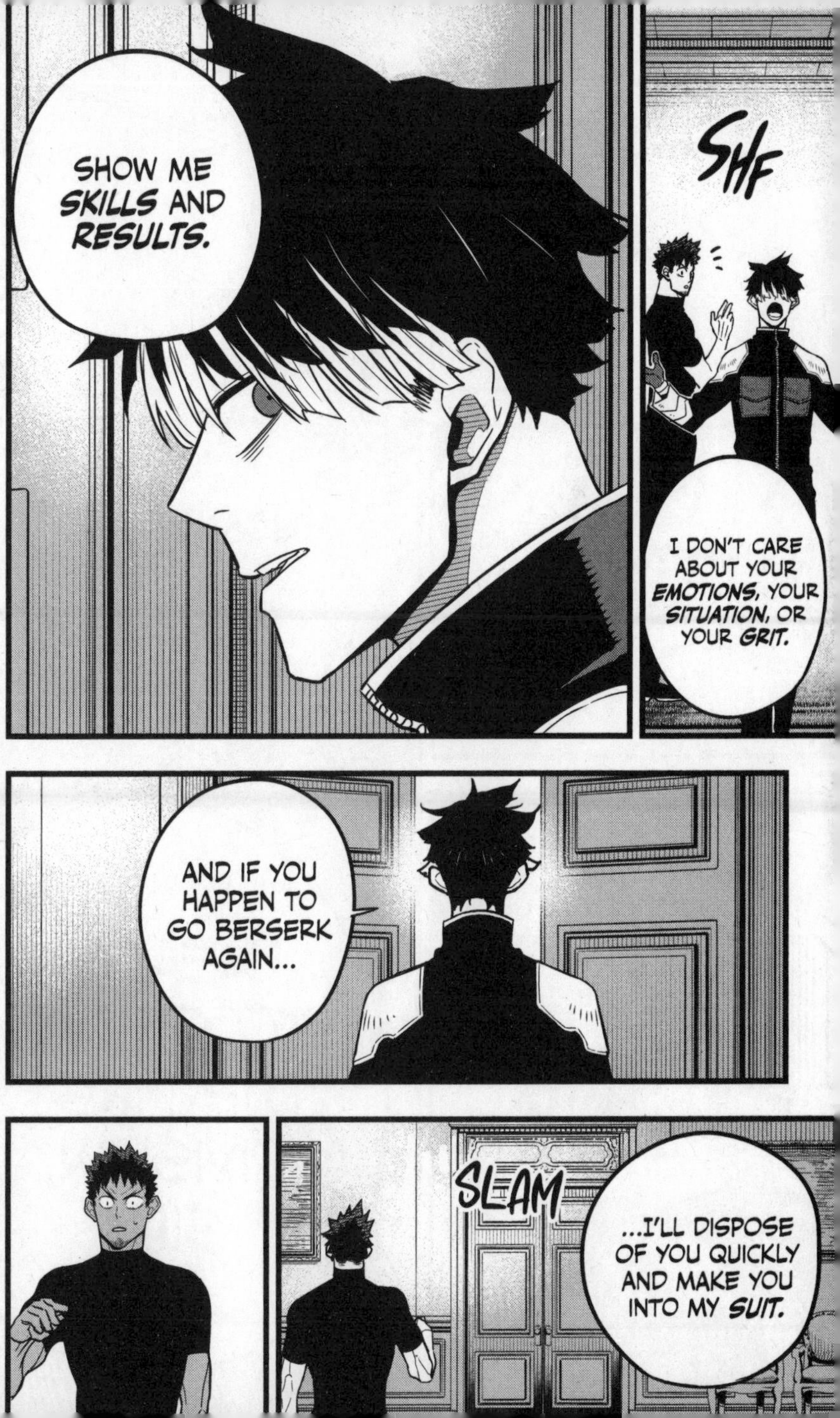
SHF
I DON'T CARE ABOUT YOUR EMOTIONS, YOUR SITUATION, OR YOUR GRIT.
SHOW ME SKILLS AND RESULTS.
AND IF YOU HAPPEN TO GO BERSERK AGAIN...
SLAM
...I'LL DISPOSE OF YOU QUICKLY AND MAKE YOU INTO MY SUIT.

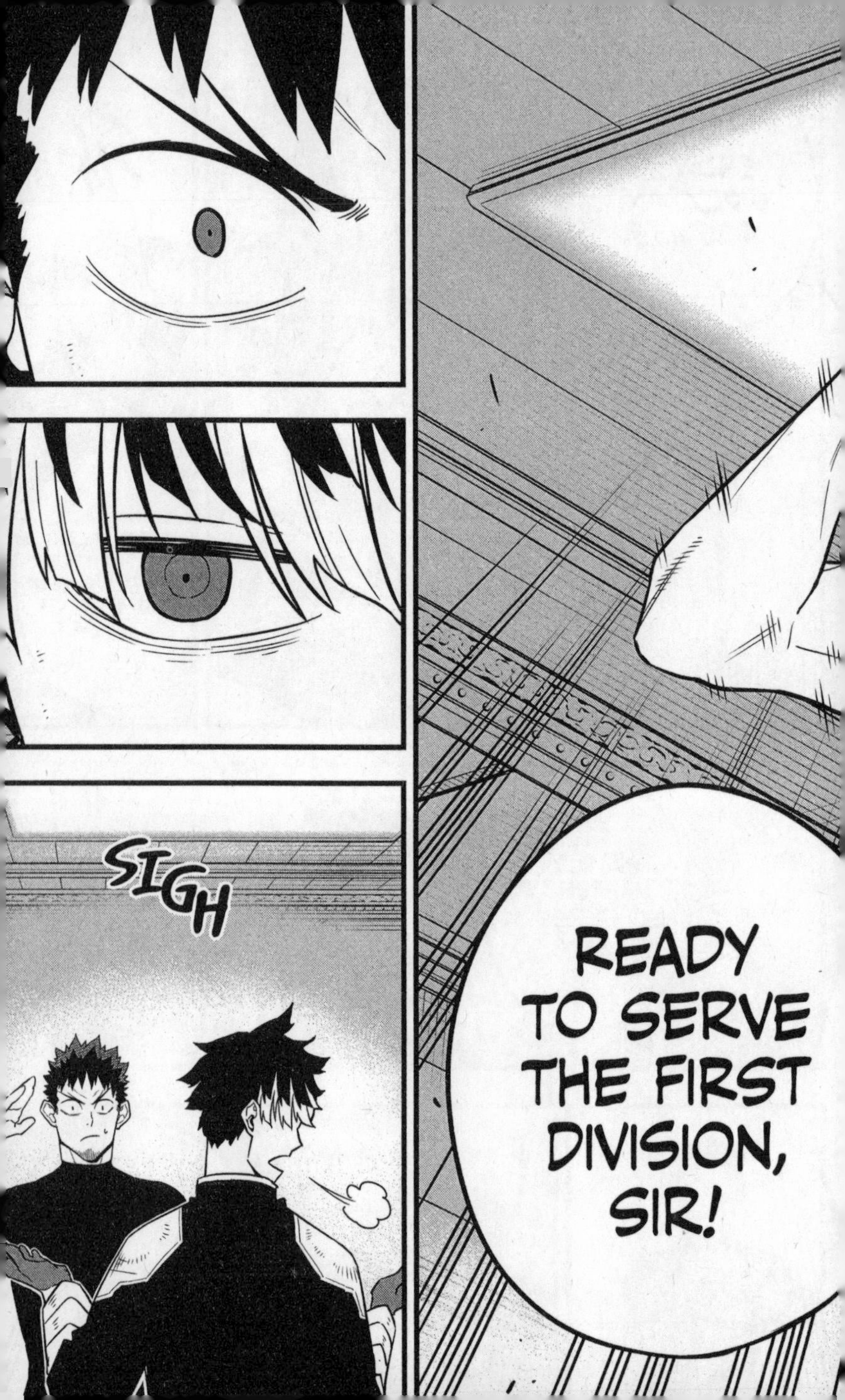
READY TO SERVE THE FIRST DIVISION, SIR!
SIGH

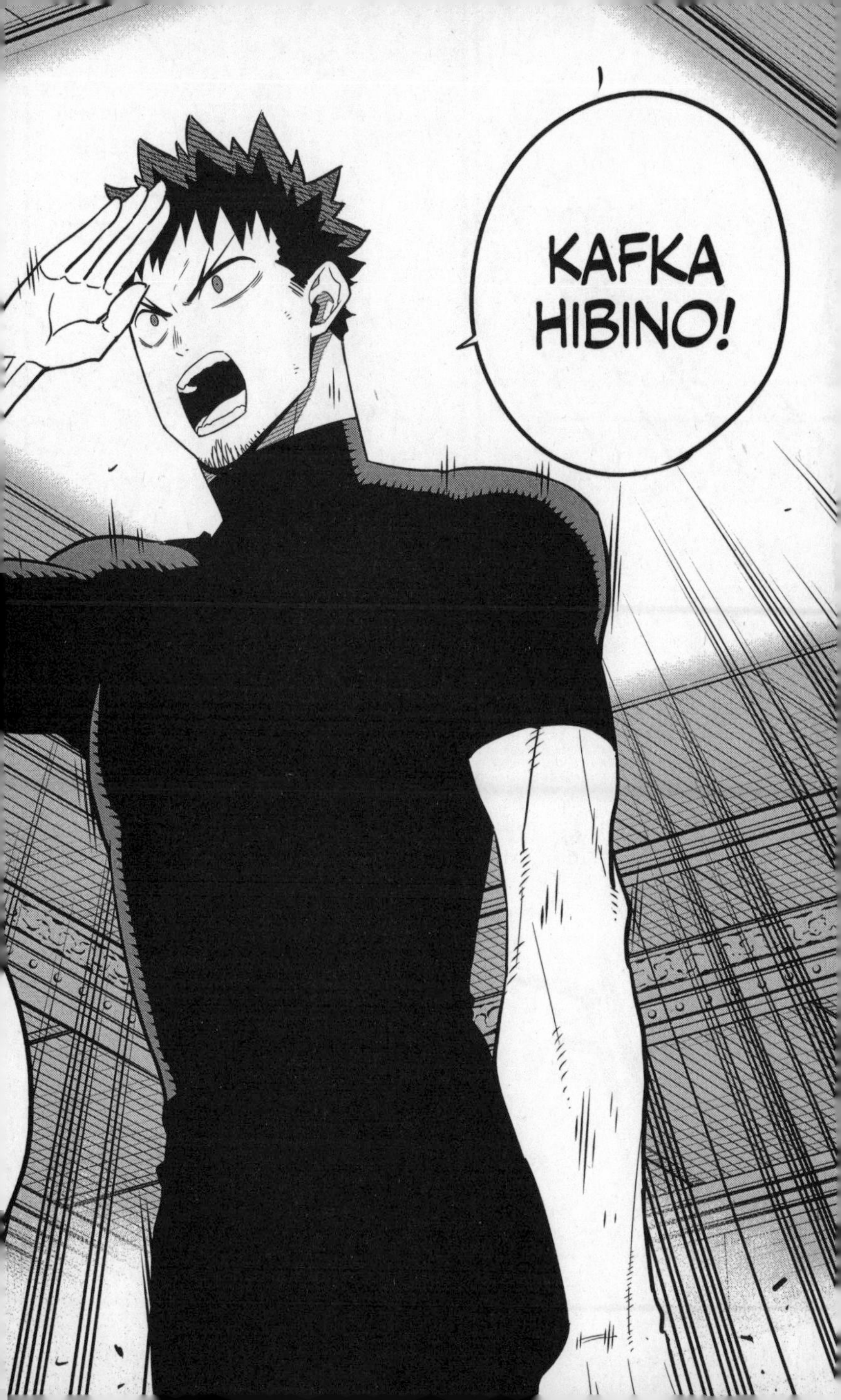
KAFKA HIBINO!

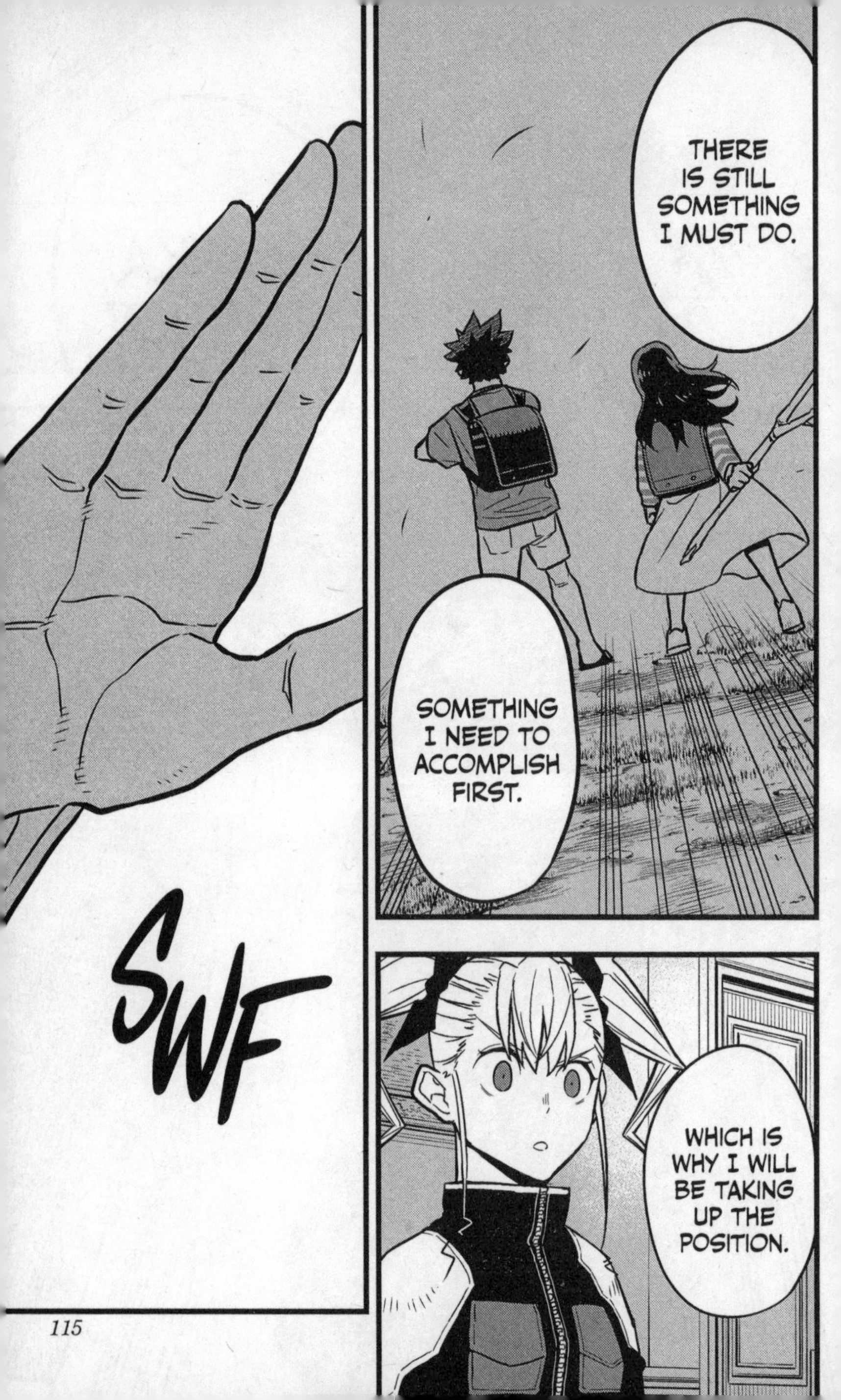
THERE IS STILL SOMETHING I MUST DO.
SOMETHING I NEED TO ACCOMPLISH FIRST.
WHICH IS WHY I WILL BE TAKING UP THE POSITION.
SWF

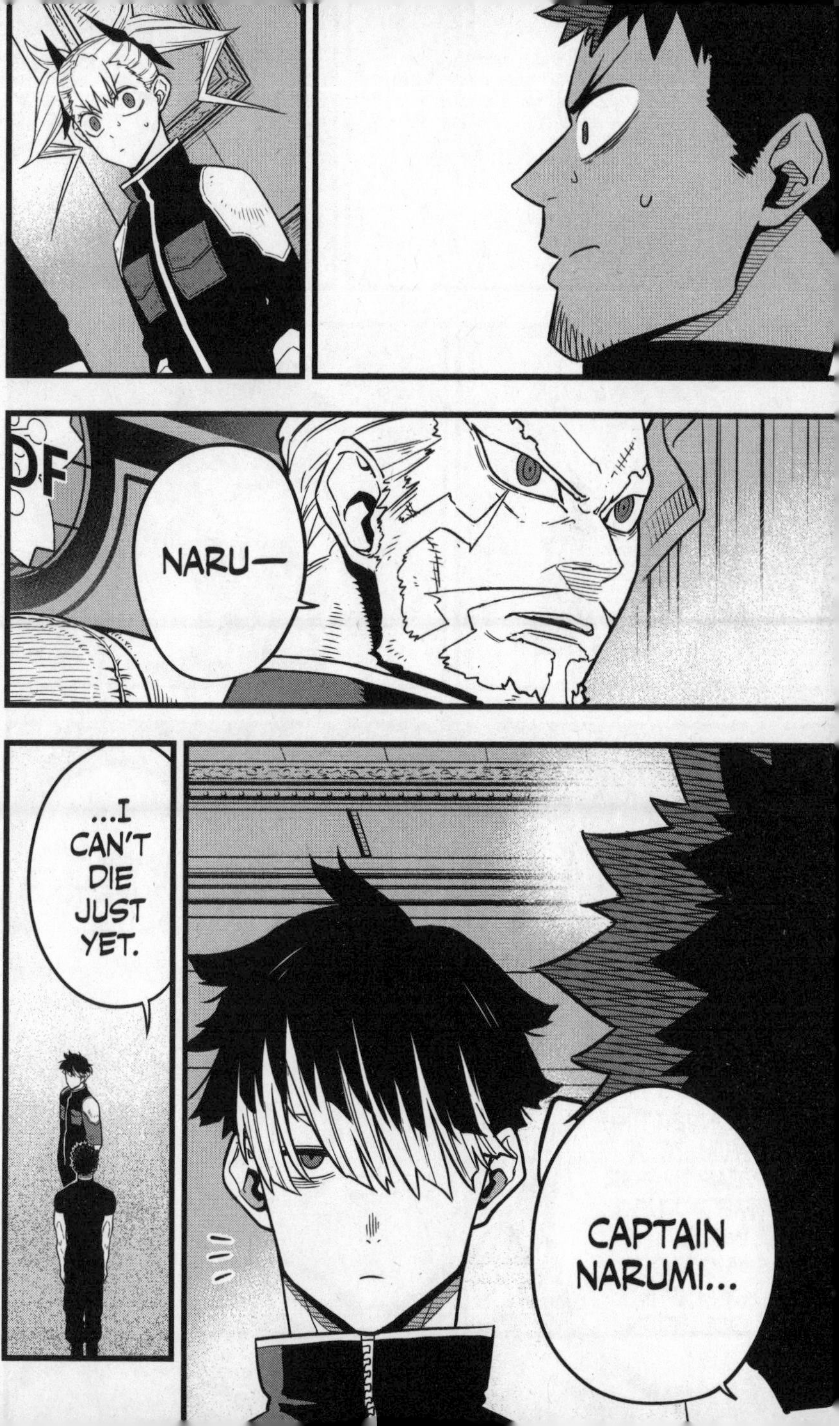
NARU—
CAPTAIN NARUMI...
...I CAN'T DIE JUST YET.

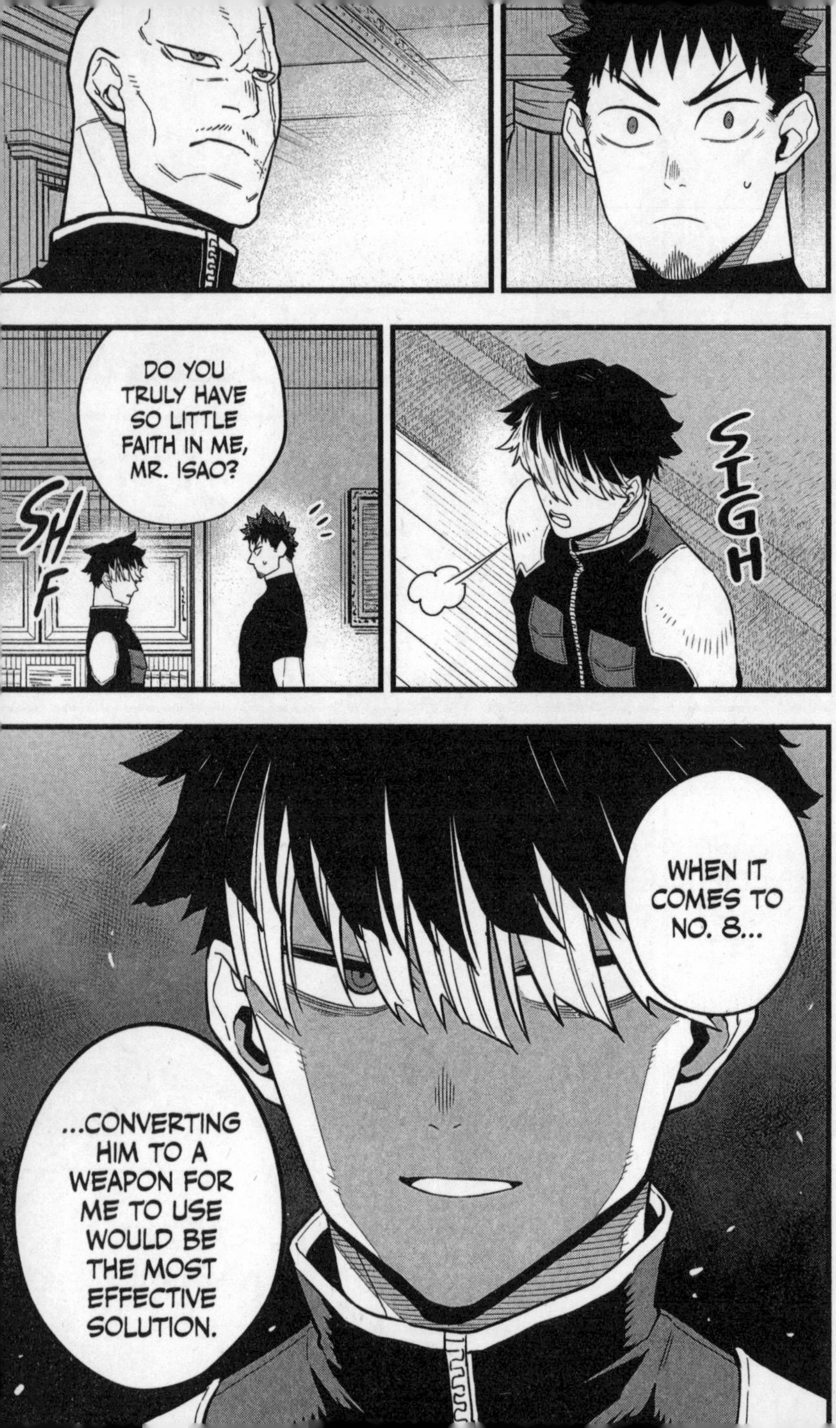
SIGH
DO YOU TRULY HAVE SO LITTLE FAITH IN ME, MR. ISAO?
SHF
WHEN IT COMES TO NO. 8...
...CONVERTING HIM TO A WEAPON FOR ME TO USE WOULD BE THE MOST EFFECTIVE SOLUTION.

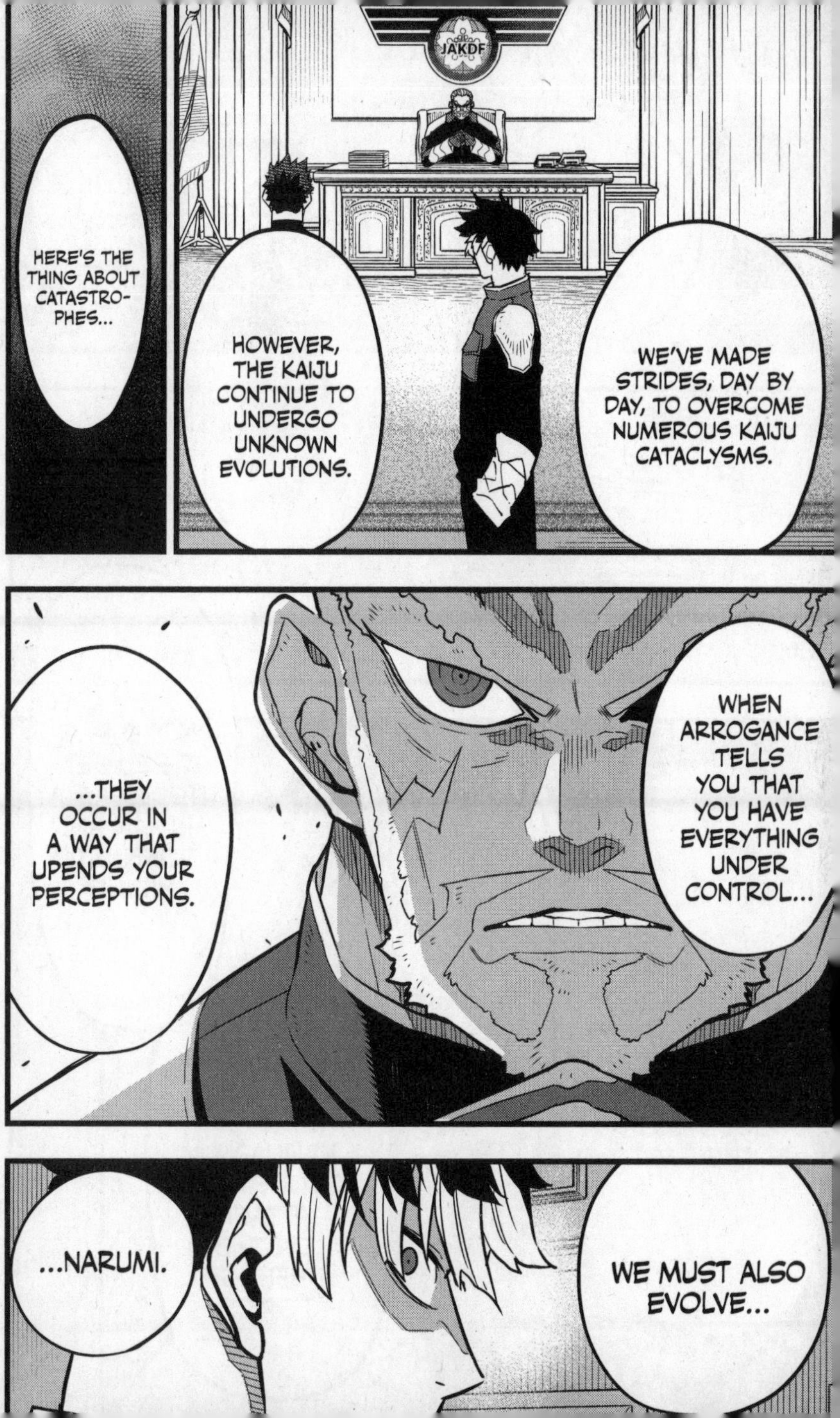
JAKDF
WE'VE MADE STRIDES, DAY BY DAY, TO OVERCOME NUMEROUS KAIJU CATACLYSMS.
HOWEVER, THE KAIJU CONTINUE TO UNDERGO UNKNOWN EVOLUTIONS.
HERE'S THE THING ABOUT CATASTRO-PHES...
WHEN ARROGANCE TELLS YOU THAT YOU HAVE EVERYTHING UNDER CONTROL...
...THEY OCCUR IN A WAY THAT UPENDS YOUR PERCEPTIONS.
WE MUST ALSO EVOLVE...
...NARUMI.

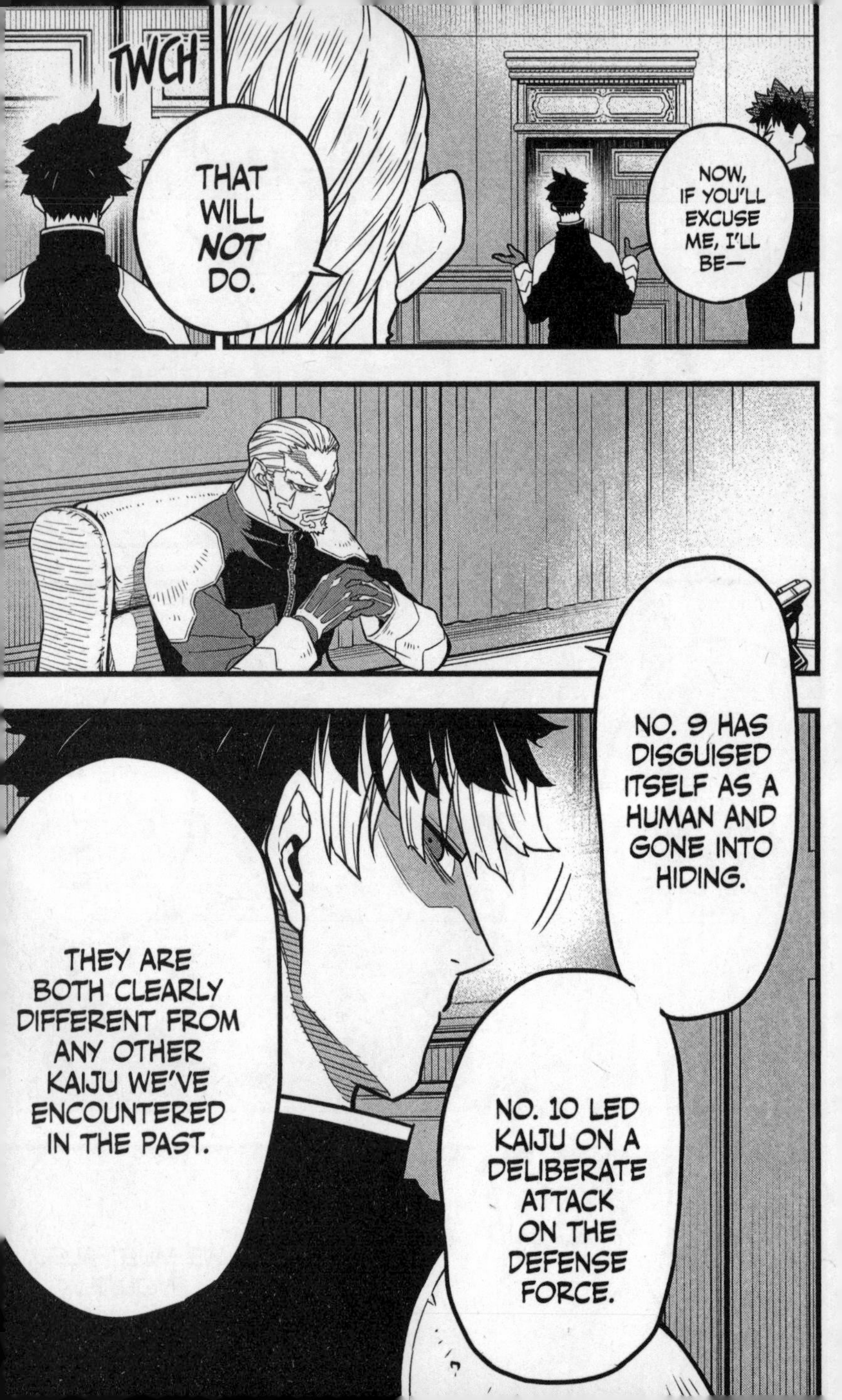
NOW, IF YOU'LL EXCUSE ME, I'LL BE—
TWCH
THAT WILL *NOT* DO.
NO. 9 HAS DISGUISED ITSELF AS A HUMAN AND GONE INTO HIDING.
NO. 10 LED KAIJU ON A DELIBERATE ATTACK ON THE DEFENSE FORCE.
THEY ARE BOTH CLEARLY DIFFERENT FROM ANY OTHER KAIJU WE'VE ENCOUNTERED IN THE PAST.

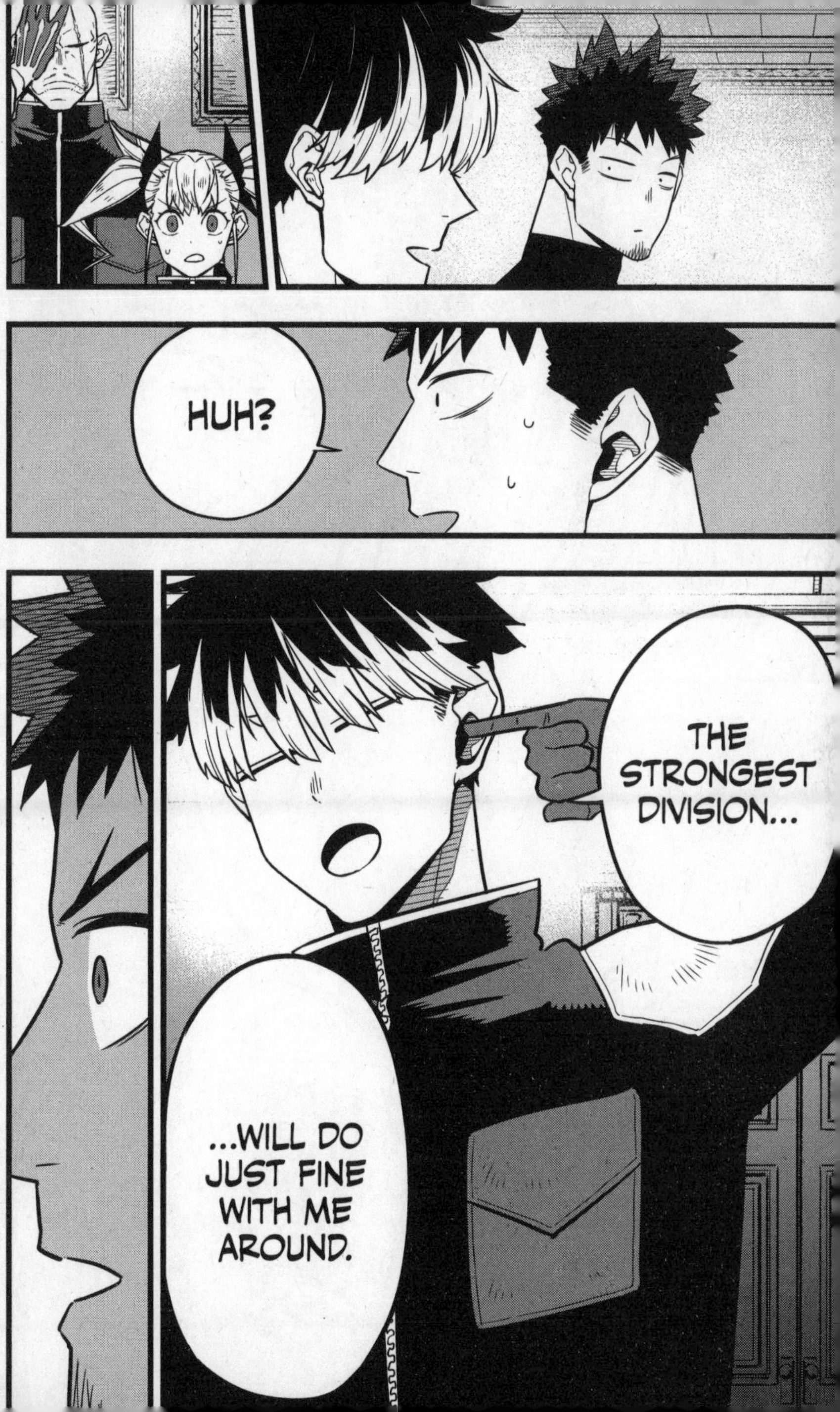
HUH?
THE STRONGEST DIVISION...
...WILL DO JUST FINE WITH ME AROUND.

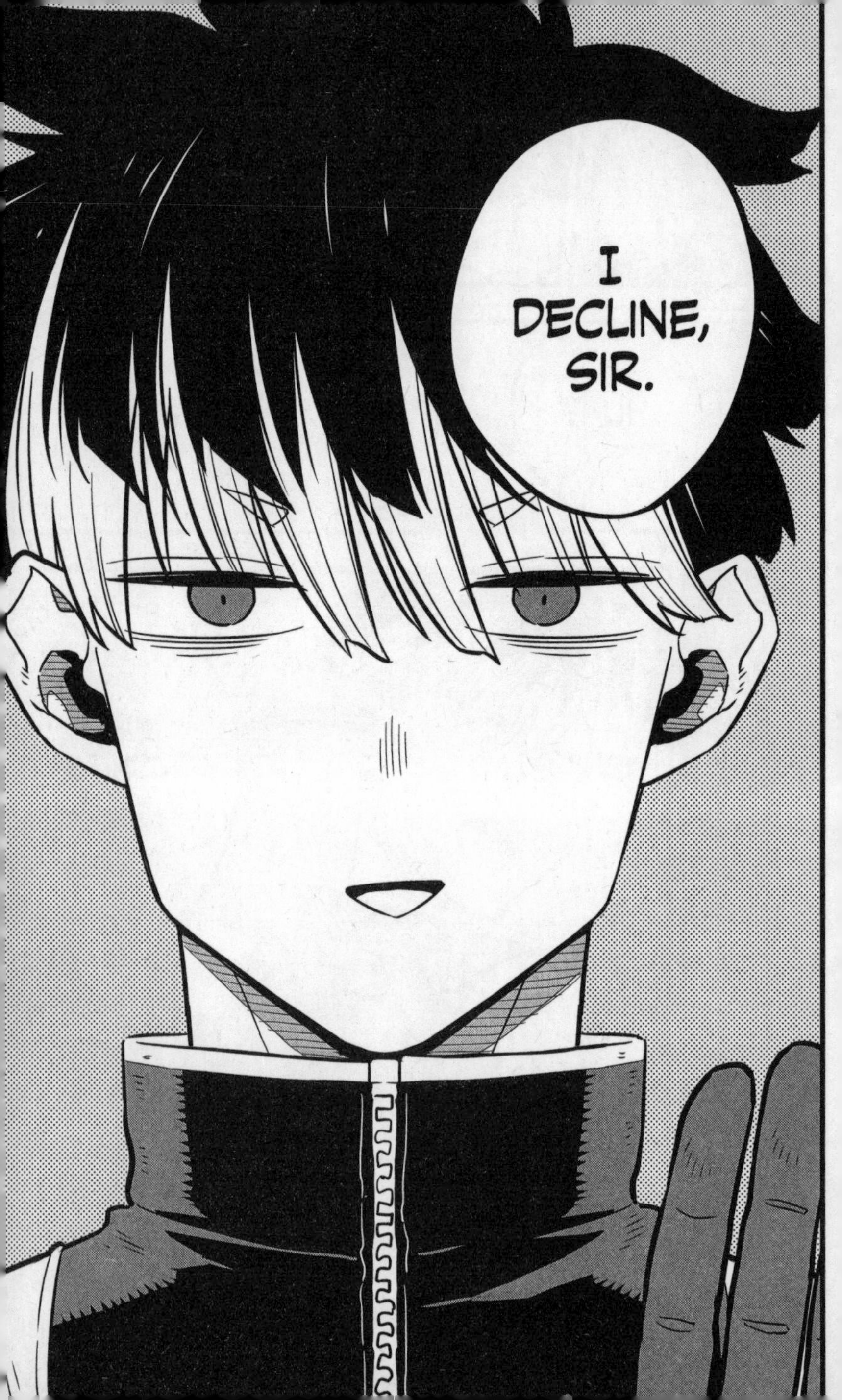
I DECLINE, SIR.

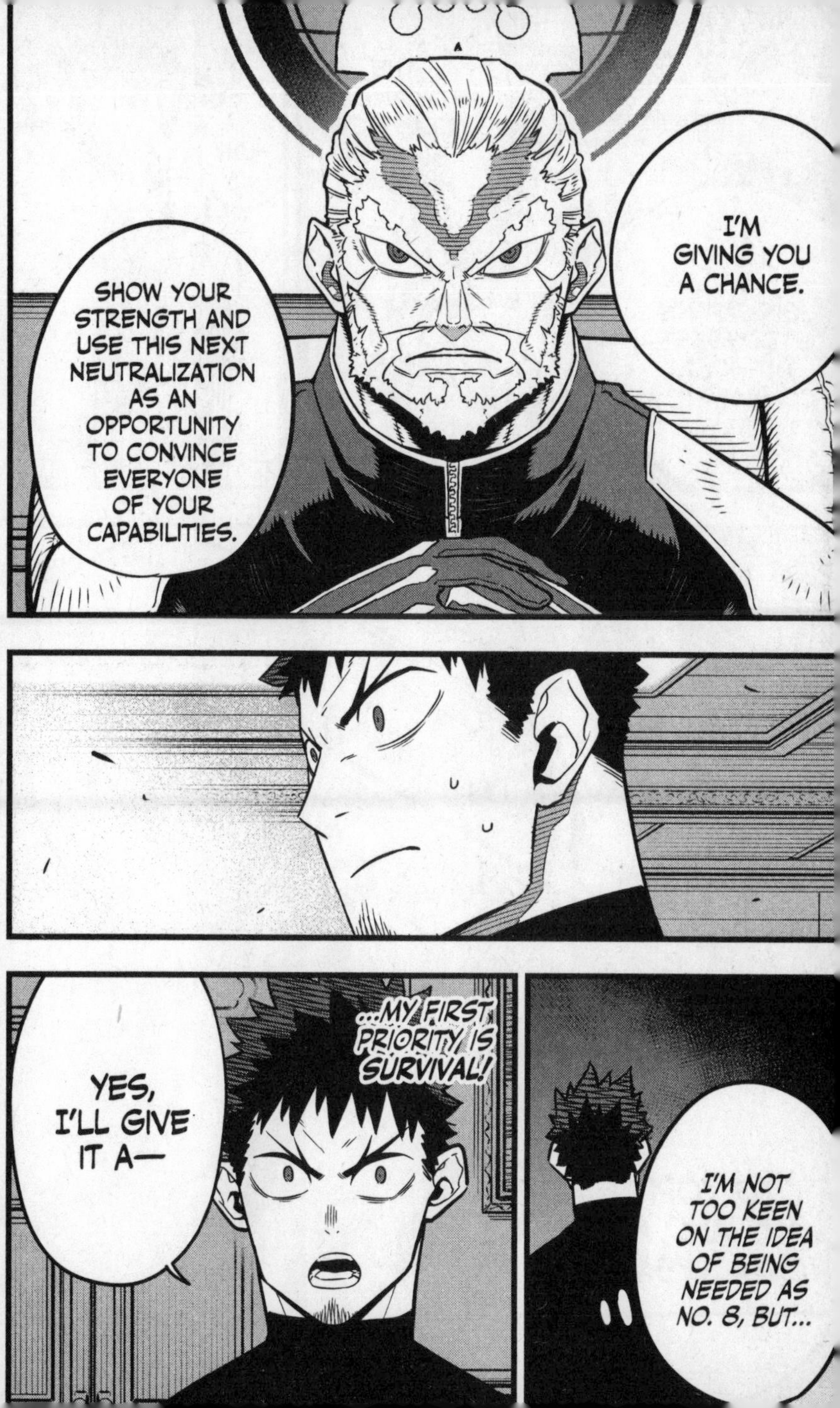
I'M GIVING YOU A CHANCE.
SHOW YOUR STRENGTH AND USE THIS NEXT NEUTRALIZATION AS AN OPPORTUNITY TO CONVINCE EVERYONE OF YOUR CAPABILITIES.
I'M NOT TOO KEEN ON THE IDEA OF BEING NEEDED AS NO. 8, BUT...
...MY FIRST PRIORITY IS SURVIVAL!
YES, I'LL GIVE IT A—

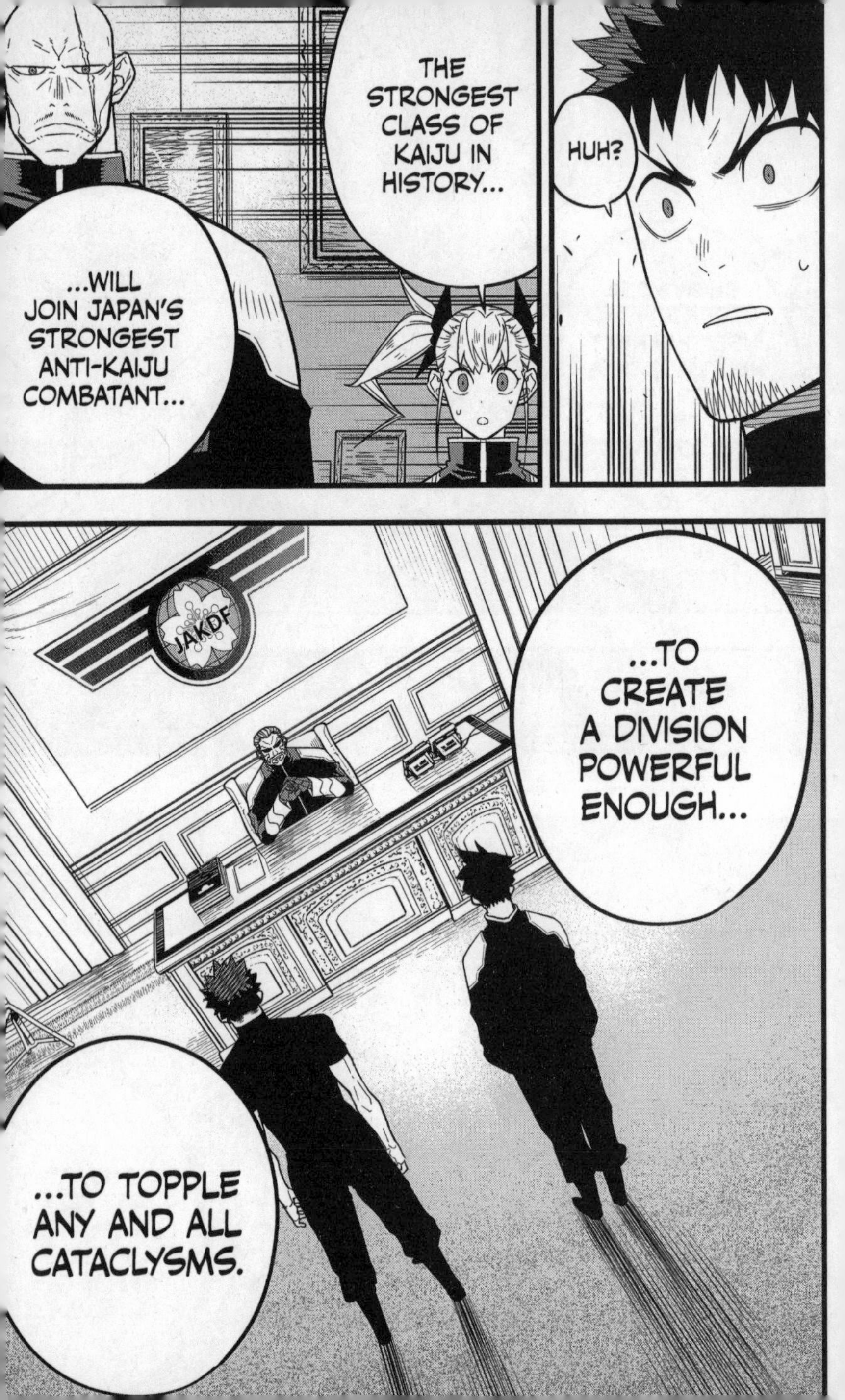
HUH?
THE STRONGEST CLASS OF KAIJU IN HISTORY...
...WILL JOIN JAPAN'S STRONGEST ANTI-KAIJU COMBATANT...
JAKDF
...TO CREATE A DIVISION POWERFUL ENOUGH...
...TO TOPPLE ANY AND ALL CATACLYSMS.

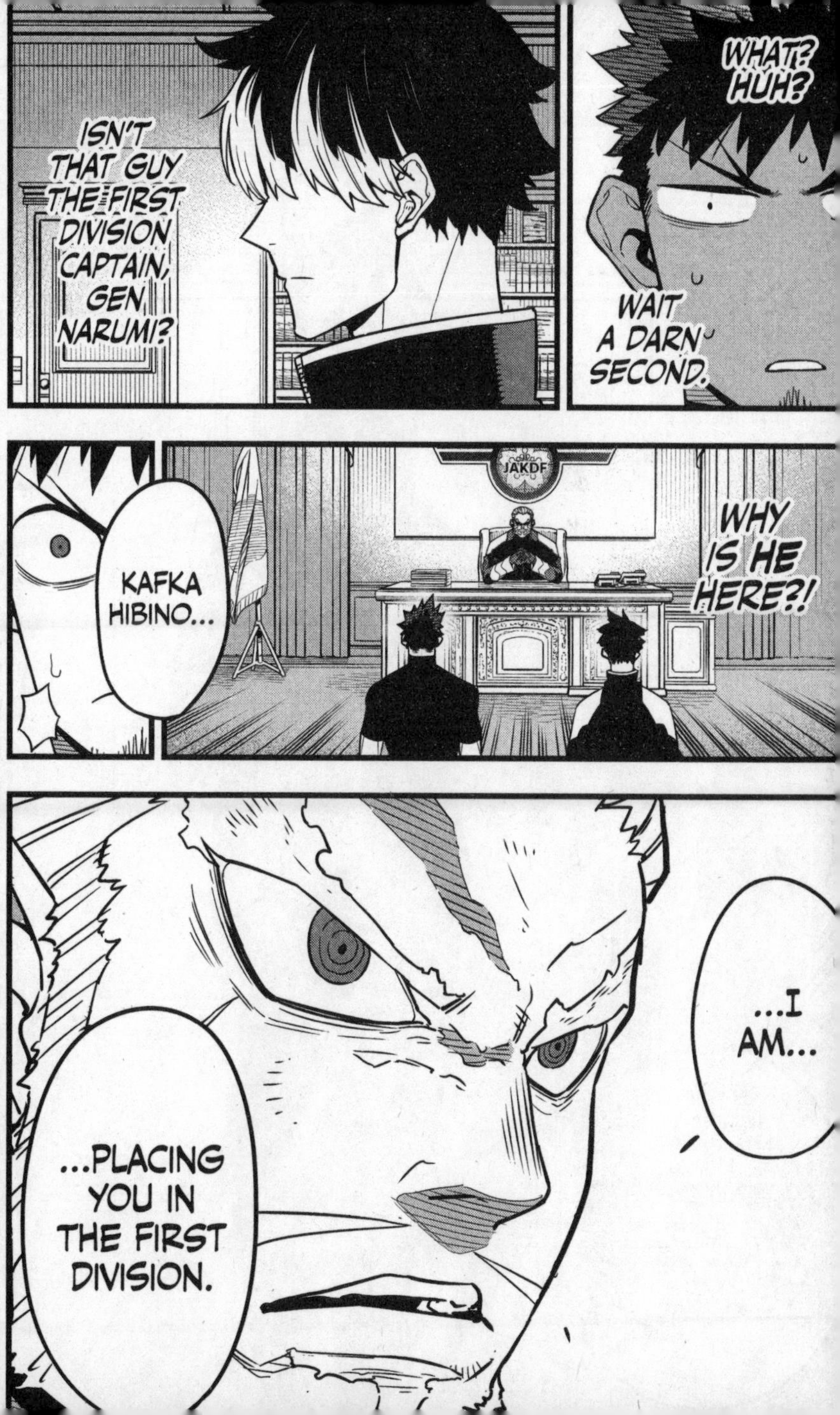
WHAT? HUH?
WAIT A DARN SECOND.
ISN'T THAT GUY THE FIRST DIVISION CAPTAIN, GEN NARUMI?
JAKDF
WHY IS HE HERE?!
KAFKA HIBINO...
...I AM...
...PLACING YOU IN THE FIRST DIVISION.

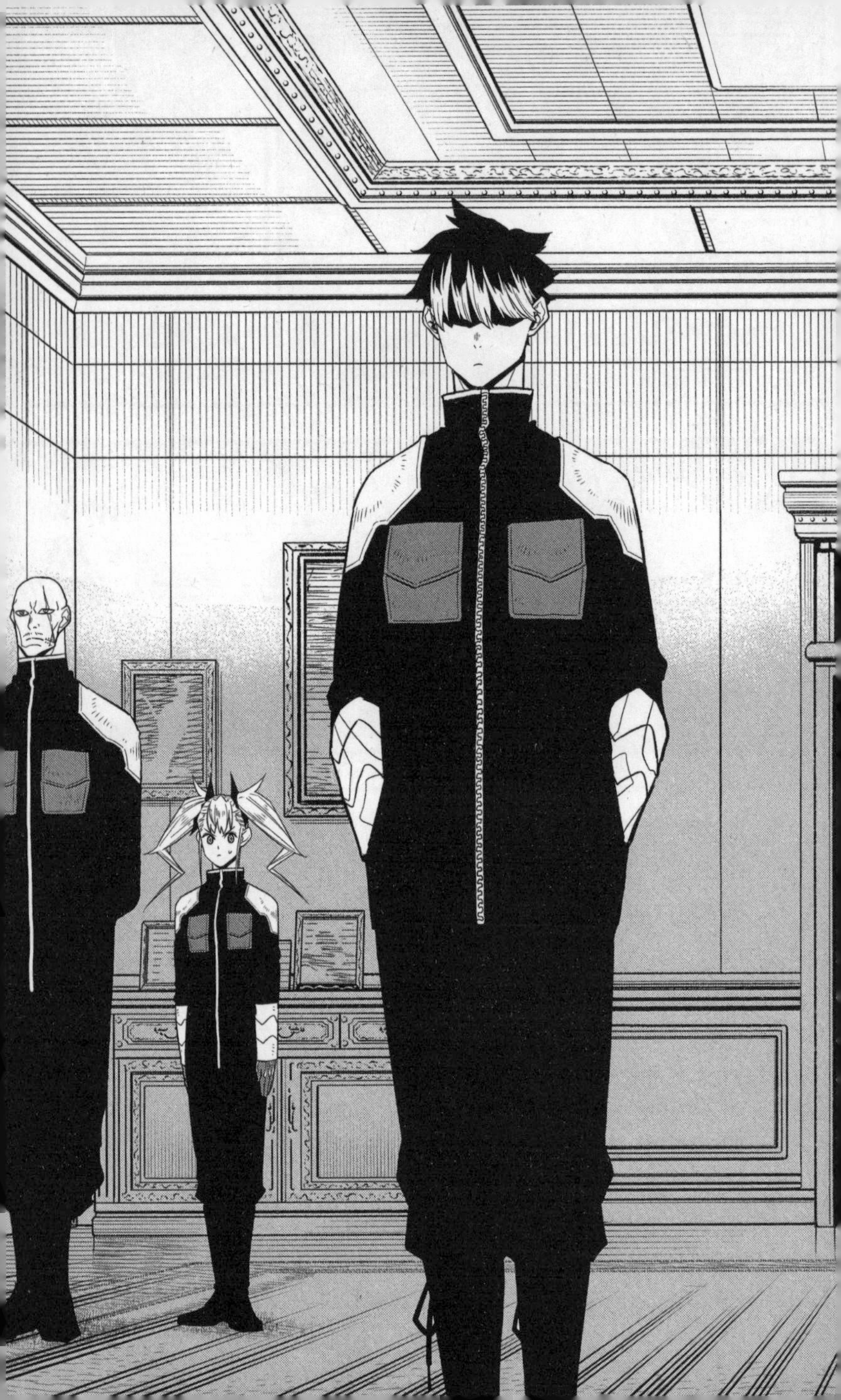

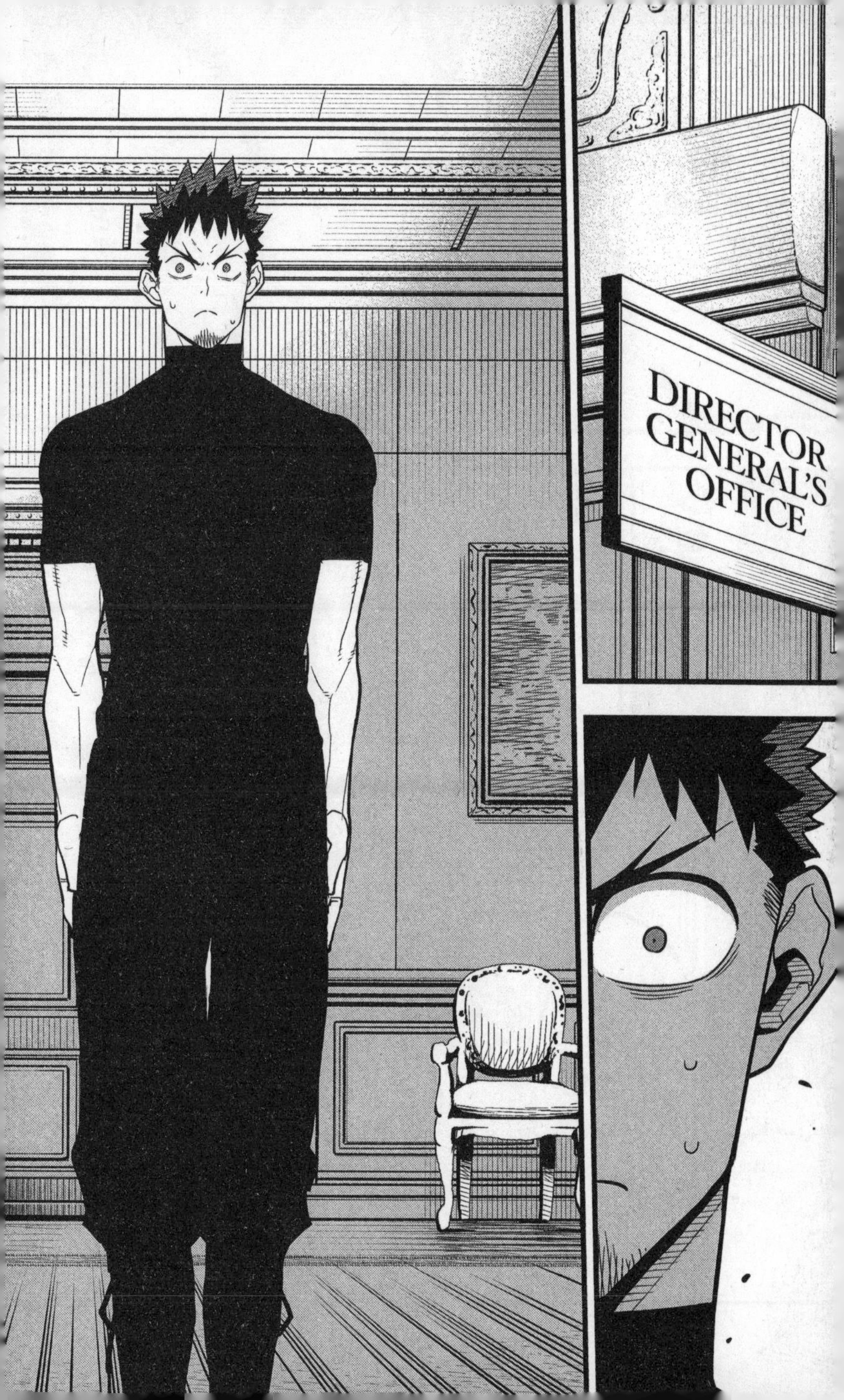
DIRECTOR GENERAL'S OFFICE

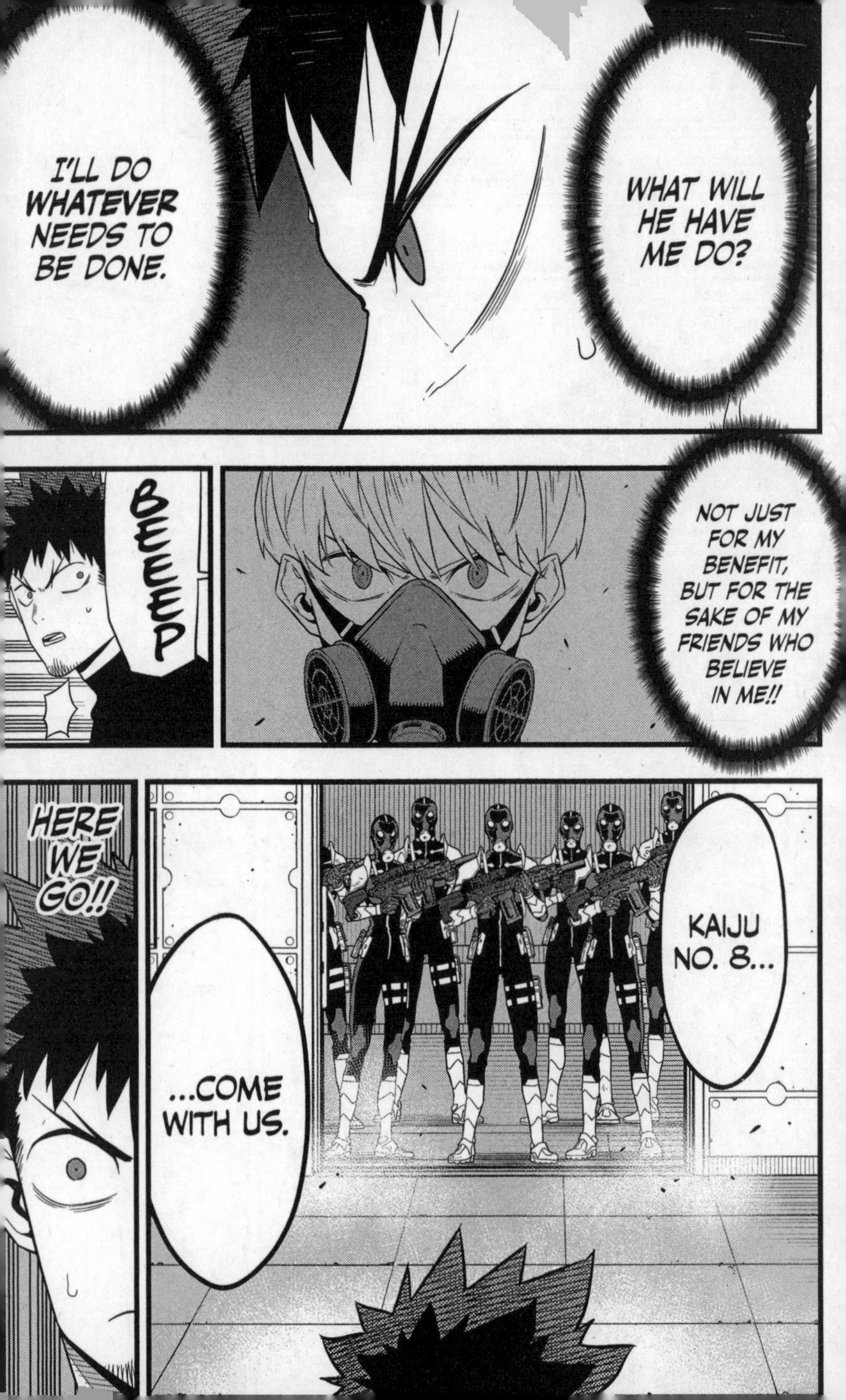
WHAT WILL HE HAVE ME DO?
I'LL DO WHATEVER NEEDS TO BE DONE.
NOT JUST FOR MY BENEFIT, BUT FOR THE SAKE OF MY FRIENDS WHO BELIEVE IN ME!!
BEEEEP
KAIJU NO. 8...
...COME WITH US.
HERE WE GO!!

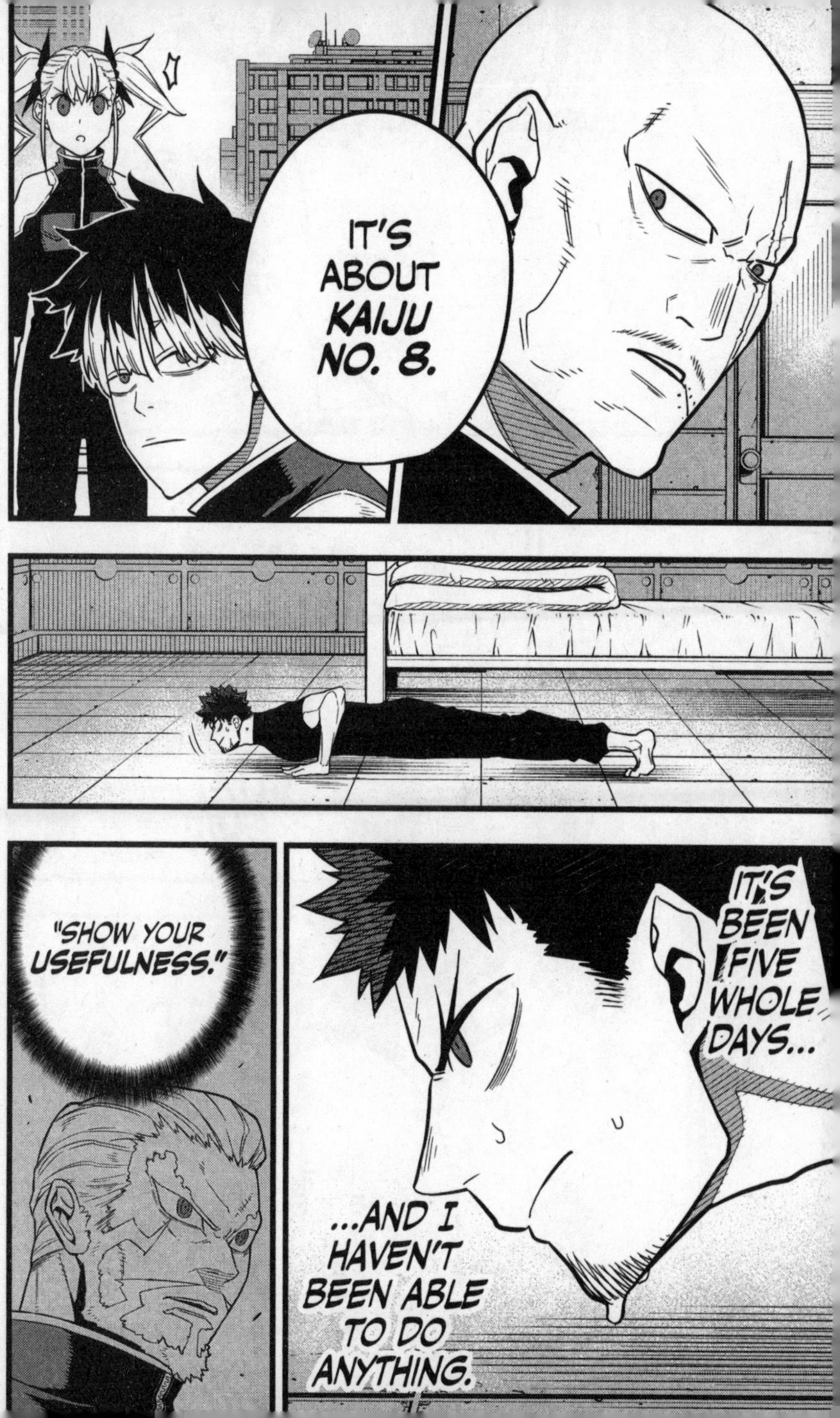
IT'S ABOUT KAIJU NO. 8.
IT'S BEEN FIVE WHOLE DAYS...
...AND I HAVEN'T BEEN ABLE TO DO ANYTHING.
"SHOW YOUR USEFULNESS."

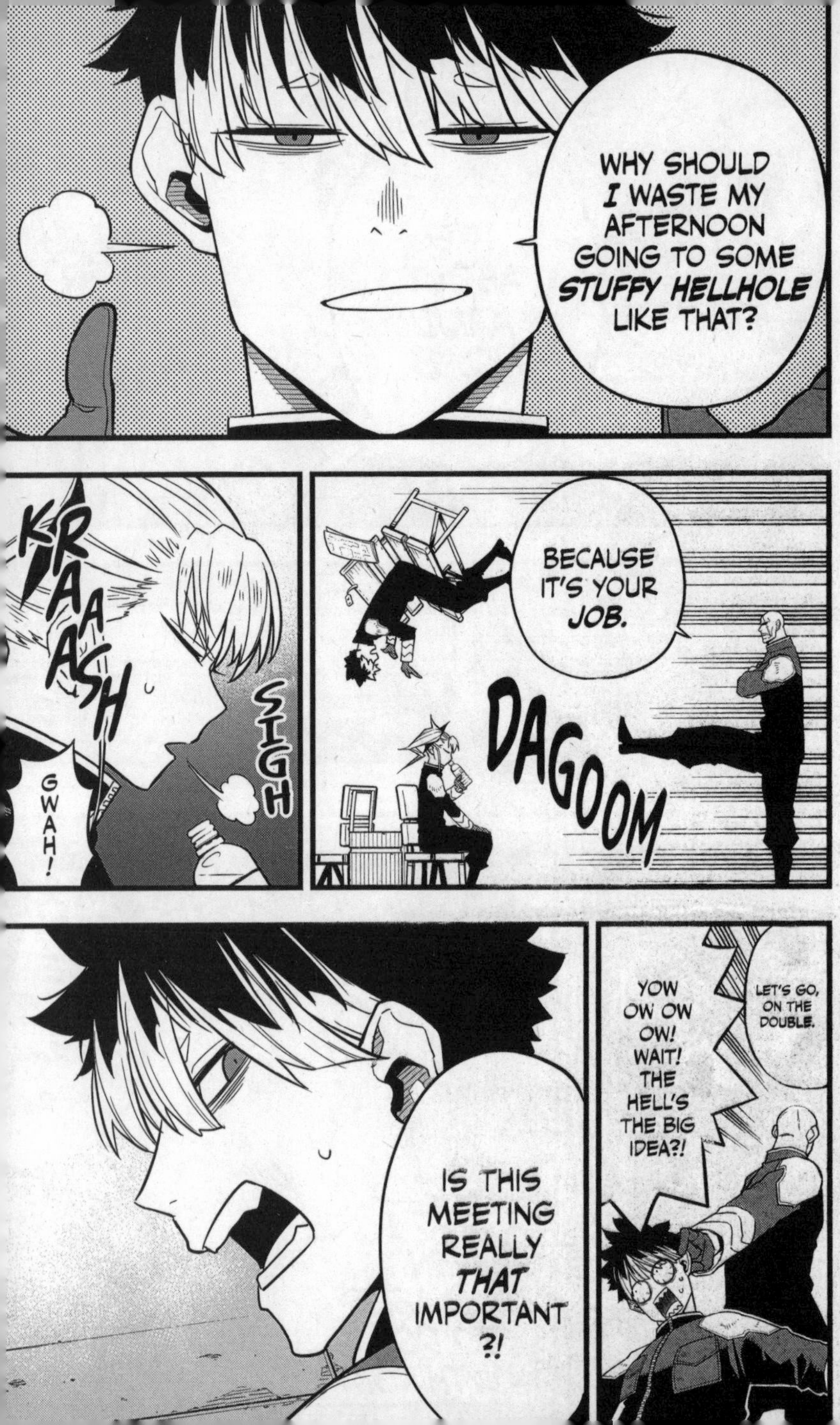
WHY SHOULD *I* WASTE MY AFTERNOON GOING TO SOME *STUFFY HELLHOLE* LIKE THAT?
BECAUSE IT'S YOUR *JOB.*
DAGOOM
KRAAASH
SIGH
GWAH!
LET'S GO, ON THE DOUBLE.
YOW OW OW OW! WAIT! THE HELL'S THE BIG IDEA?!
IS THIS MEETING REALLY *THAT* IMPORTANT?!

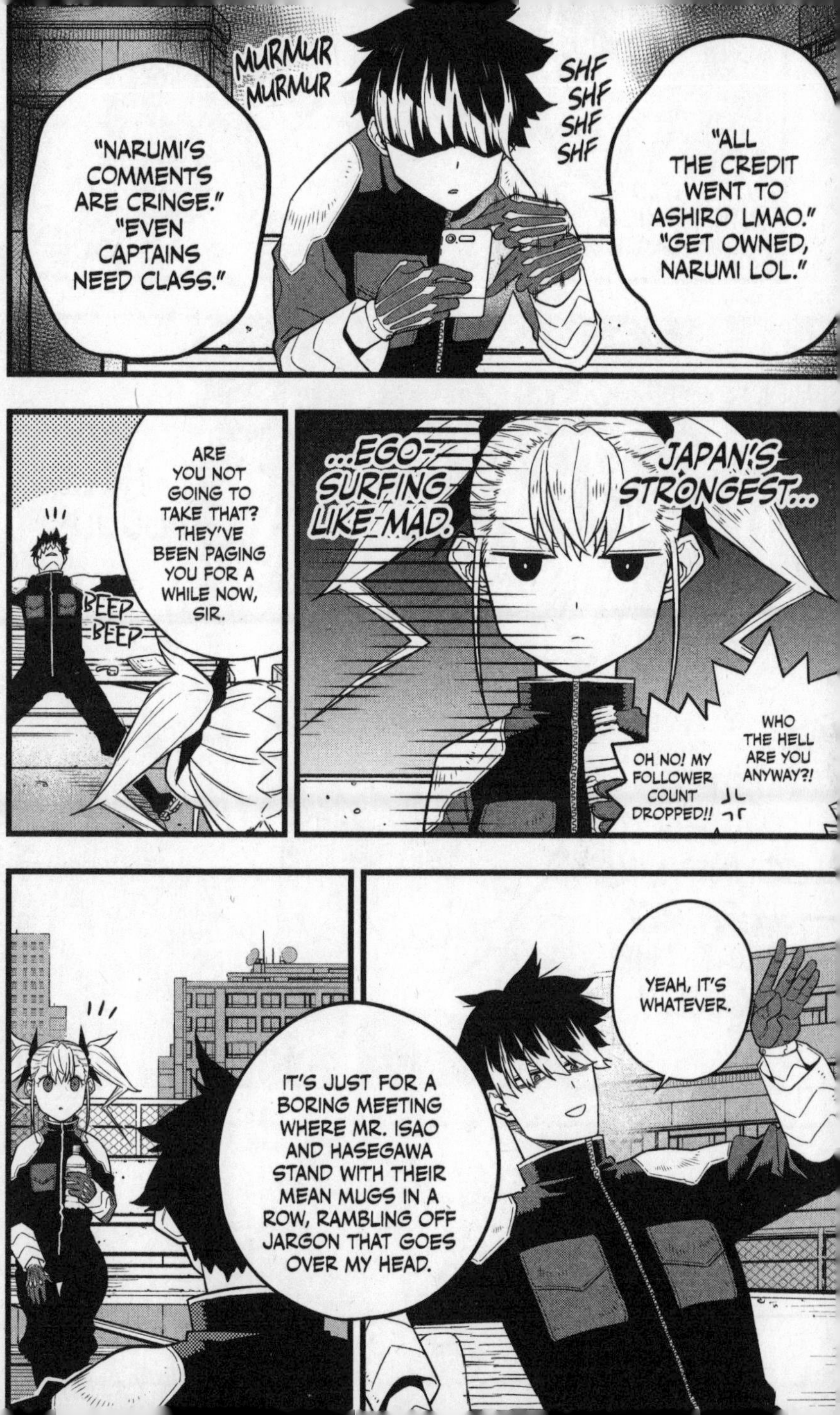

"ALL THE CREDIT WENT TO ASHIRO LMAO." "GET OWNED, NARUMI LOL."
SHF SHF SHF SHF
MURMUR MURMUR
"NARUMI'S COMMENTS ARE CRINGE." "EVEN CAPTAINS NEED CLASS."
JAPAN'S STRONGEST...
...EGO-SURFING LIKE MAD.
WHO THE HELL ARE YOU ANYWAY?!
OH NO! MY FOLLOWER COUNT DROPPED!!
ARE YOU NOT GOING TO TAKE THAT? THEY'VE BEEN PAGING YOU FOR A WHILE NOW, SIR.
BEEP BEEP
YEAH, IT'S WHATEVER.
IT'S JUST FOR A BORING MEETING WHERE MR. ISAO AND HASEGAWA STAND WITH THEIR MEAN MUGS IN A ROW, RAMBLING OFF JARGON THAT GOES OVER MY HEAD.

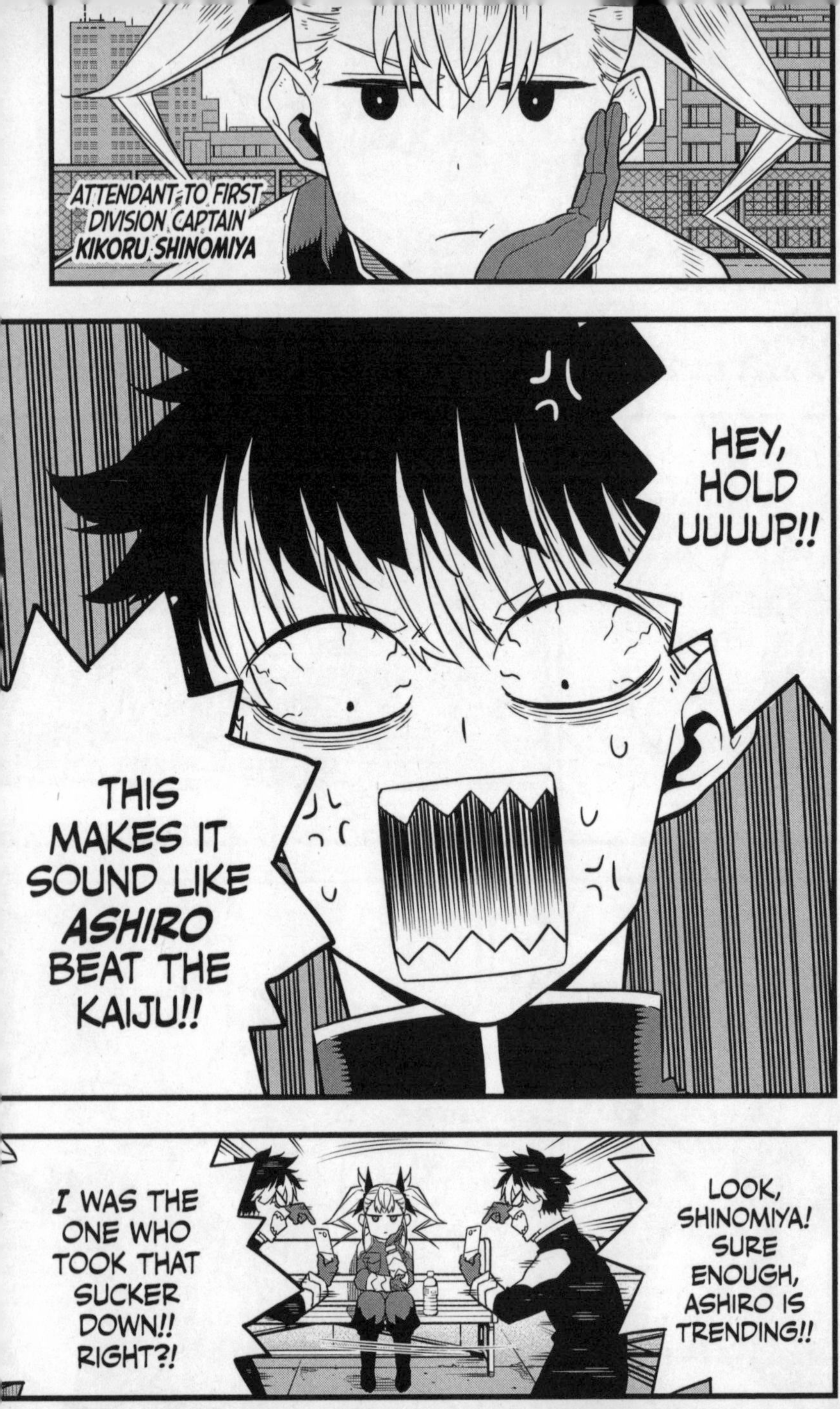
ATTENDANT TO FIRST DIVISION CAPTAIN KIKORU SHINOMIYA
HEY, HOLD UUUUP!!
THIS MAKES IT SOUND LIKE *ASHIRO* BEAT THE KAIJU!!
LOOK, SHINOMIYA! SURE ENOUGH, ASHIRO IS TRENDING!!
I WAS THE ONE WHO TOOK THAT SUCKER DOWN!! RIGHT?!

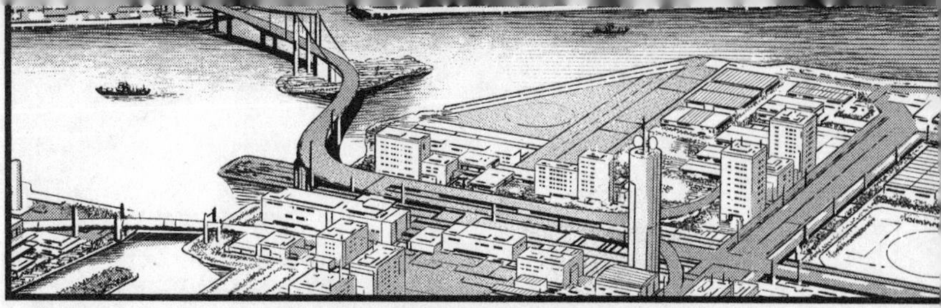

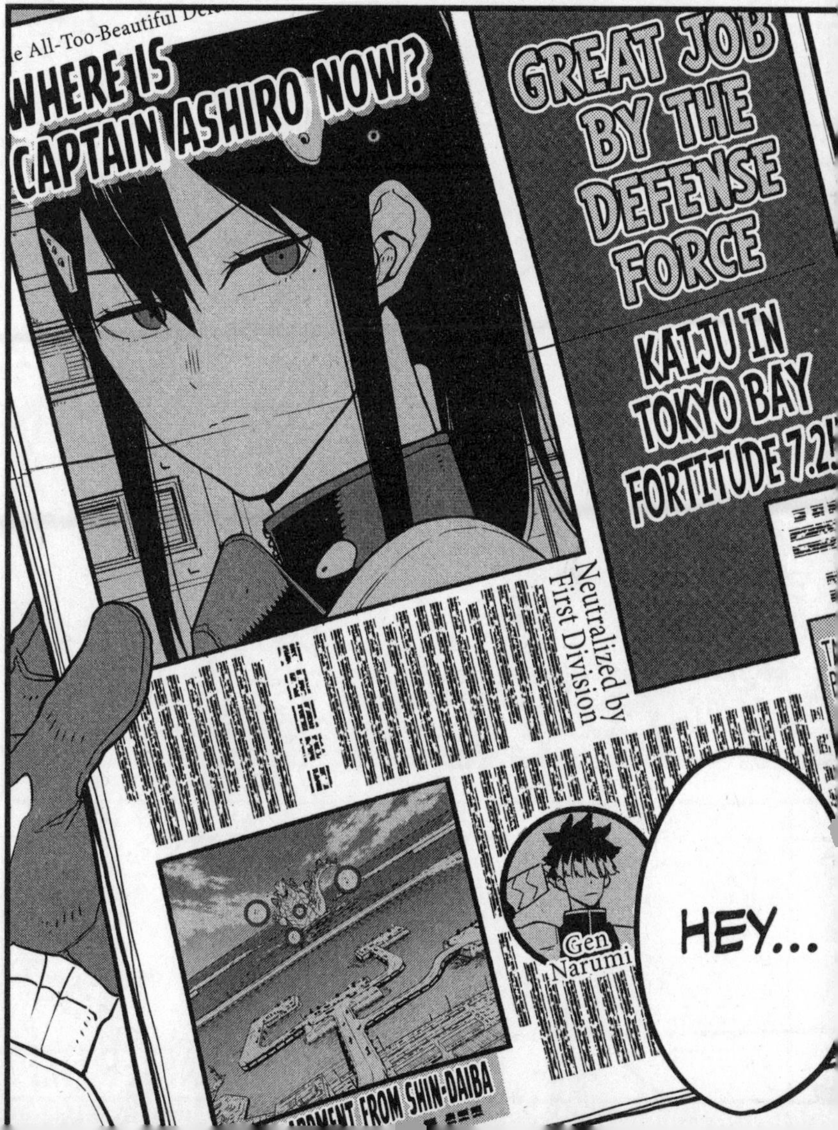
WHERE IS CAPTAIN ASHIRO NOW?
GREAT JOB BY THE DEFENSE FORCE
KAIJU IN TOKYO BAY FORTITUDE 7.2
Neutralized by First Division
FROM SHIN-DAIBA
Gen Narumi
HEY...

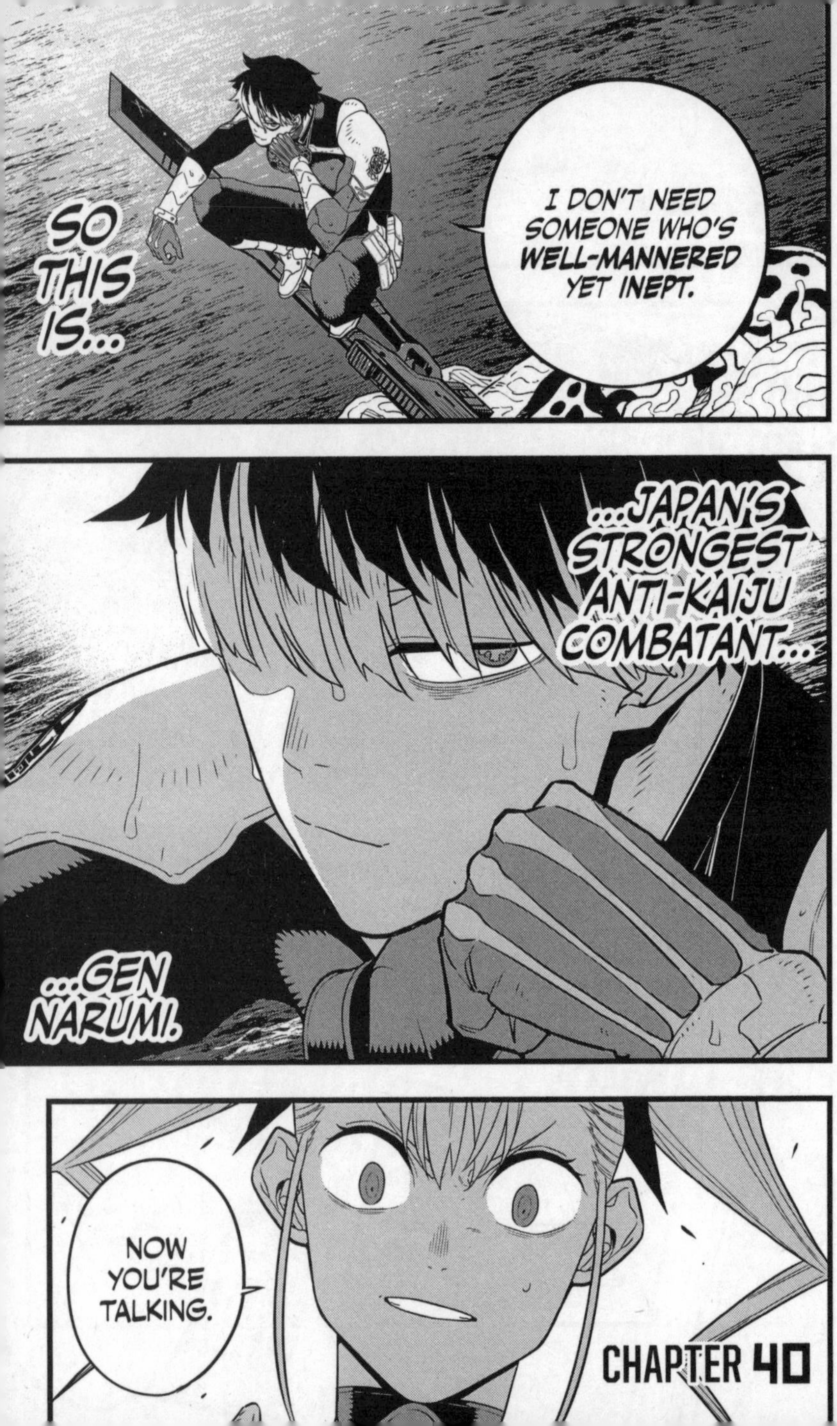
I DON'T NEED SOMEONE WHO'S WELL-MANNERED YET INEPT.
SO THIS IS...
...JAPAN'S STRONGEST ANTI-KAIJU COMBATANT...
...GEN NARUMI.
NOW YOU'RE TALKING.
CHAPTER 40

AFTER RETURNING FROM THE MISSION

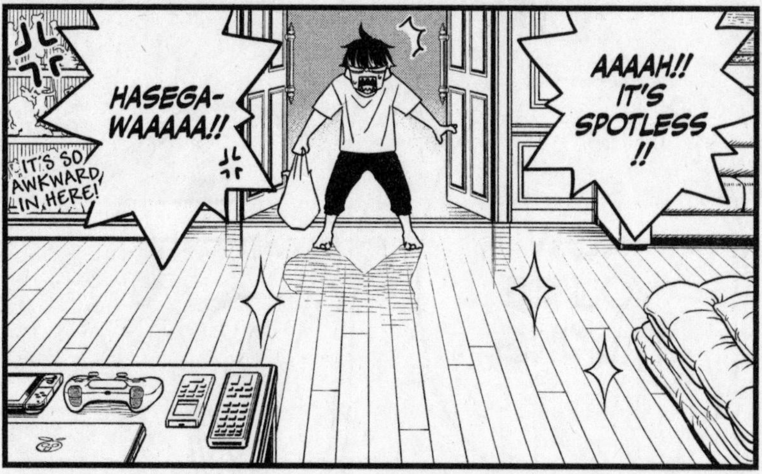
AAAAH!! IT'S SPOTLESS!!
HASEGA-WAAAAAA!!
IT'S SO AWKWARD IN HERE!

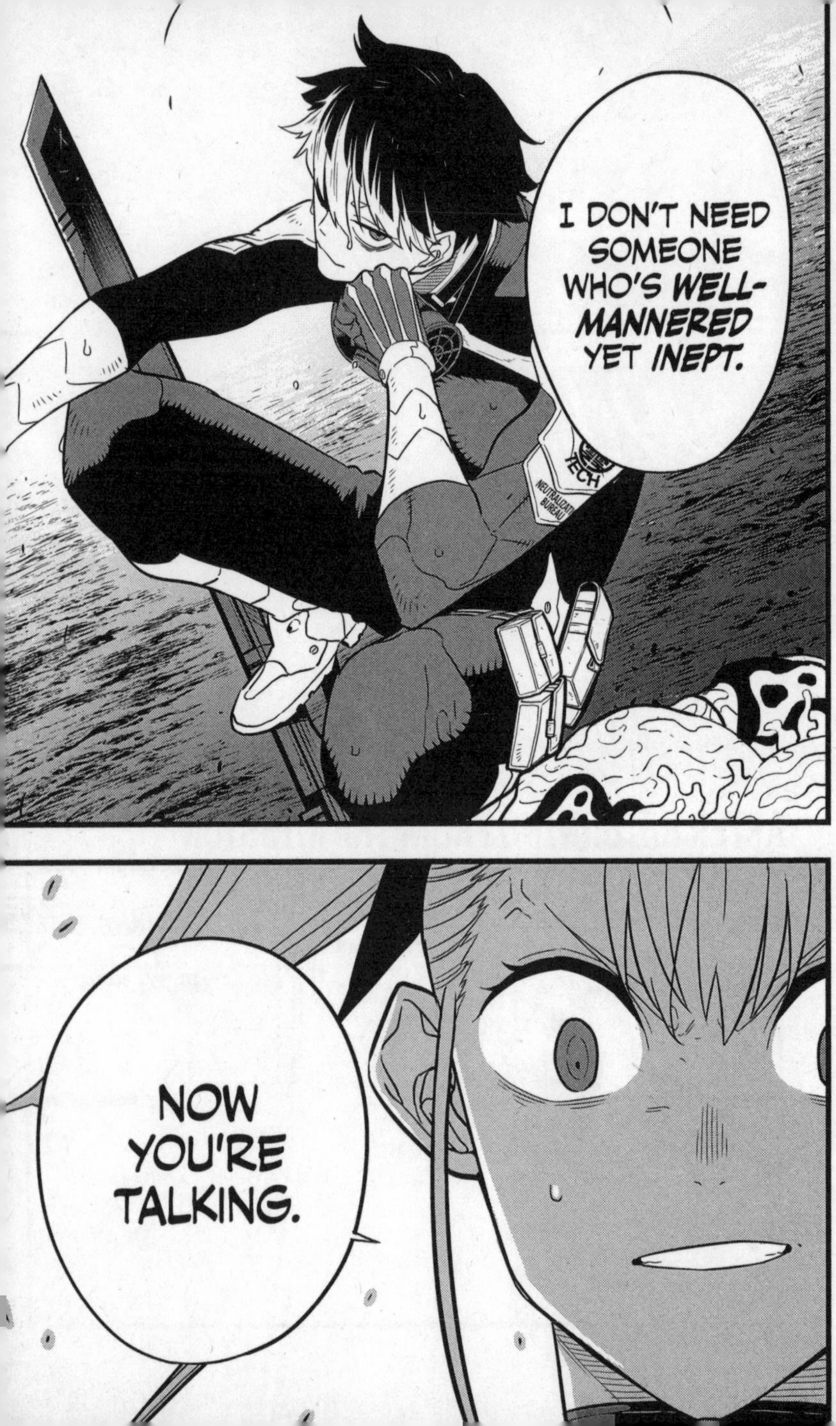
I DON'T NEED SOMEONE WHO'S WELL-MANNERED YET INEPT.
TECH
NEUTRALIZATION BUREAU
NOW YOU'RE TALKING.

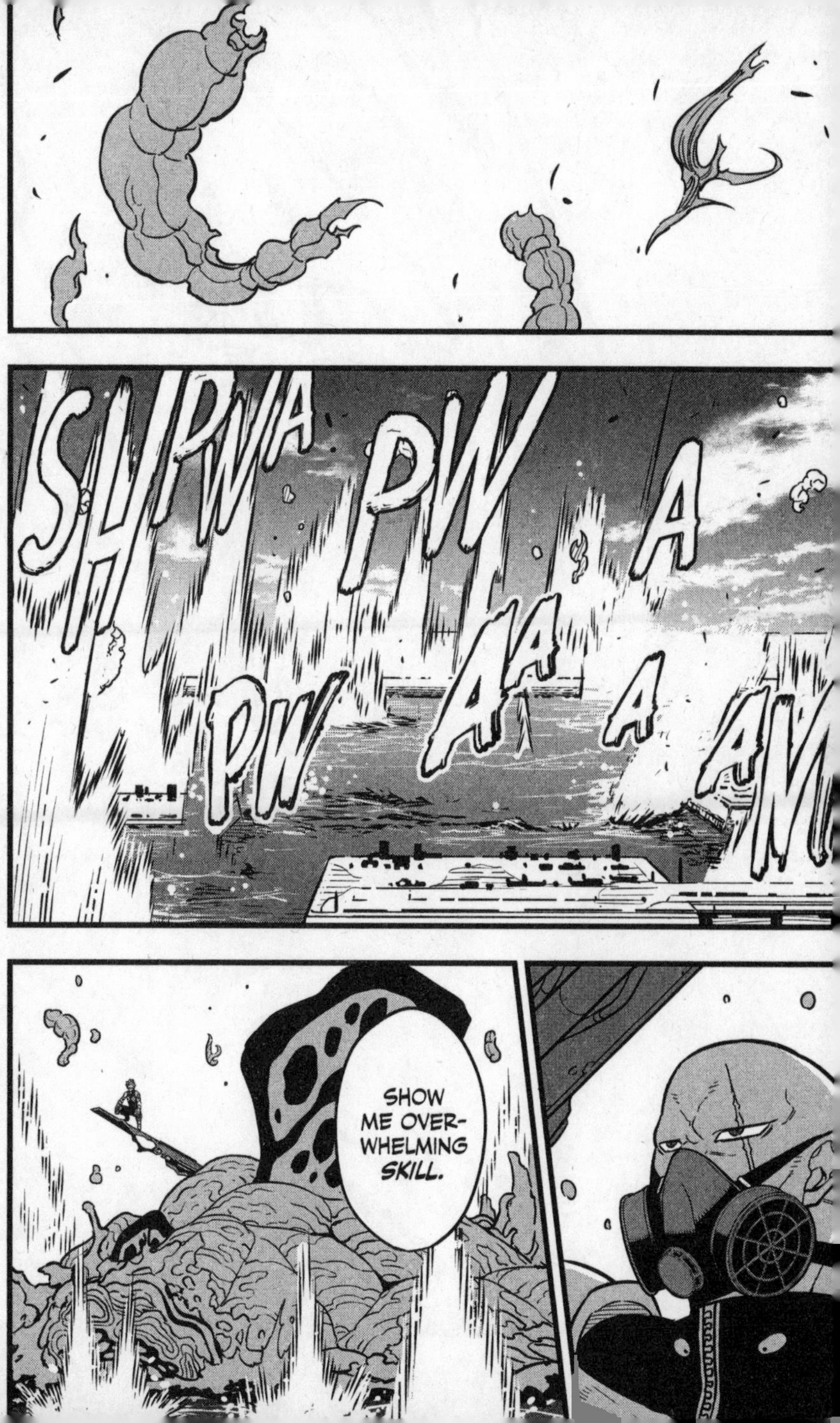
SHPWA PW A
PW AA A AM
SHOW ME OVER-WHELMING SKILL.

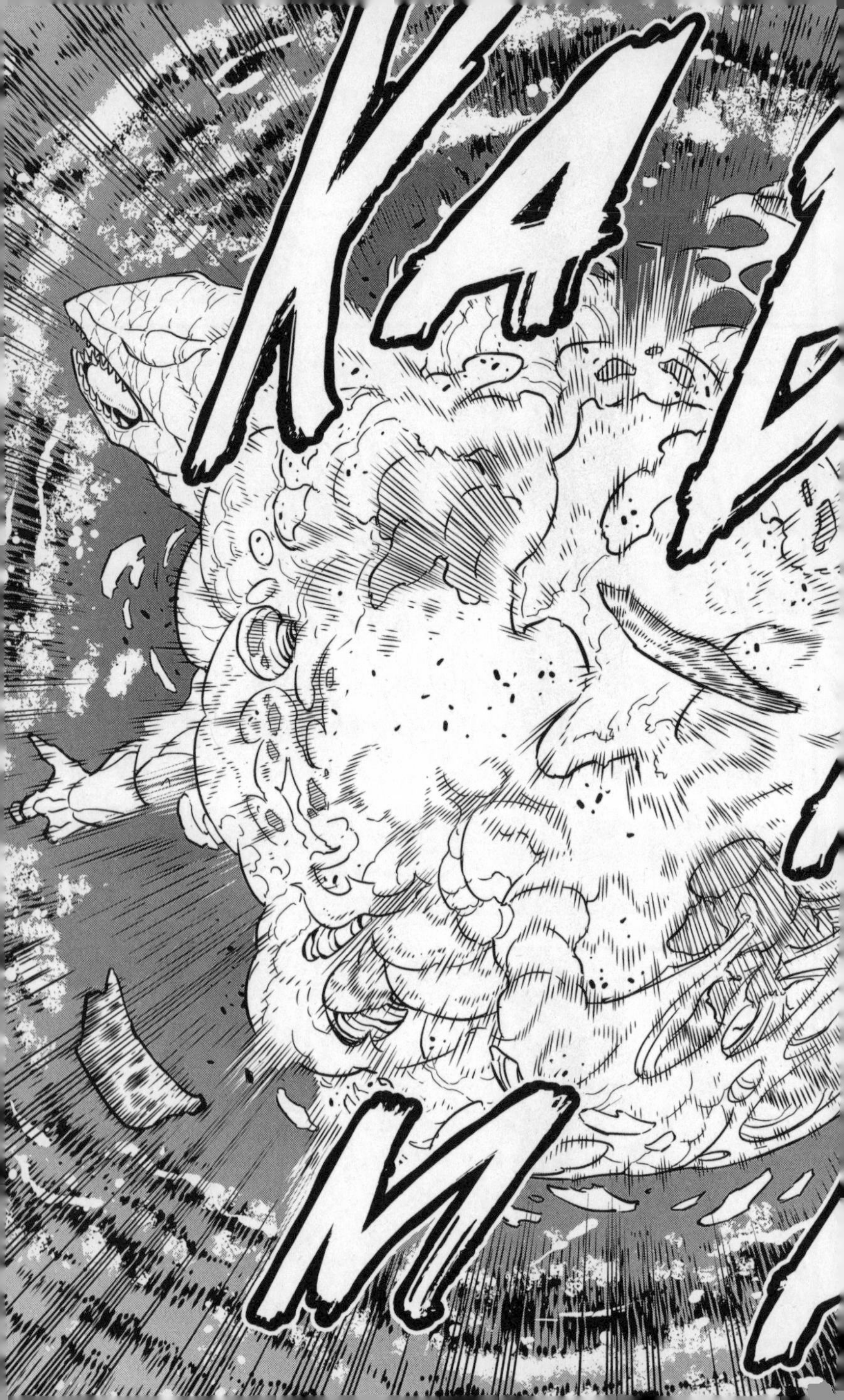
KA
M

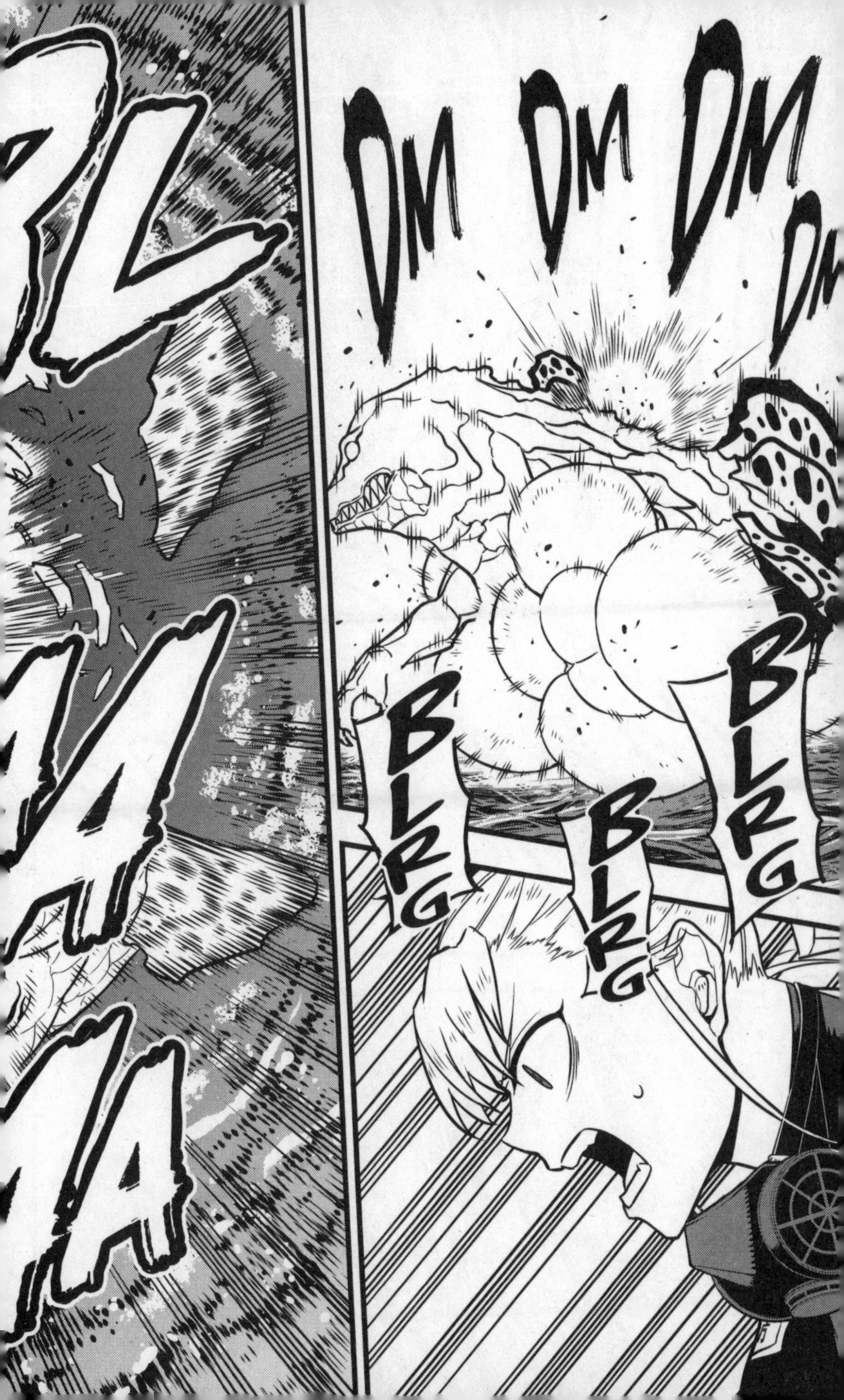
DM DM DM DM
BLRG
BLRG
BLRG

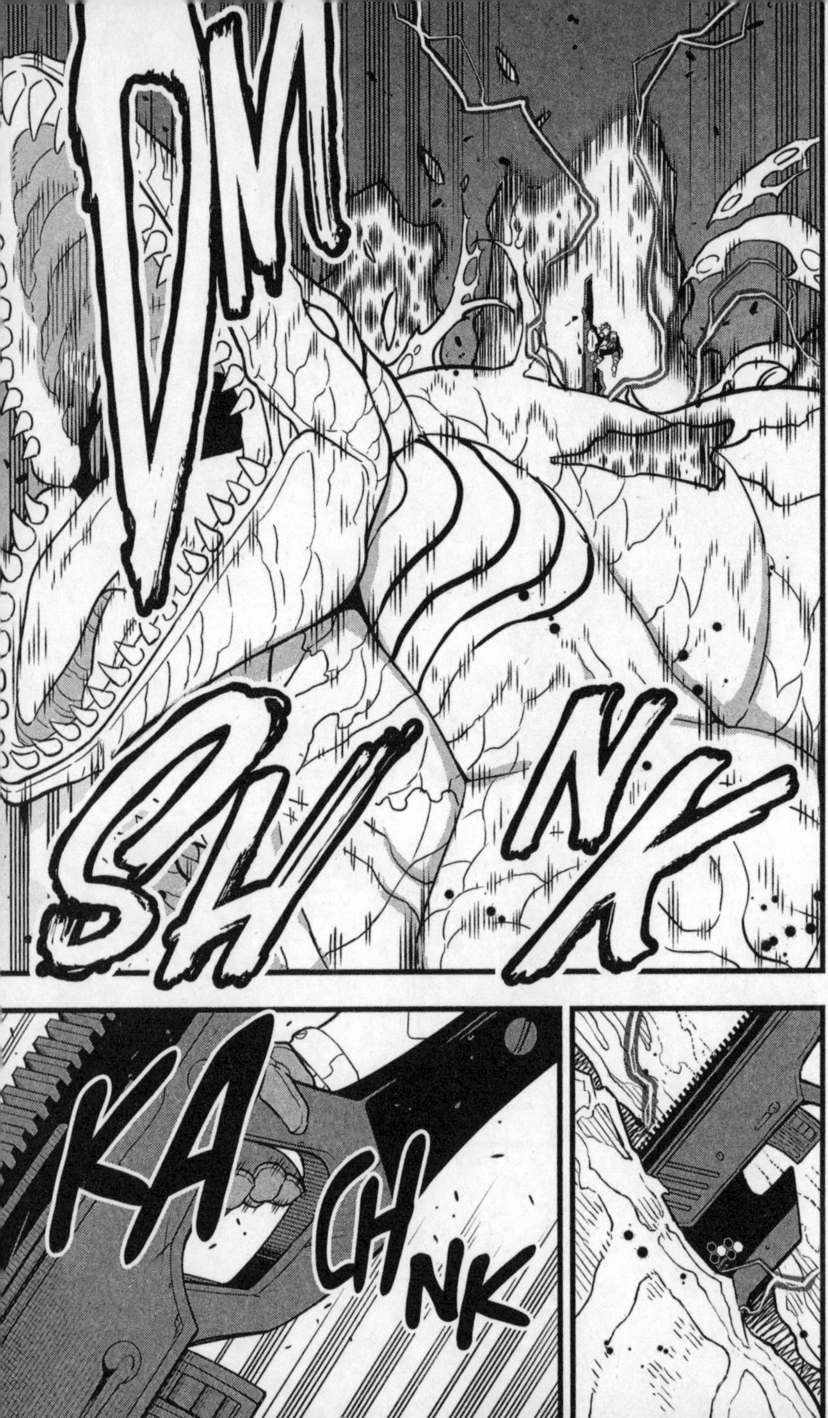

SHNK
KACHNK

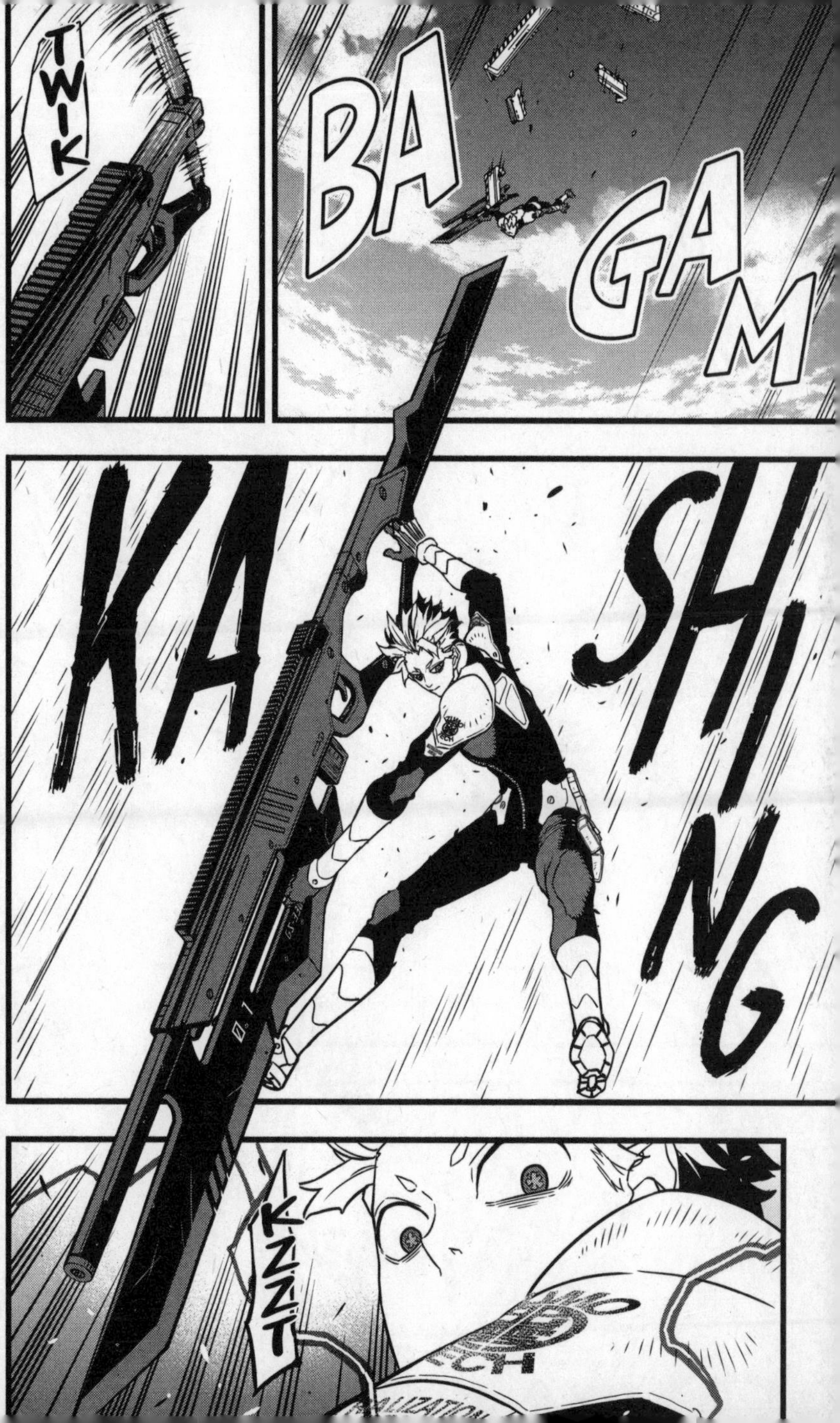
BA GAM
TWIK
KASHING
KZZZT

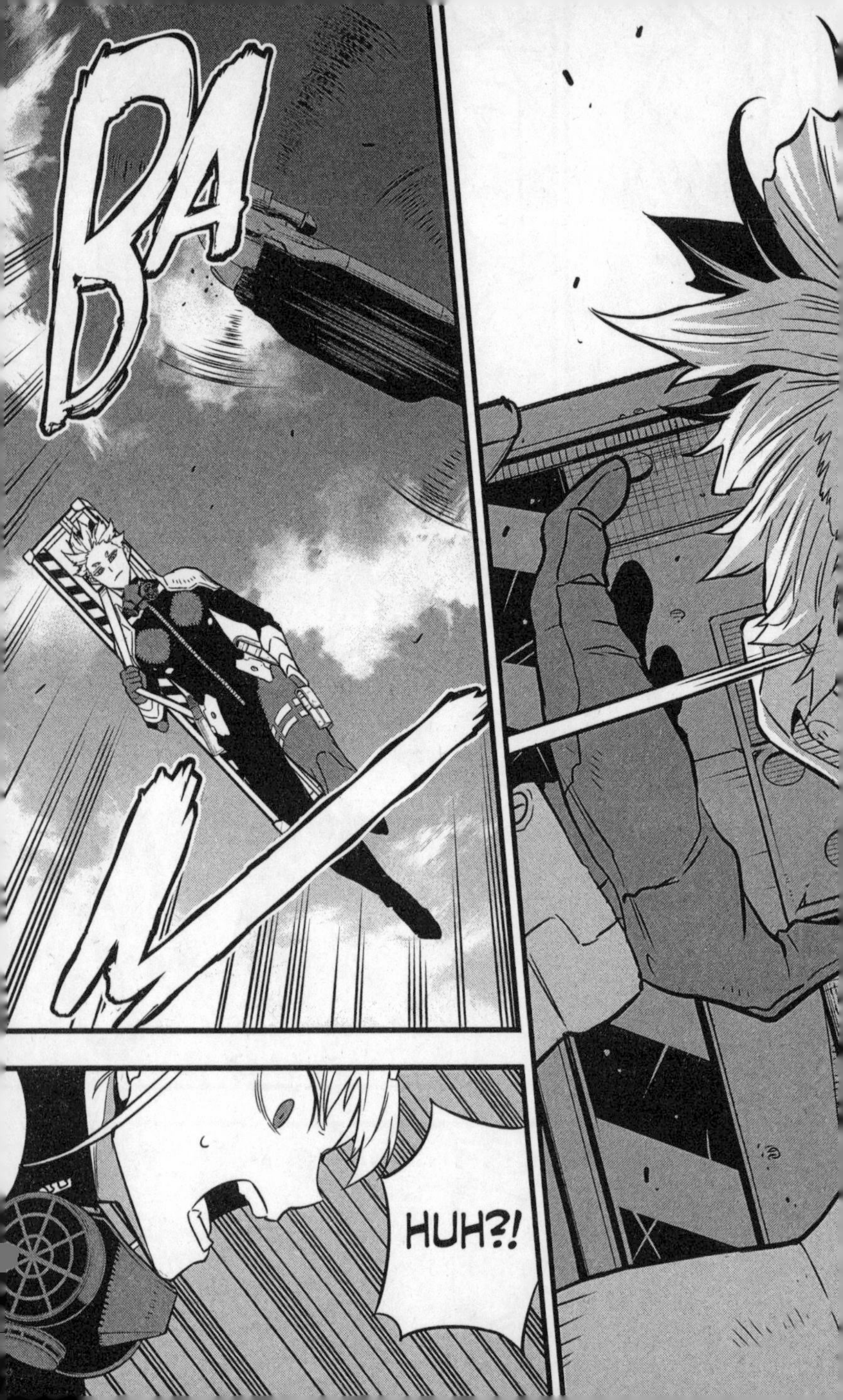
BA
DA
HUH?!

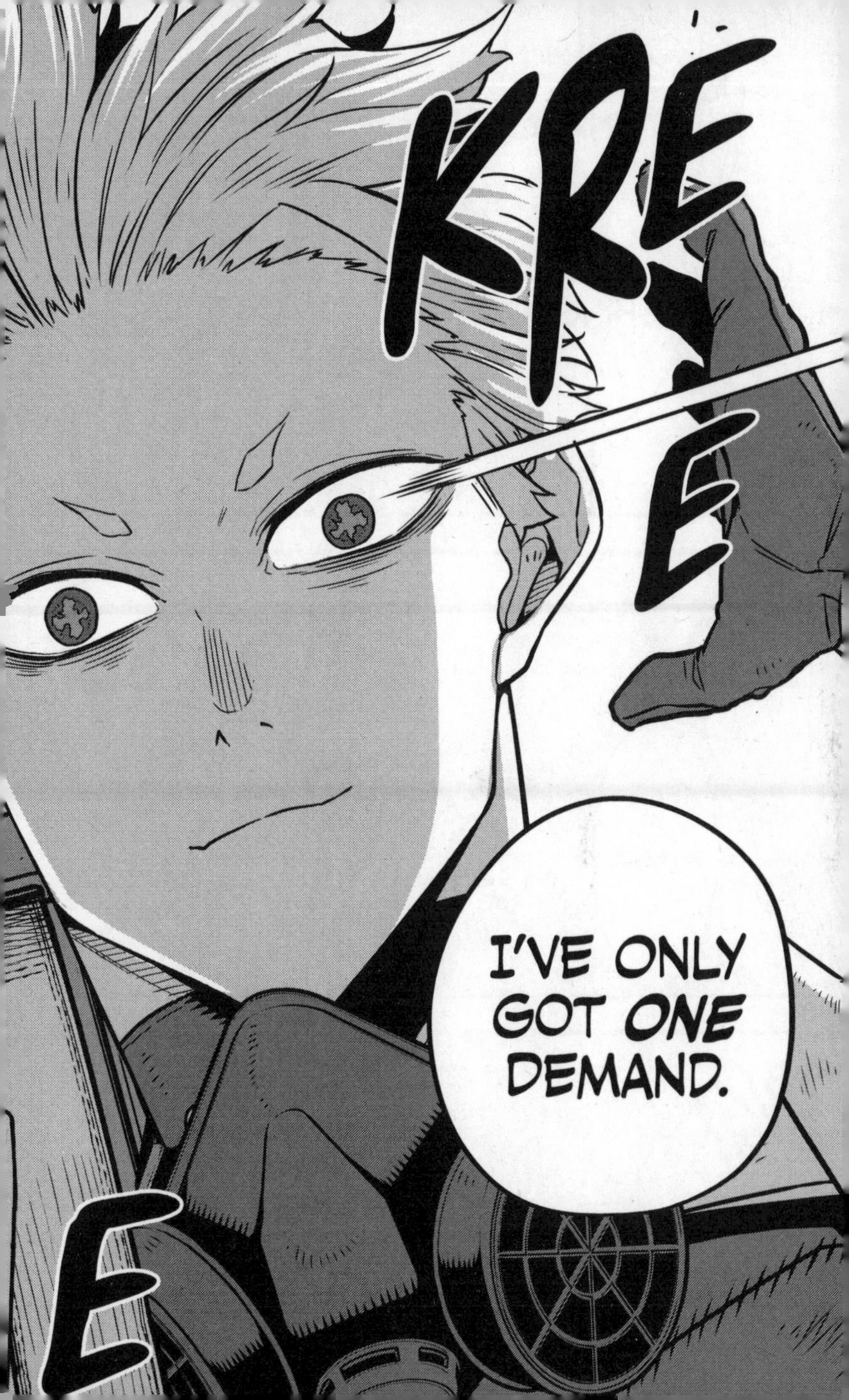
KREEE
I'VE ONLY GOT ONE DEMAND.

...KIKORU SHINOMIYA?

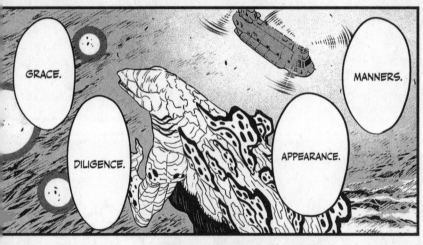

GRACE.

DILIGENCE.

MANNERS.

APPEARANCE.

SWSH

NONE OF THAT IS WHAT I WANT FROM YOU.

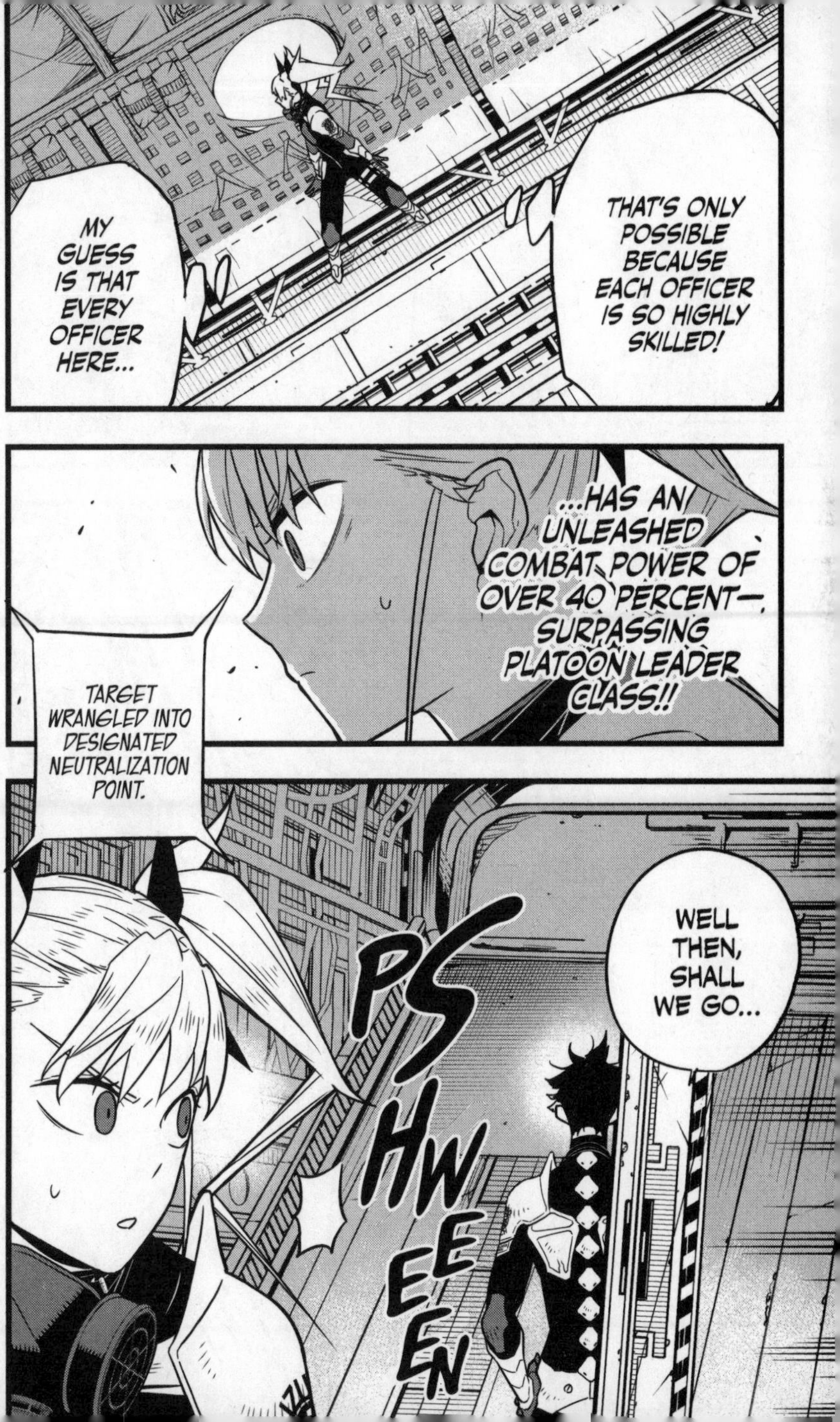
THAT'S ONLY POSSIBLE BECAUSE EACH OFFICER IS SO HIGHLY SKILLED!
MY GUESS IS THAT EVERY OFFICER HERE...
...HAS AN UNLEASHED COMBAT POWER OF OVER 40 PERCENT— SURPASSING PLATOON LEADER CLASS!!
TARGET WRANGLED INTO DESIGNATED NEUTRALIZATION POINT.
WELL THEN, SHALL WE GO...
PSHWEEEN

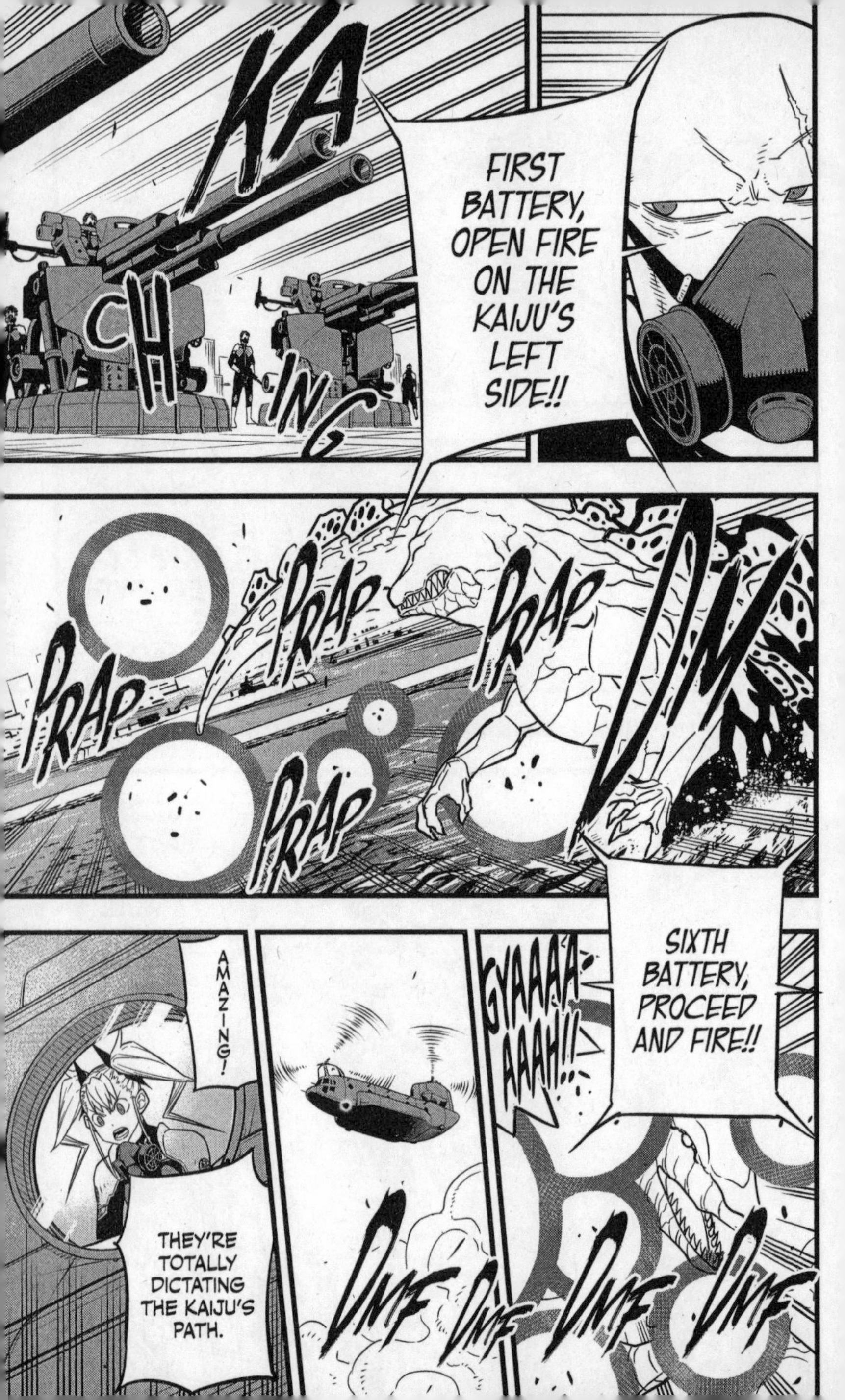
FIRST BATTERY, OPEN FIRE ON THE KAIJU'S LEFT SIDE!!
KA
CHING
DM
PRAP
PRAP
PRAP
PRAP
SIXTH BATTERY, PROCEED AND FIRE!!
GYAAAAAAAH!!
DMF DMF DMF DMF
AMAZING!
THEY'RE TOTALLY DICTATING THE KAIJU'S PATH.

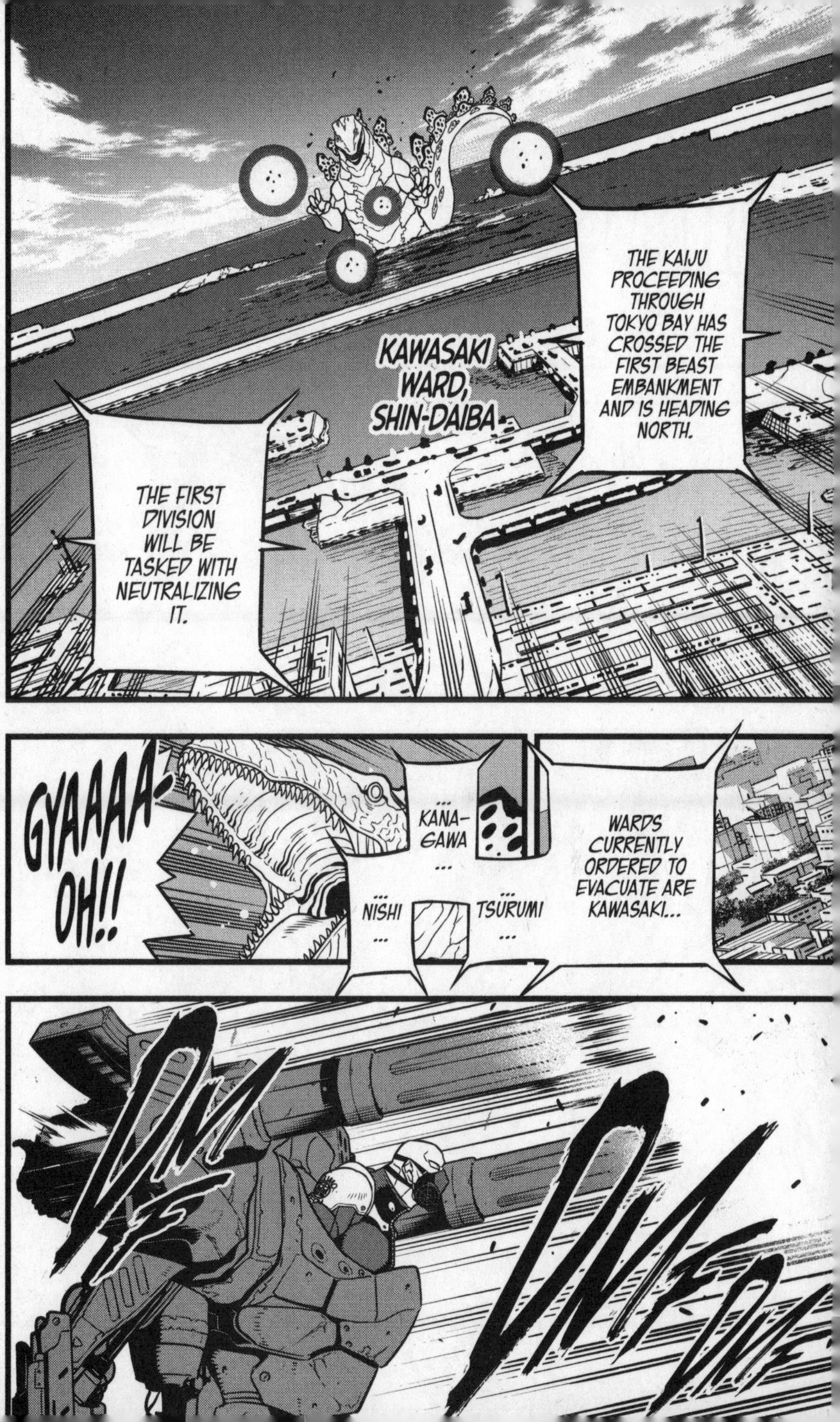
THE KAIJU PROCEEDING THROUGH TOKYO BAY HAS CROSSED THE FIRST BEAST EMBANKMENT AND IS HEADING NORTH.
KAWASAKI WARD, SHIN-DAIBA
THE FIRST DIVISION WILL BE TASKED WITH NEUTRALIZING IT.
WARDS CURRENTLY ORDERED TO EVACUATE ARE KAWASAKI...
...KANAGAWA...
...TSURUMI...
...NISHI...
GYAAAA-OH!!

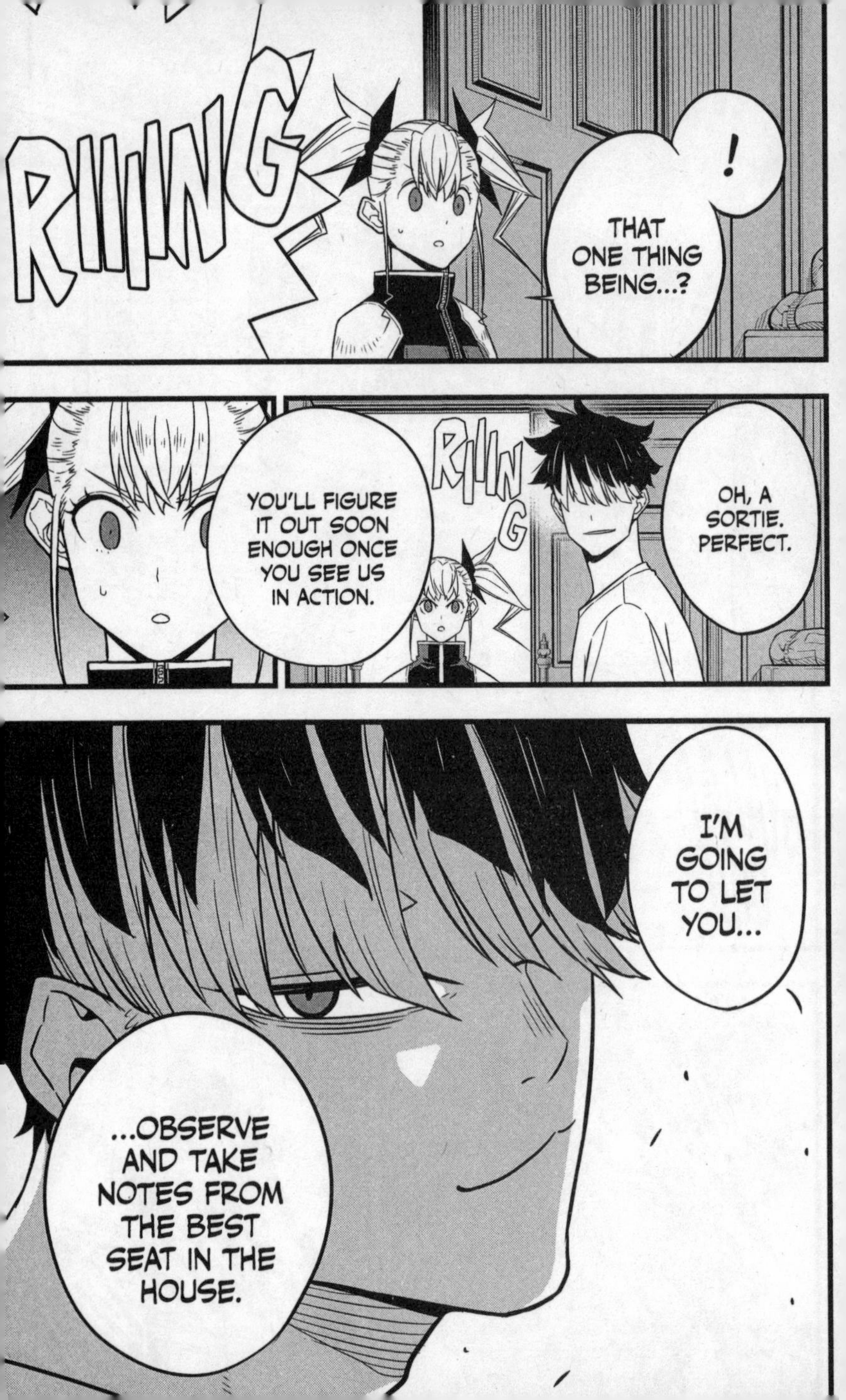
!
THAT ONE THING BEING...?
RIIIING
OH, A SORTIE. PERFECT.
RIIING
YOU'LL FIGURE IT OUT SOON ENOUGH ONCE YOU SEE US IN ACTION.
I'M GOING TO LET YOU...
...OBSERVE AND TAKE NOTES FROM THE BEST SEAT IN THE HOUSE.

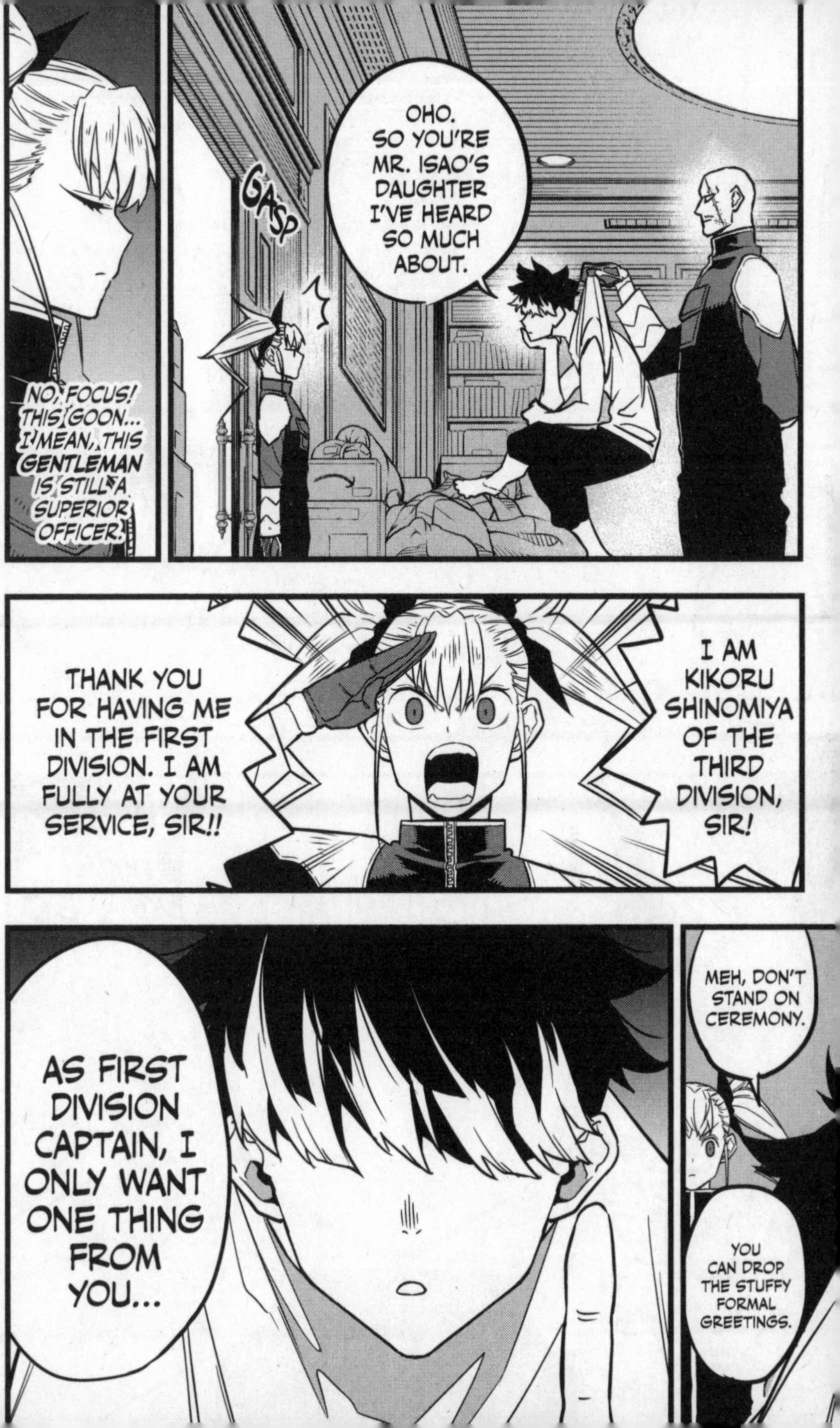
OHO. SO YOU'RE MR. ISAO'S DAUGHTER I'VE HEARD SO MUCH ABOUT.
GASP
NO, FOCUS! THIS GOON... I MEAN, THIS GENTLEMAN IS STILL A SUPERIOR OFFICER.
I AM KIKORU SHINOMIYA OF THE THIRD DIVISION, SIR!
THANK YOU FOR HAVING ME IN THE FIRST DIVISION. I AM FULLY AT YOUR SERVICE, SIR!!
MEH, DON'T STAND ON CEREMONY.
YOU CAN DROP THE STUFFY FORMAL GREETINGS.
AS FIRST DIVISION CAPTAIN, I ONLY WANT ONE THING FROM YOU...

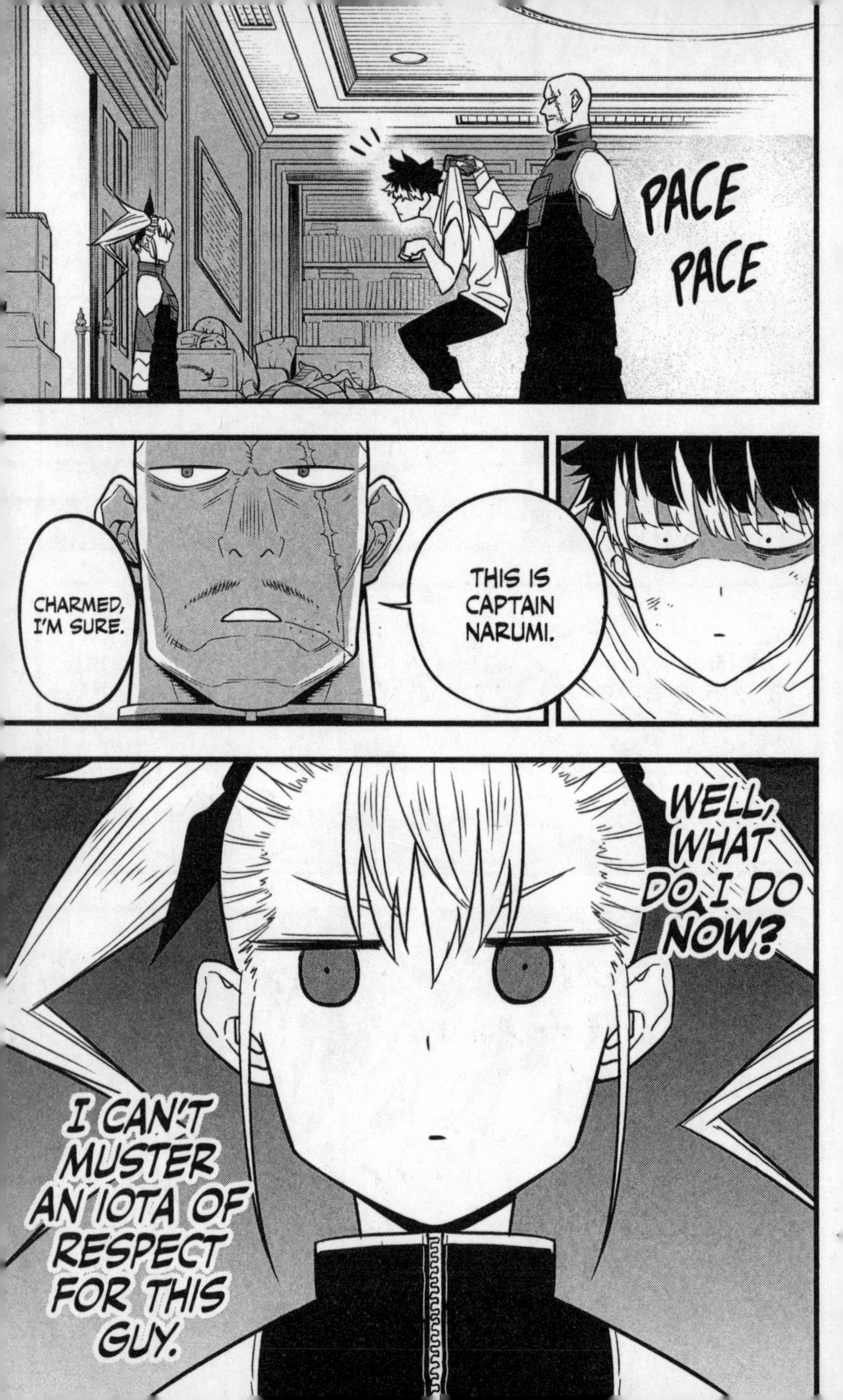
PACE PACE
THIS IS CAPTAIN NARUMI.
CHARMED, I'M SURE.
WELL, WHAT DO I DO NOW?
I CAN'T MUSTER AN IOTA OF RESPECT FOR THIS GUY.

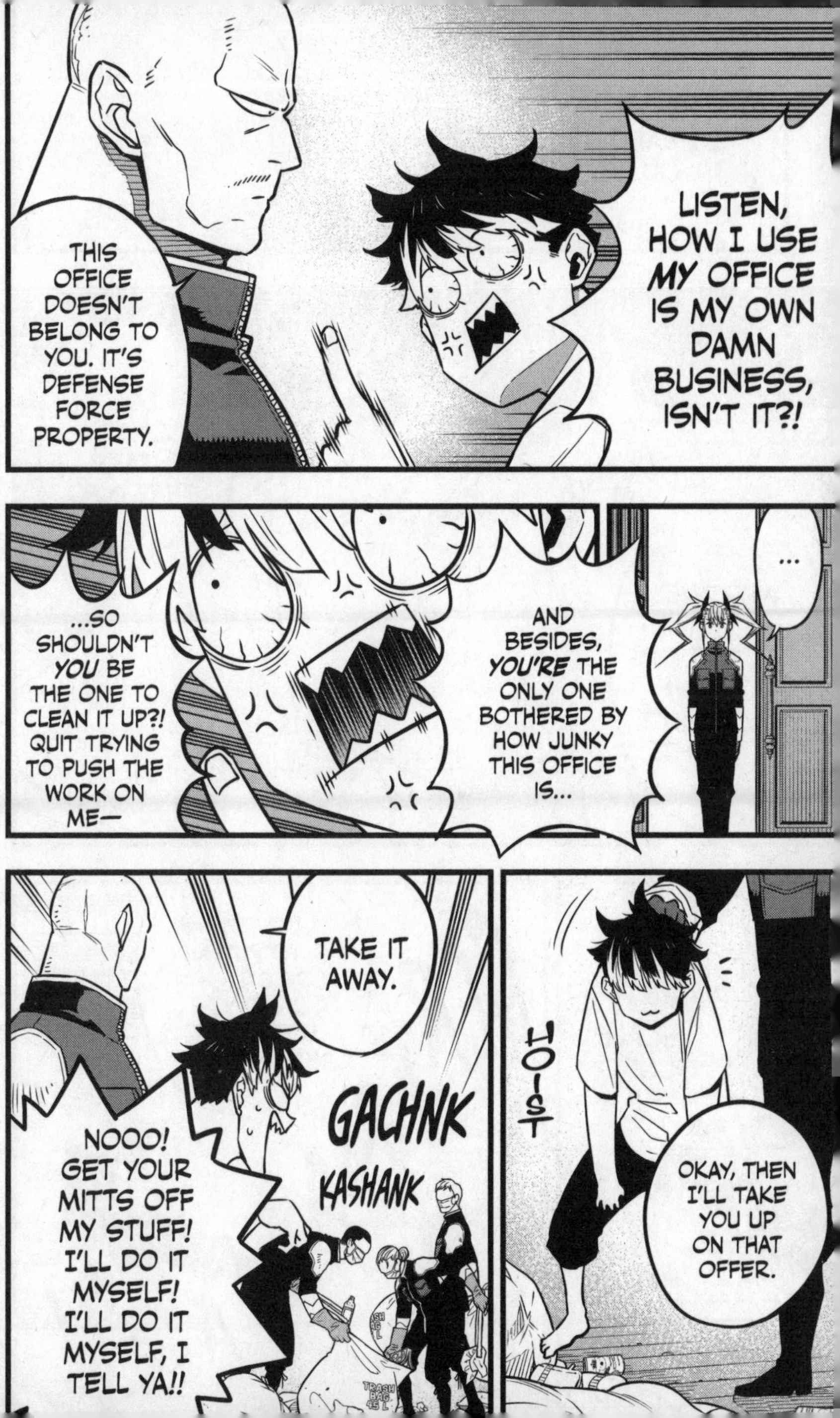
LISTEN, HOW I USE MY OFFICE IS MY OWN DAMN BUSINESS, ISN'T IT?!
THIS OFFICE DOESN'T BELONG TO YOU. IT'S DEFENSE FORCE PROPERTY.
...
AND BESIDES, YOU'RE THE ONLY ONE BOTHERED BY HOW JUNKY THIS OFFICE IS...
...SO SHOULDN'T YOU BE THE ONE TO CLEAN IT UP?! QUIT TRYING TO PUSH THE WORK ON ME—
HOIST
OKAY, THEN I'LL TAKE YOU UP ON THAT OFFER.
TAKE IT AWAY.
GACHNK
KASHANK
NOOO! GET YOUR MITTS OFF MY STUFF! I'LL DO IT MYSELF! I'LL DO IT MYSELF, I TELL YA!!
TRASH BAG 45 L

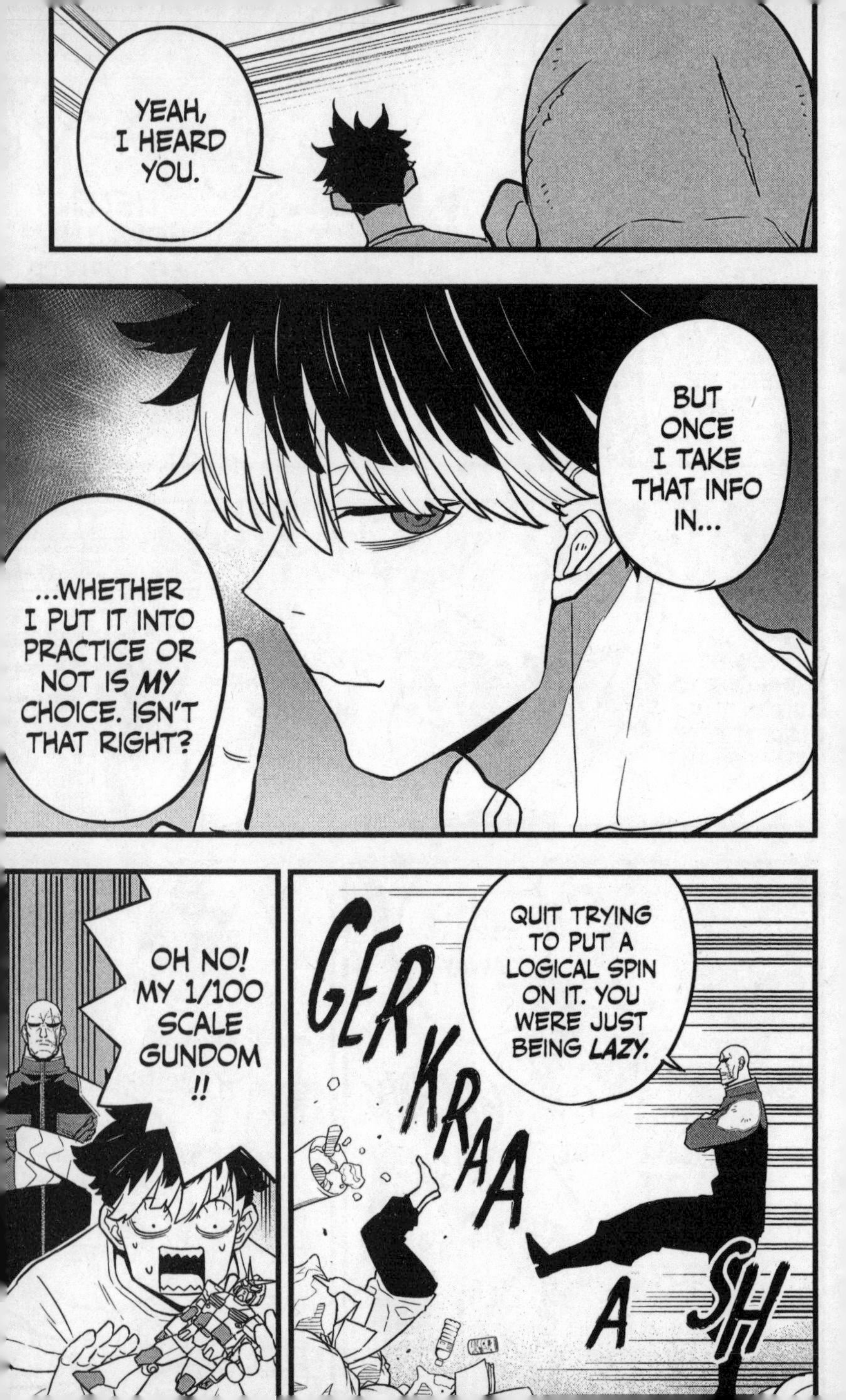
YEAH, I HEARD YOU.
BUT ONCE I TAKE THAT INFO IN...
...WHETHER I PUT IT INTO PRACTICE OR NOT IS *MY* CHOICE. ISN'T THAT RIGHT?
QUIT TRYING TO PUT A LOGICAL SPIN ON IT. YOU WERE JUST BEING *LAZY*.
GERKRAAAASH
OH NO! MY 1/100 SCALE GUNDOM !!

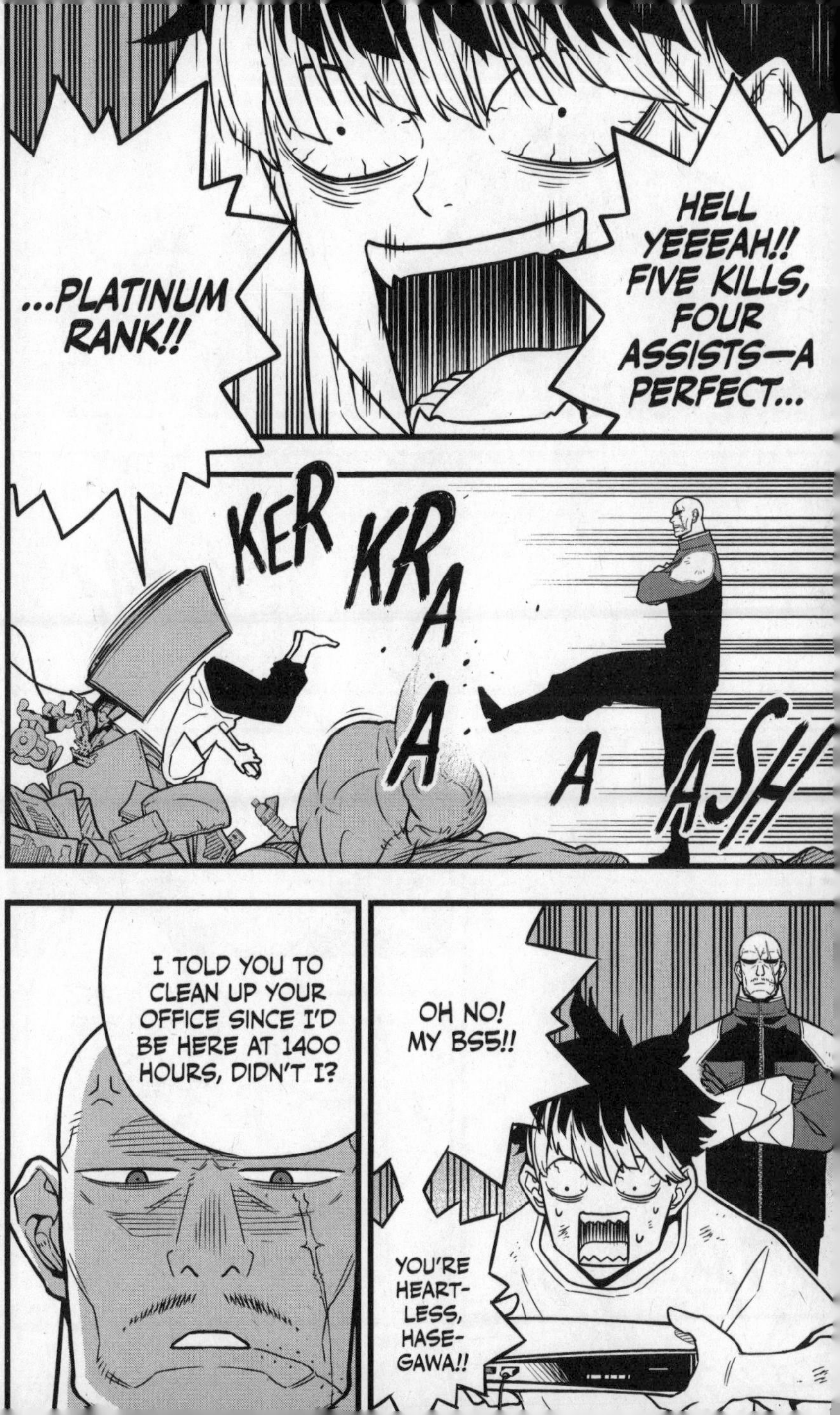

HELL YEEEAH!! FIVE KILLS, FOUR ASSISTS—A PERFECT...
...PLATINUM RANK!!
KER
KRAAAA
ASH
OH NO! MY BS5!!
YOU'RE HEART-LESS, HASE-GAWA!!
I TOLD YOU TO CLEAN UP YOUR OFFICE SINCE I'D BE HERE AT 1400 HOURS, DIDN'T I?

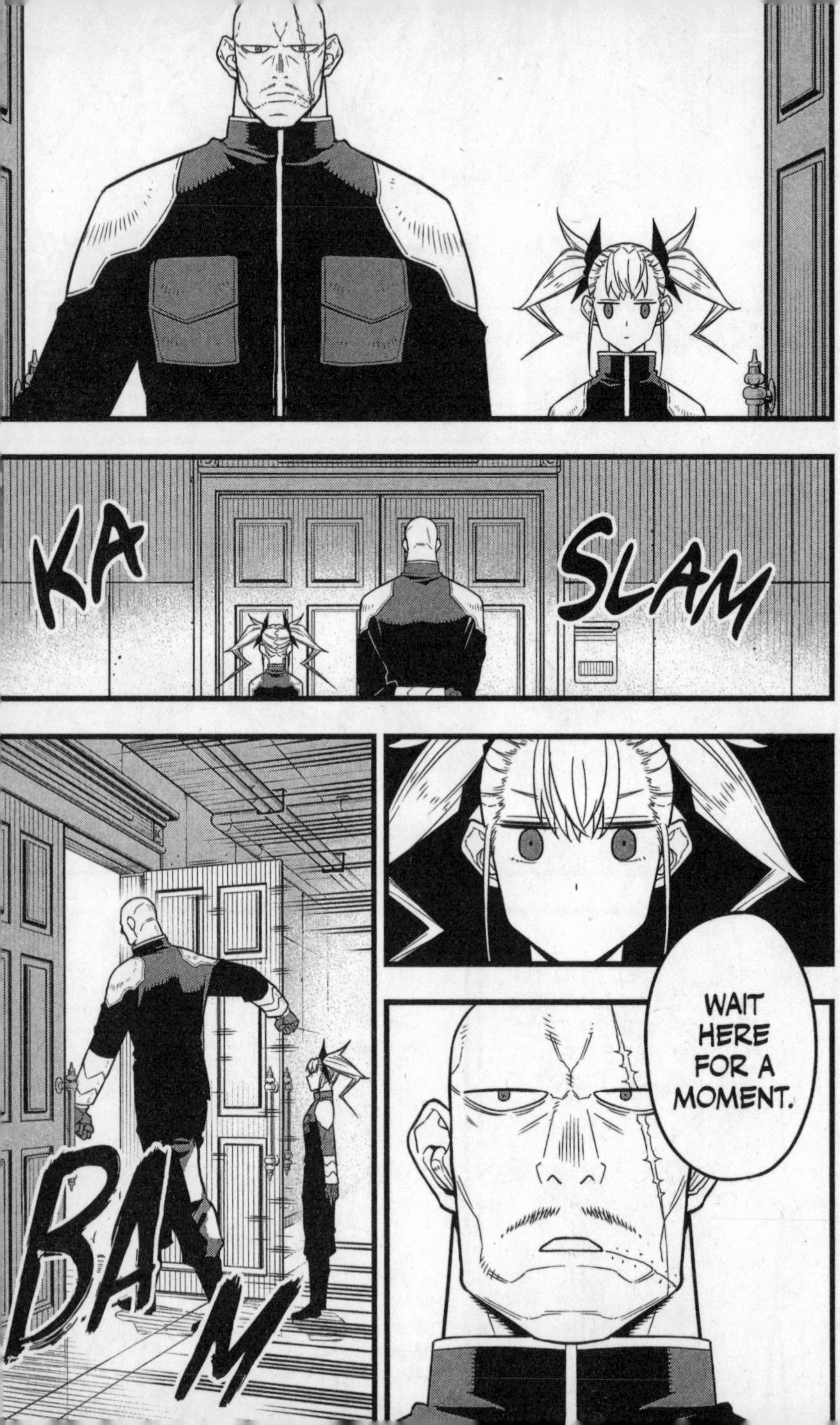
KA SLAM
WAIT HERE FOR A MOMENT.
BAM

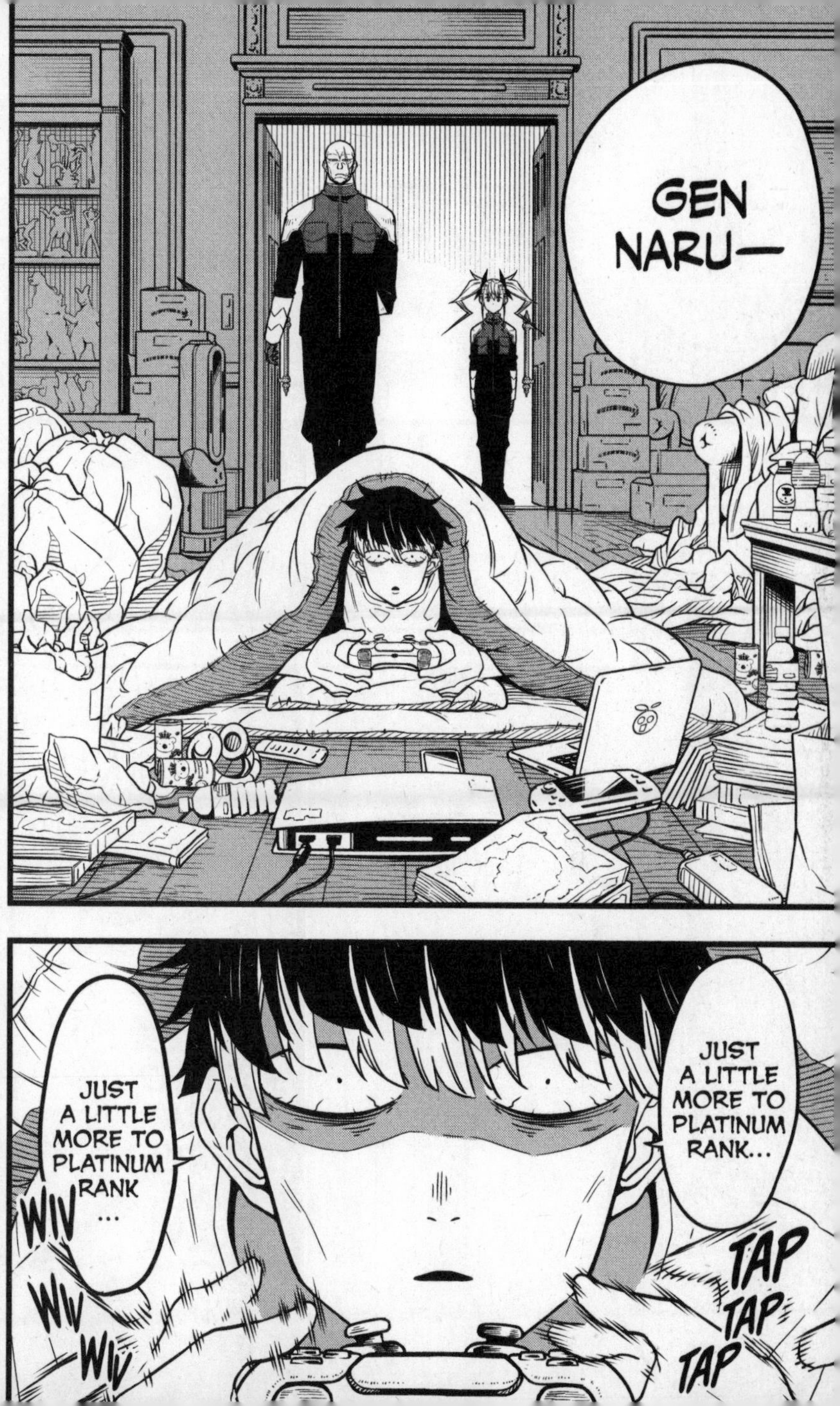
GEN NARU—
JUST A LITTLE MORE TO PLATINUM RANK...
TAP TAP TAP
JUST A LITTLE MORE TO PLATINUM RANK ...
WIV WIV WIV

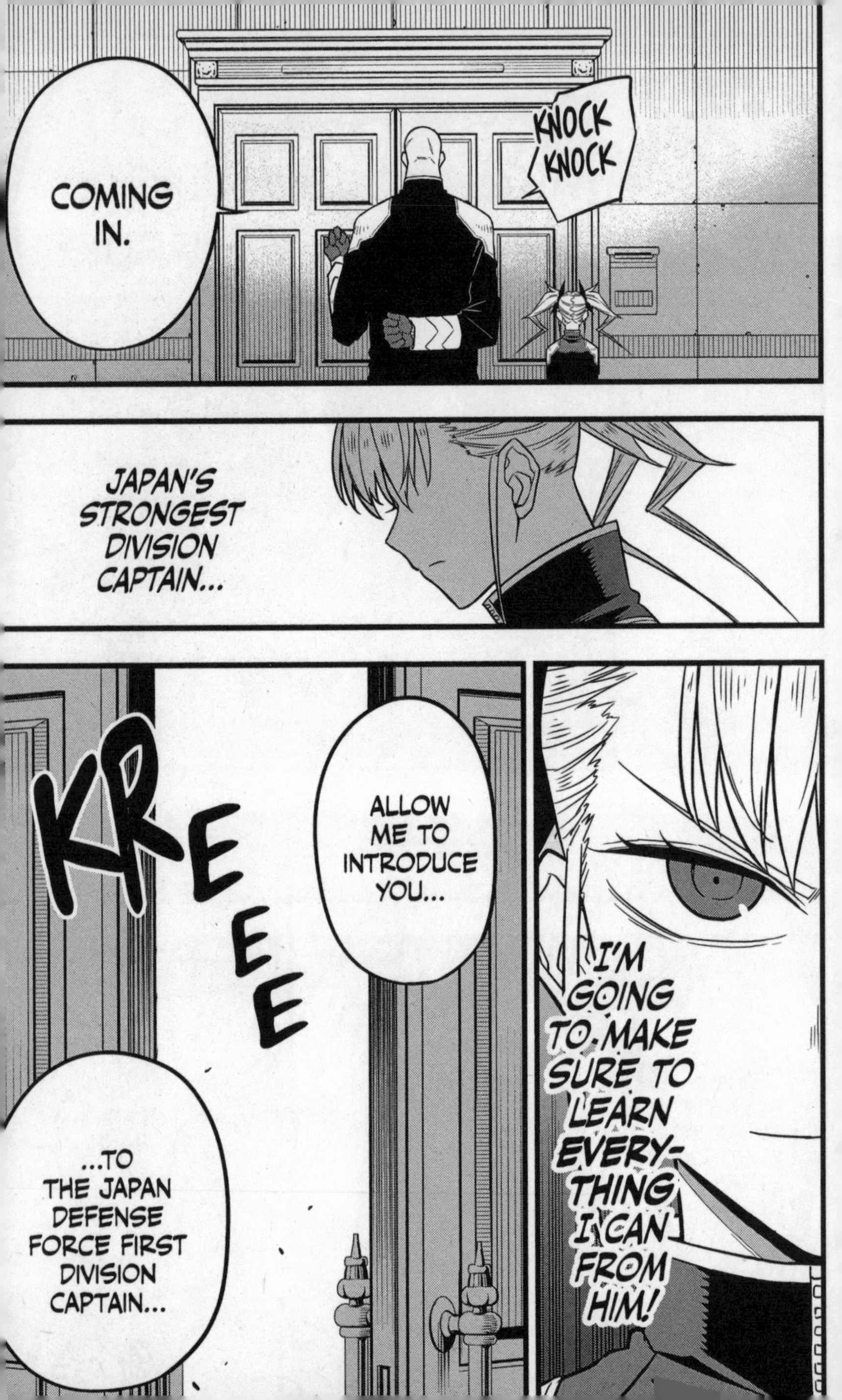
KNOCK KNOCK
COMING IN.
JAPAN'S STRONGEST DIVISION CAPTAIN...
I'M GOING TO MAKE SURE TO LEARN EVERY-THING I CAN FROM HIM!
ALLOW ME TO INTRODUCE YOU...
KREEE
...TO THE JAPAN DEFENSE FORCE FIRST DIVISION CAPTAIN...

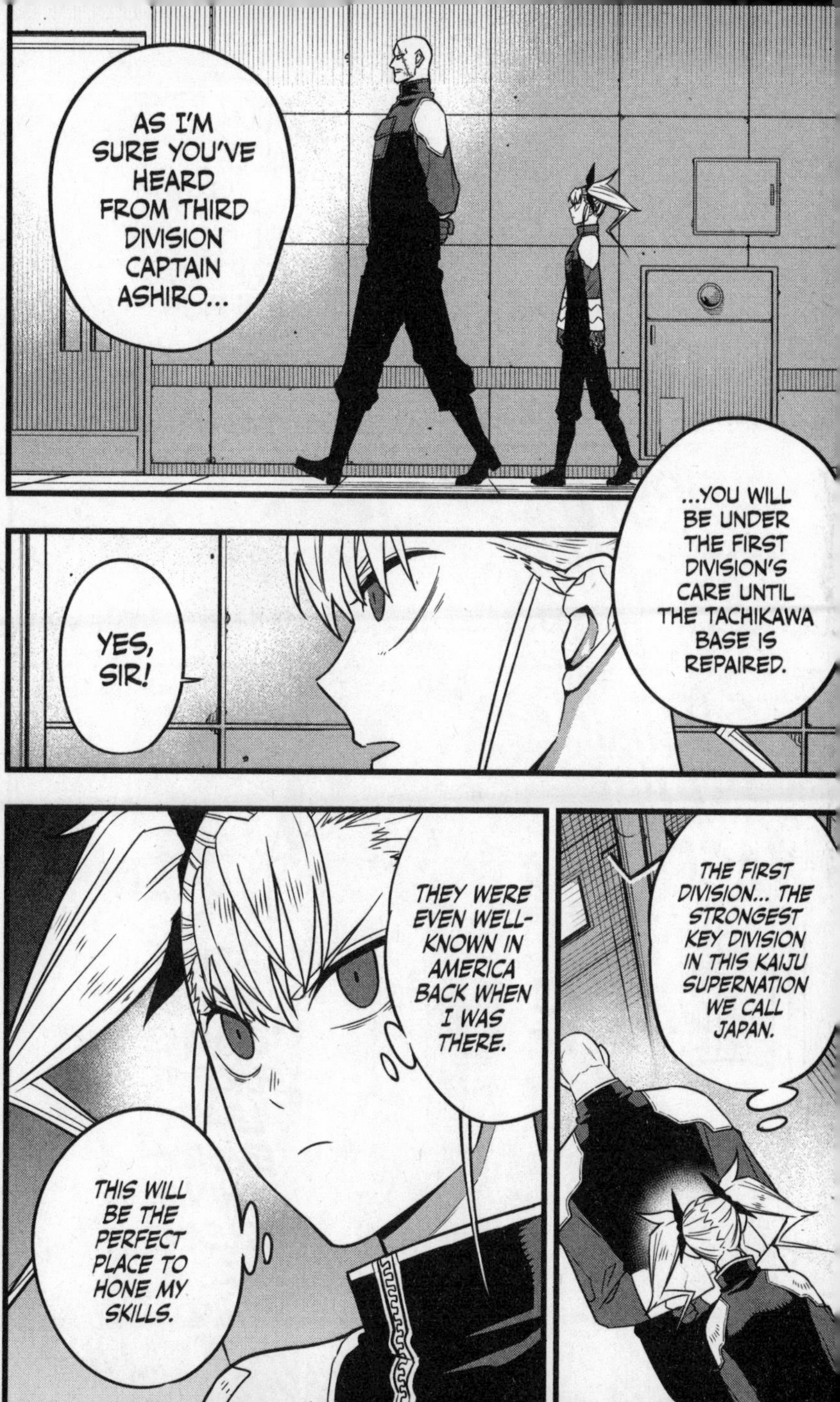
AS I'M SURE YOU'VE HEARD FROM THIRD DIVISION CAPTAIN ASHIRO...
...YOU WILL BE UNDER THE FIRST DIVISION'S CARE UNTIL THE TACHIKAWA BASE IS REPAIRED.
YES, SIR!
THE FIRST DIVISION... THE STRONGEST KEY DIVISION IN THIS KAIJU SUPERNATION WE CALL JAPAN.
THEY WERE EVEN WELL-KNOWN IN AMERICA BACK WHEN I WAS THERE.
THIS WILL BE THE PERFECT PLACE TO HONE MY SKILLS.

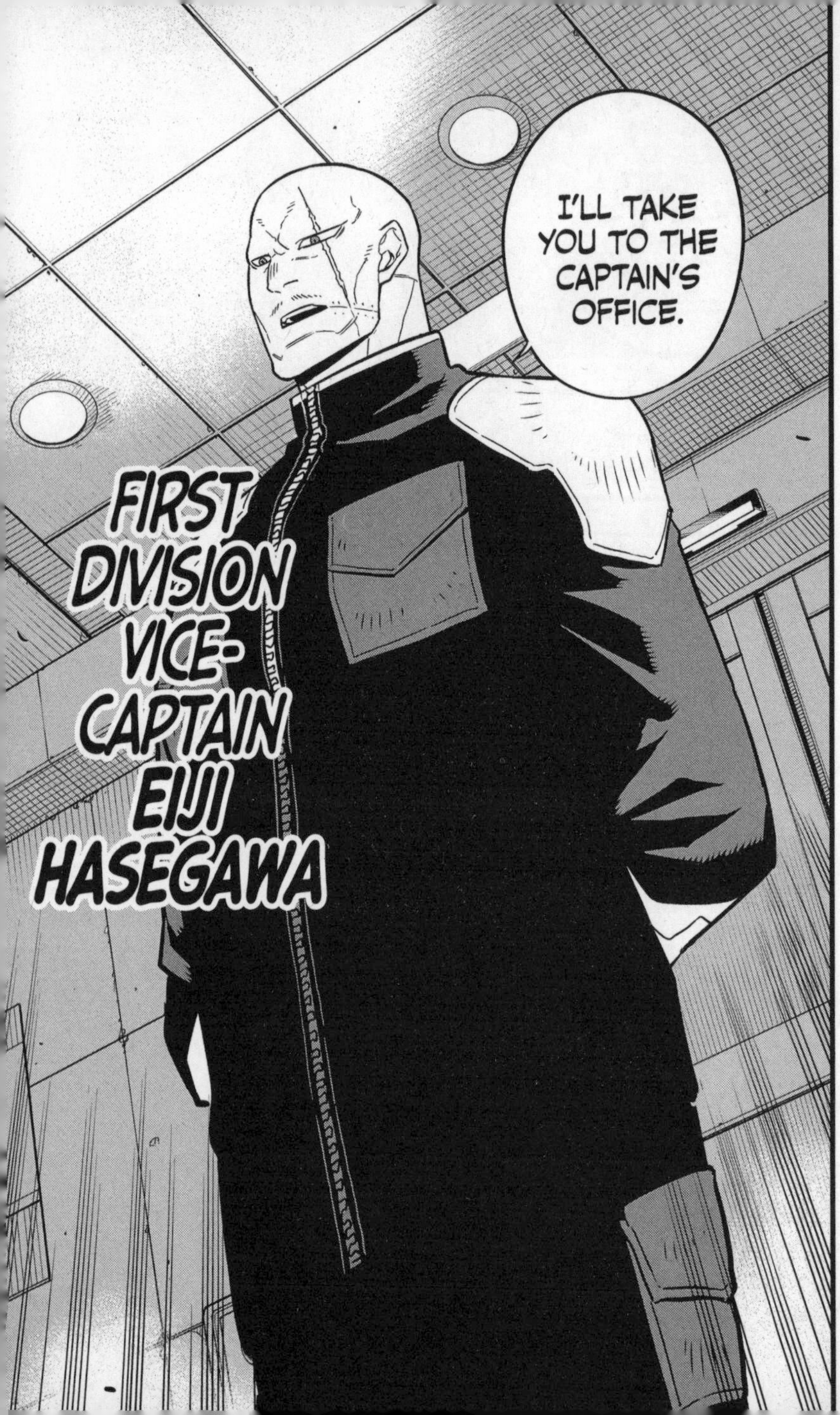
I'LL TAKE YOU TO THE CAPTAIN'S OFFICE.
FIRST DIVISION VICE-CAPTAIN EIJI HASEGAWA

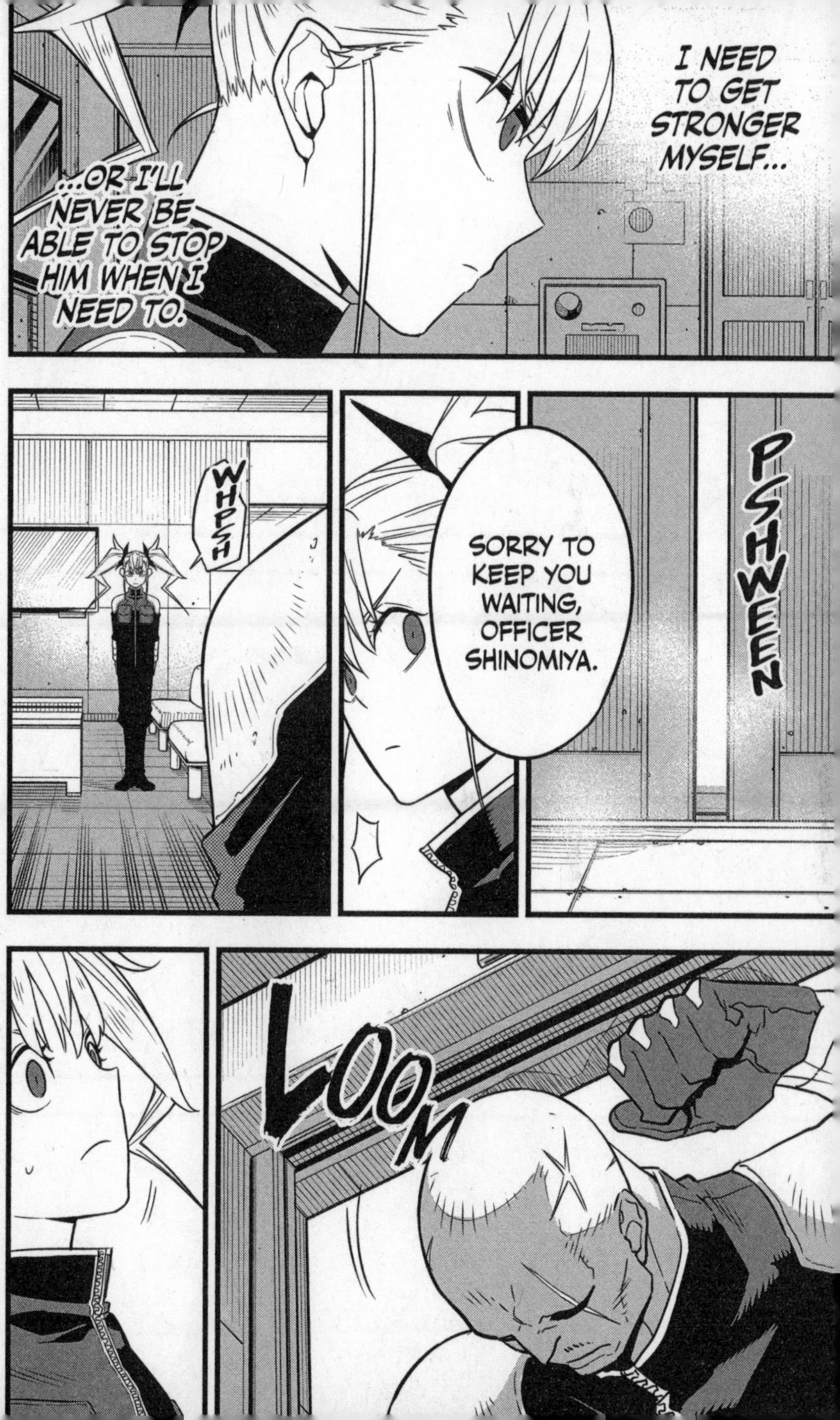
I NEED TO GET STRONGER MYSELF...
...OR I'LL NEVER BE ABLE TO STOP HIM WHEN I NEED TO.
PSHWEEN
SORRY TO KEEP YOU WAITING, OFFICER SHINOMIYA.
WHPSH
LOOM

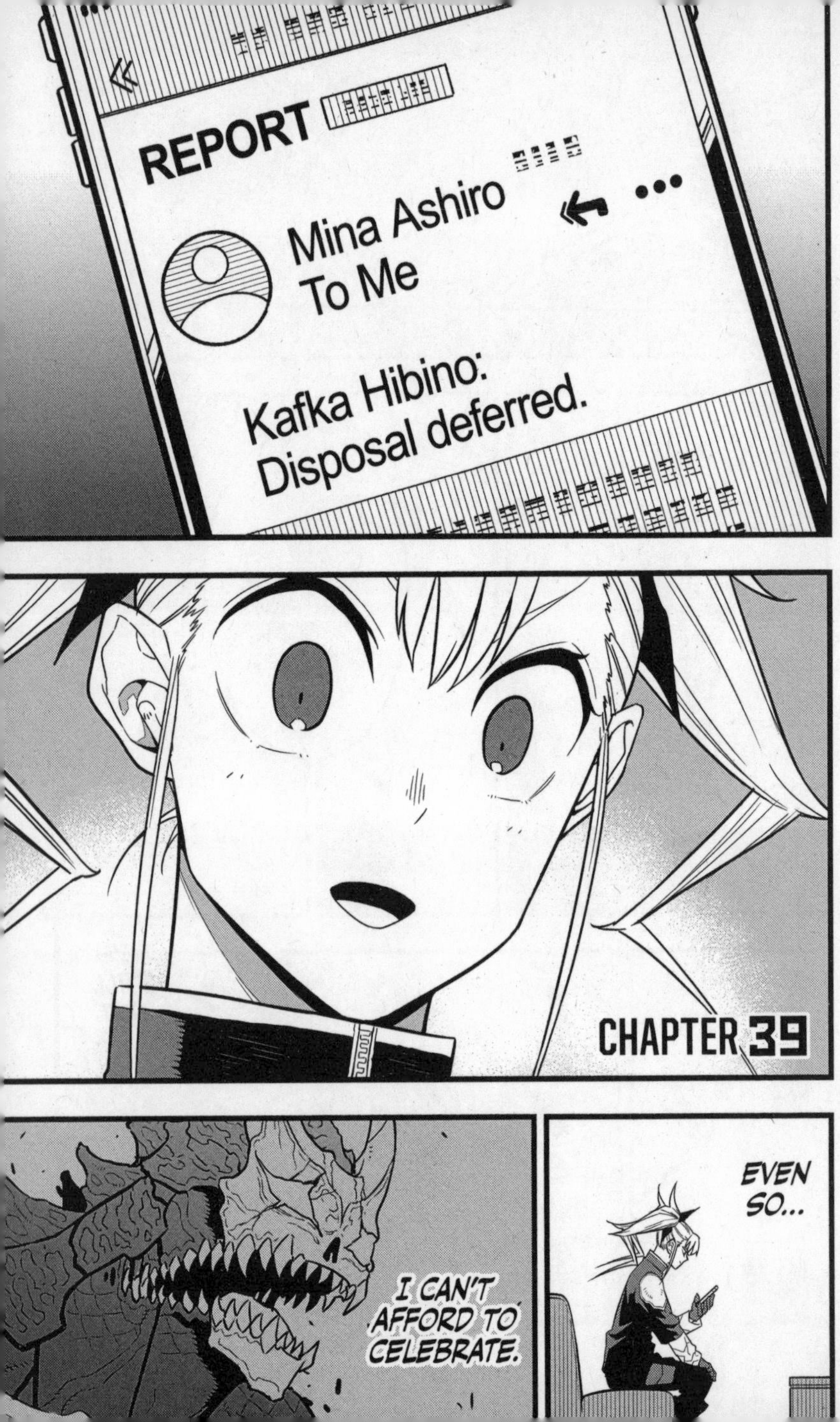
REPORT
Mina Ashiro
To Me
Kafka Hibino:
Disposal deferred.
CHAPTER 39
EVEN SO...
I CAN'T AFFORD TO CELEBRATE.

JUST BEFORE KAFKA WOKE UP

HE'S STILL NOT UP?
THE ANESTHESIA SHOULD HAVE WORN OFF BY NOW.
IT SEEMS HE'S A HEAVY SLEEPER, SIR...

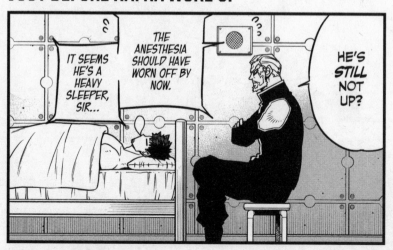

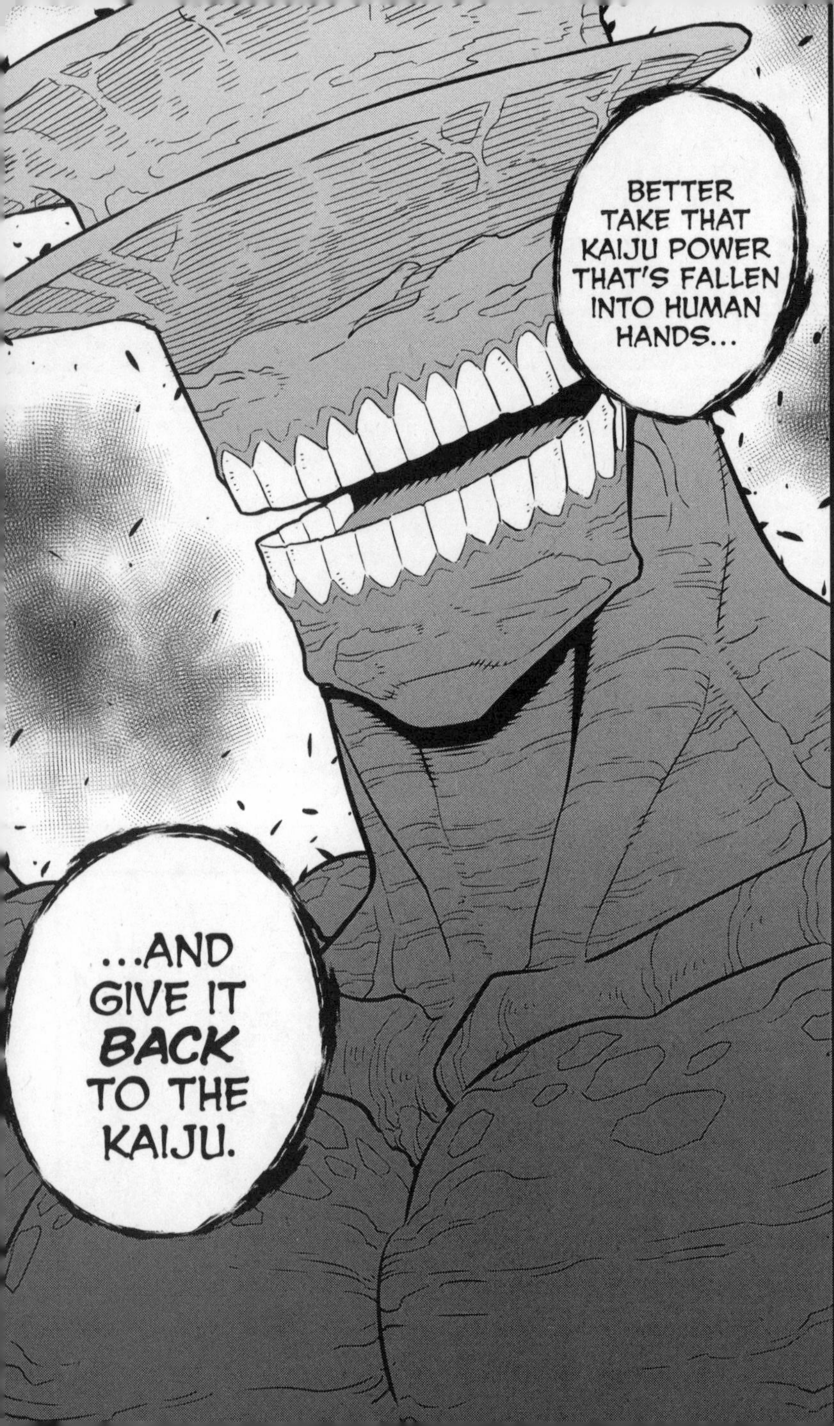
BETTER TAKE THAT KAIJU POWER THAT'S FALLEN INTO HUMAN HANDS...
...AND GIVE IT **BACK** TO THE KAIJU.

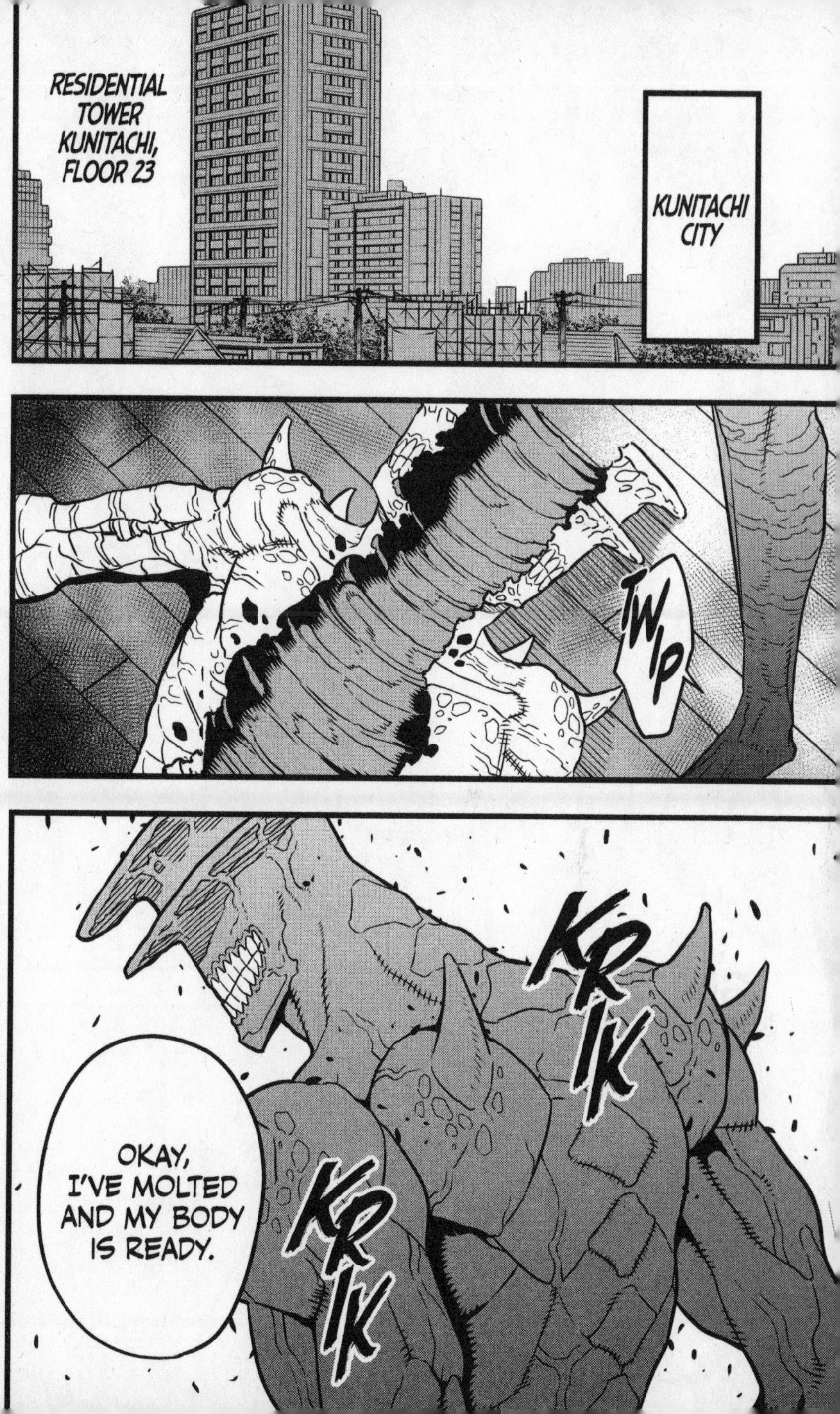
KUNITACHI CITY
RESIDENTIAL TOWER KUNITACHI, FLOOR 23
TWIP
KRIK
OKAY, I'VE MOLTED AND MY BODY IS READY.
KRIK

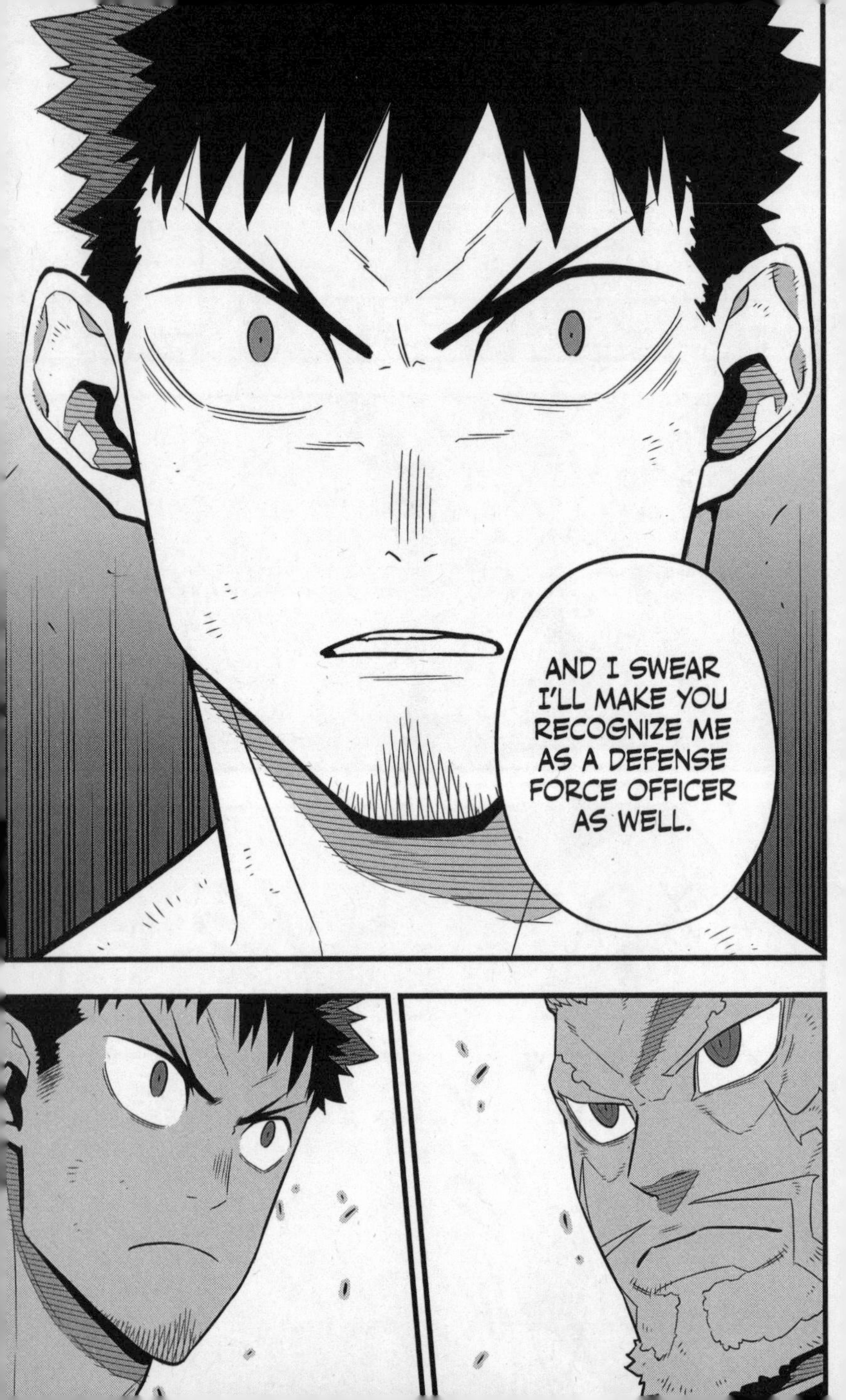
AND I SWEAR I'LL MAKE YOU RECOGNIZE ME AS A DEFENSE FORCE OFFICER AS WELL.

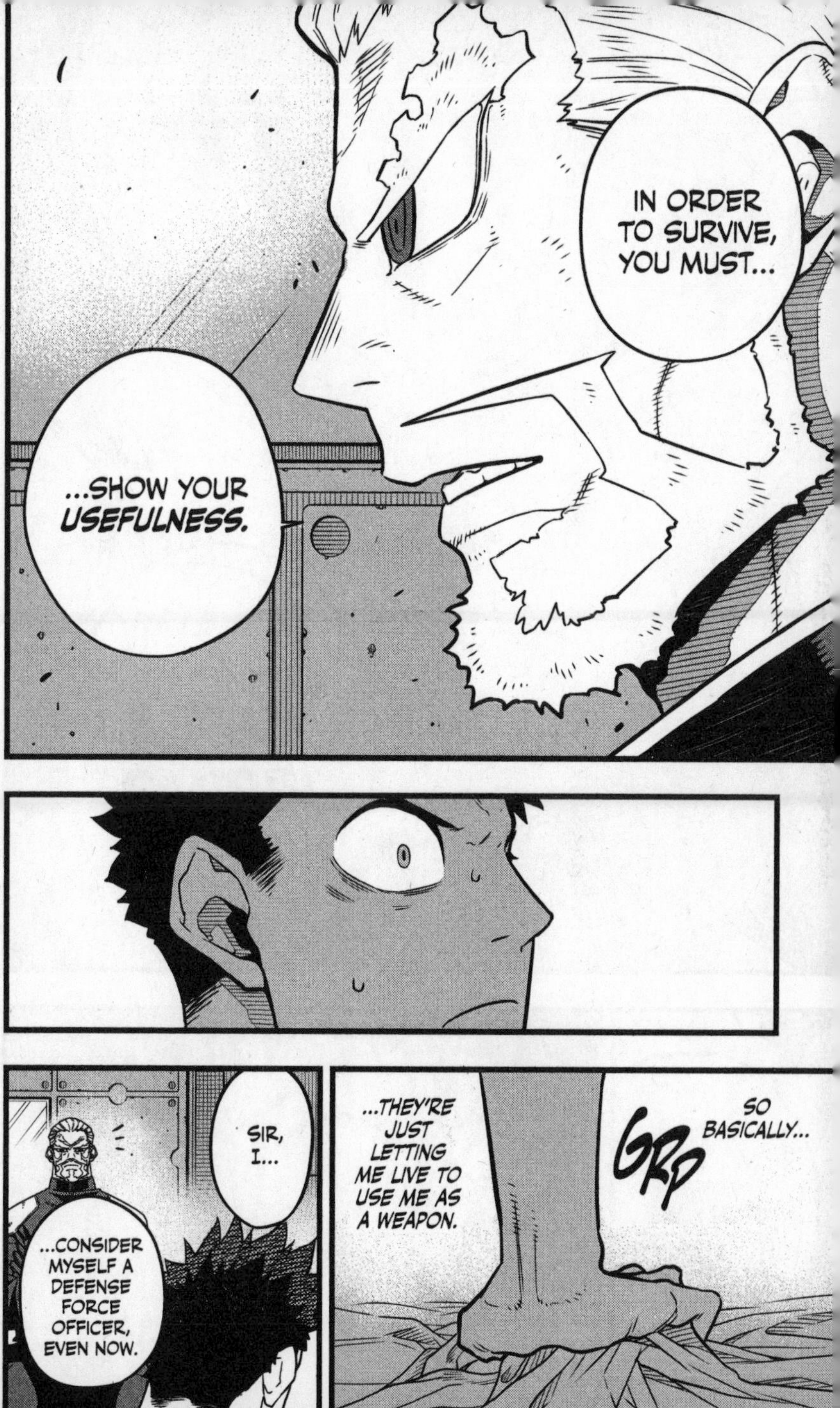
IN ORDER TO SURVIVE, YOU MUST...
...SHOW YOUR USEFULNESS.
SO BASICALLY...
GRP
...THEY'RE JUST LETTING ME LIVE TO USE ME AS A WEAPON.
SIR, I...
...CONSIDER MYSELF A DEFENSE FORCE OFFICER, EVEN NOW.

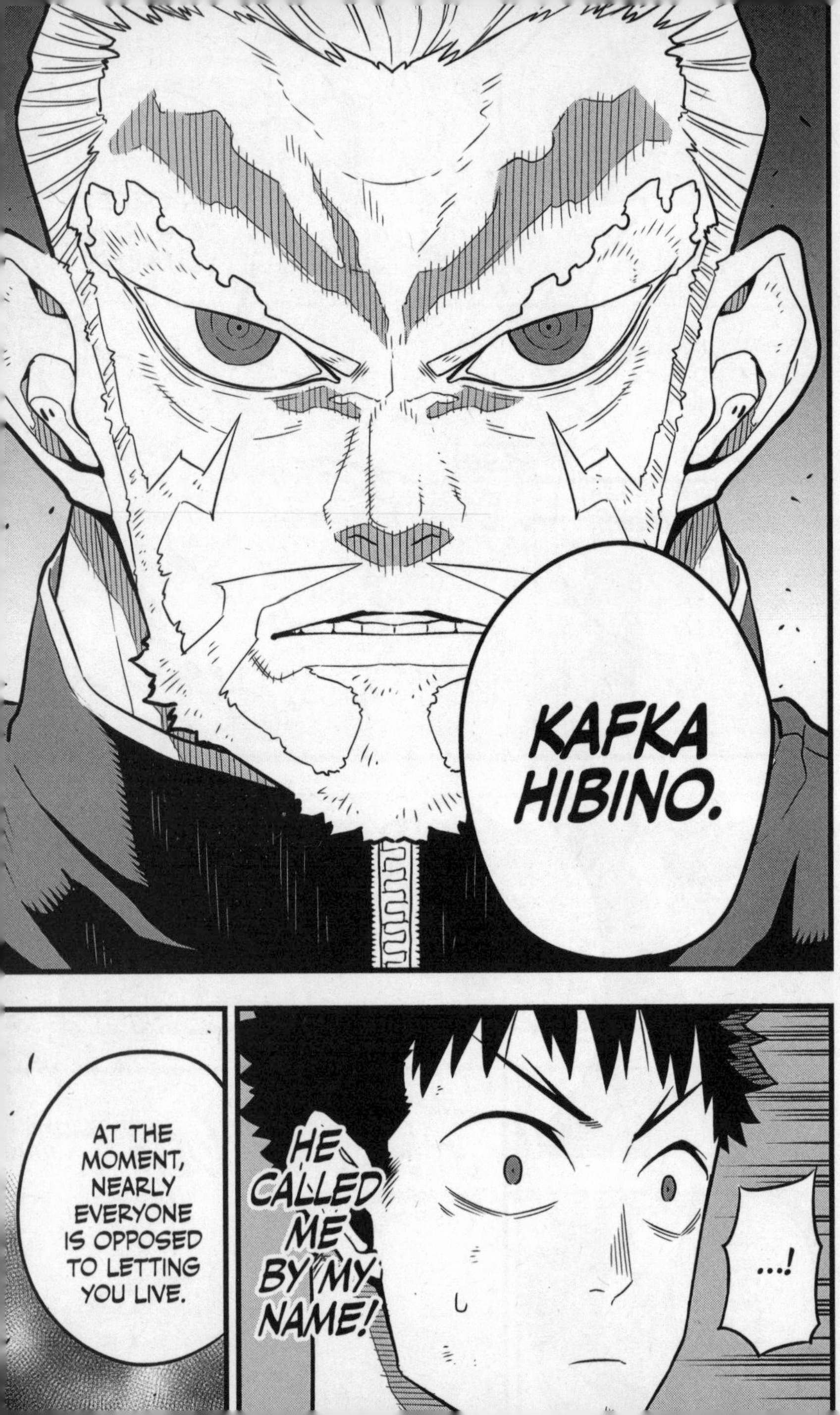
KAFKA HIBINO.
...!
HE CALLED ME BY MY NAME!
AT THE MOMENT, NEARLY EVERYONE IS OPPOSED TO LETTING YOU LIVE.

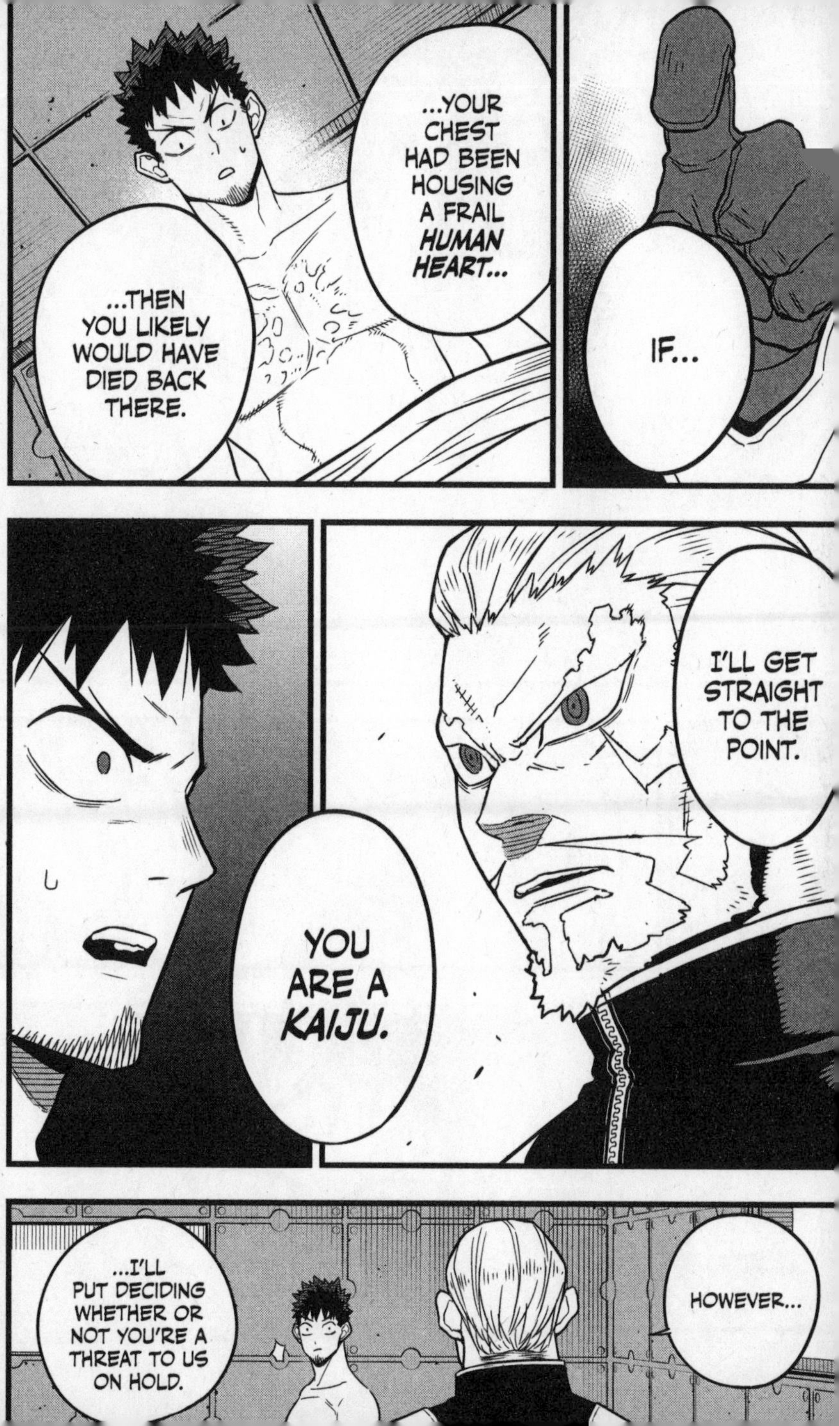
IF...
...YOUR CHEST HAD BEEN HOUSING A FRAIL *HUMAN HEART*...
...THEN YOU LIKELY WOULD HAVE DIED BACK THERE.
I'LL GET STRAIGHT TO THE POINT.
YOU ARE A *KAIJU.*
HOWEVER...
...I'LL PUT DECIDING WHETHER OR NOT YOU'RE A THREAT TO US ON HOLD.

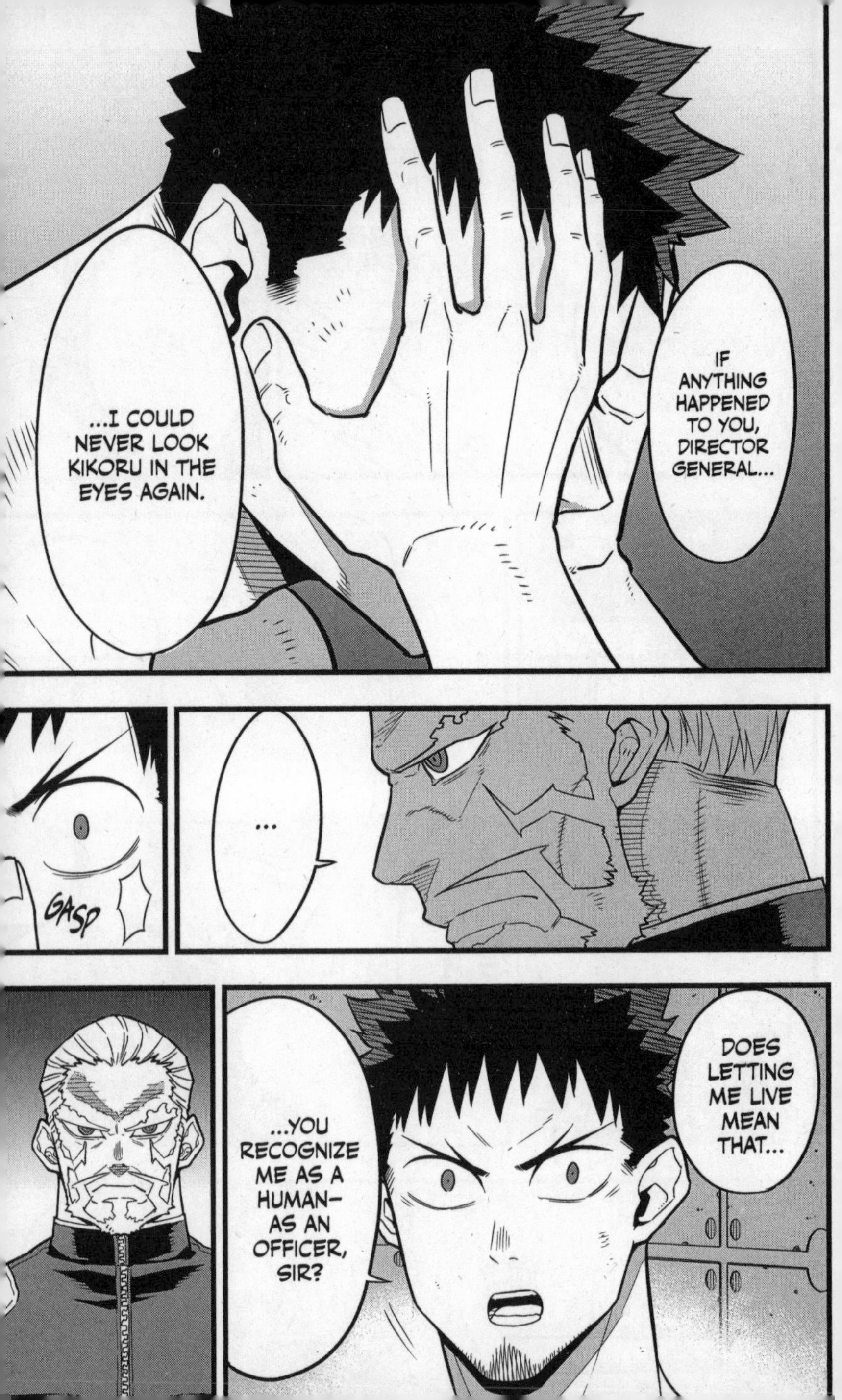
IF ANYTHING HAPPENED TO YOU, DIRECTOR GENERAL...
...I COULD NEVER LOOK KIKORU IN THE EYES AGAIN.
...
GASP
DOES LETTING ME LIVE MEAN THAT...
...YOU RECOGNIZE ME AS A HUMAN— AS AN OFFICER, SIR?

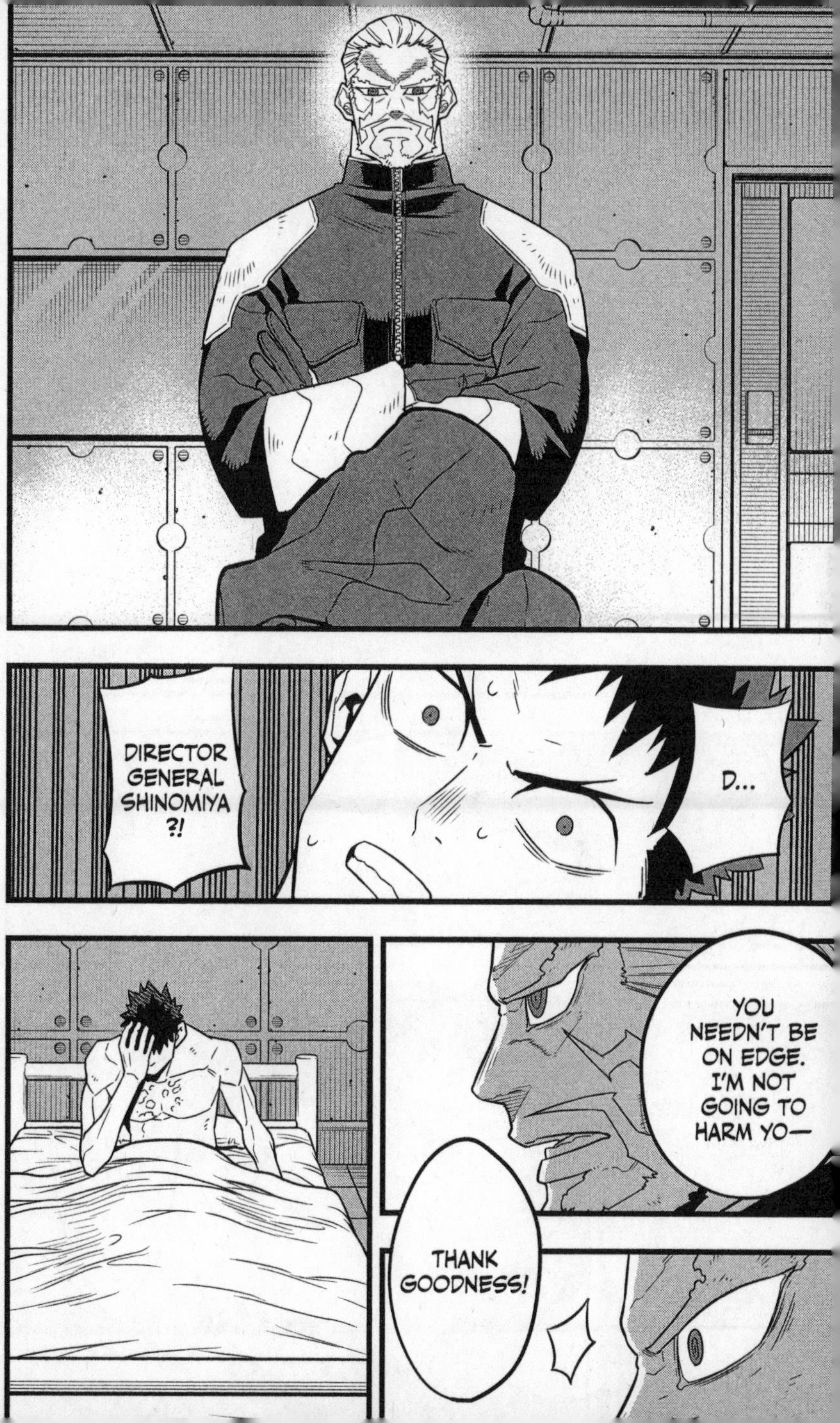
D...
DIRECTOR GENERAL SHINOMIYA ?!
YOU NEEDN'T BE ON EDGE. I'M NOT GOING TO HARM YO—
THANK GOODNESS!

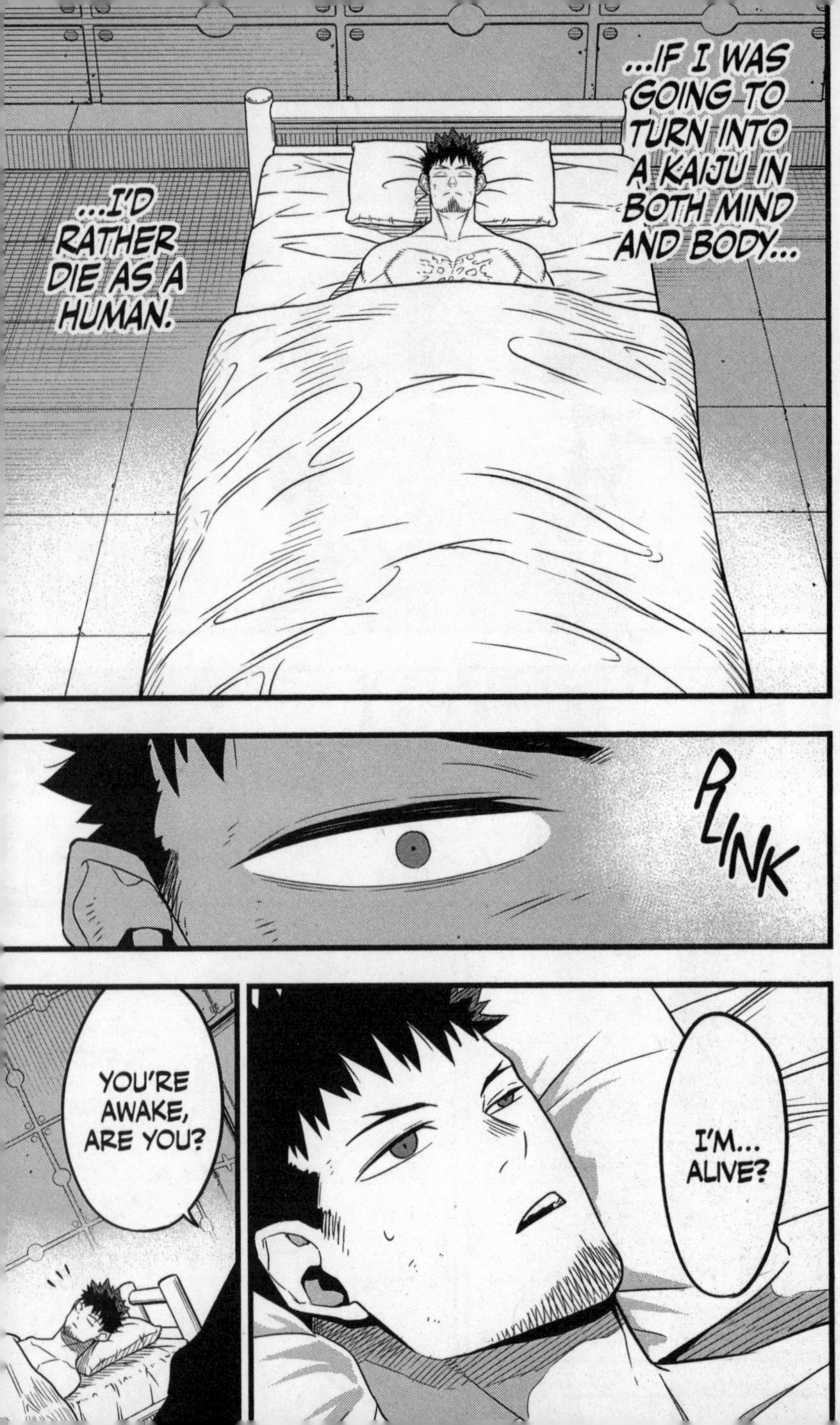
...IF I WAS GOING TO TURN INTO A KAIJU IN BOTH MIND AND BODY...
...I'D RATHER DIE AS A HUMAN.
BLINK
I'M... ALIVE?
YOU'RE AWAKE, ARE YOU?

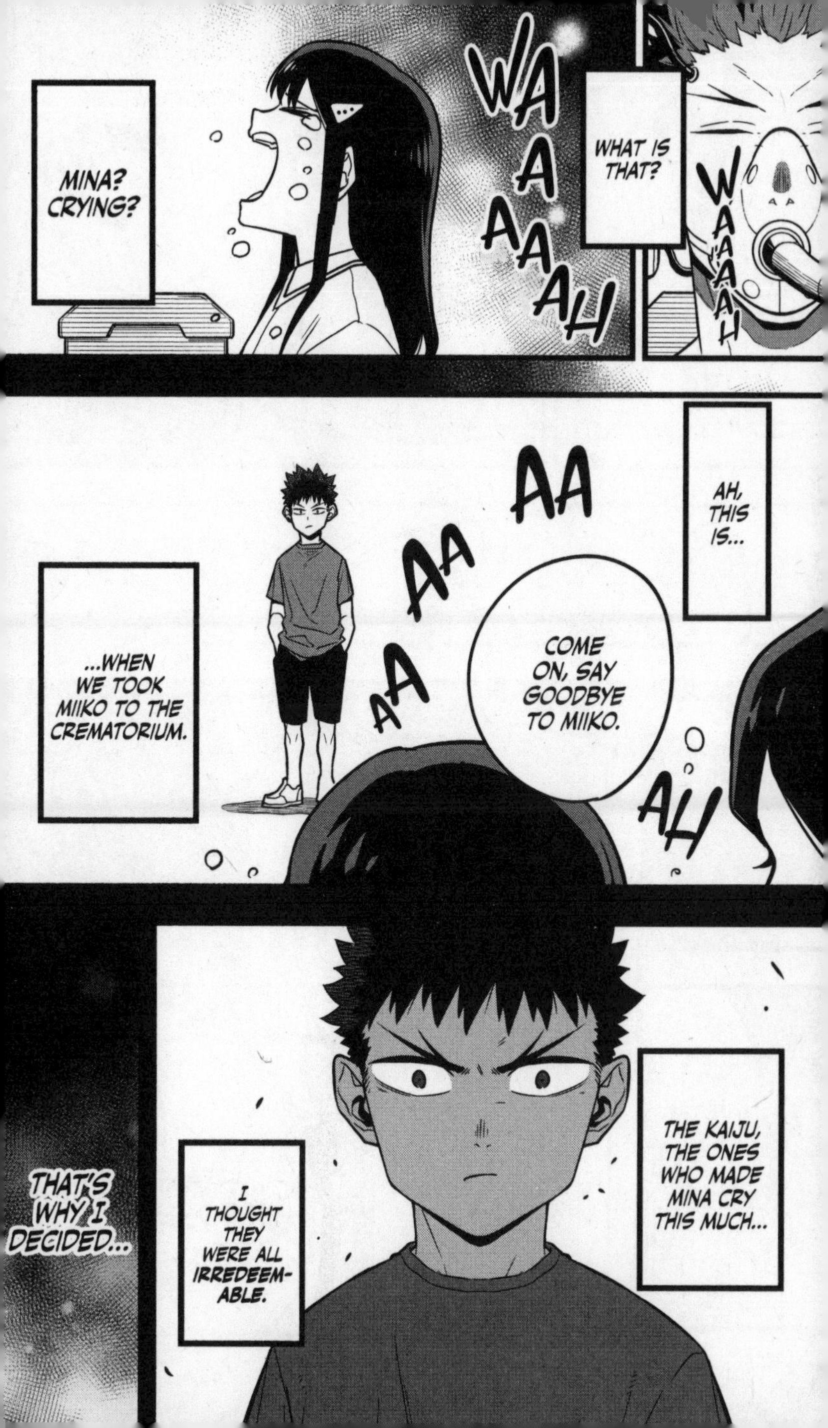
WHAT IS THAT?
WAAAAAH
WAAAAAAH
MINA? CRYING?
AH, THIS IS...
COME ON, SAY GOODBYE TO MIIKO.
AAAAAA
AH
...WHEN WE TOOK MIIKO TO THE CREMATORIUM.
THE KAIJU, THE ONES WHO MADE MINA CRY THIS MUCH...
I THOUGHT THEY WERE ALL IRREDEEM-ABLE.
THAT'S WHY I DECIDED...

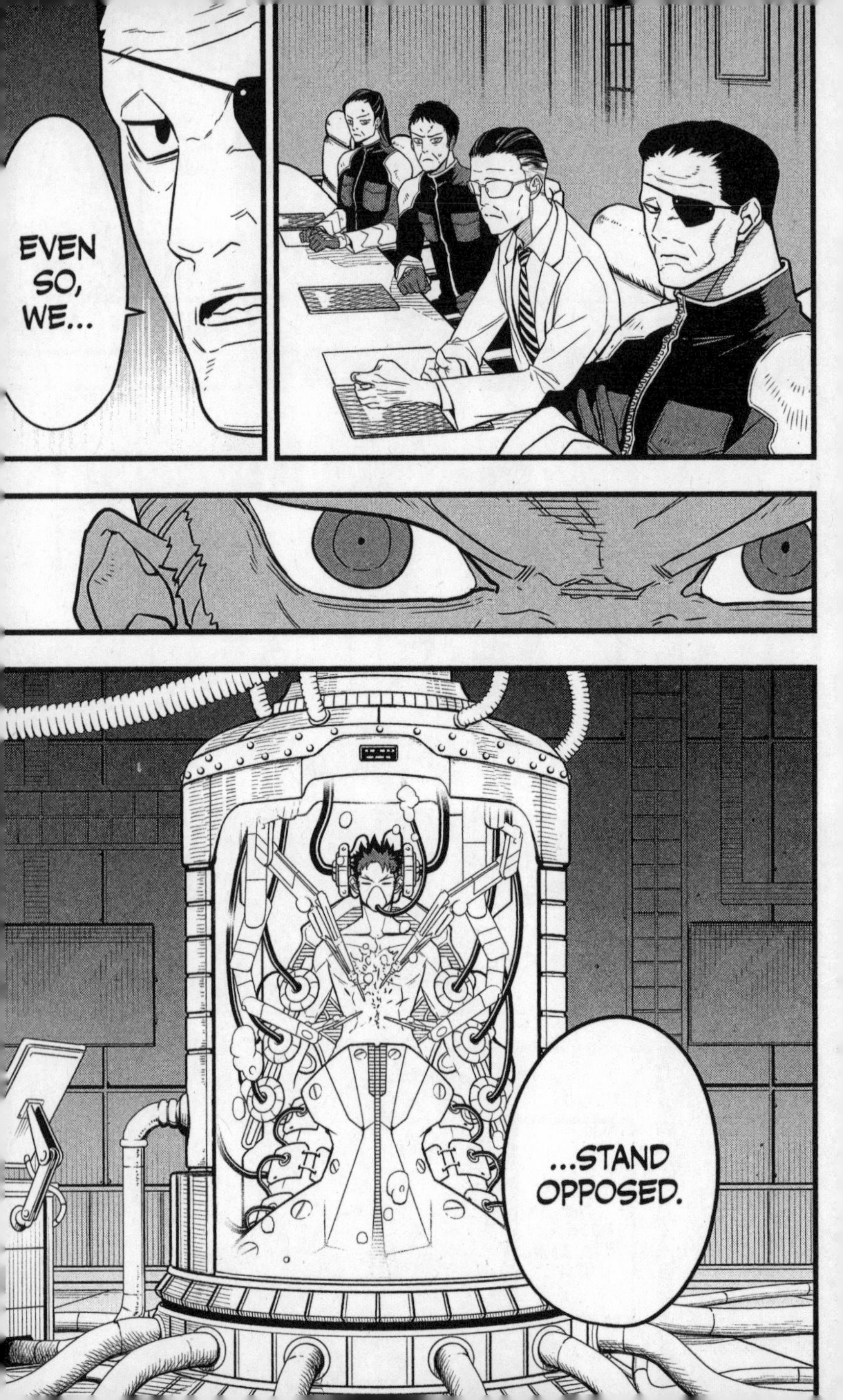
EVEN SO, WE...
...STAND OPPOSED.

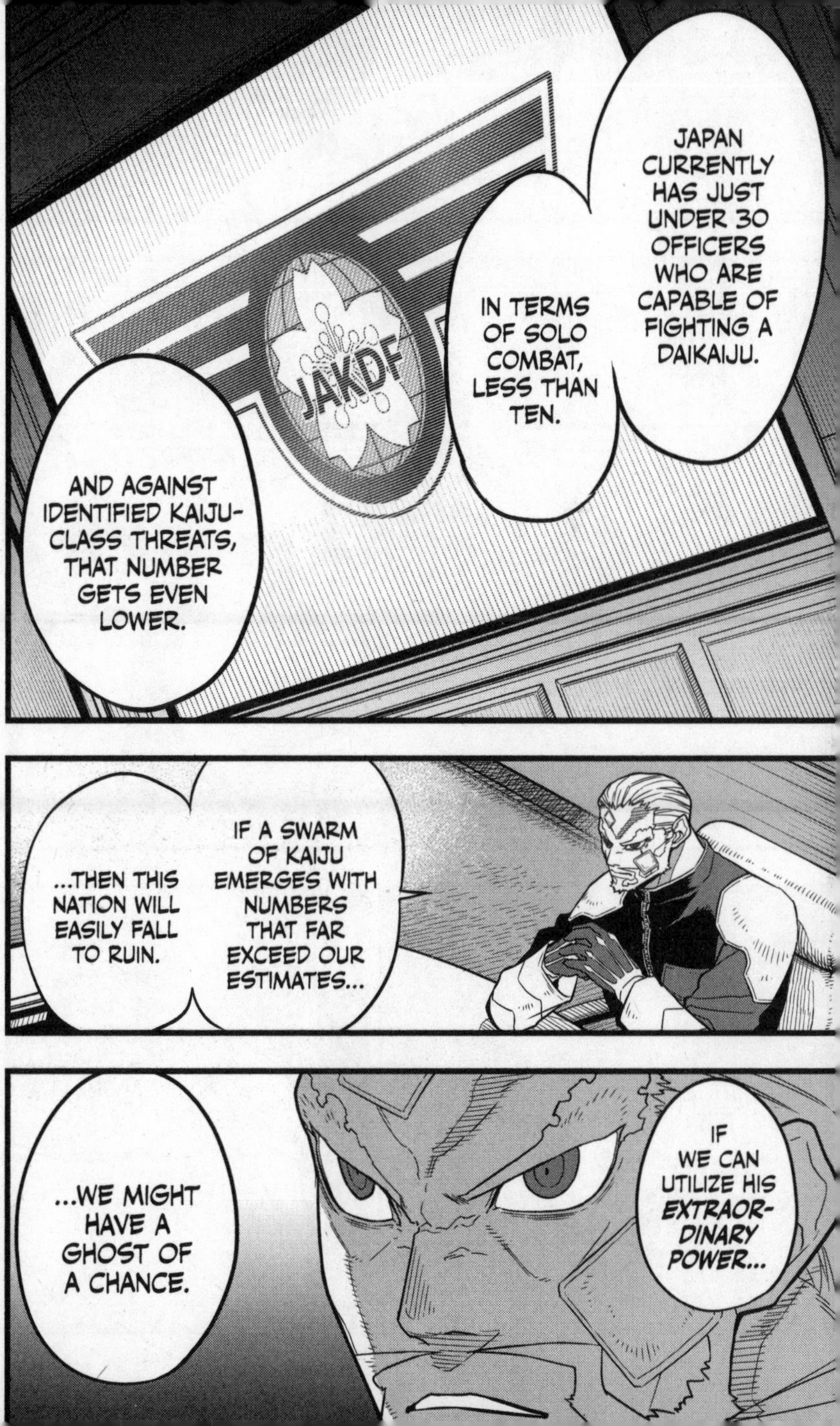
JAKDF
JAPAN CURRENTLY HAS JUST UNDER 30 OFFICERS WHO ARE CAPABLE OF FIGHTING A DAIKAIJU.
IN TERMS OF SOLO COMBAT, LESS THAN TEN.
AND AGAINST IDENTIFIED KAIJU-CLASS THREATS, THAT NUMBER GETS EVEN LOWER.
IF A SWARM OF KAIJU EMERGES WITH NUMBERS THAT FAR EXCEED OUR ESTIMATES...
...THEN THIS NATION WILL EASILY FALL TO RUIN.
IF WE CAN UTILIZE HIS *EXTRAORDINARY POWER*...
...WE MIGHT HAVE A GHOST OF A CHANCE.

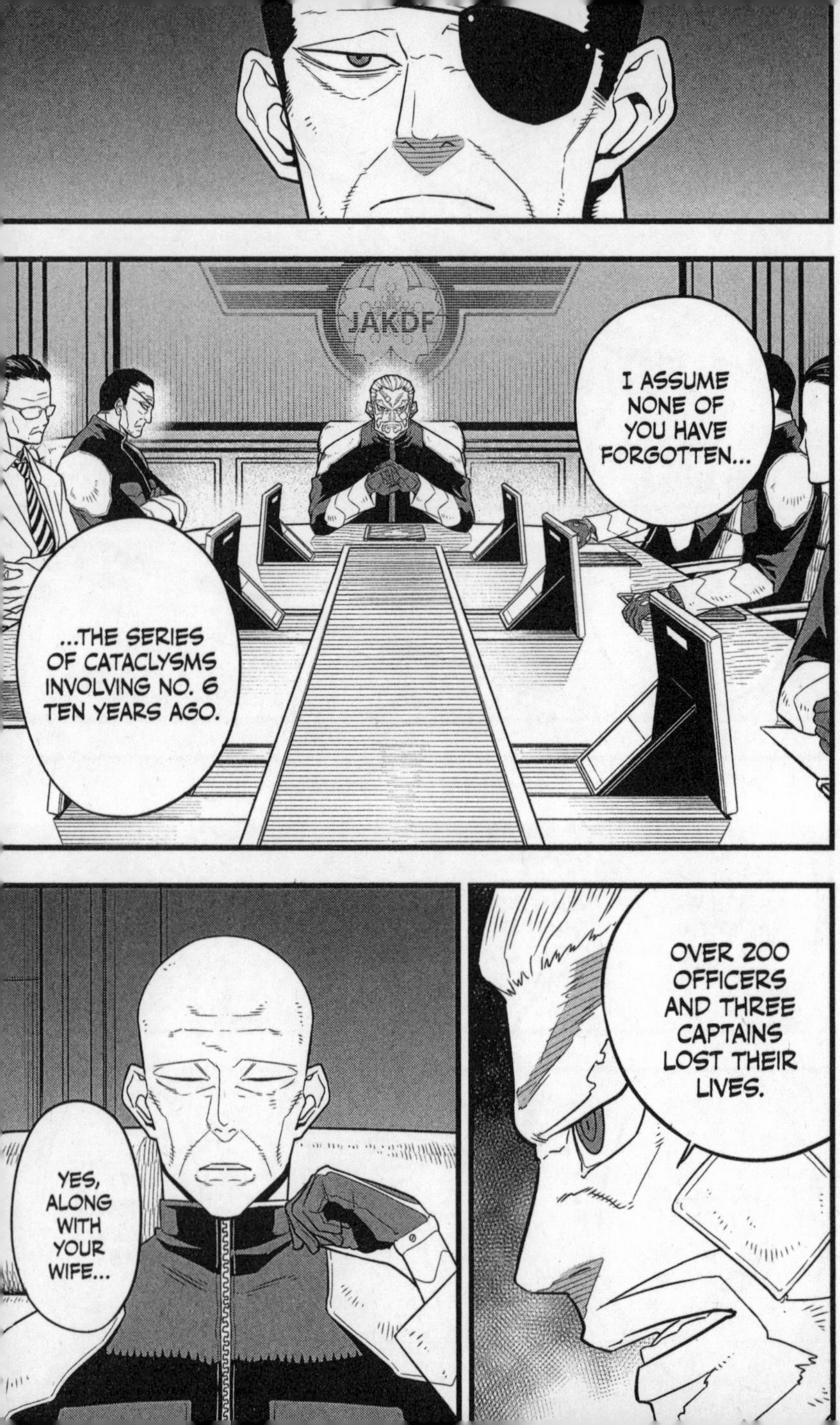
I ASSUME NONE OF YOU HAVE FORGOTTEN...
...THE SERIES OF CATACLYSMS INVOLVING NO. 6 TEN YEARS AGO.
OVER 200 OFFICERS AND THREE CAPTAINS LOST THEIR LIVES.
YES, ALONG WITH YOUR WIFE...

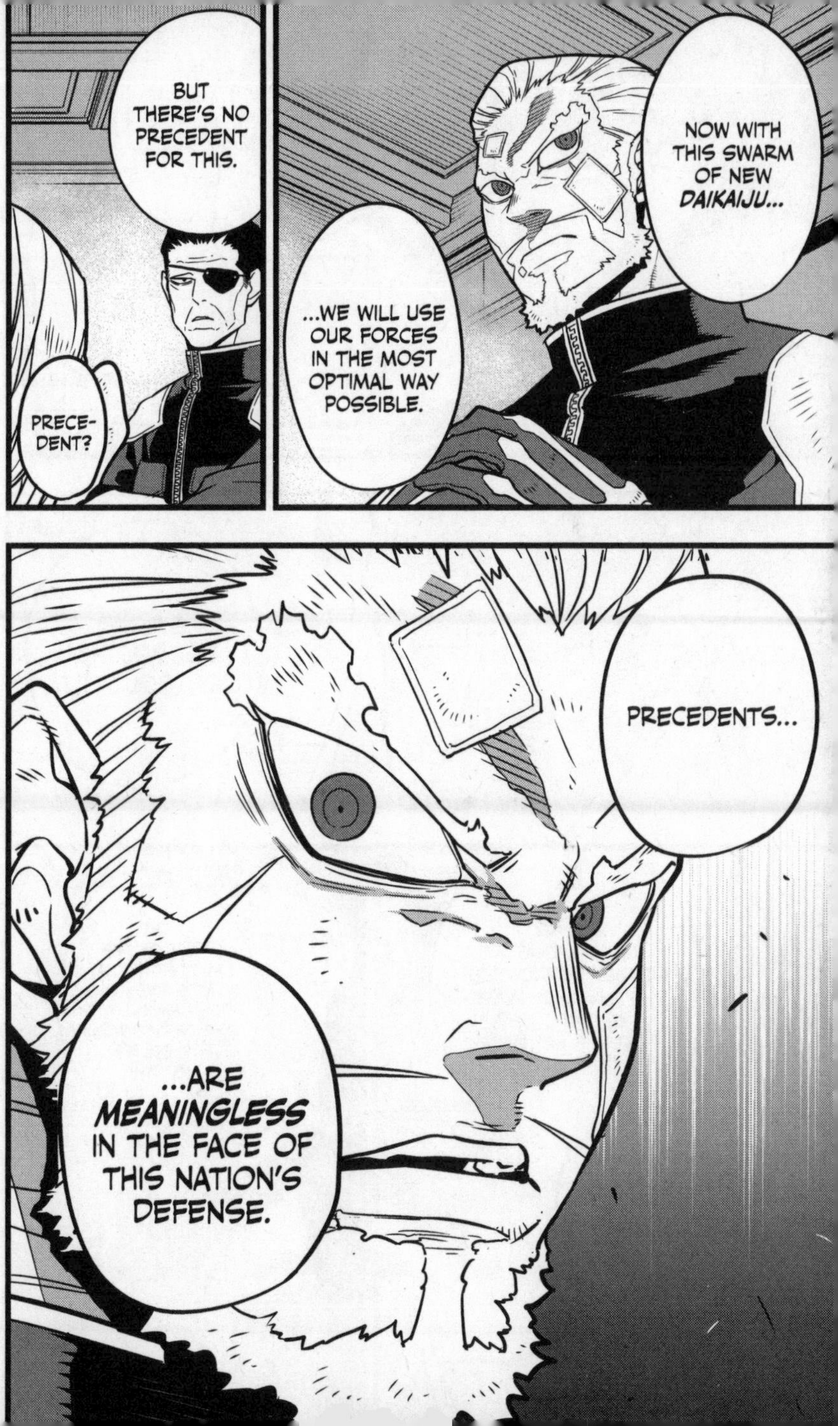
NOW WITH THIS SWARM OF NEW *DAIKAIJU*...
...WE WILL USE OUR FORCES IN THE MOST OPTIMAL WAY POSSIBLE.
BUT THERE'S NO PRECEDENT FOR THIS.
PRECE-DENT?
PRECEDENTS...
...ARE *MEANINGLESS* IN THE FACE OF THIS NATION'S DEFENSE.

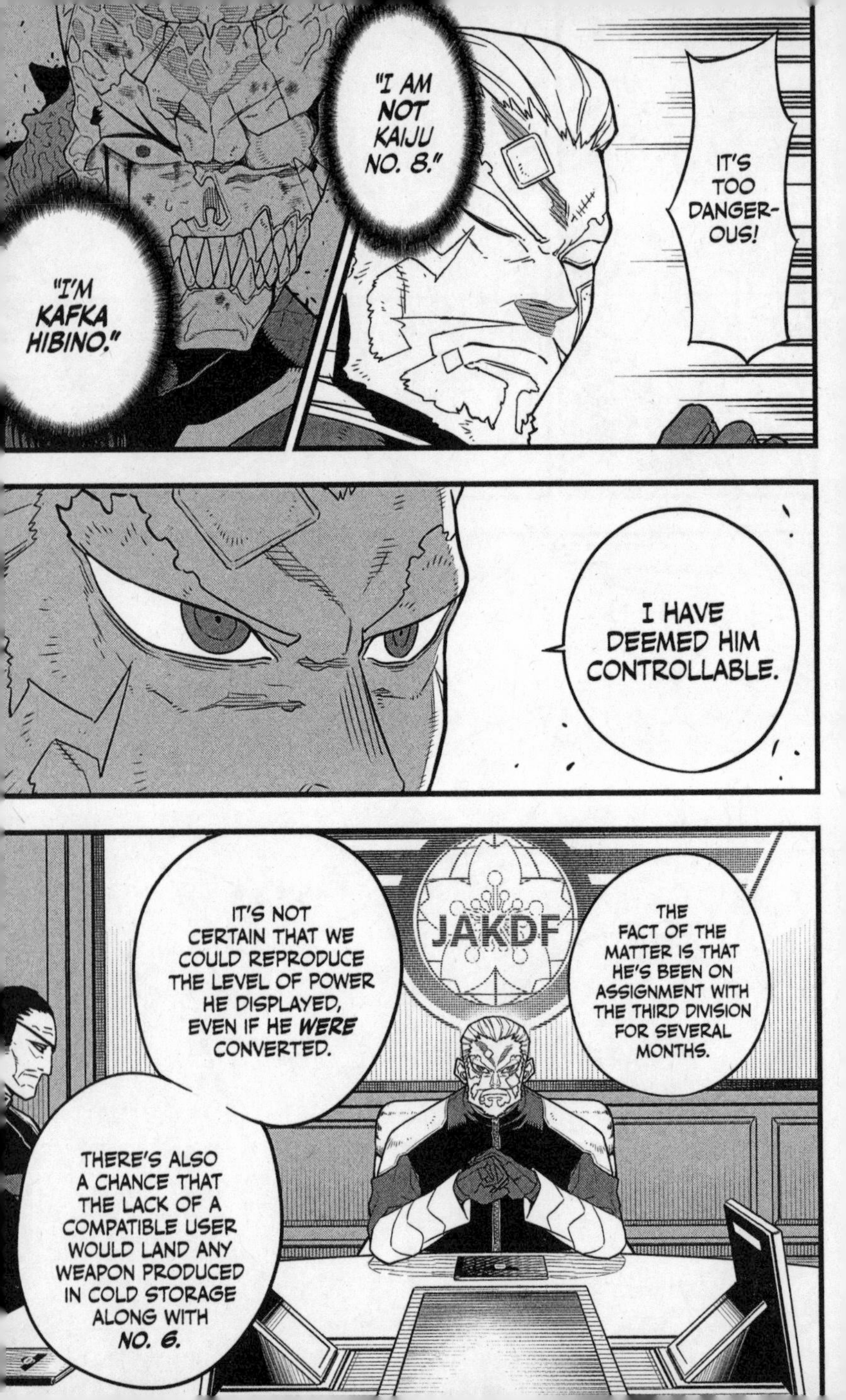
IT'S TOO DANGER-OUS!
"I AM NOT KAIJU NO. 8."
"I'M KAFKA HIBINO."
I HAVE DEEMED HIM CONTROLLABLE.
THE FACT OF THE MATTER IS THAT HE'S BEEN ON ASSIGNMENT WITH THE THIRD DIVISION FOR SEVERAL MONTHS.
JAKDF
IT'S NOT CERTAIN THAT WE COULD REPRODUCE THE LEVEL OF POWER HE DISPLAYED, EVEN IF HE *WERE* CONVERTED.
THERE'S ALSO A CHANCE THAT THE LACK OF A COMPATIBLE USER WOULD LAND ANY WEAPON PRODUCED IN COLD STORAGE ALONG WITH **NO. 6.**

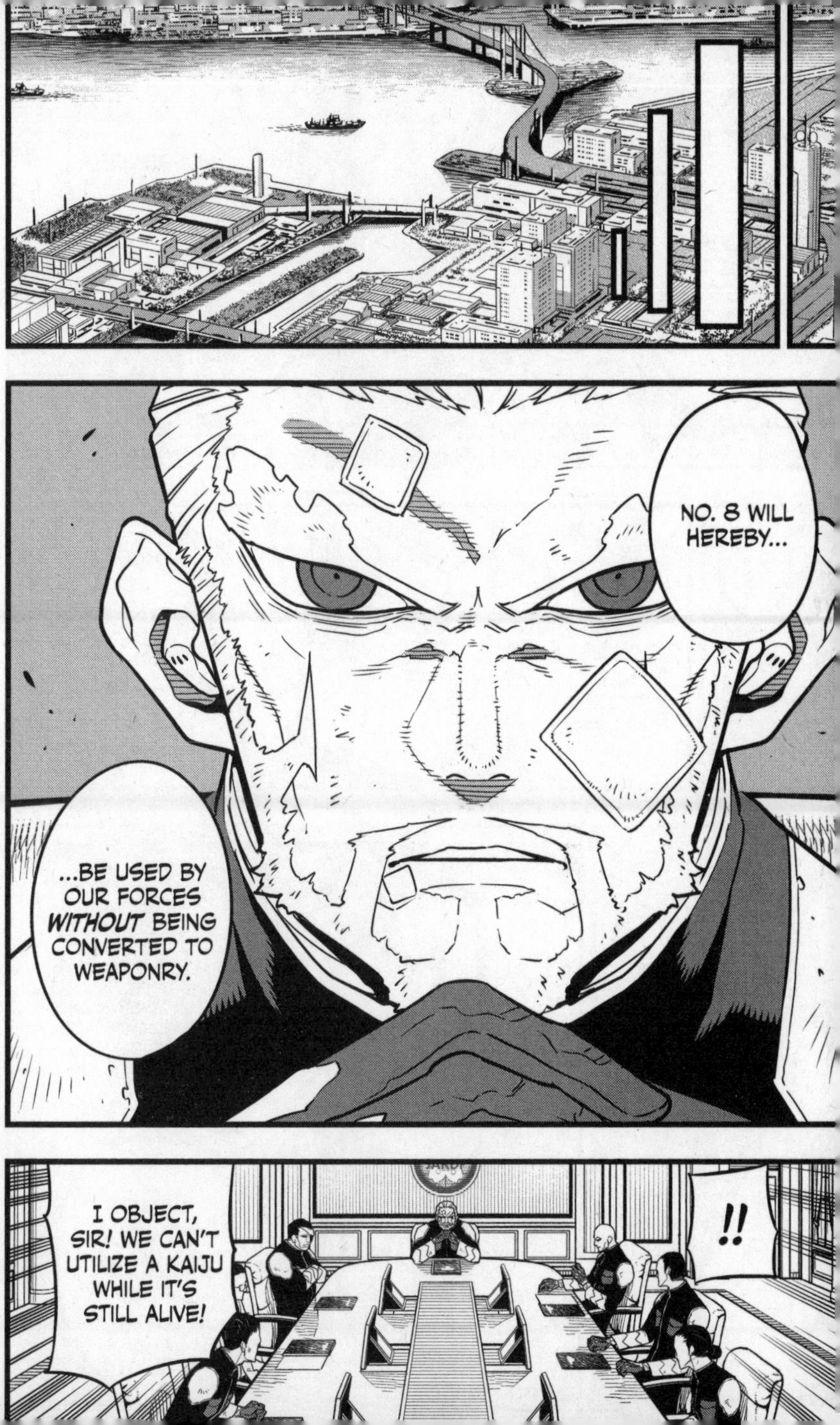
NO. 8 WILL HEREBY...
...BE USED BY OUR FORCES *WITHOUT* BEING CONVERTED TO WEAPONRY.
!!
I OBJECT, SIR! WE CAN'T UTILIZE A KAIJU WHILE IT'S STILL ALIVE!

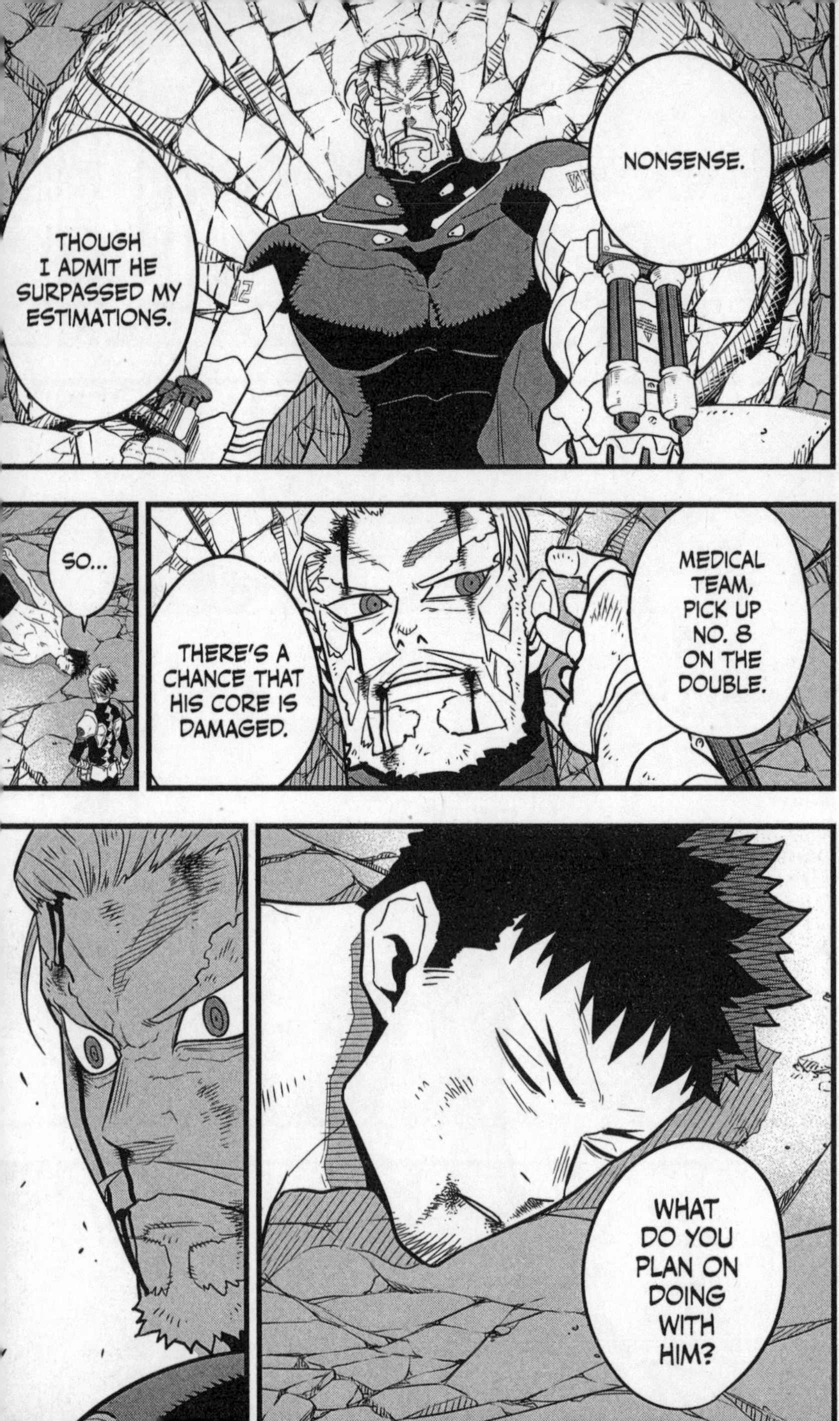
NONSENSE.
THOUGH I ADMIT HE SURPASSED MY ESTIMATIONS.
MEDICAL TEAM, PICK UP NO. 8 ON THE DOUBLE.
THERE'S A CHANCE THAT HIS CORE IS DAMAGED.
SO...
WHAT DO YOU PLAN ON DOING WITH HIM?

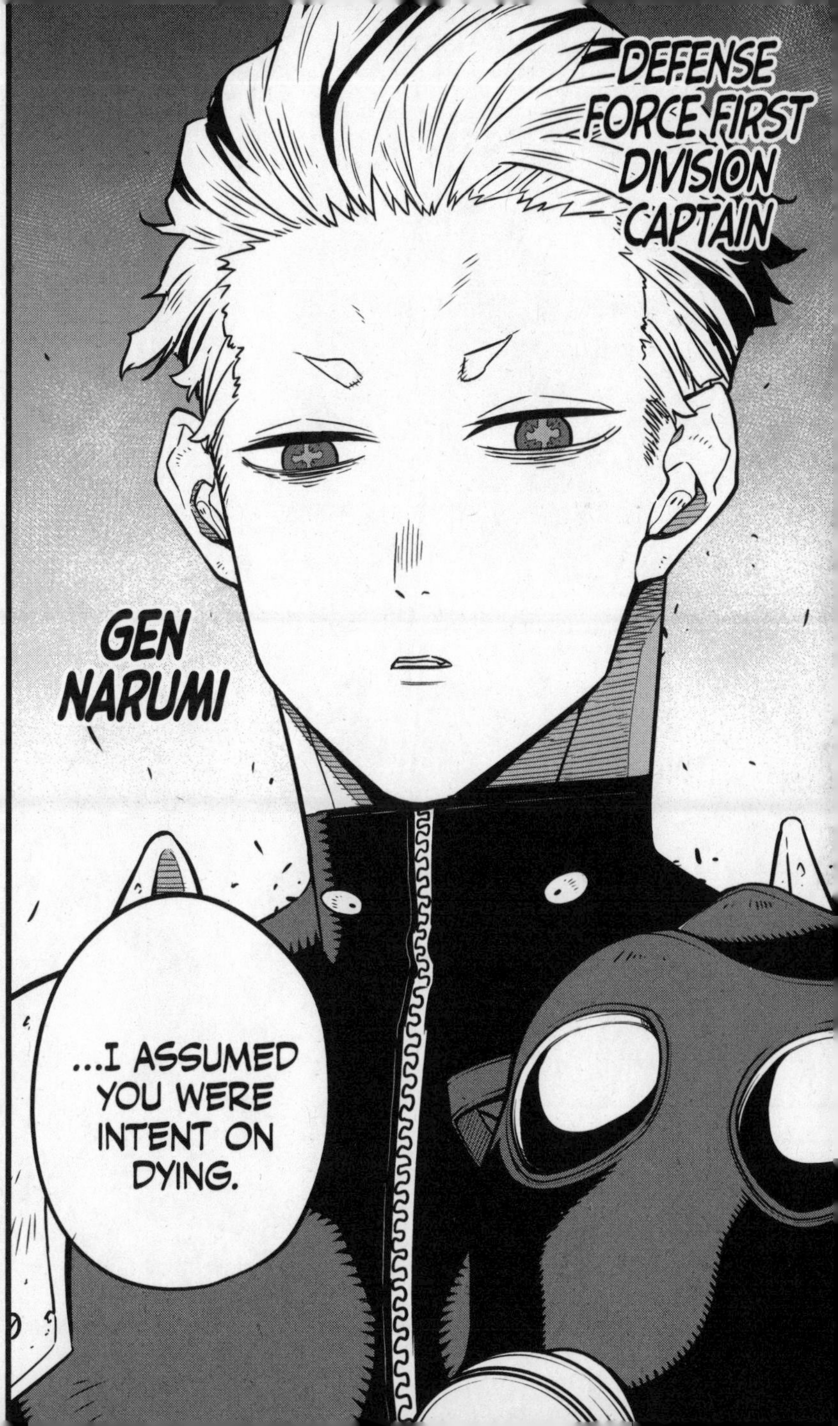
DEFENSE FORCE FIRST DIVISION CAPTAIN
GEN NARUMI
...I ASSUMED YOU WERE INTENT ON DYING.

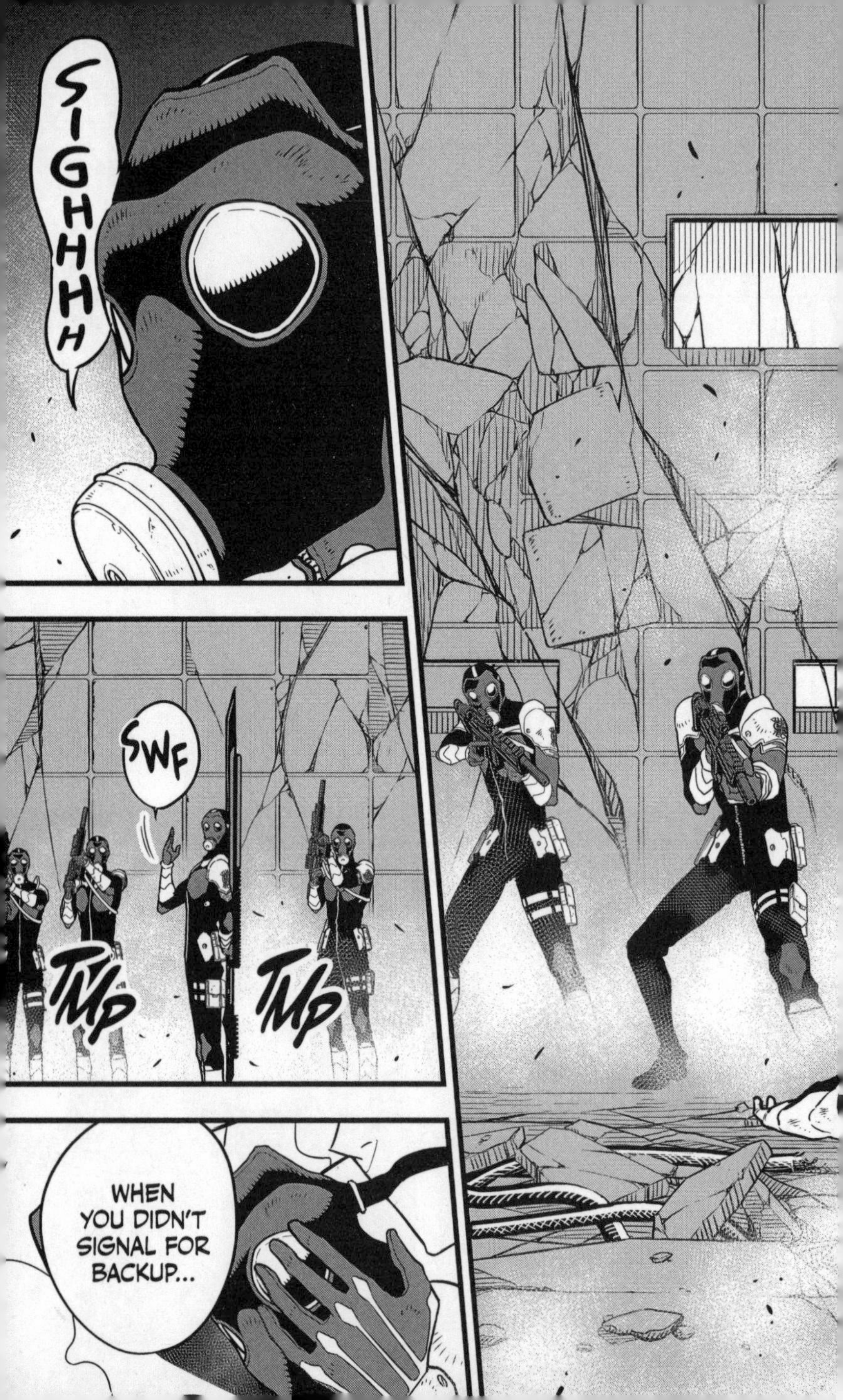
SIGHHHH
SWF
TMP
TMP
WHEN YOU DIDN'T SIGNAL FOR BACKUP...

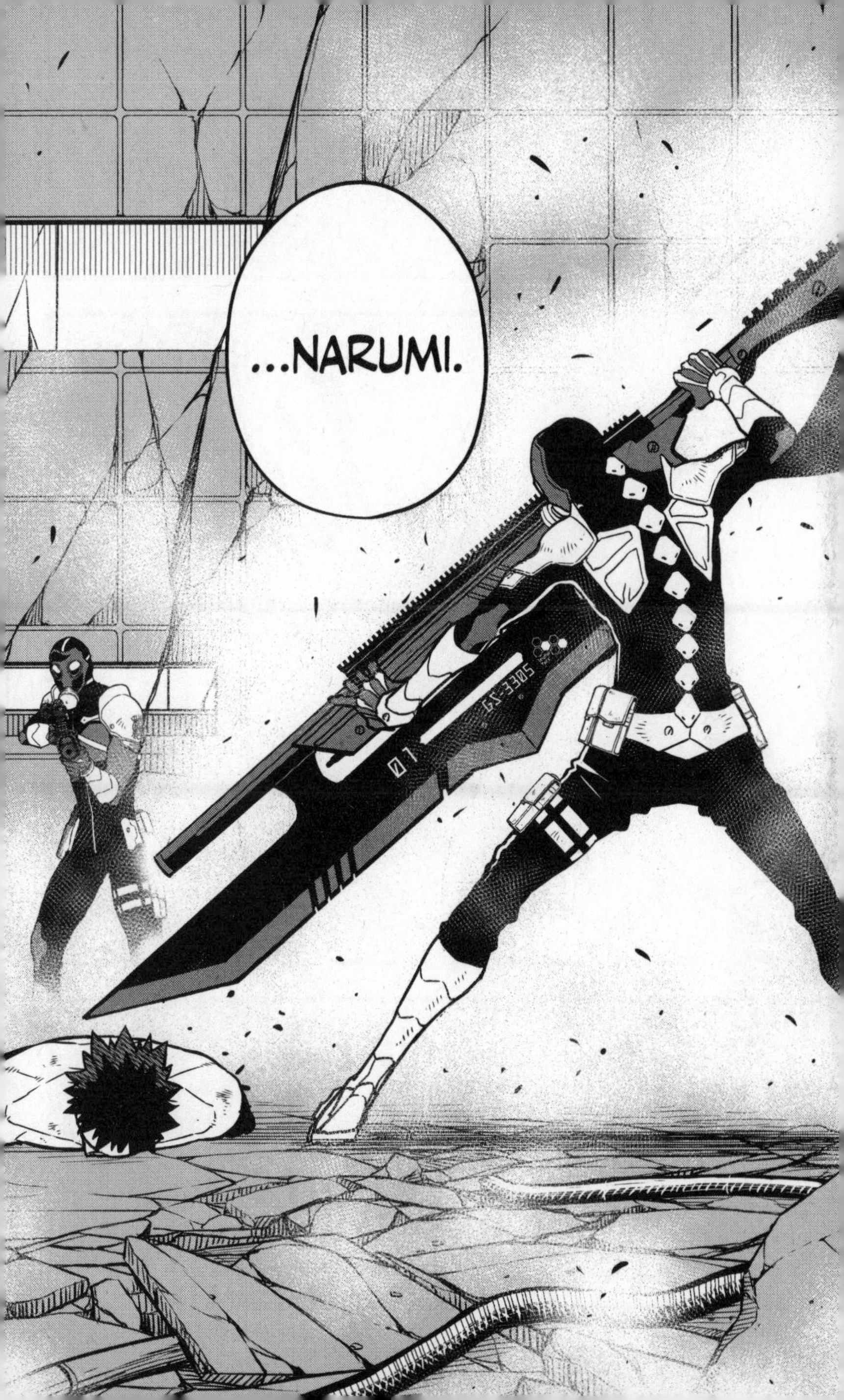
...NARUMI.

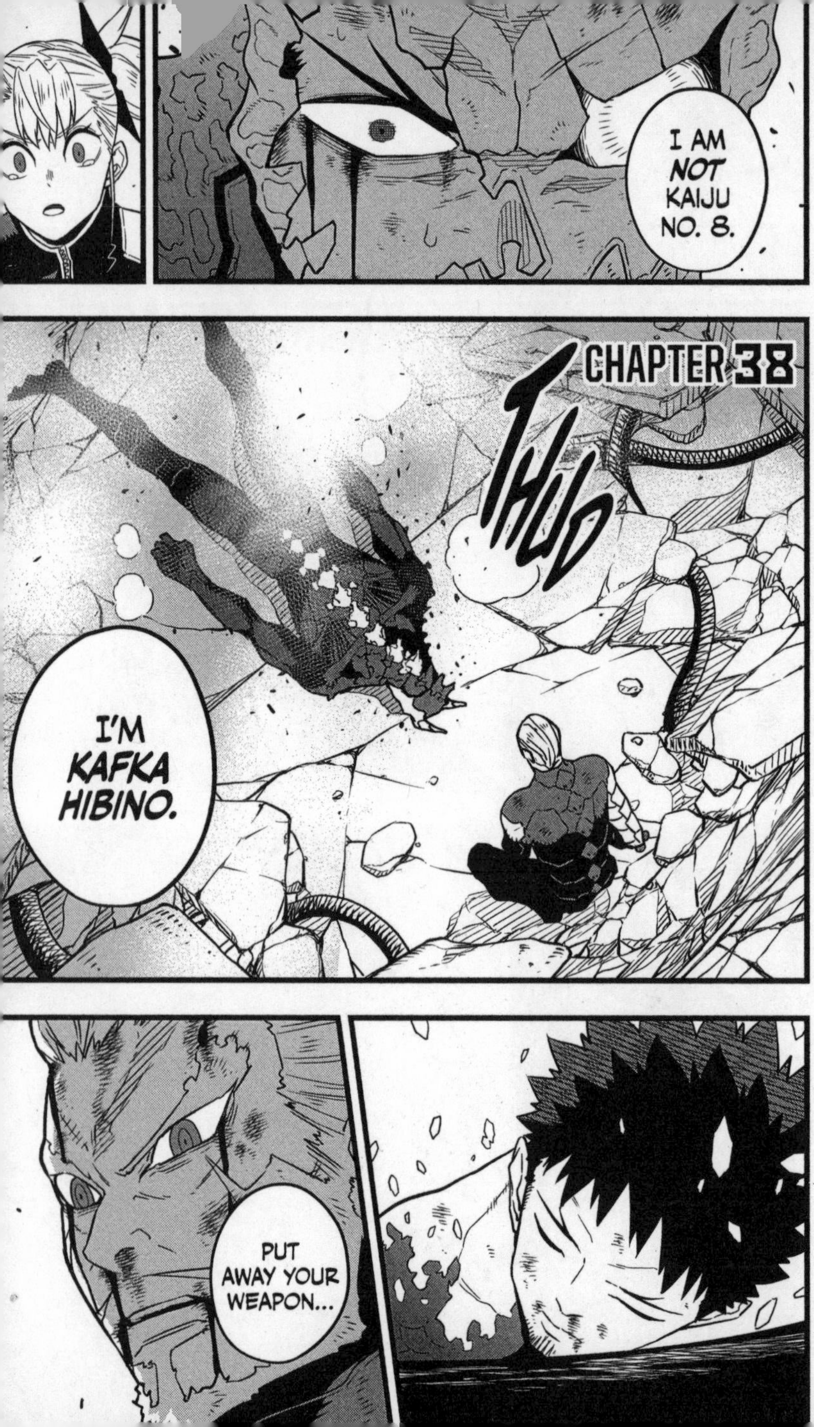
I AM NOT KAIJU NO. 8.
CHAPTER 38
THUD
I'M KAFKA HIBINO.
PUT AWAY YOUR WEAPON...

AKARI MINASE

Birthday:
February 23

Height:
153 cm

Likes:
Wood furniture, plaid-patterned items, making sweets

Author Comment:
One of the members of the Third Division who is particularly friendly with Kikoru. Kind and caring, she has a lot of secret fans among the Defense Force's ranks.

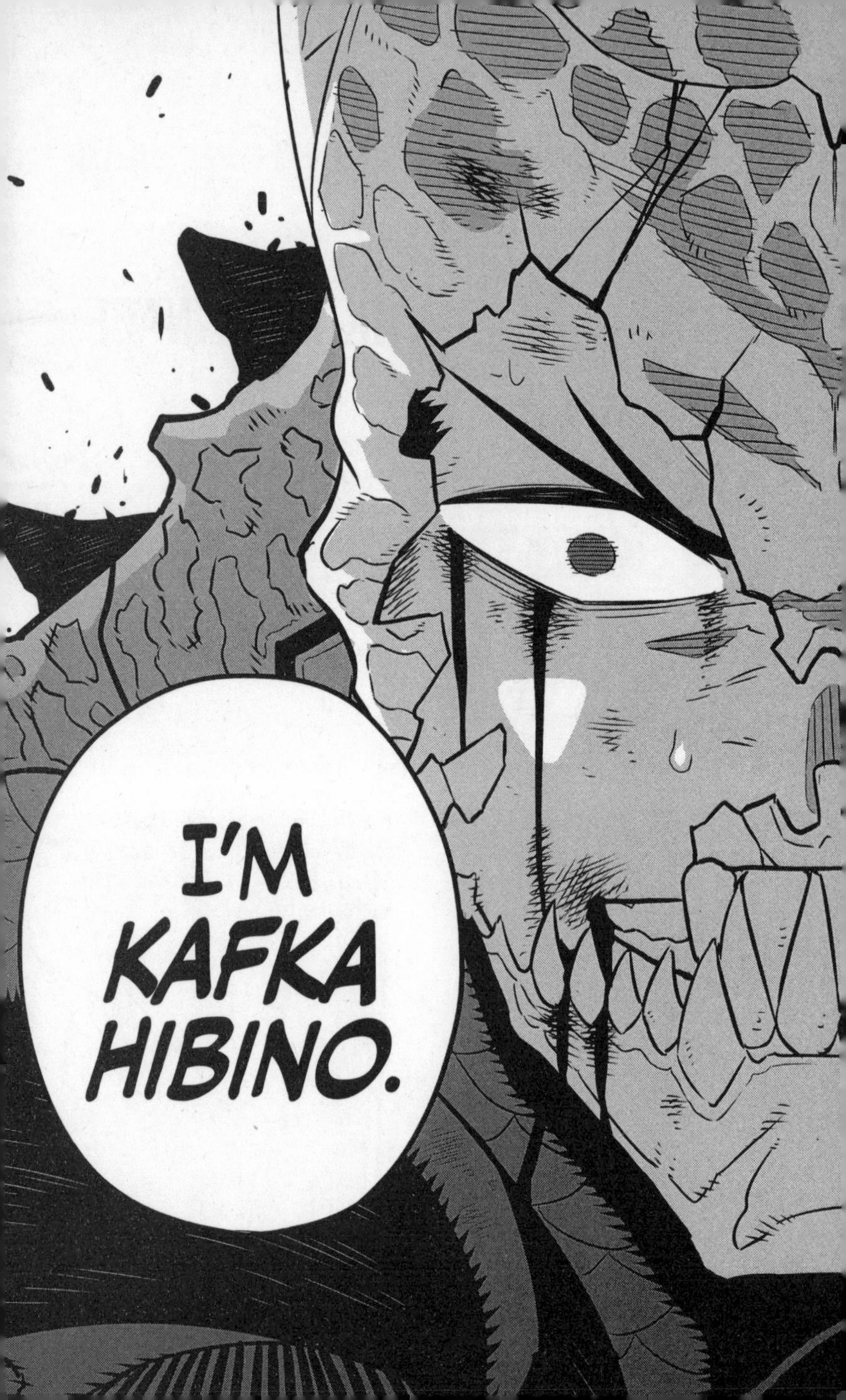
I'M KAFKA HIBINO.

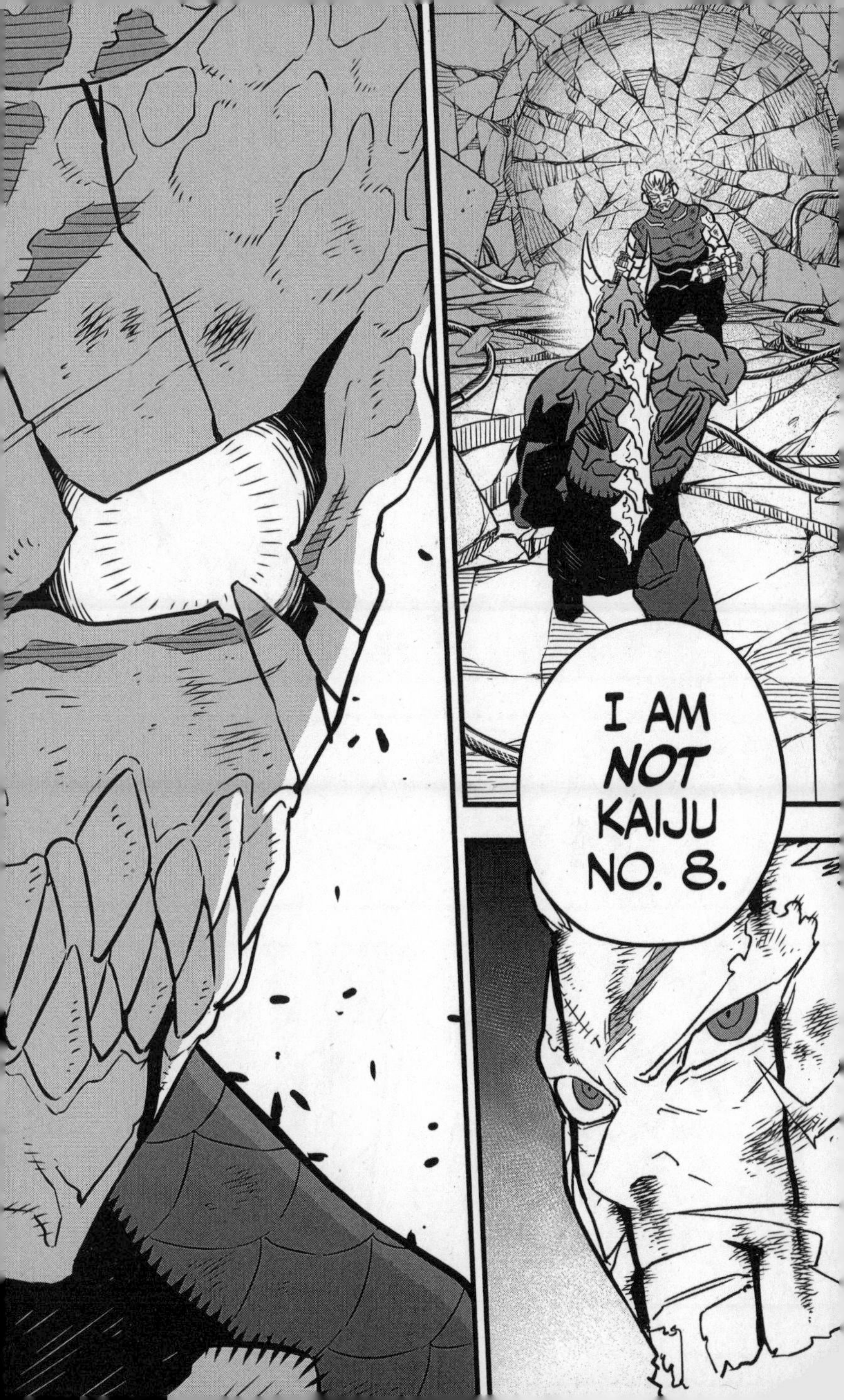
I AM NOT KAIJU NO. 8.

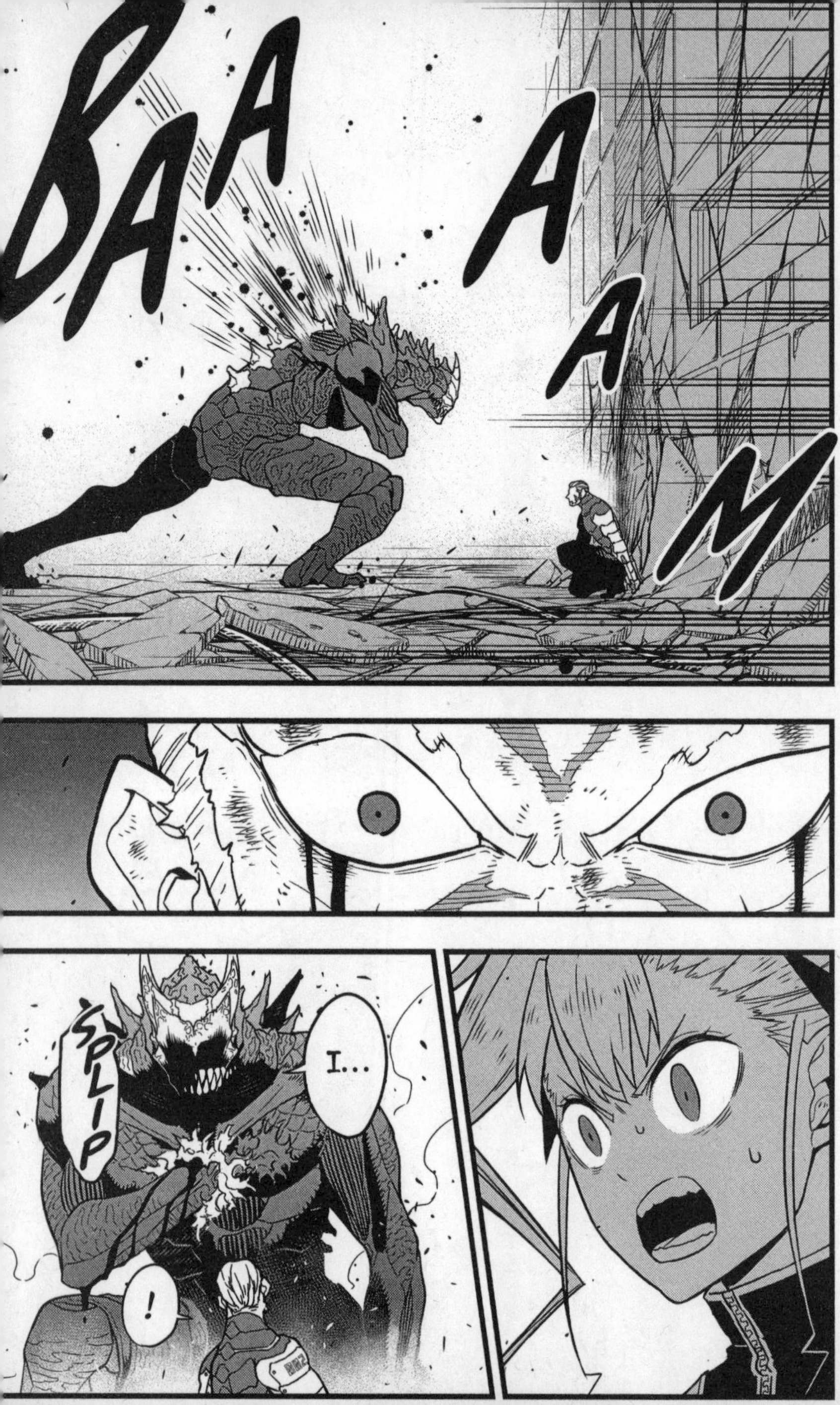
BAAAAM
I...
SPLIP
!

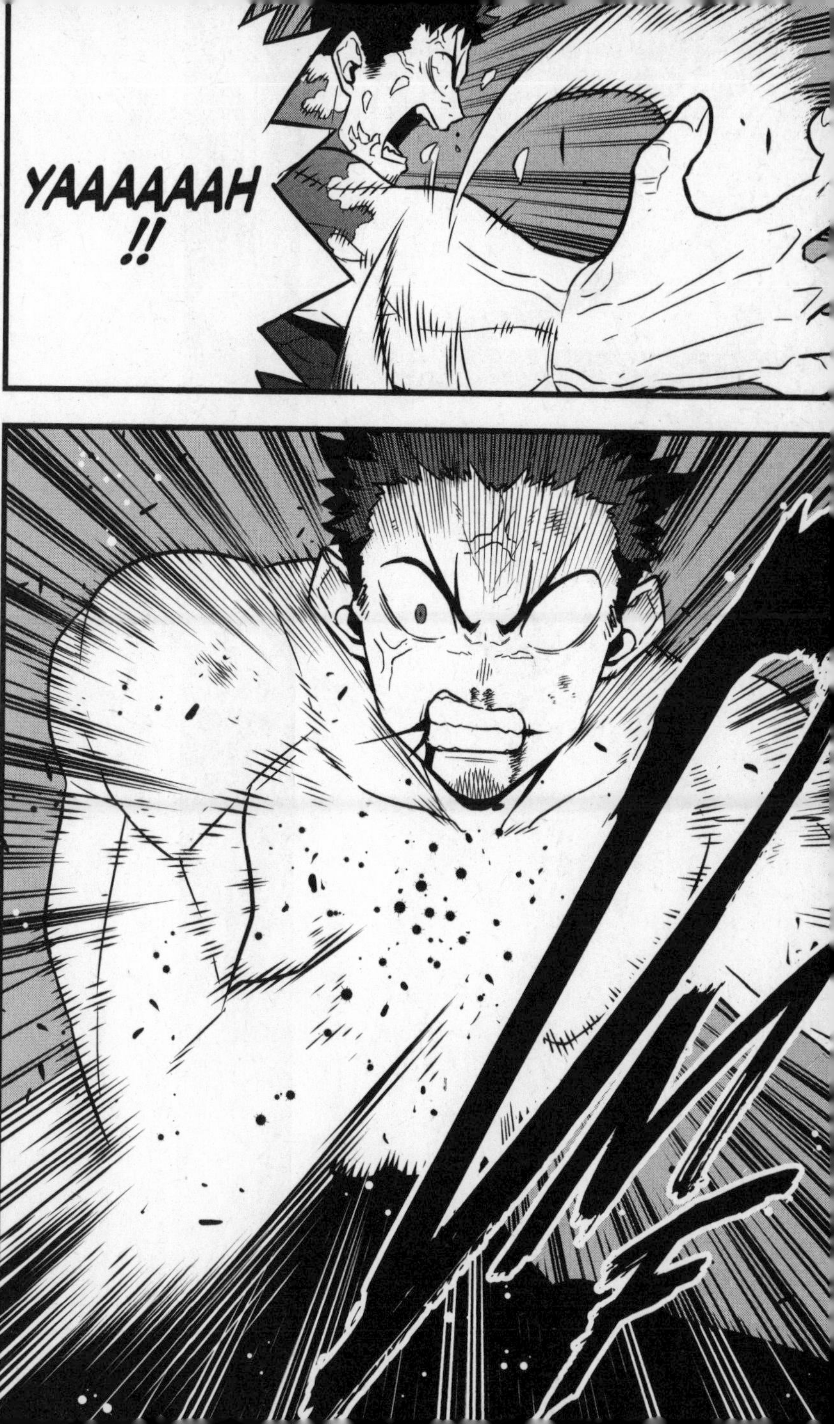
YAAAAAAH
!!

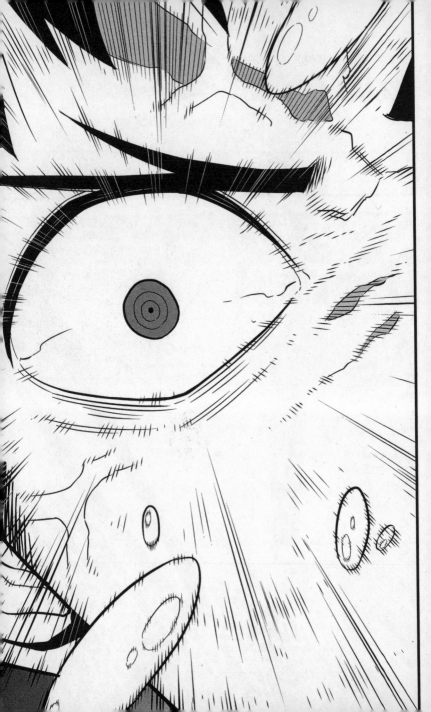

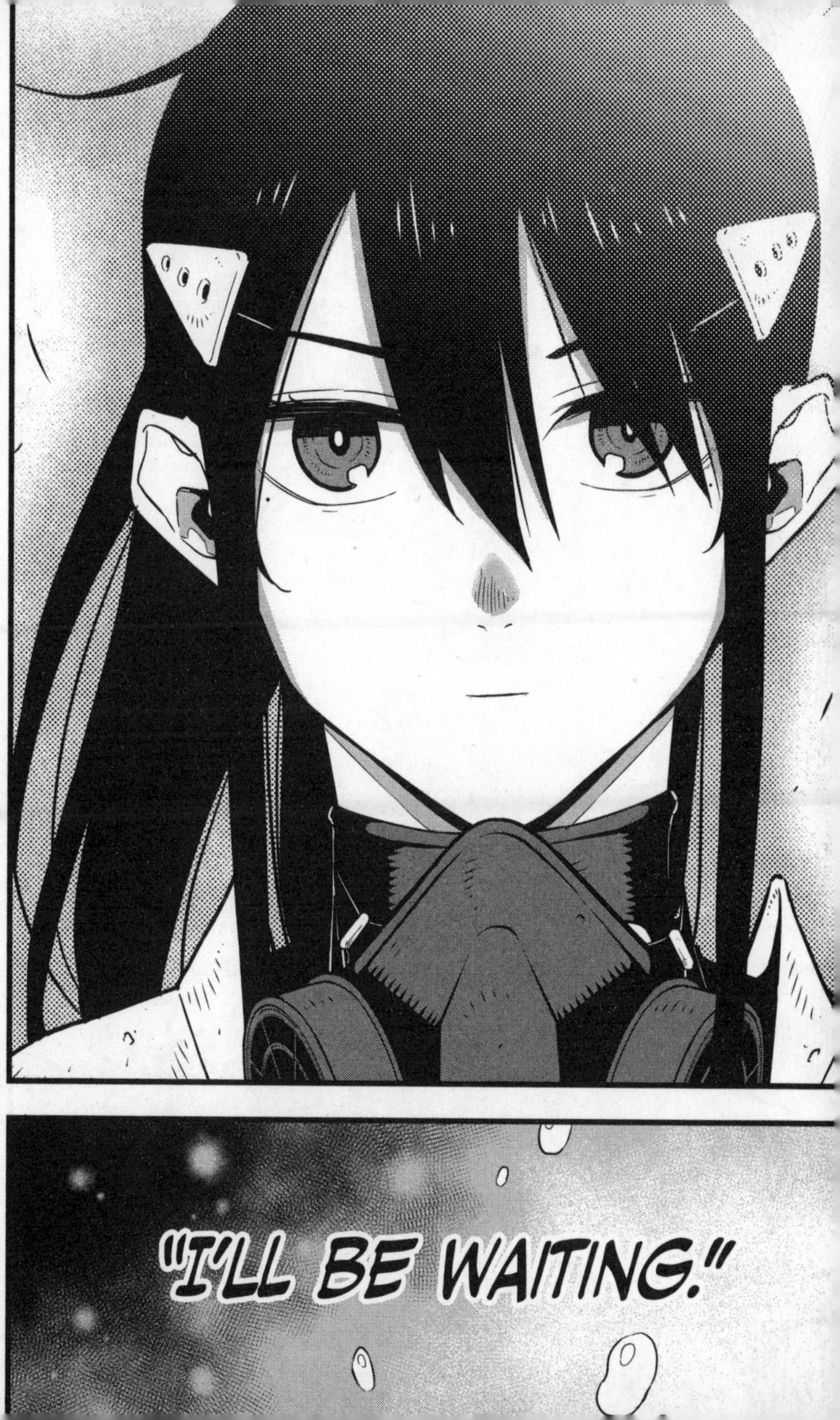
"I'LL BE WAITING."

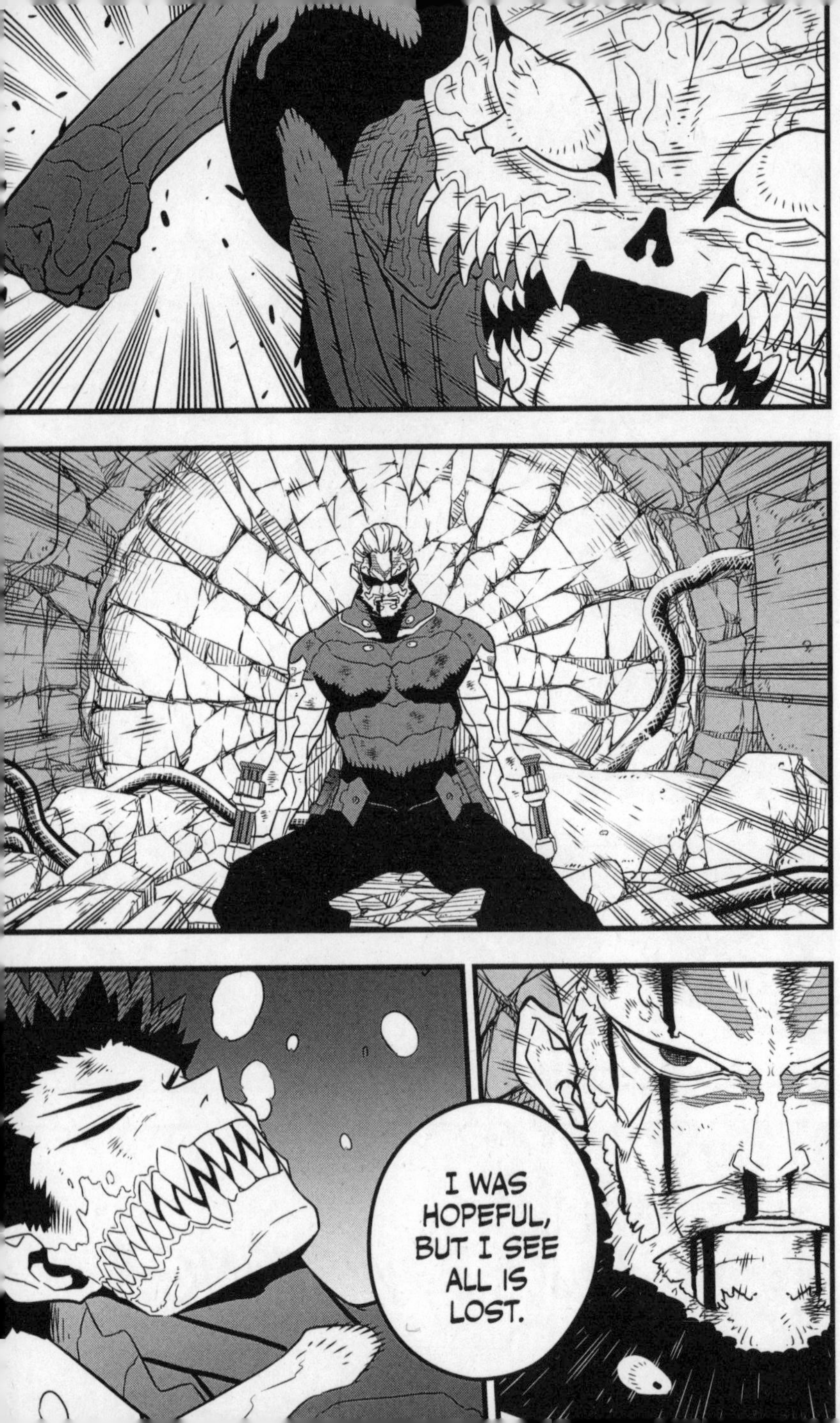
I WAS HOPEFUL, BUT I SEE ALL IS LOST.

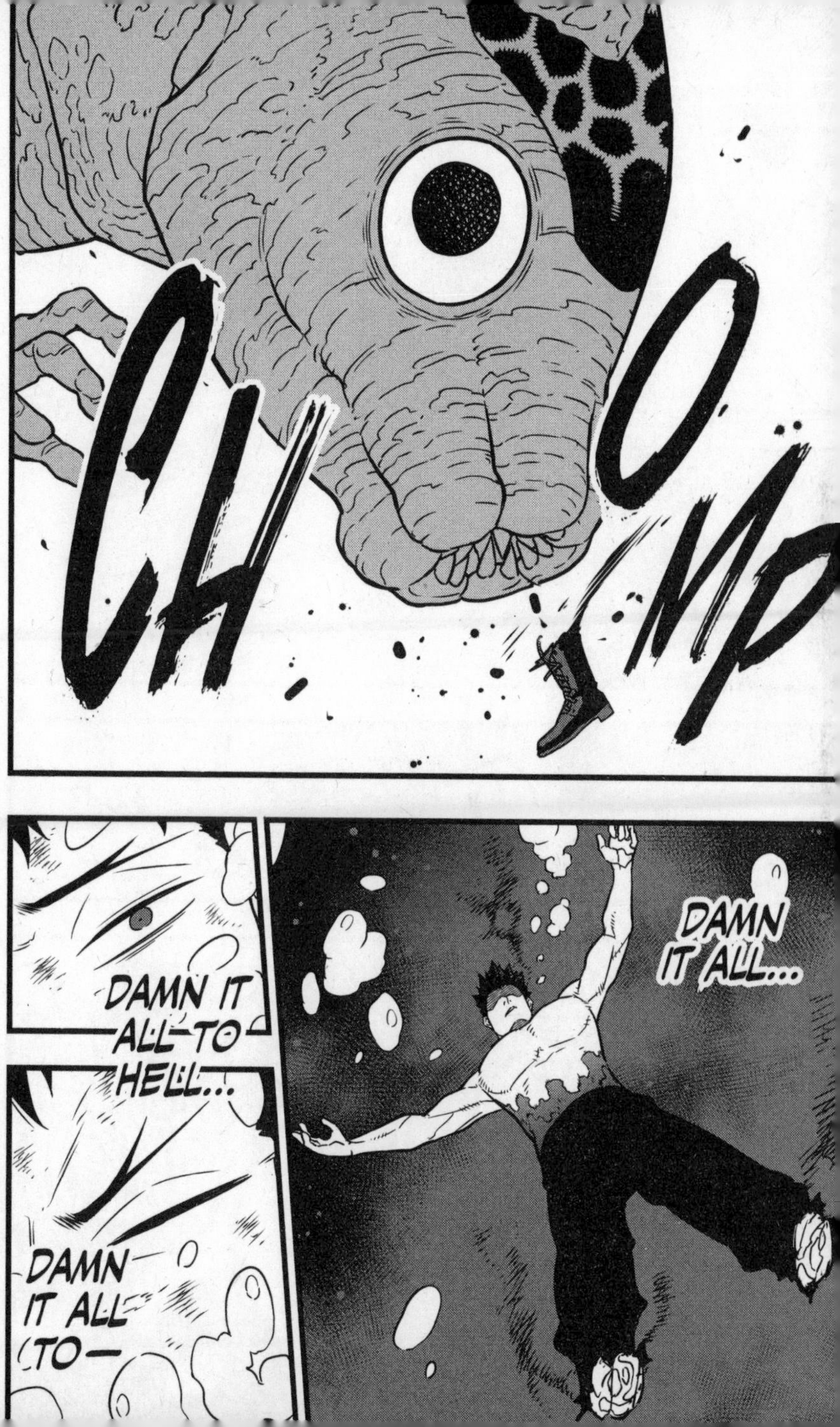
CHOMP
DAMN IT ALL...
DAMN IT ALL TO HELL...
DAMN IT ALL TO—

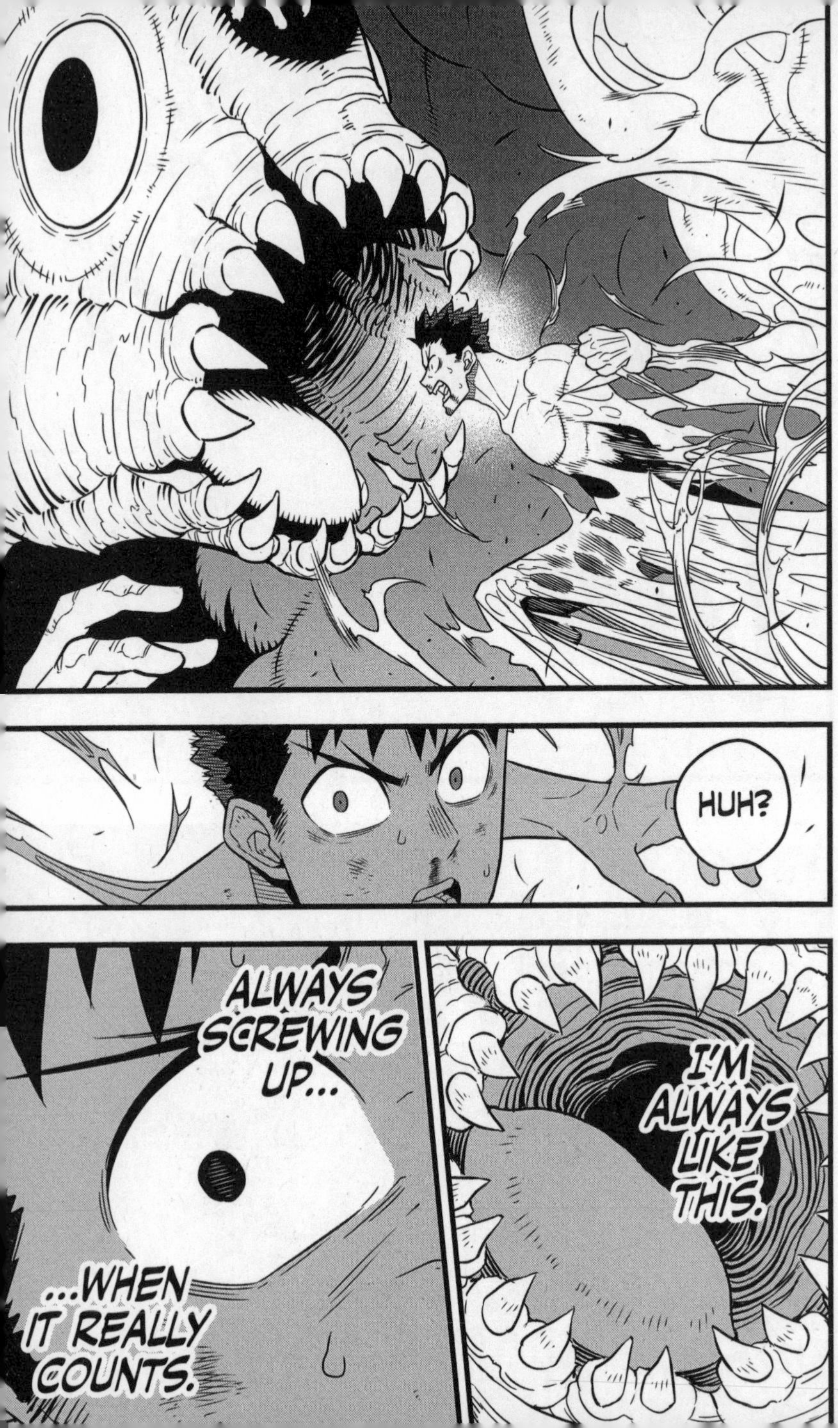
HUH?
I'M ALWAYS LIKE THIS.
ALWAYS SCREWING UP...
...WHEN IT REALLY COUNTS.

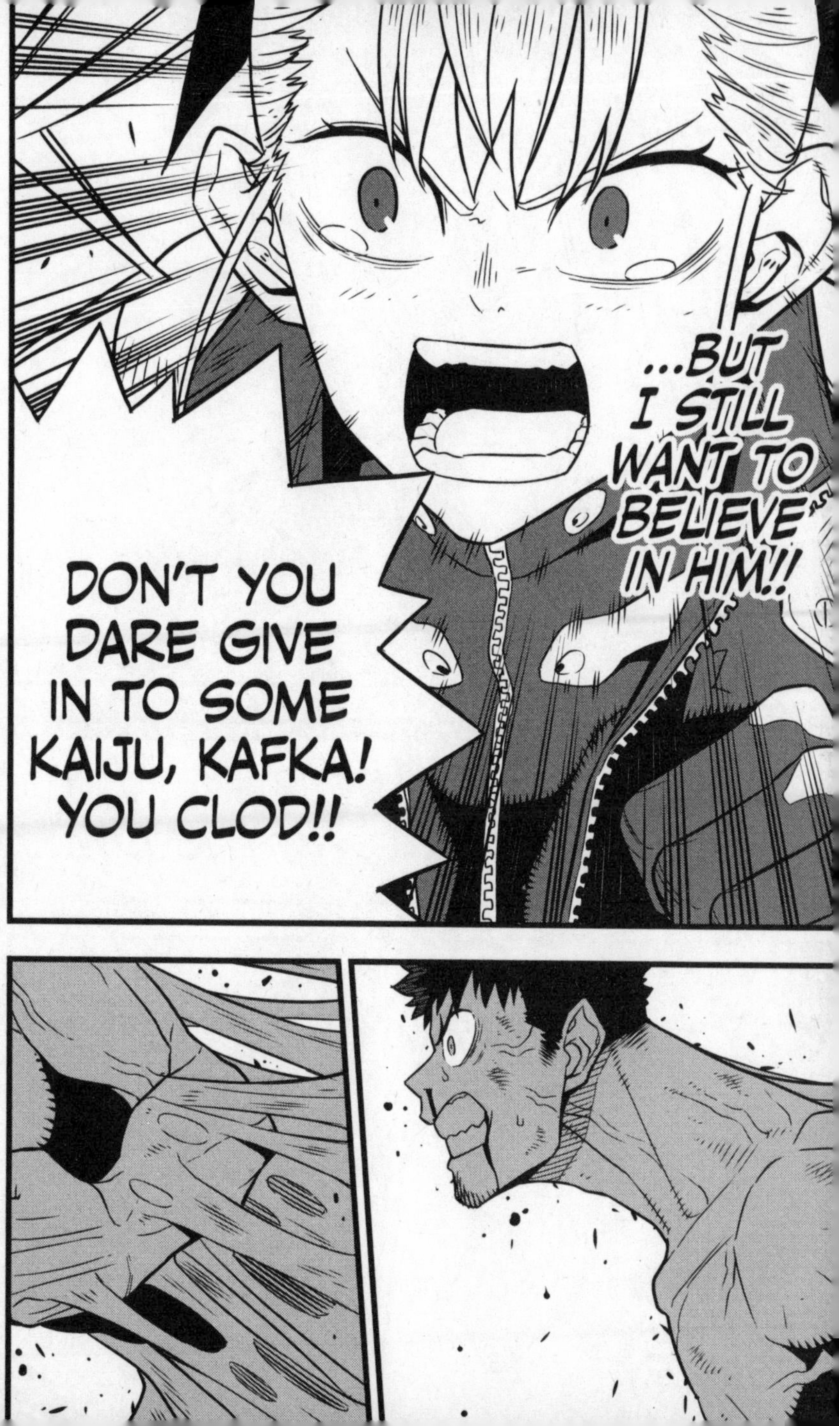
...BUT I STILL WANT TO BELIEVE IN HIM!!
DON'T YOU DARE GIVE IN TO SOME KAIJU, KAFKA! YOU CLOD!!

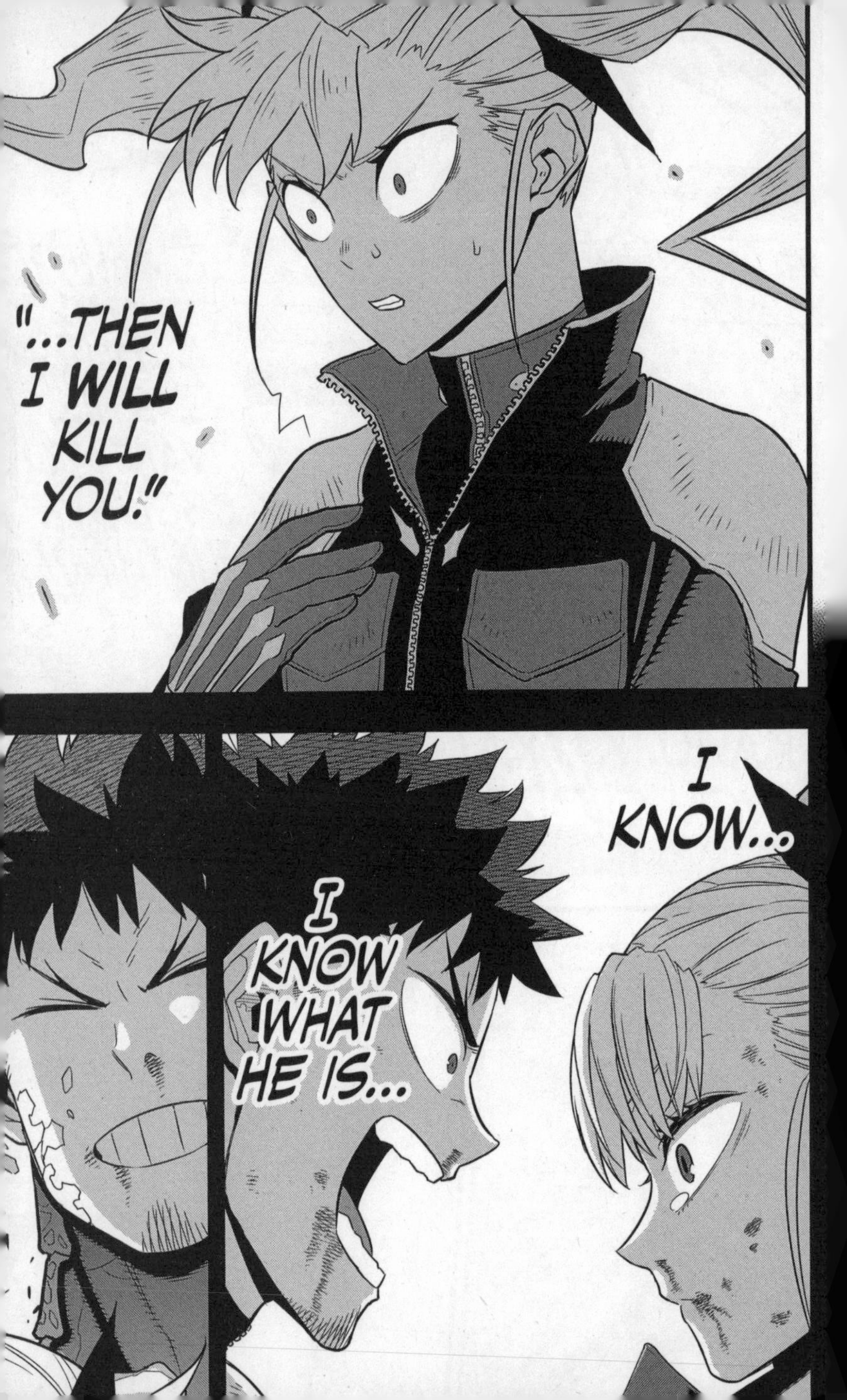
"...THEN I WILL KILL YOU."
I KNOW...
I KNOW WHAT HE IS...

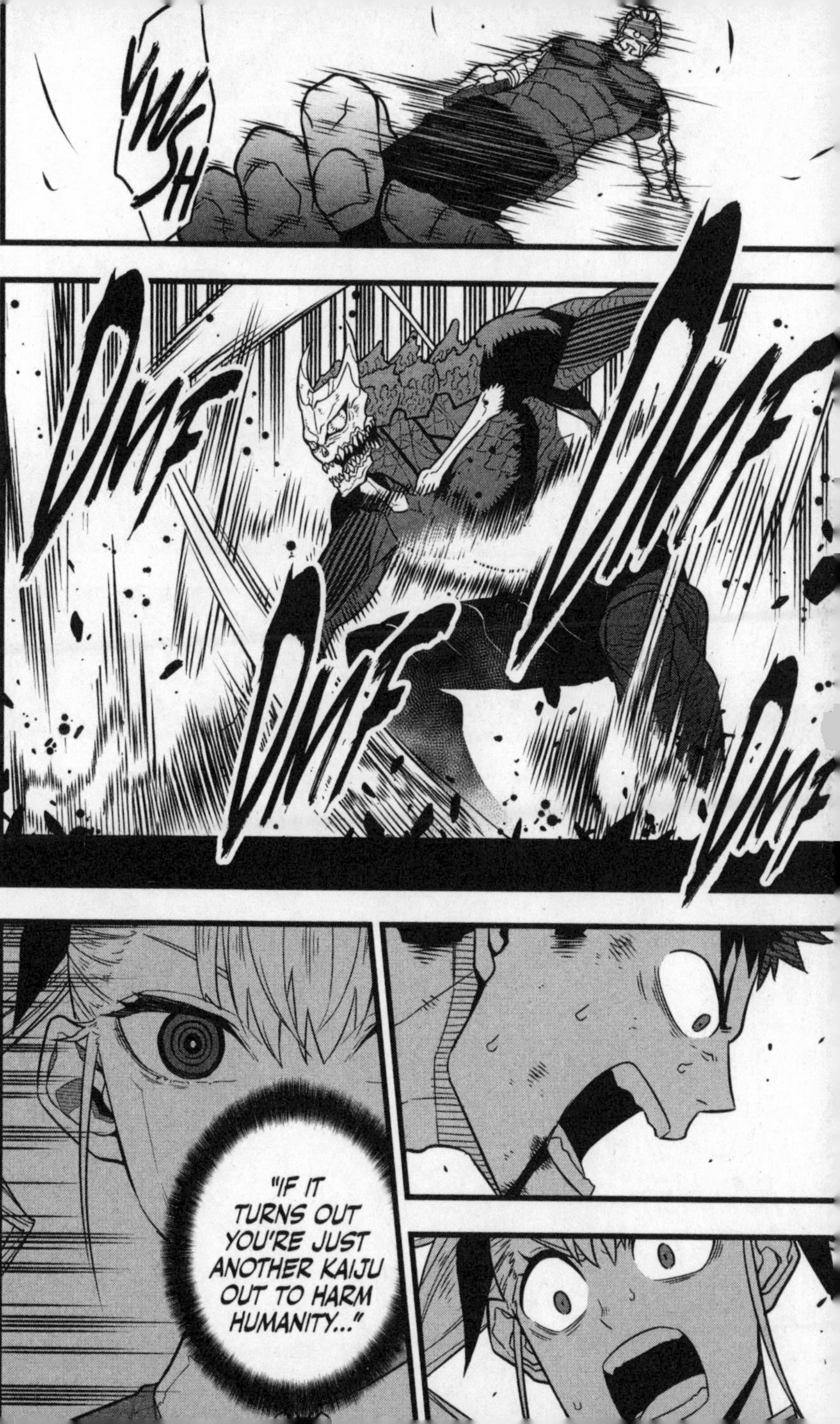
VWSH
"IF IT TURNS OUT YOU'RE JUST ANOTHER KAIJU OUT TO HARM HUMANITY..."

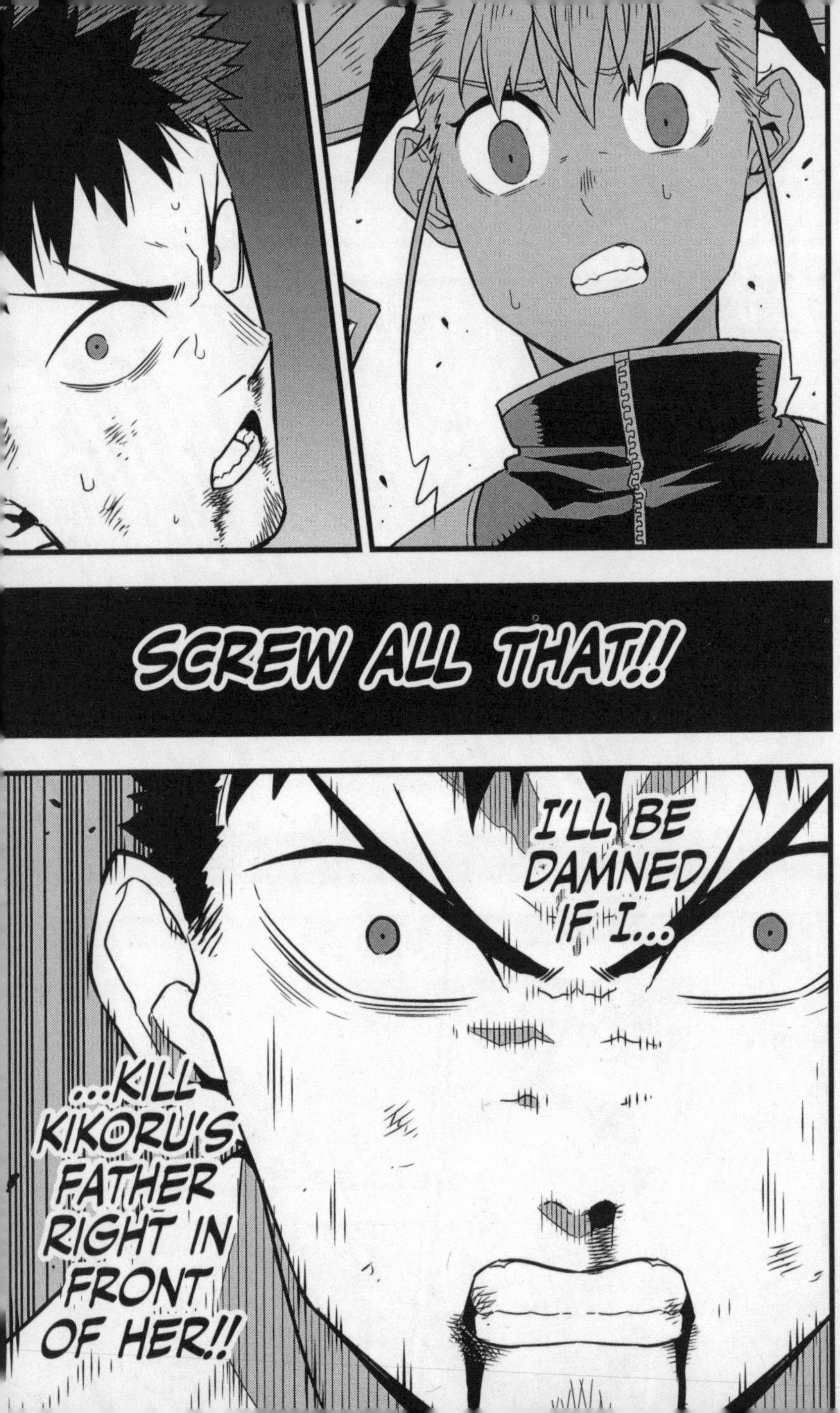
SCREW ALL THAT!!
I'LL BE DAMNED IF I...
...KILL KIKORU'S FATHER RIGHT IN FRONT OF HER!!

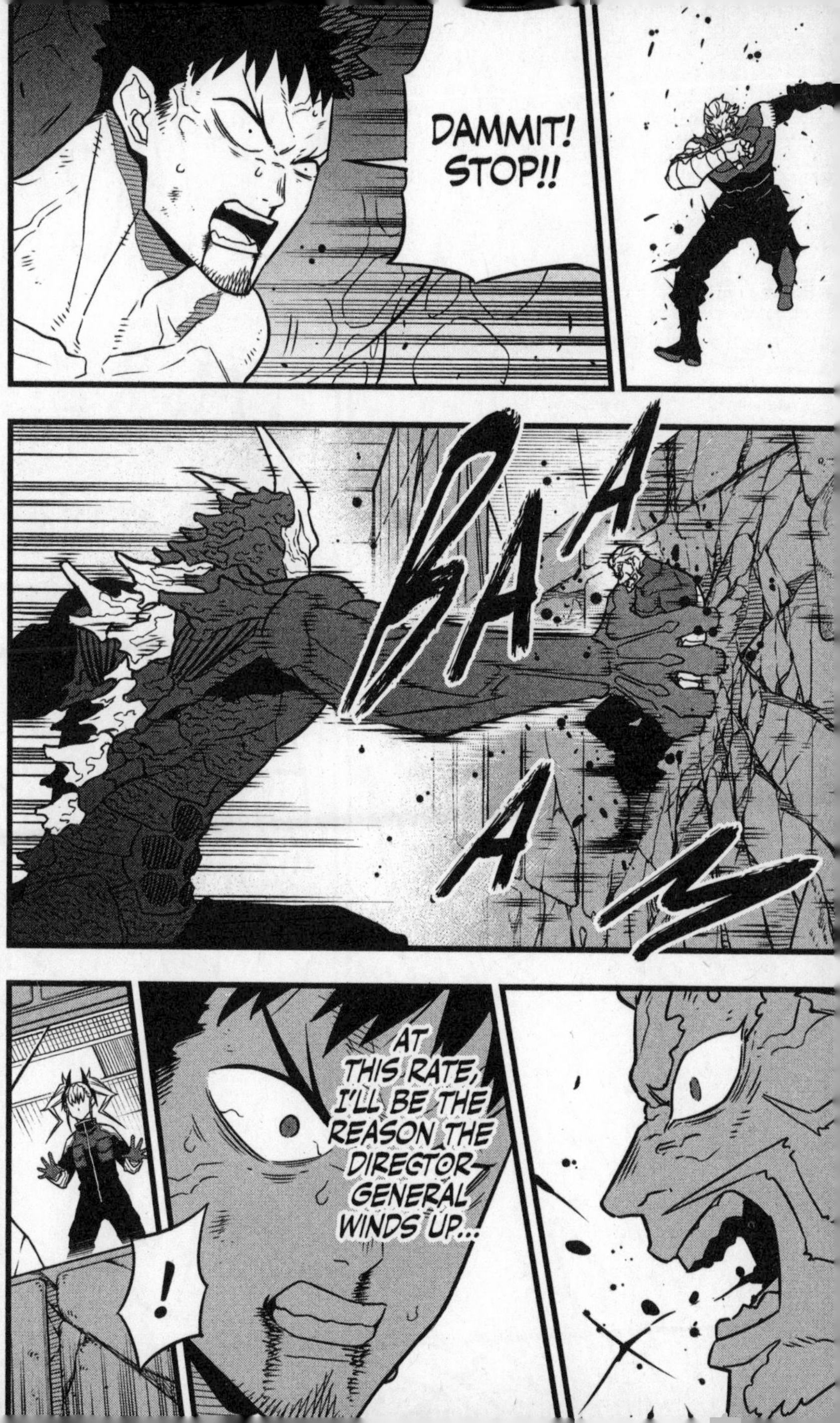
DAMMIT! STOP!!
BAAAM
AT THIS RATE, I'LL BE THE REASON THE DIRECTOR-GENERAL WINDS UP...
!

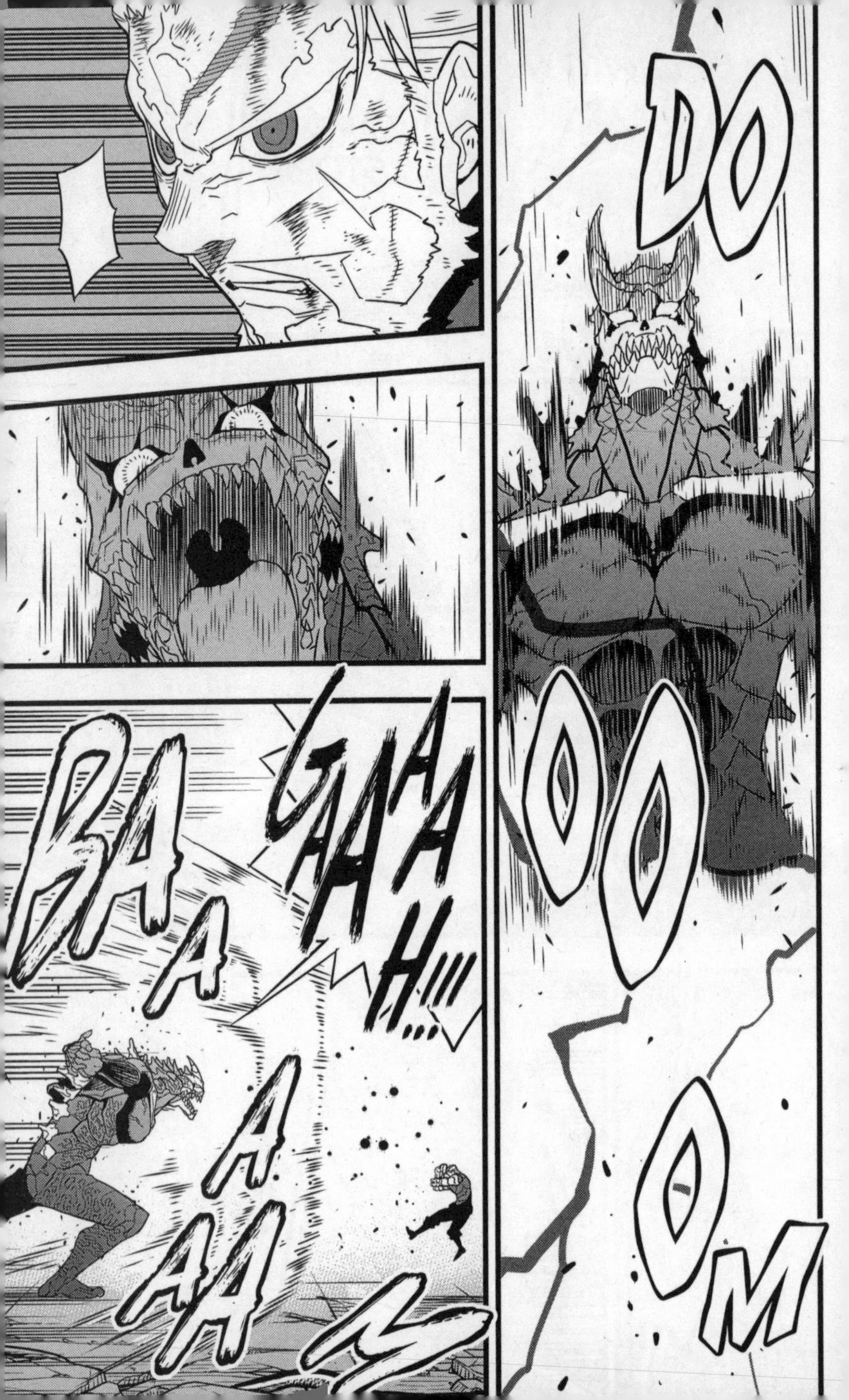
DOOOOOM
GAAAAH!!!...
BAAAAAA

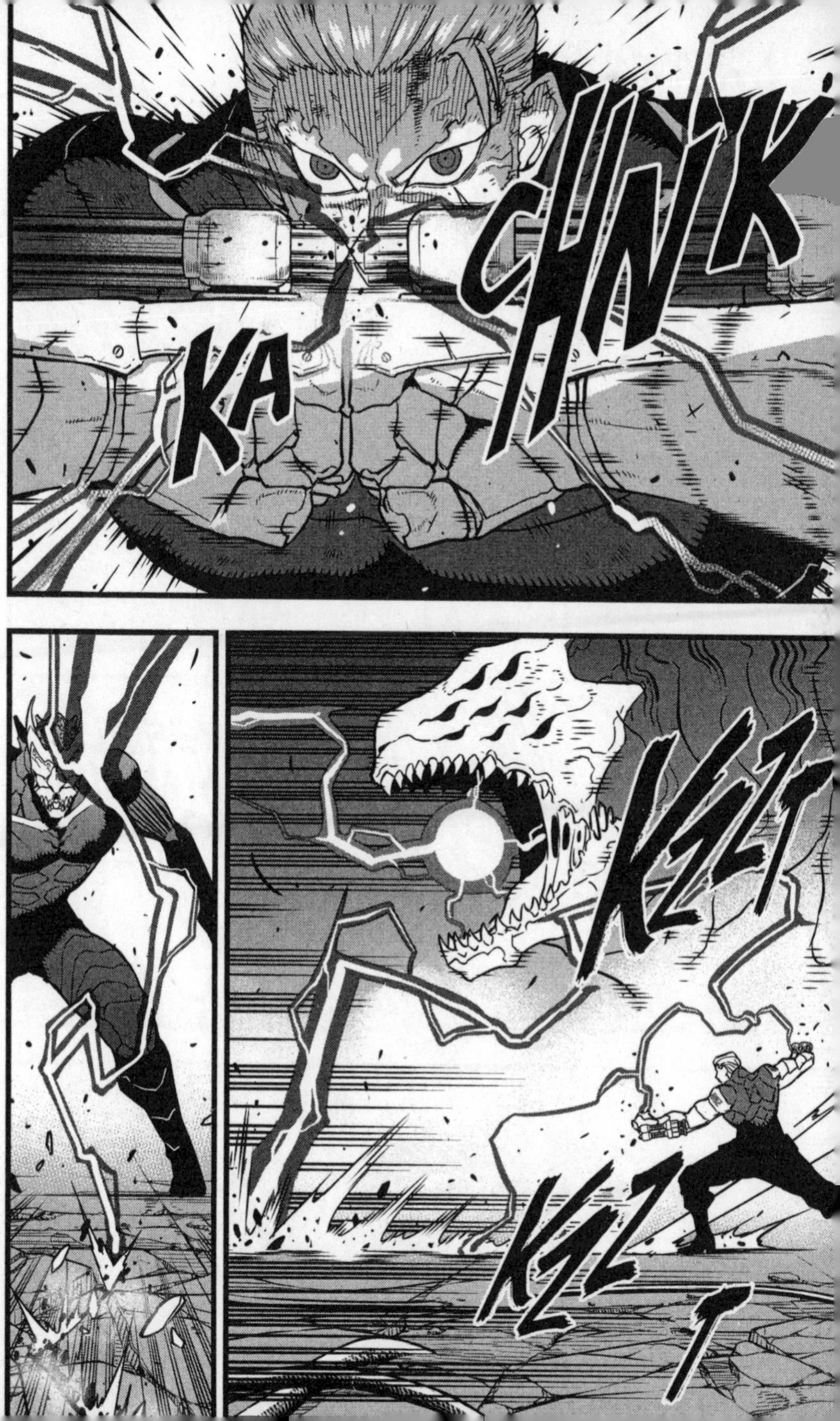
KA
CHNK
KZZT
KZZT

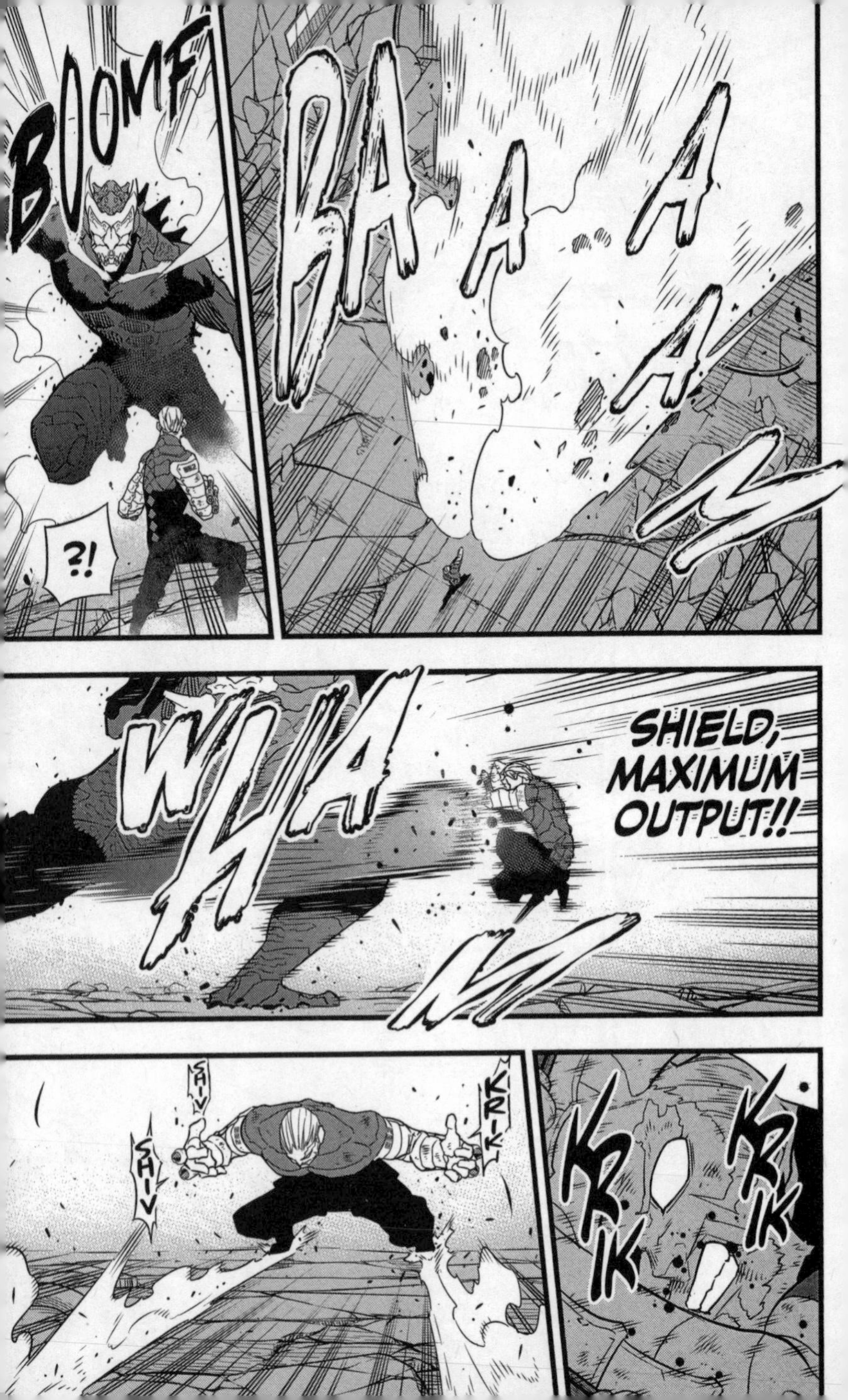
BAAAAM
BOOMF
?!
SHIELD, MAXIMUM OUTPUT!!
WHAM
KRIK
KRIK
SHIV
SHIV
KRIK

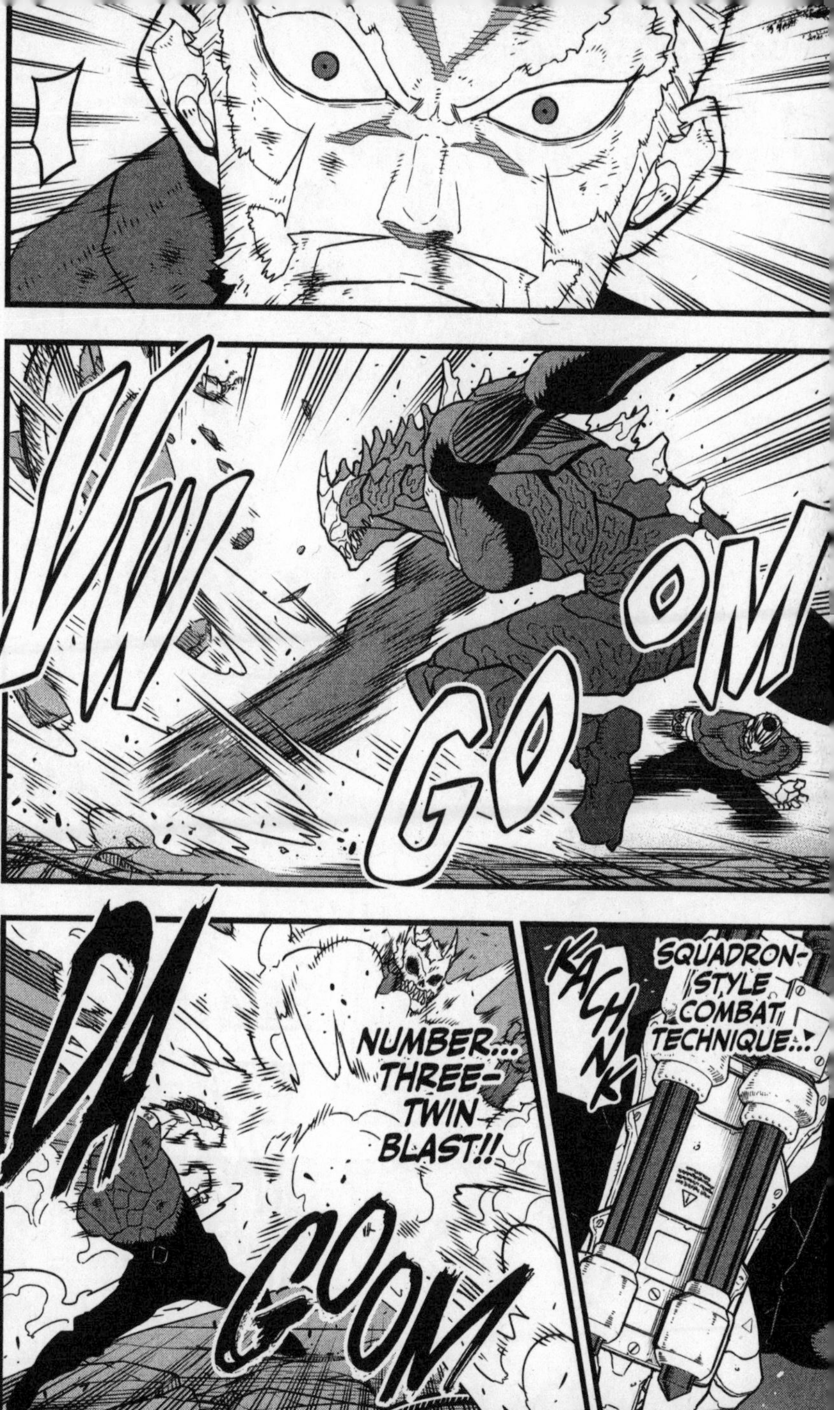
VW
GOOM
KACHNK
SQUADRON-STYLE COMBAT TECHNIQUE...
NUMBER... THREE-TWIN BLAST!!
GOOM

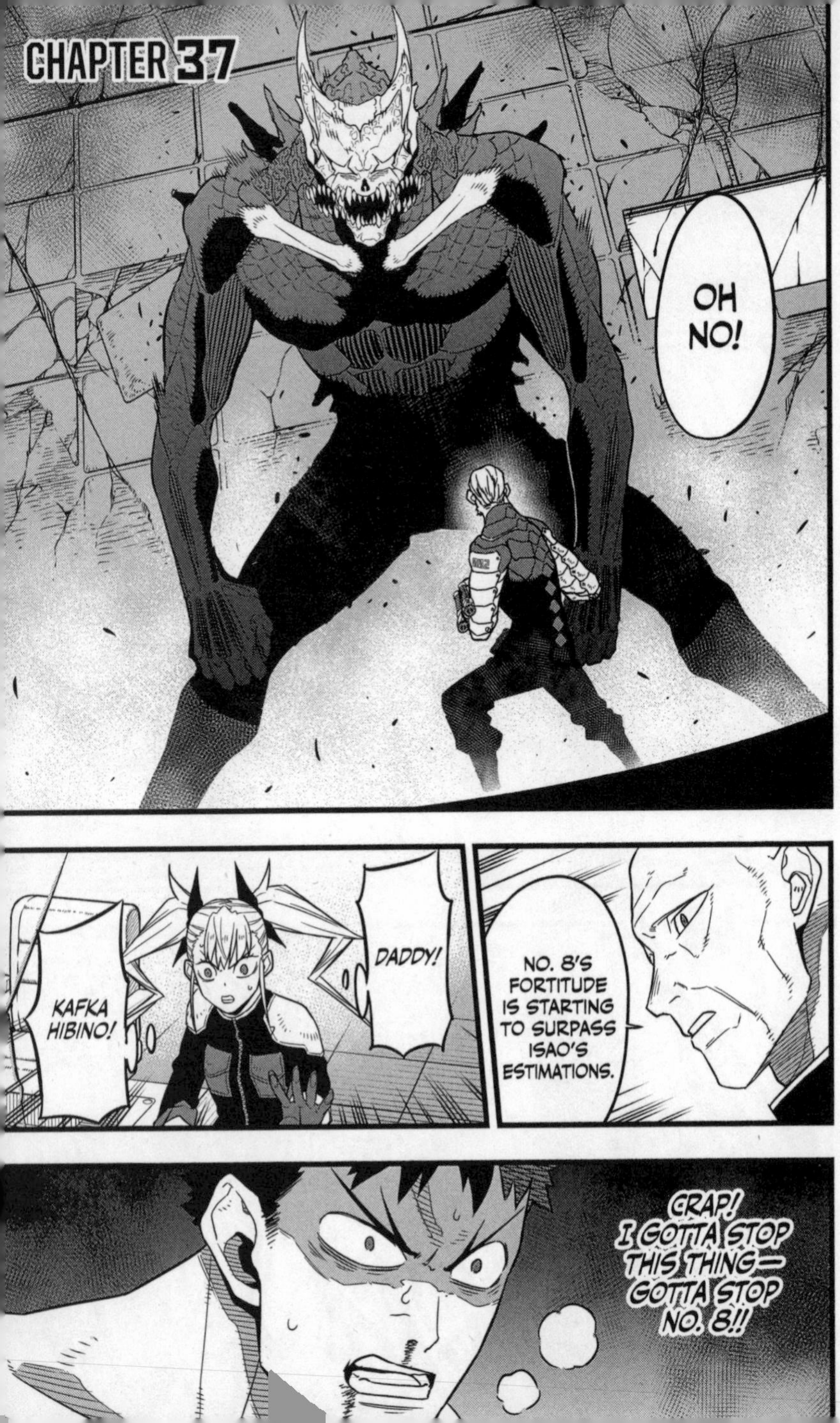
CHAPTER 37
OH NO!
NO. 8'S FORTITUDE IS STARTING TO SURPASS ISAO'S ESTIMATIONS.
DADDY!
KAFKA HIBINO!
CRAP! I GOTTA STOP THIS THING— GOTTA STOP NO. 8!!

KAIJU NO. 8

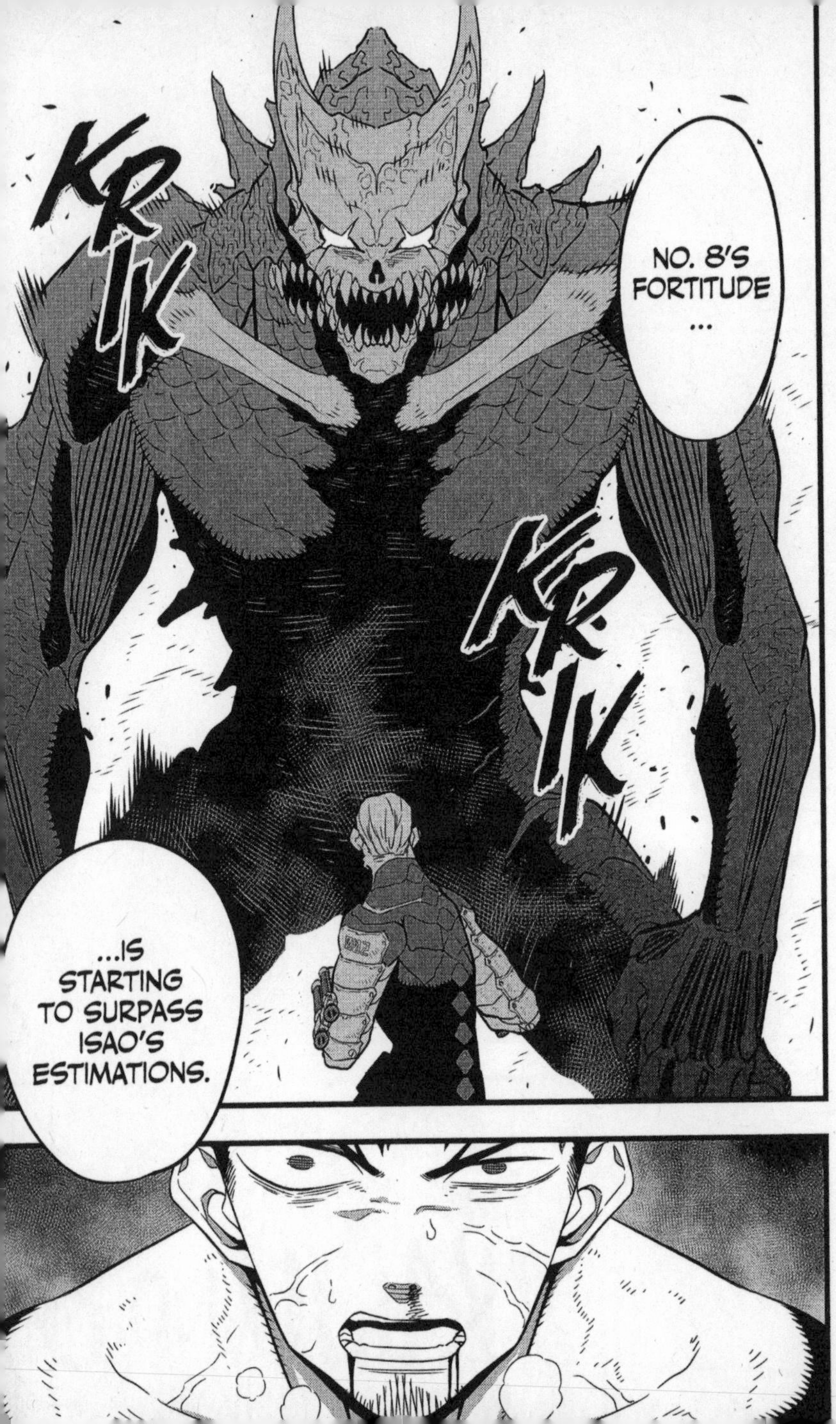
NO. 8'S FORTITUDE ...
KRIK
KRIK
...IS STARTING TO SURPASS ISAO'S ESTIMATIONS.

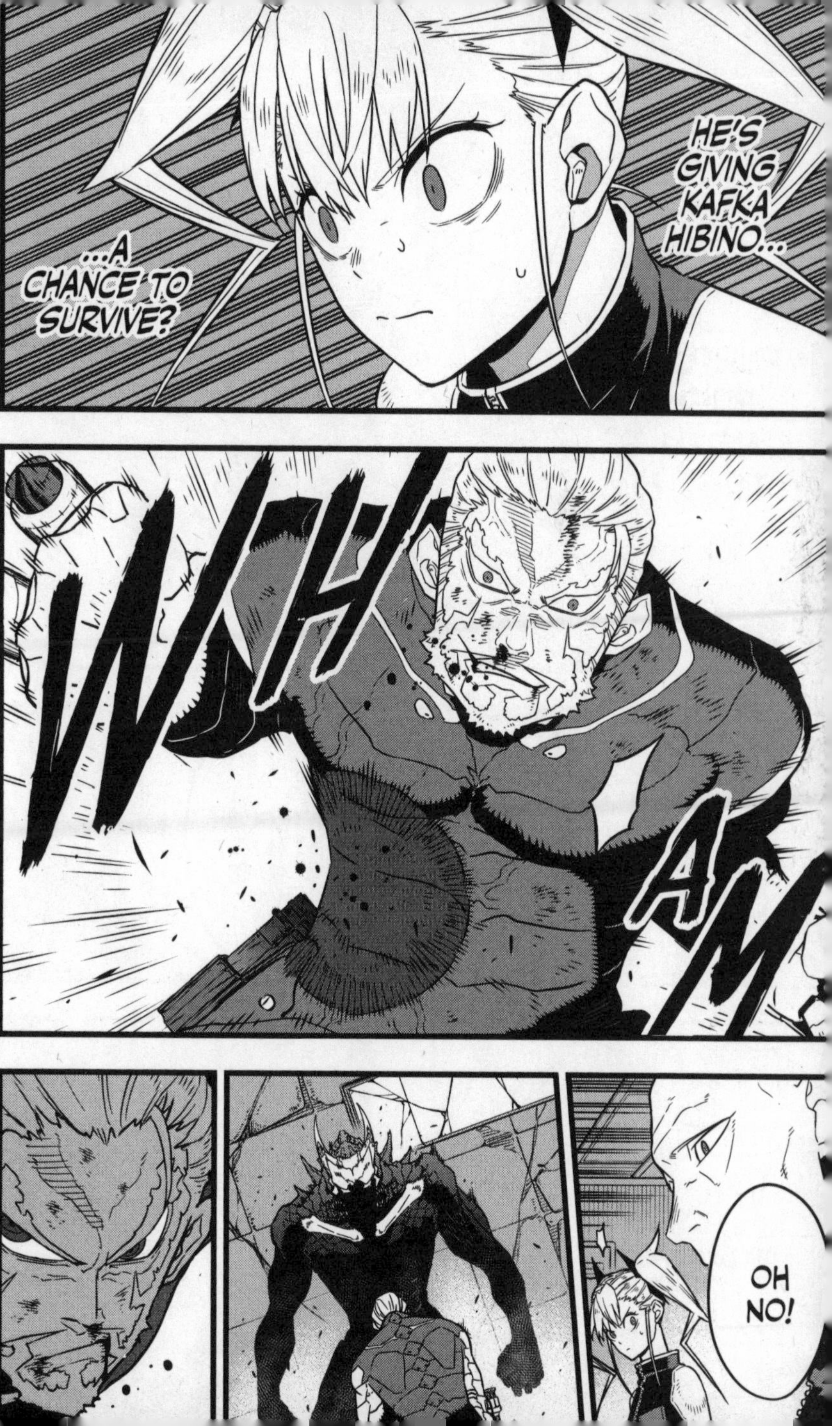
HE'S GIVING KAFKA HIBINO...
...A CHANCE TO SURVIVE?
WHAM
OH NO!

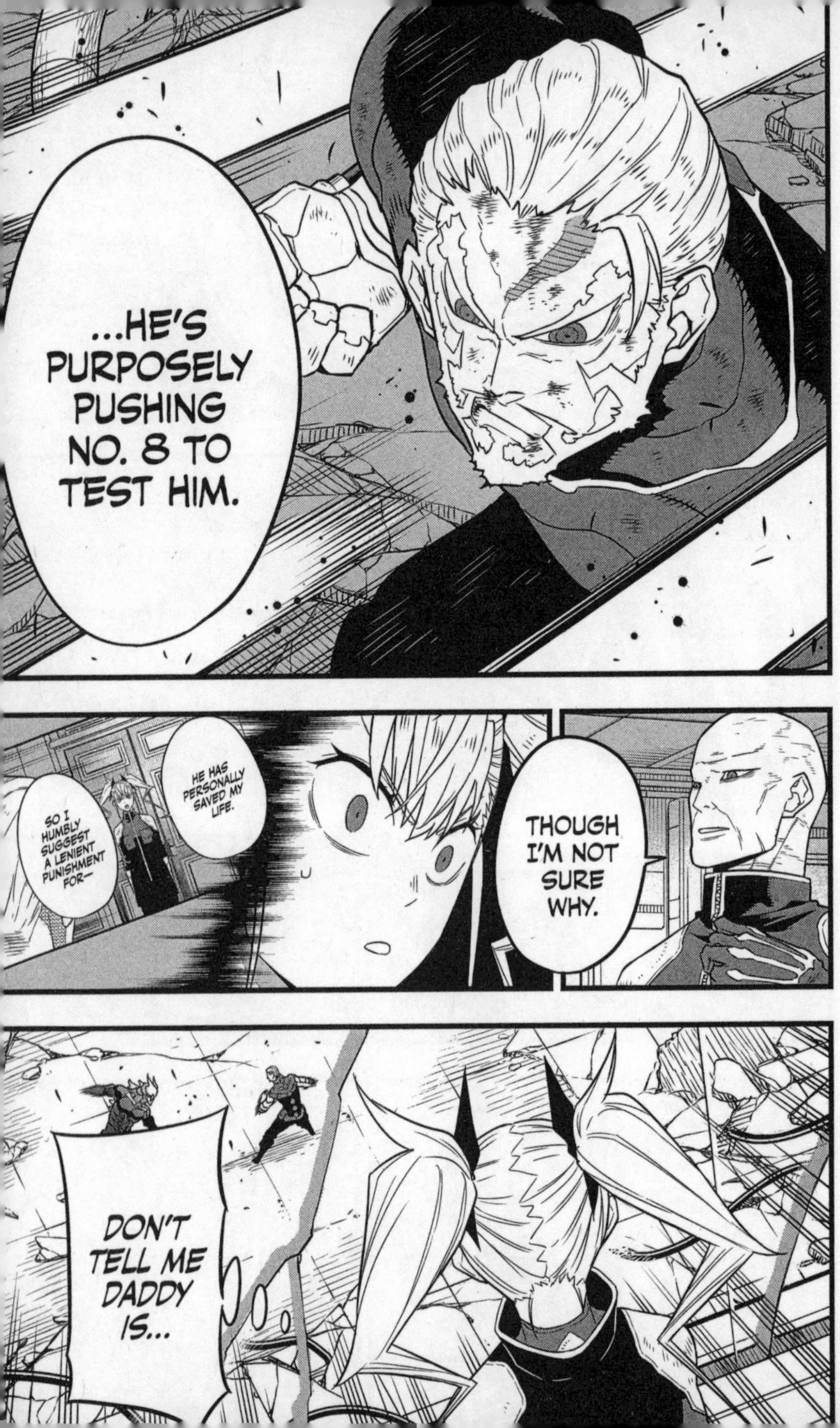
...HE'S PURPOSELY PUSHING NO. 8 TO TEST HIM.
THOUGH I'M NOT SURE WHY.
HE HAS PERSONALLY SAVED MY LIFE.
SO I HUMBLY SUGGEST A LENIENT PUNISHMENT FOR—
DON'T TELL ME DADDY IS...

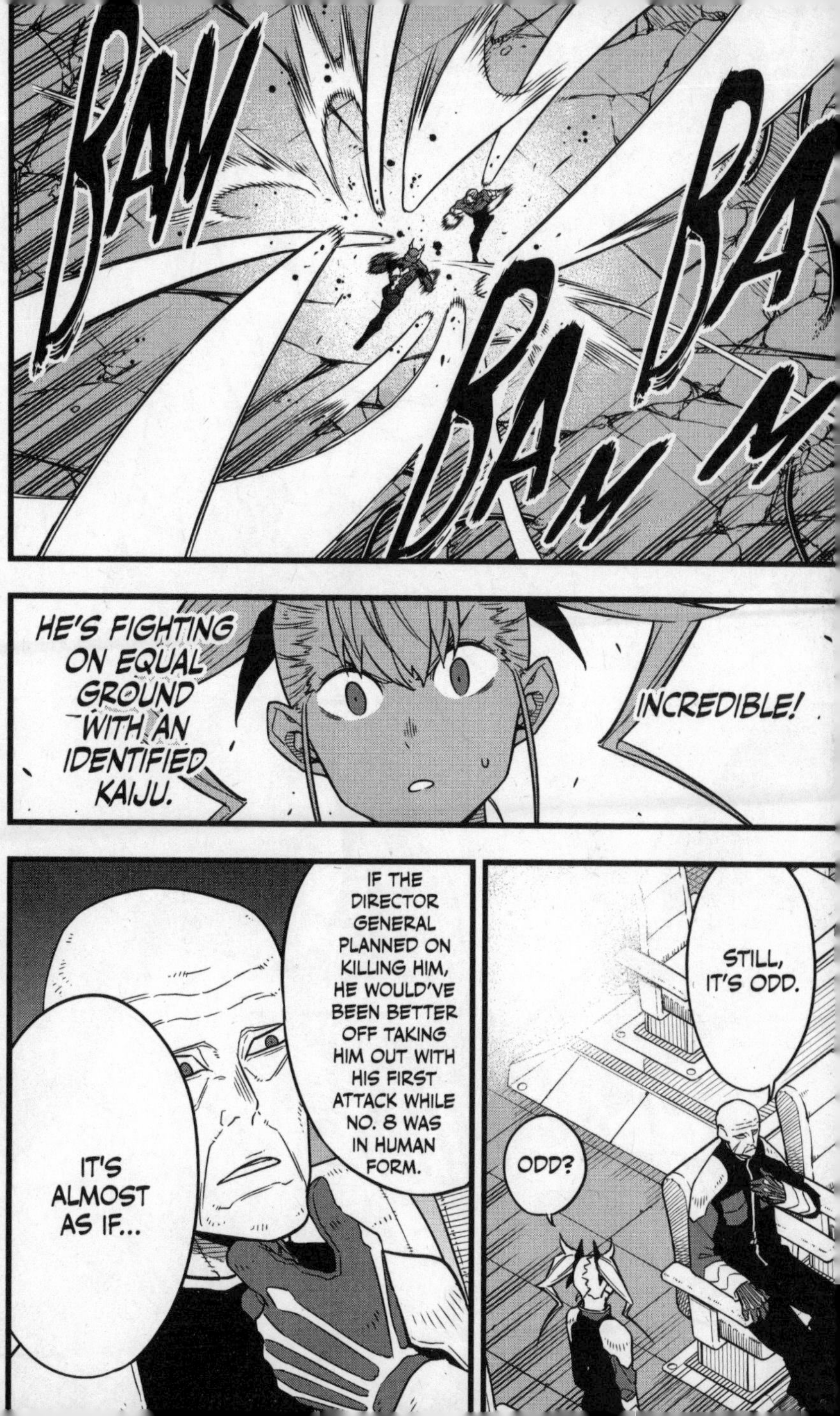
BA
BADAM
BAM
INCREDIBLE!
HE'S FIGHTING ON EQUAL GROUND WITH AN IDENTIFIED KAIJU.
STILL, IT'S ODD.
ODD?
IF THE DIRECTOR GENERAL PLANNED ON KILLING HIM, HE WOULD'VE BEEN BETTER OFF TAKING HIM OUT WITH HIS FIRST ATTACK WHILE NO. 8 WAS IN HUMAN FORM.
IT'S ALMOST AS IF...

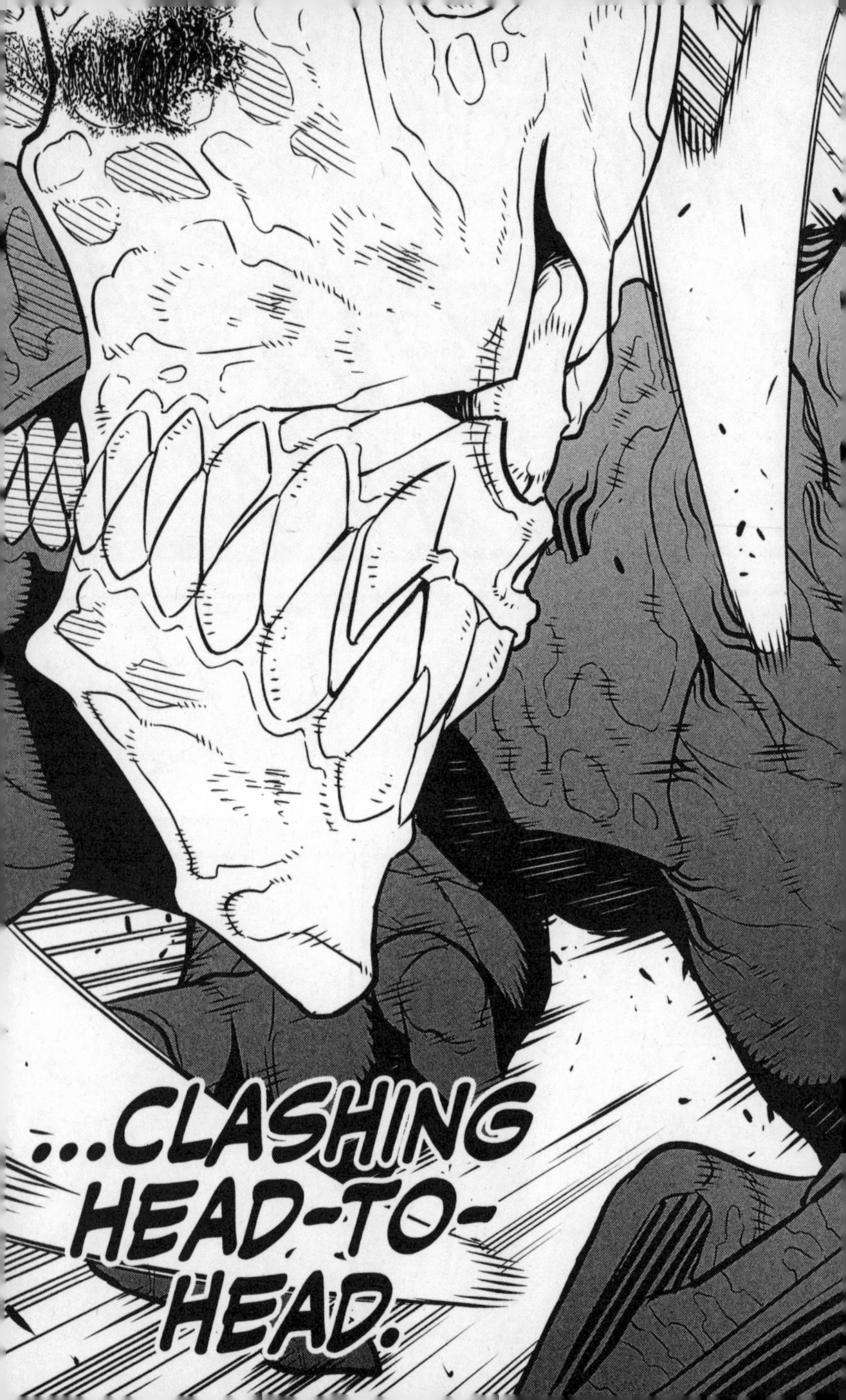
...CLASHING HEAD-TO-HEAD.

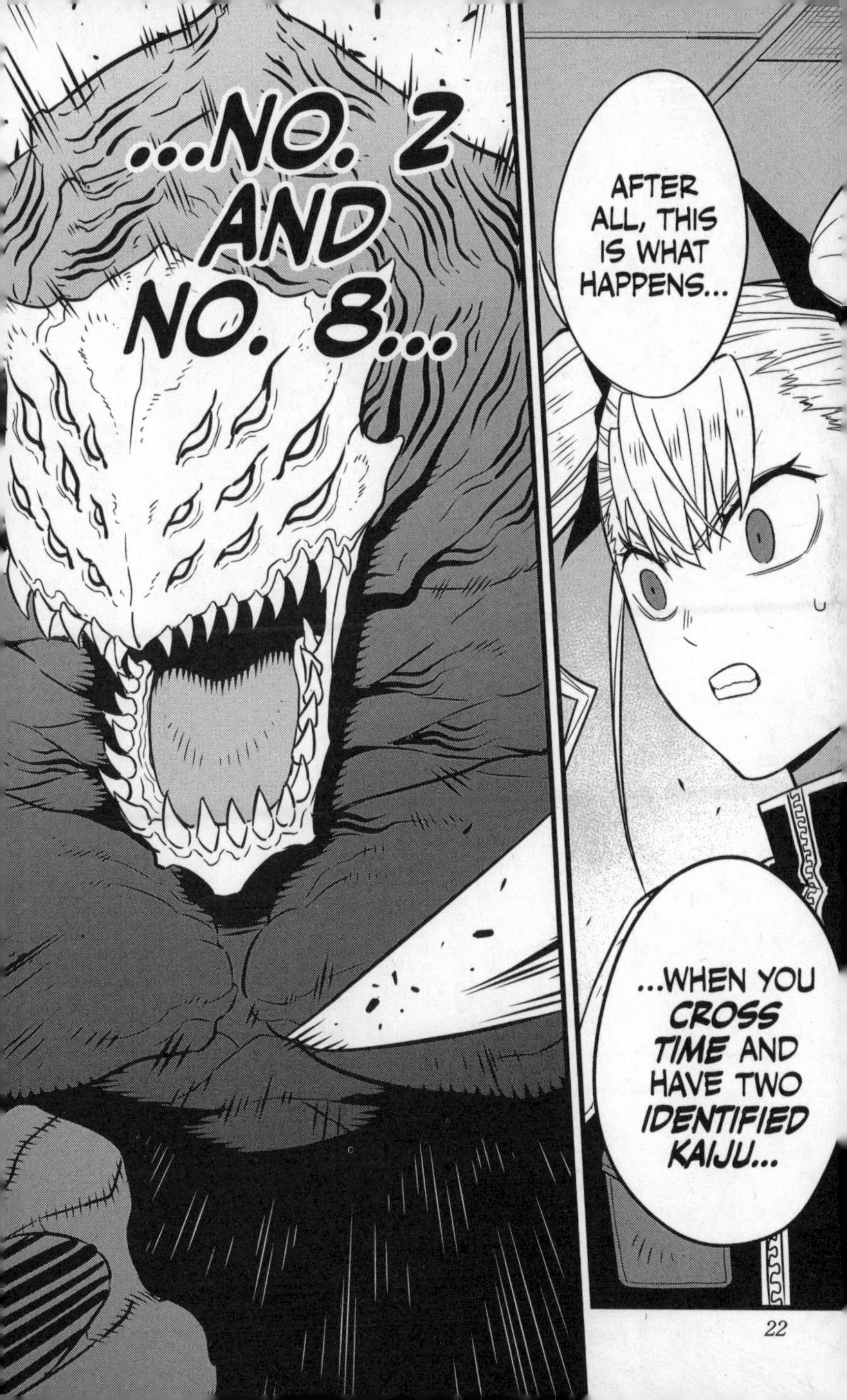
AFTER ALL, THIS IS WHAT HAPPENS...
...WHEN YOU CROSS TIME AND HAVE TWO IDENTIFIED KAIJU...
...NO. 2 AND NO. 8...

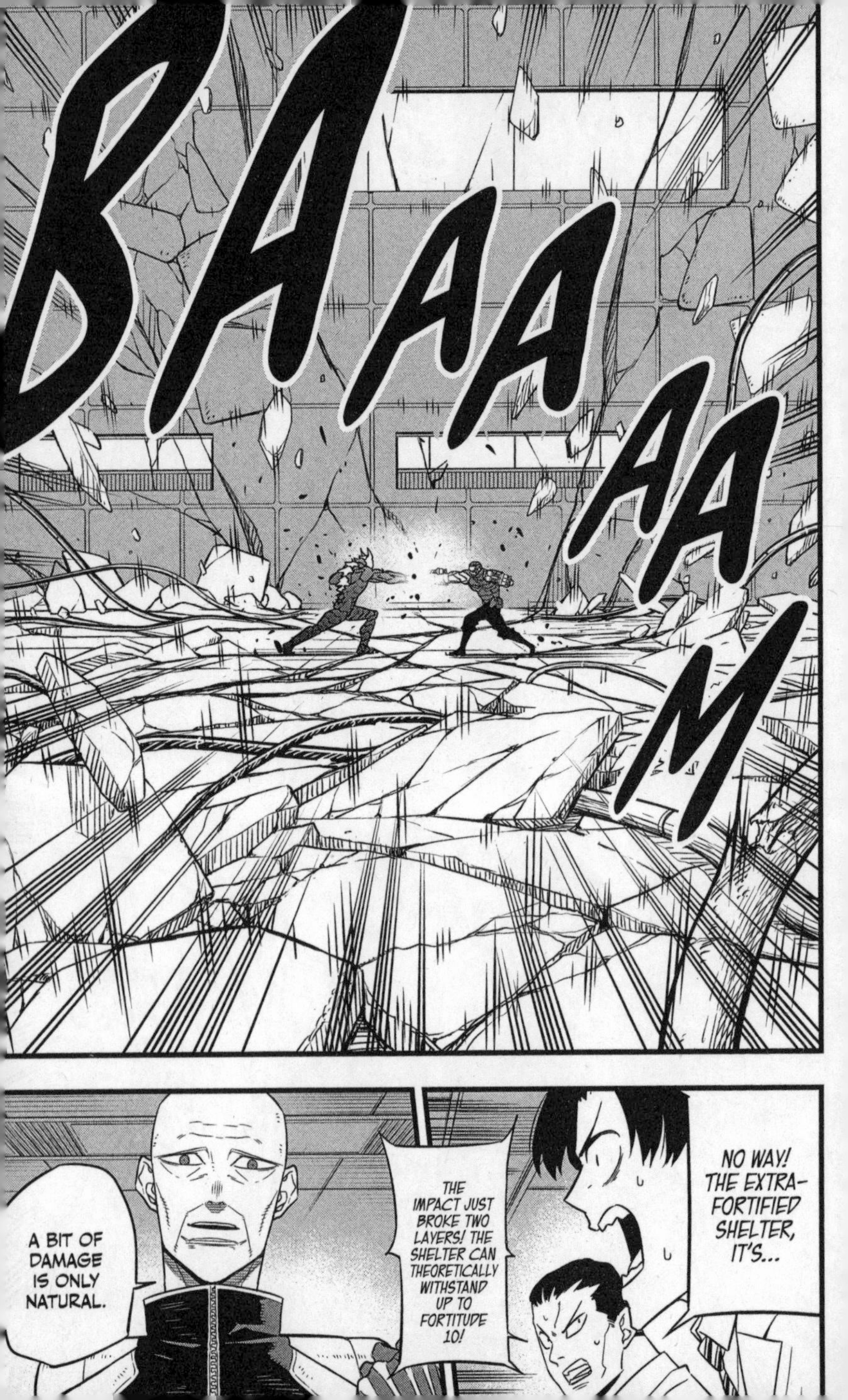
BAAAAAM
NO WAY! THE EXTRA-FORTIFIED SHELTER, IT'S...
THE IMPACT JUST BROKE TWO LAYERS! THE SHELTER CAN THEORETICALLY WITHSTAND UP TO FORTITUDE 10!
A BIT OF DAMAGE IS ONLY NATURAL.

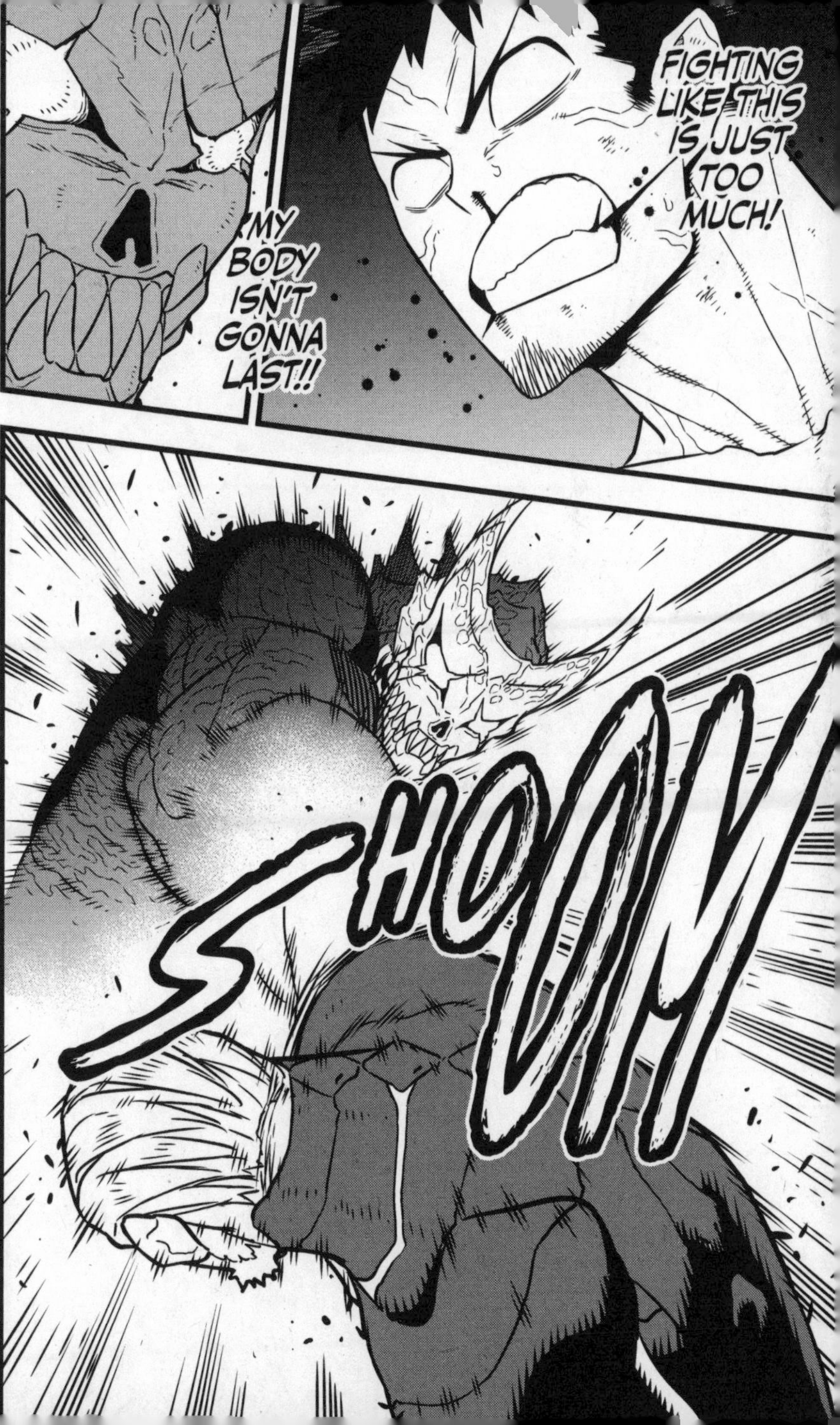
FIGHTING LIKE THIS IS JUST TOO MUCH!
MY BODY ISN'T GONNA LAST!!
SHOOM

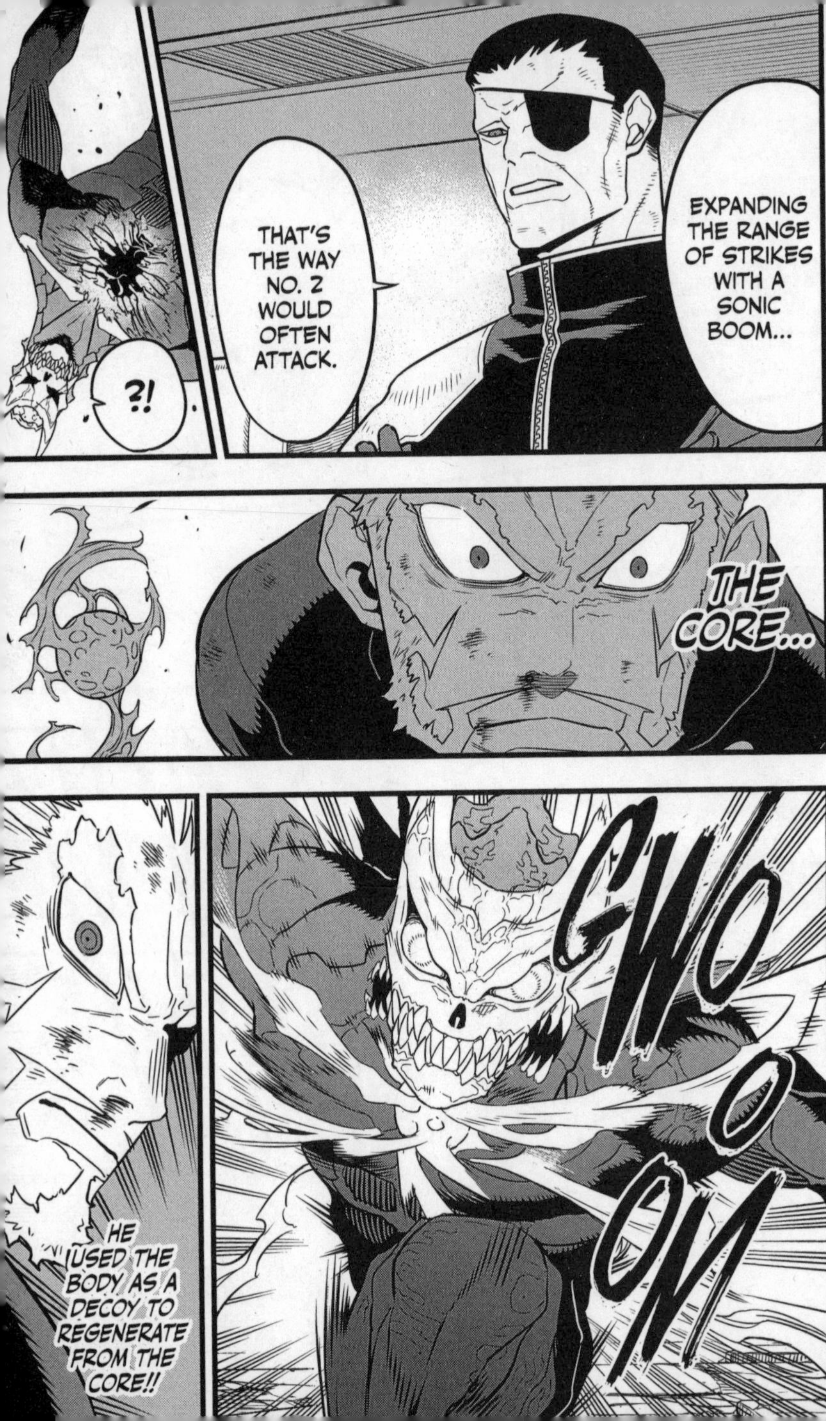
EXPANDING THE RANGE OF STRIKES WITH A SONIC BOOM...
THAT'S THE WAY NO. 2 WOULD OFTEN ATTACK.
?!
THE CORE...
GWOOOON
HE USED THE BODY AS A DECOY TO REGENERATE FROM THE CORE!!

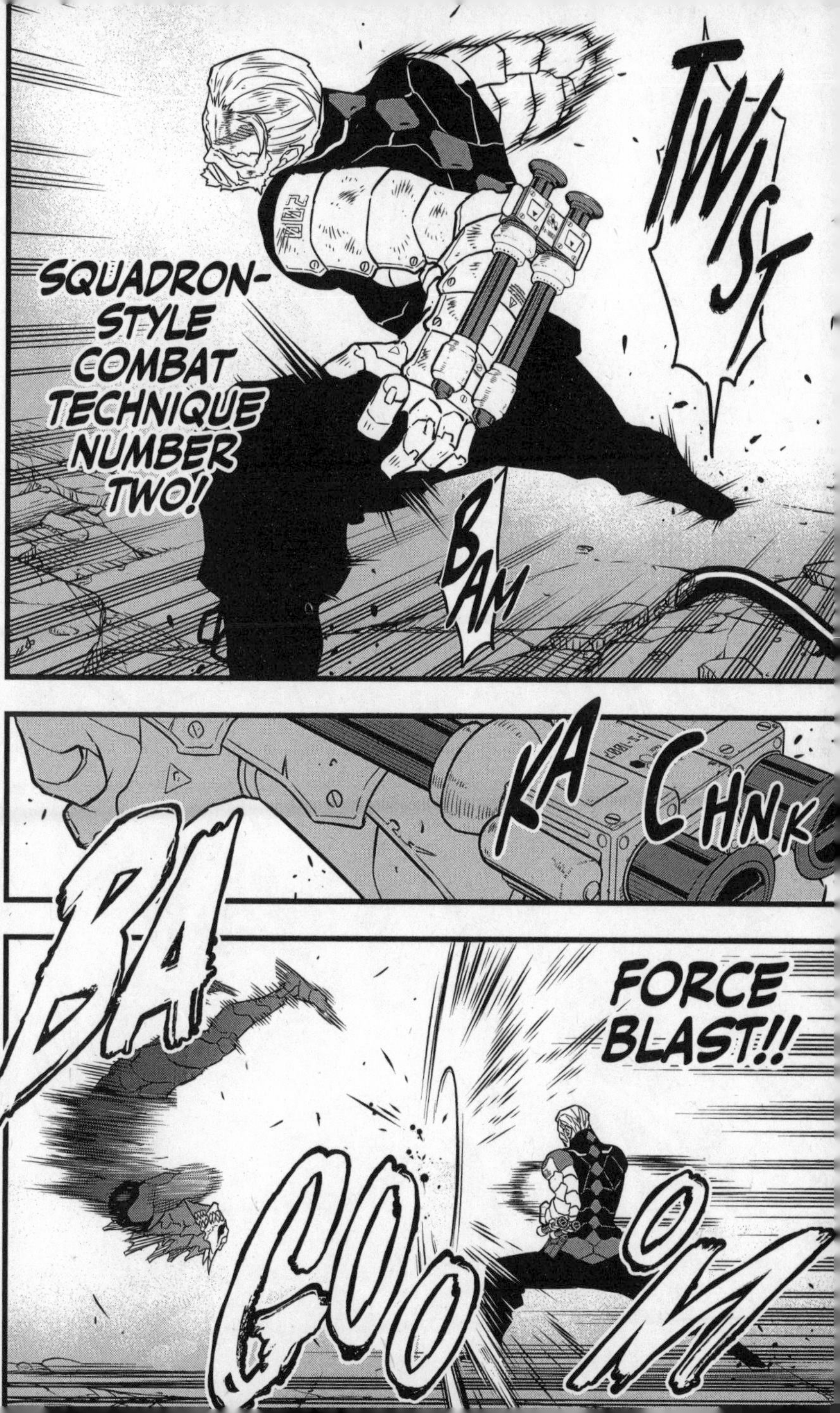
TWIST
SQUADRON-STYLE COMBAT TECHNIQUE NUMBER TWO!
BAM
KA CHNK
FORCE BLAST!!
BA
COOOM

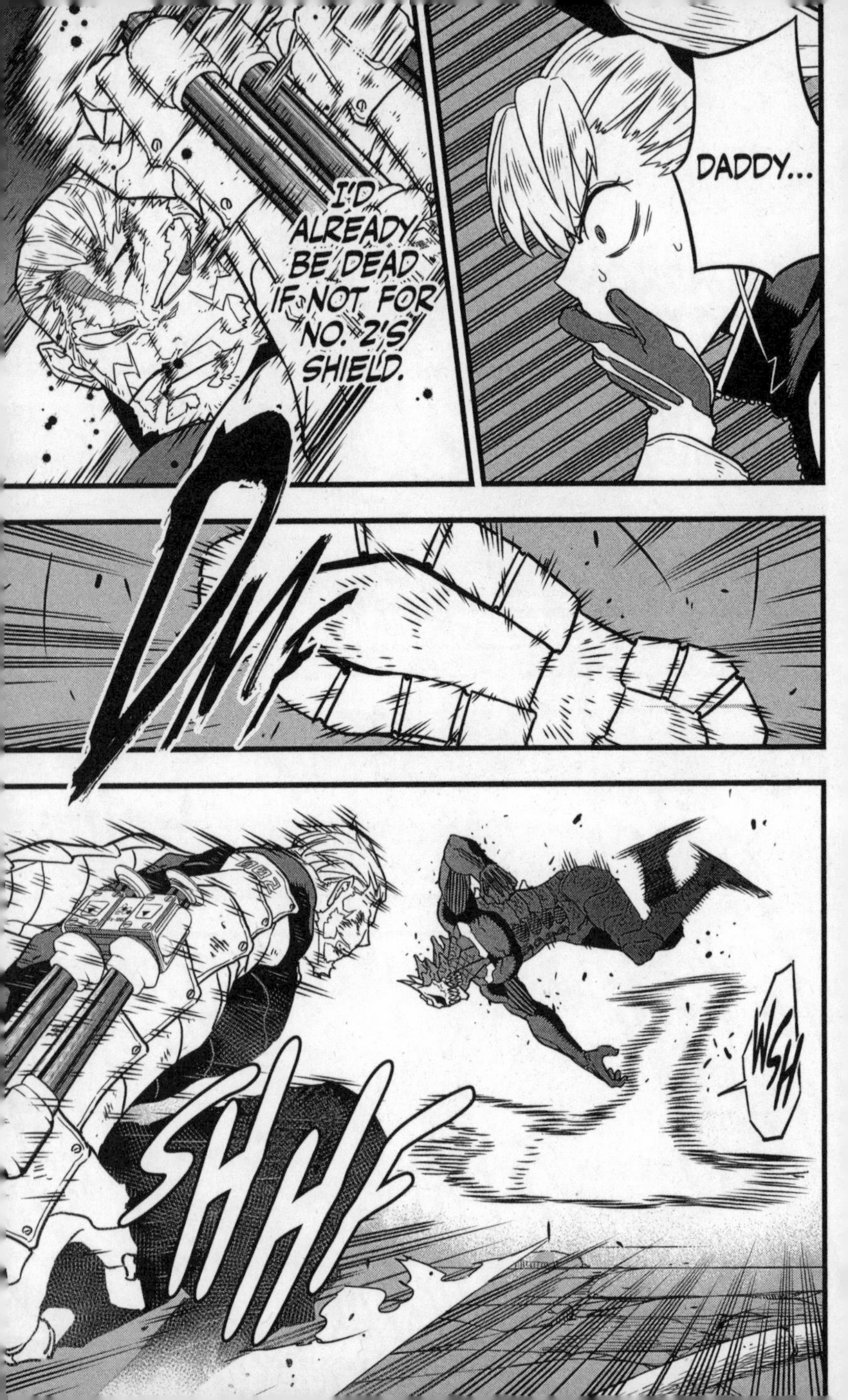
DADDY...
I'D ALREADY BE DEAD IF NOT FOR NO. 2'S SHIELD.

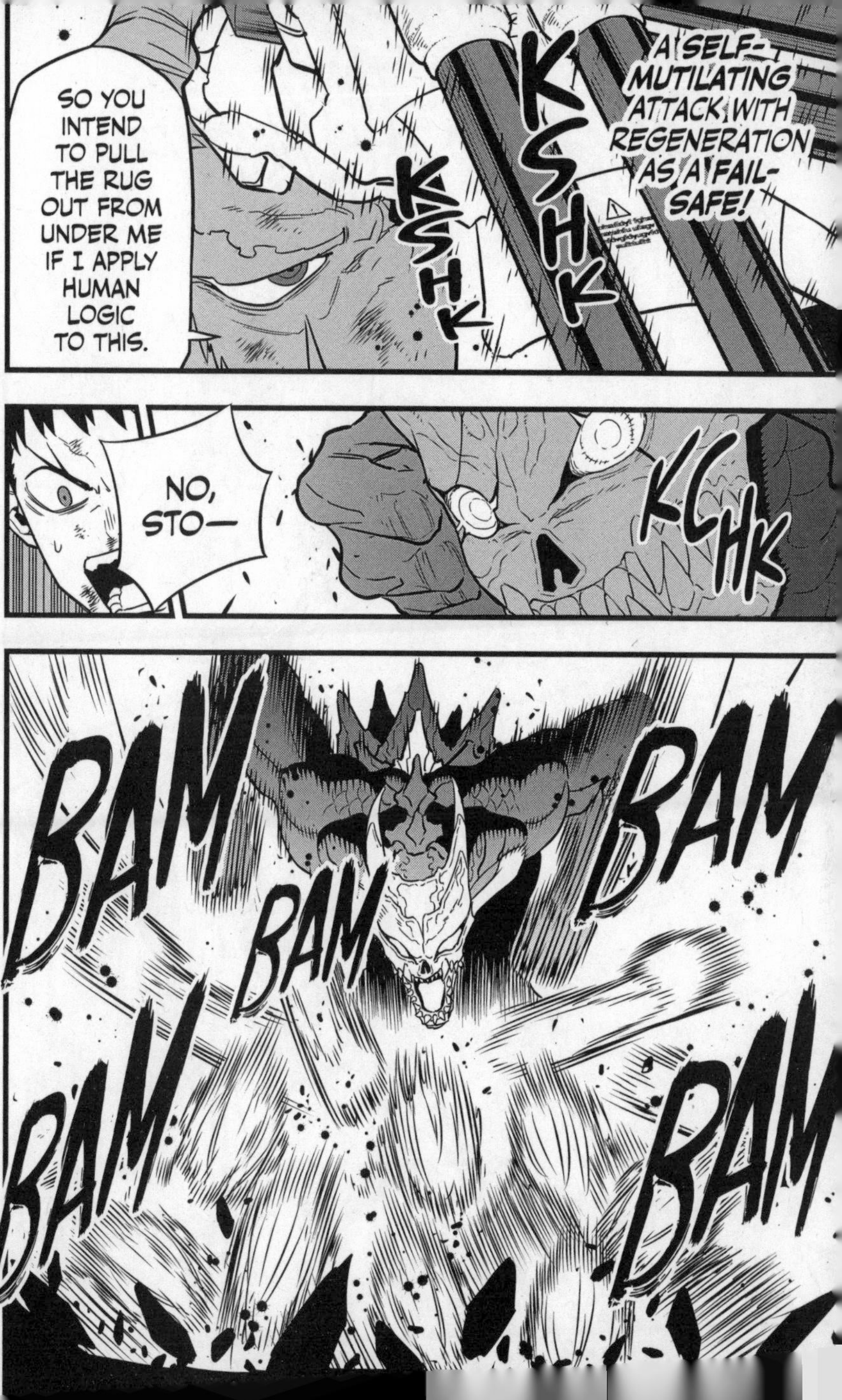
A SELF-MUTILATING ATTACK WITH REGENERATION AS A FAIL-SAFE!
KSHK
KSHK
SO YOU INTEND TO PULL THE RUG OUT FROM UNDER ME IF I APPLY HUMAN LOGIC TO THIS.
KCHK
NO, STO—
BAM
BAM
BAM
BAM
BAM

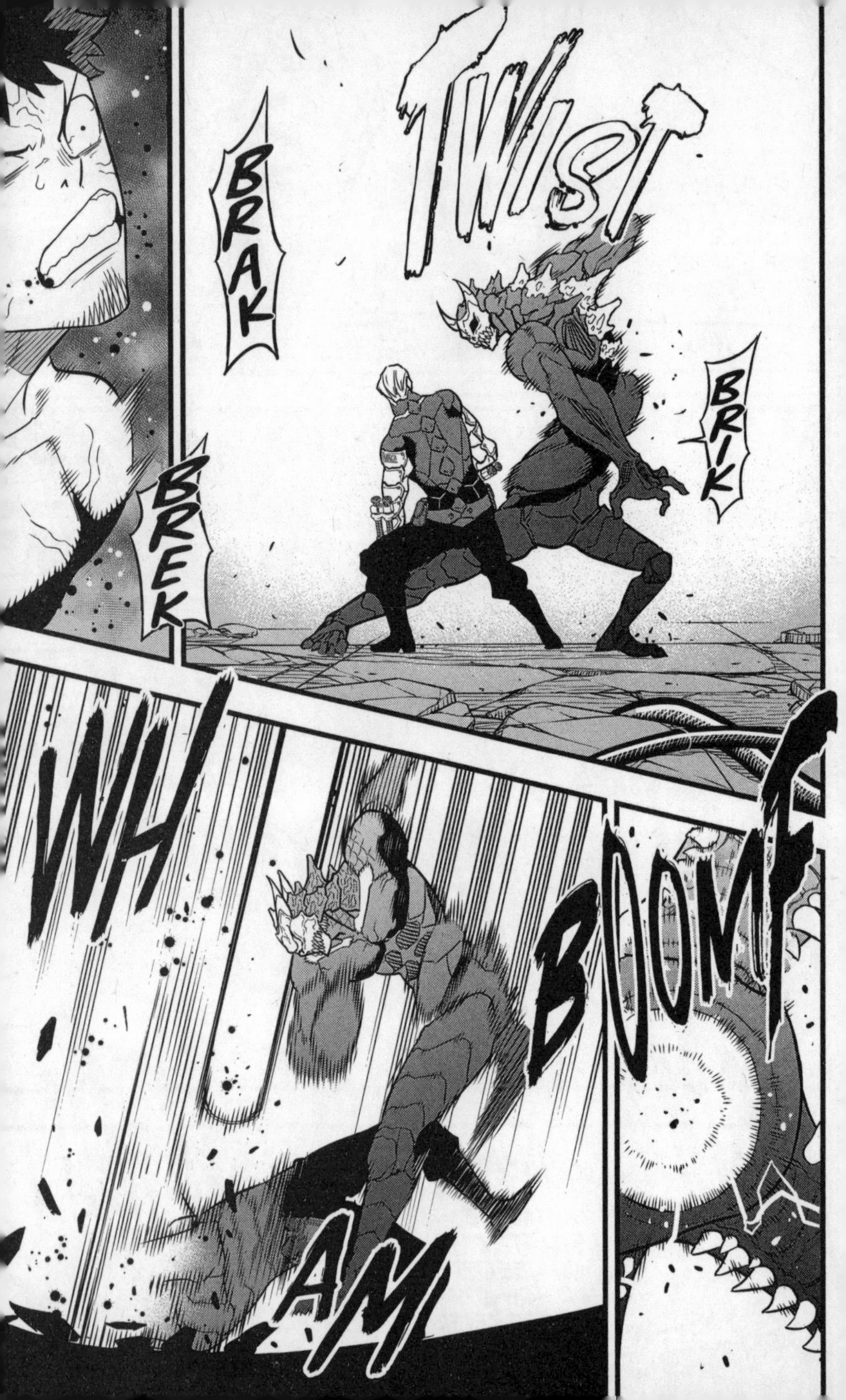
TWIST
BRIK
BRAK
BREK
BOOM
WH
AM

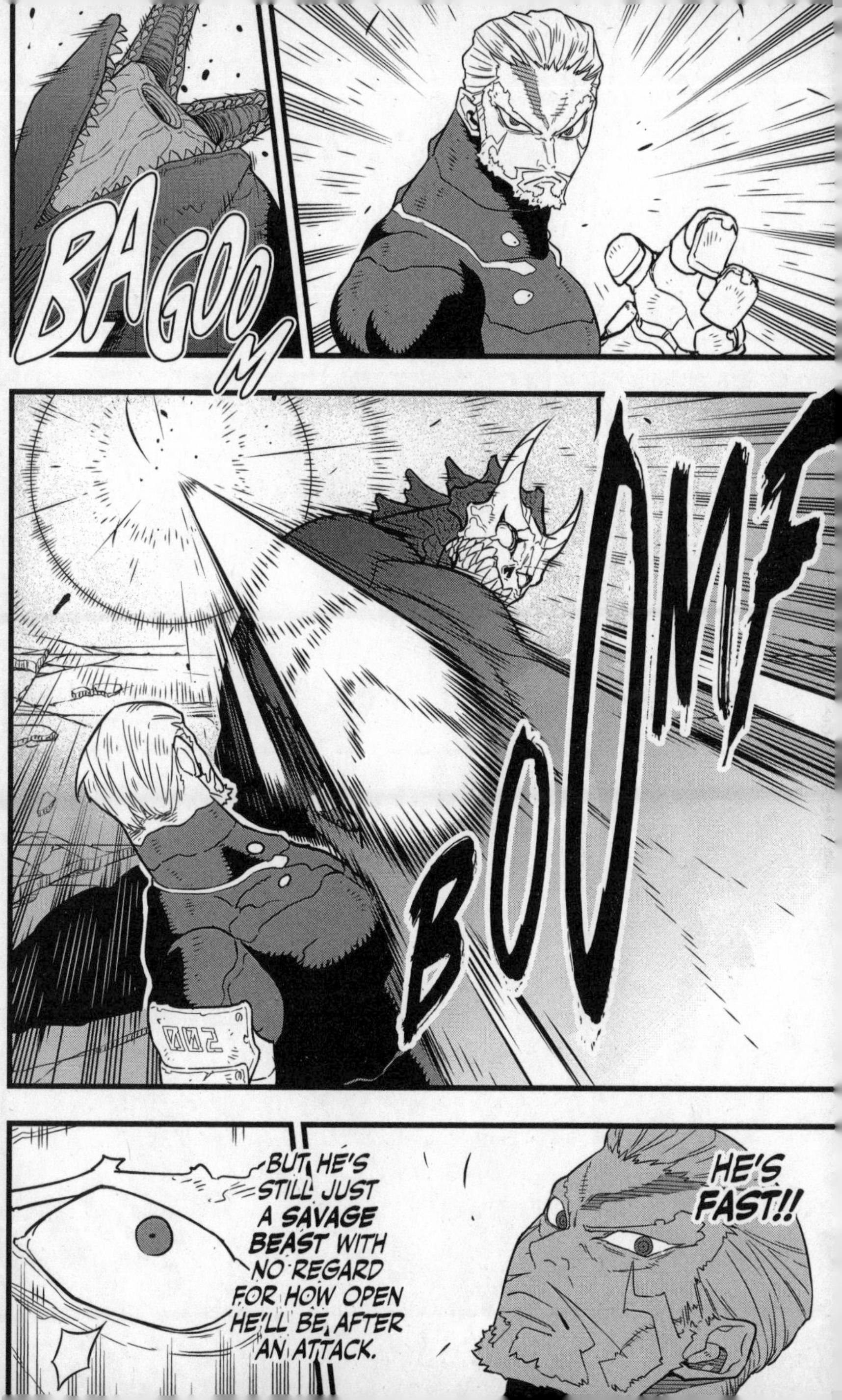
BAGOOM
BOOM
HE'S FAST!!
BUT HE'S STILL JUST A SAVAGE BEAST WITH NO REGARD FOR HOW OPEN HE'LL BE AFTER AN ATTACK.

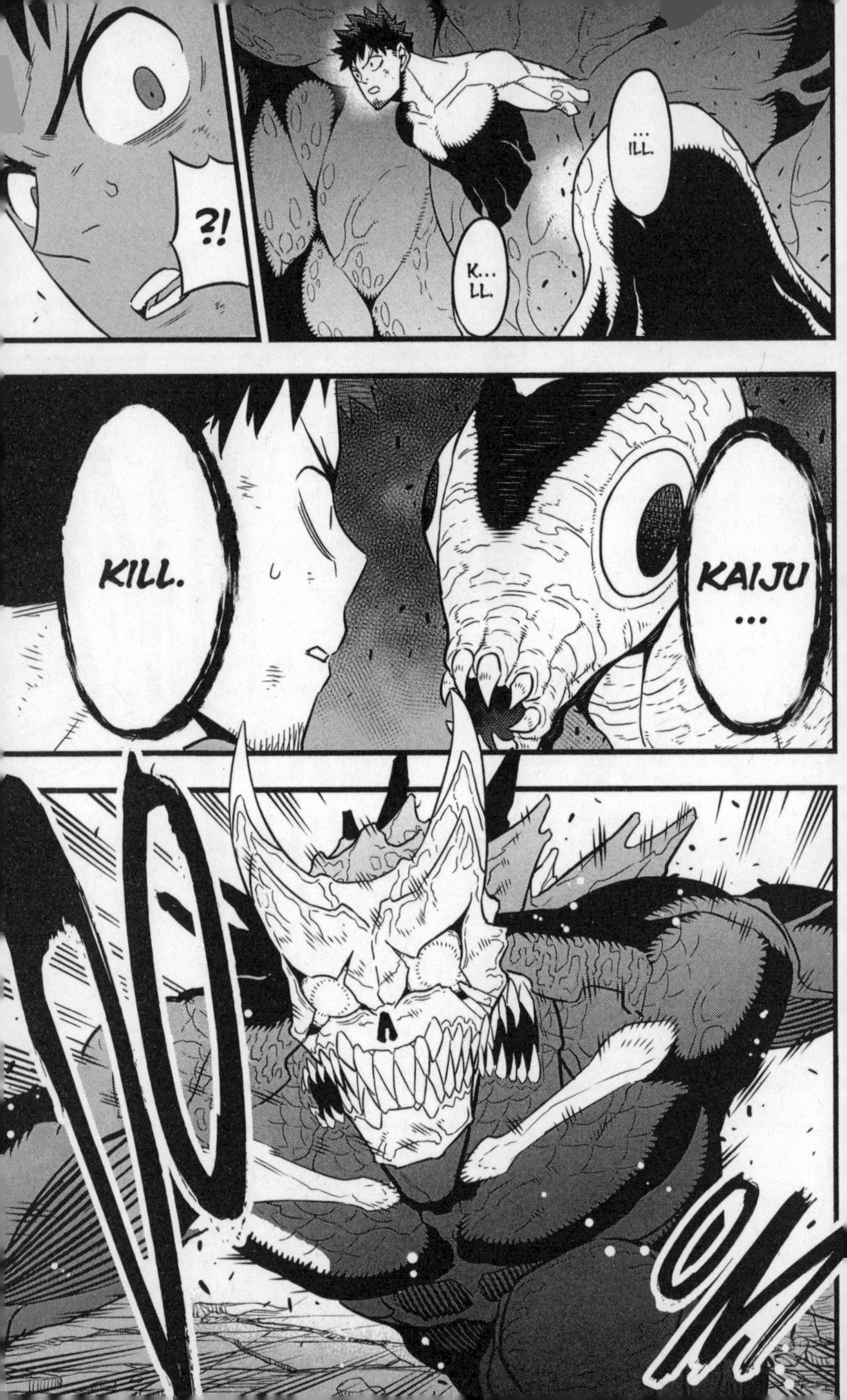
...ILL.
K... LL.
?!
KAIJU ...
KILL.

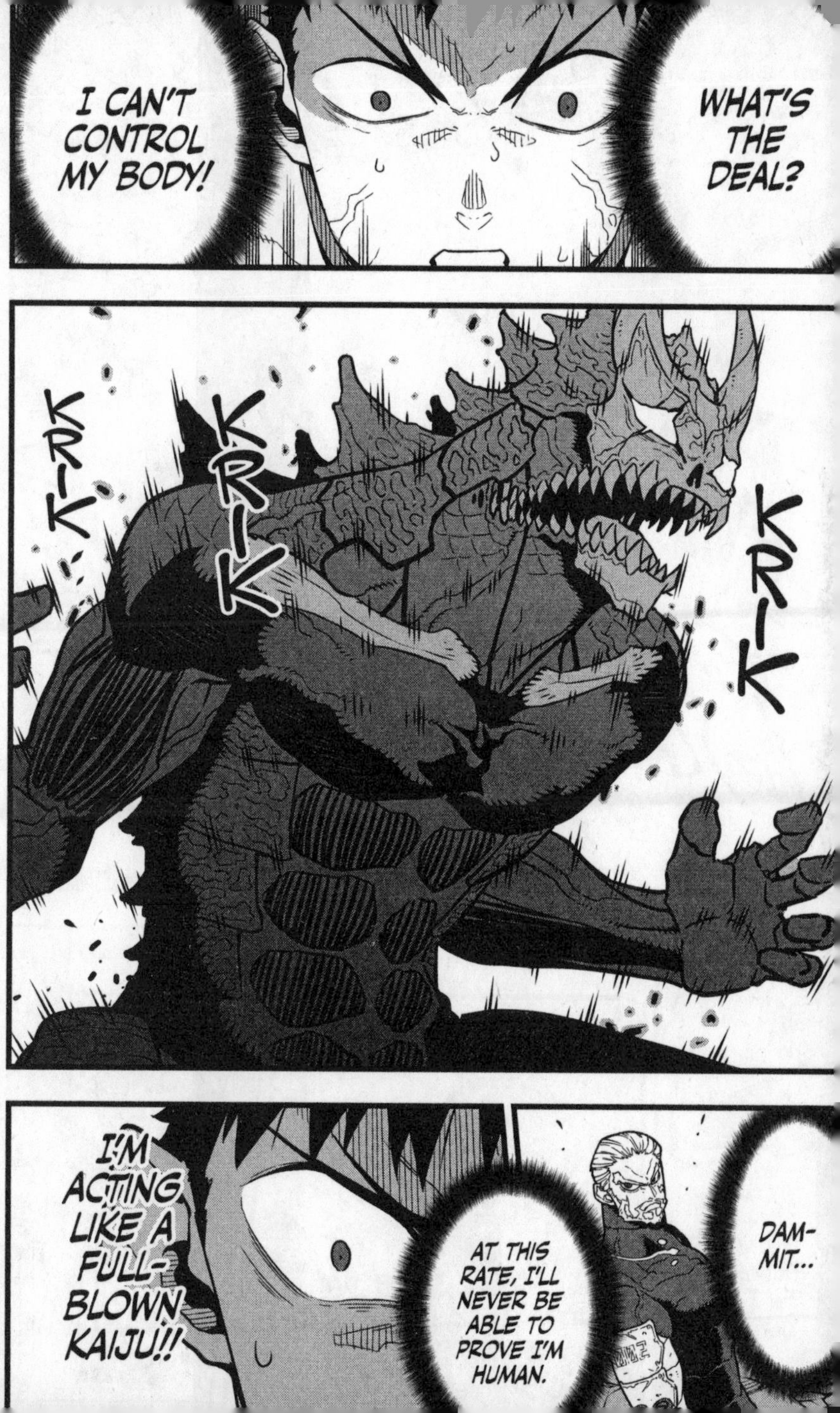
WHAT'S THE DEAL?
I CAN'T CONTROL MY BODY!
KRIK
KRIK
KRIK
DAM-MIT...
AT THIS RATE, I'LL NEVER BE ABLE TO PROVE I'M HUMAN.
I'M ACTING LIKE A FULL-BLOWN KAIJU!!

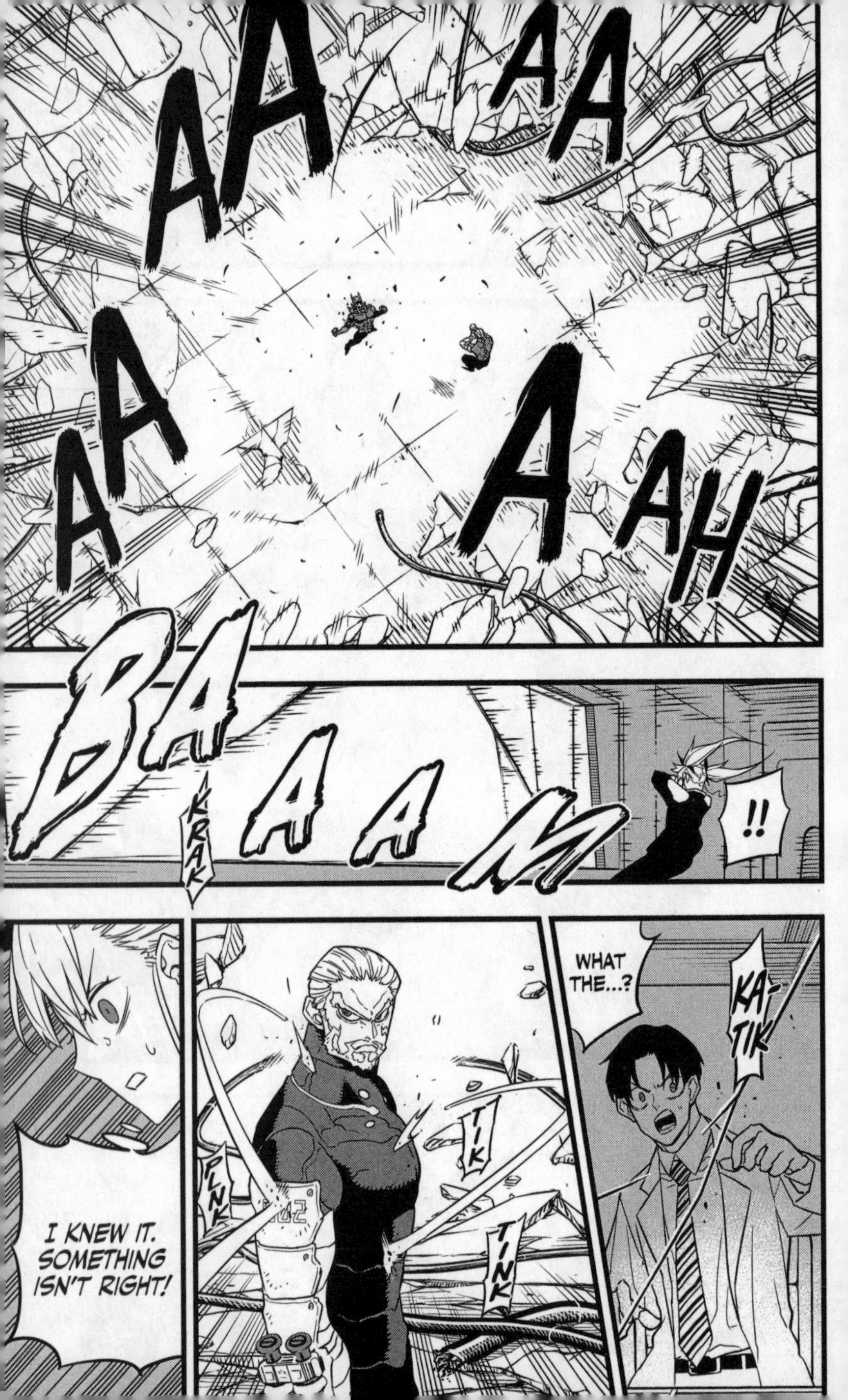

AAAAAAAAH
BAAAAM
KRAK
!!
WHAT THE...?
KA-TIK
TIK
PLINK
TINK
I KNEW IT. SOMETHING ISN'T RIGHT!

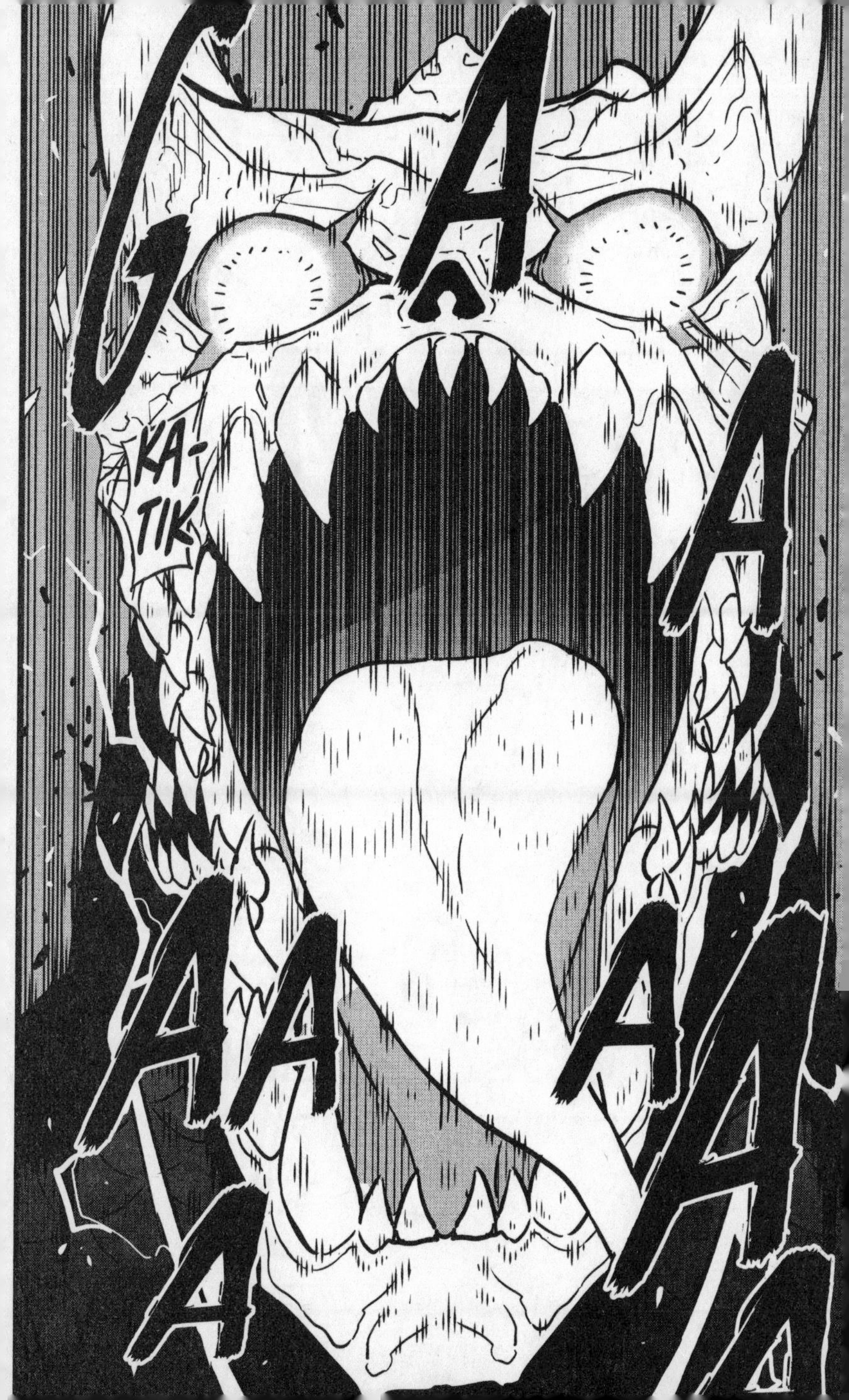
GAAAAAAAAA
KA-TIK

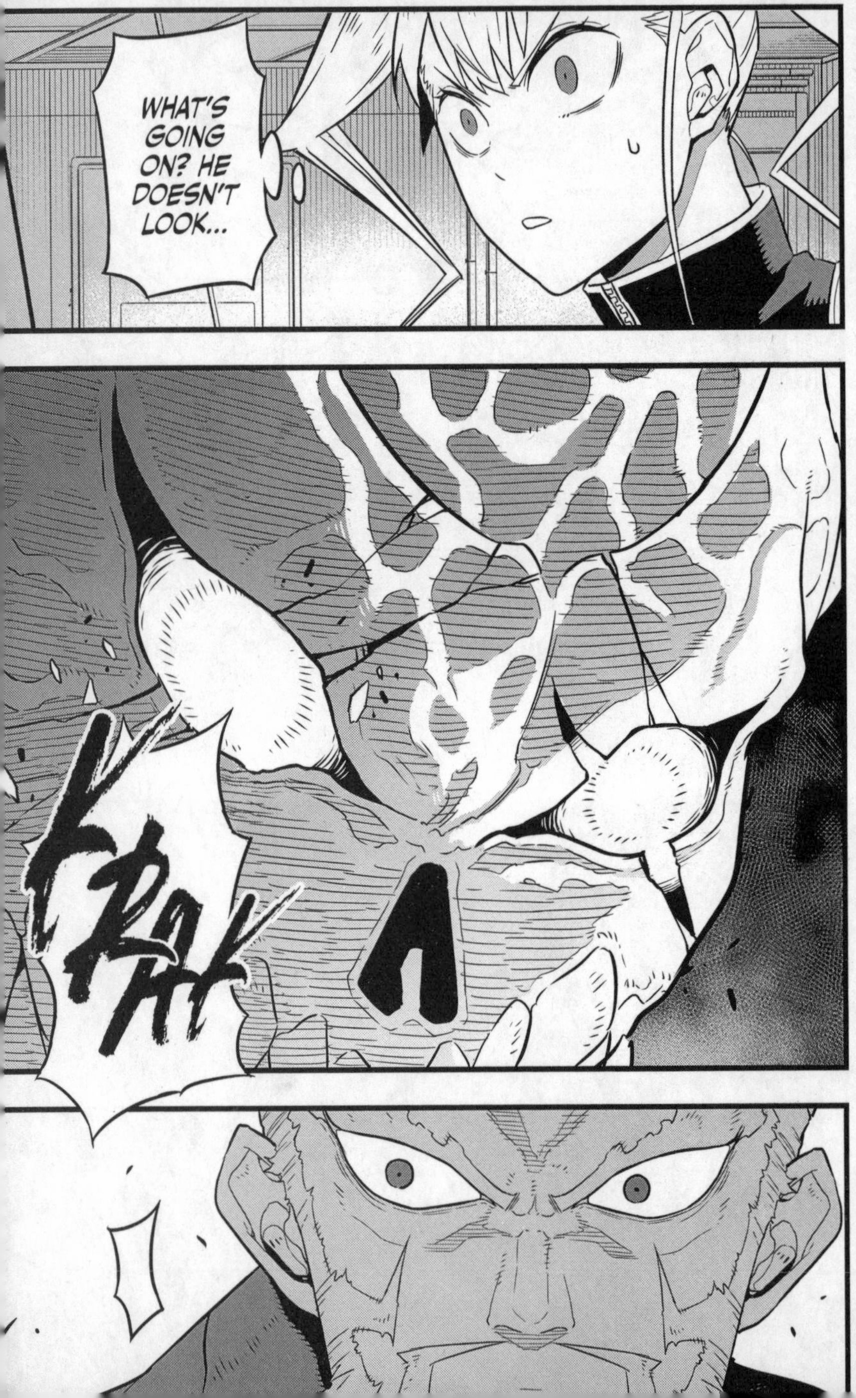
WHAT'S GOING ON? HE DOESN'T LOOK...
KRAK
!

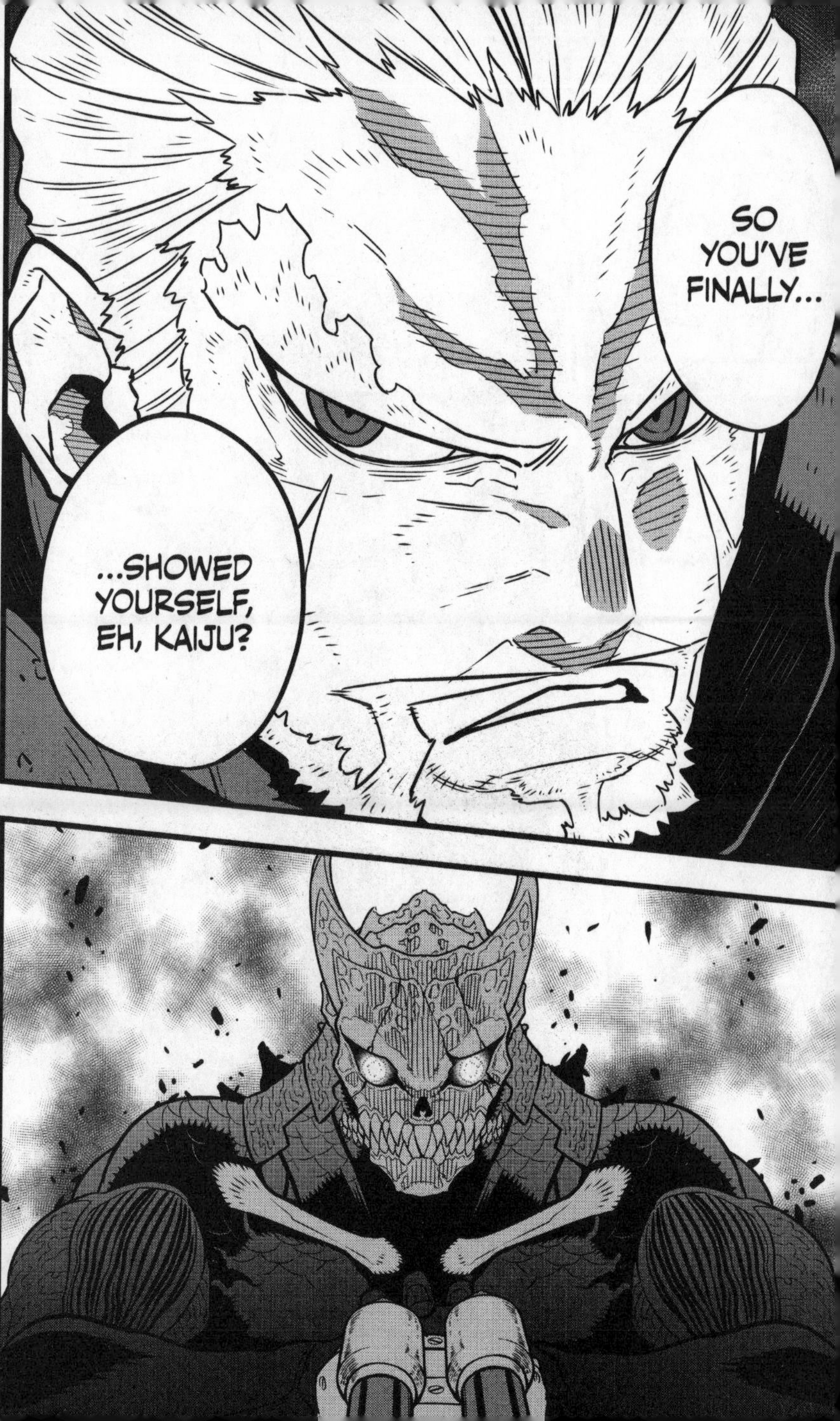
SO YOU'VE FINALLY...
...SHOWED YOURSELF, EH, KAIJU?

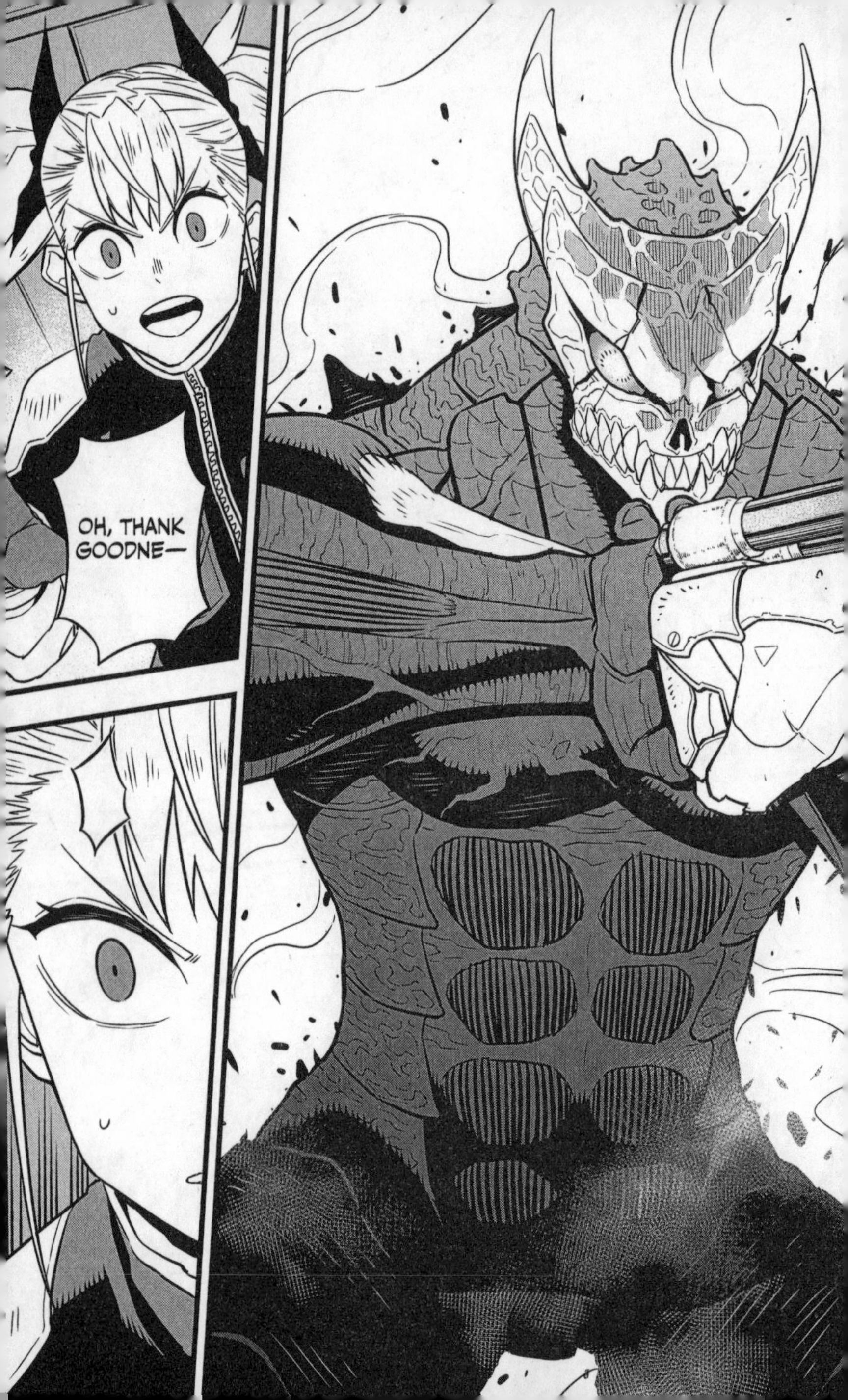
OH, THANK GOODNE—

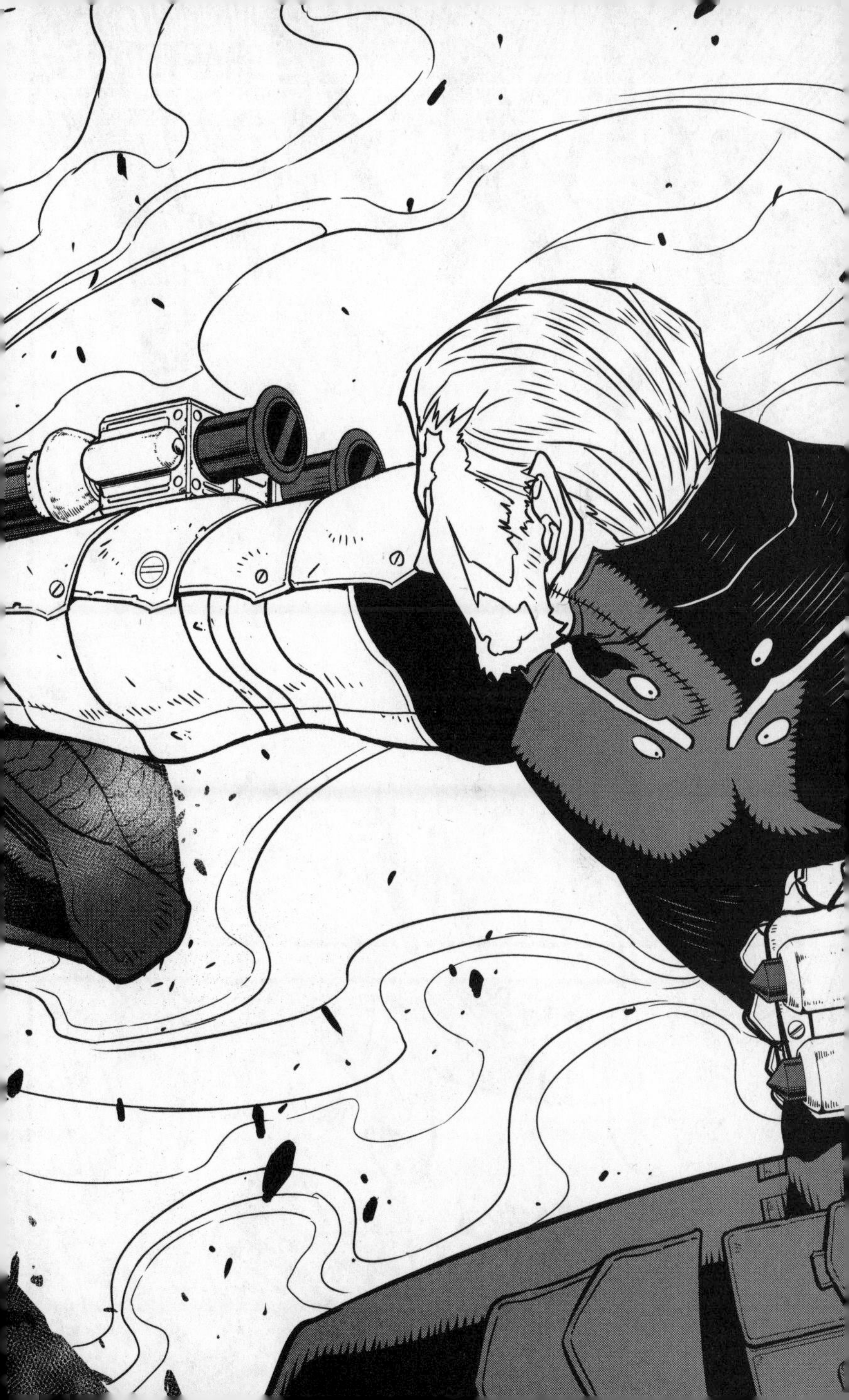

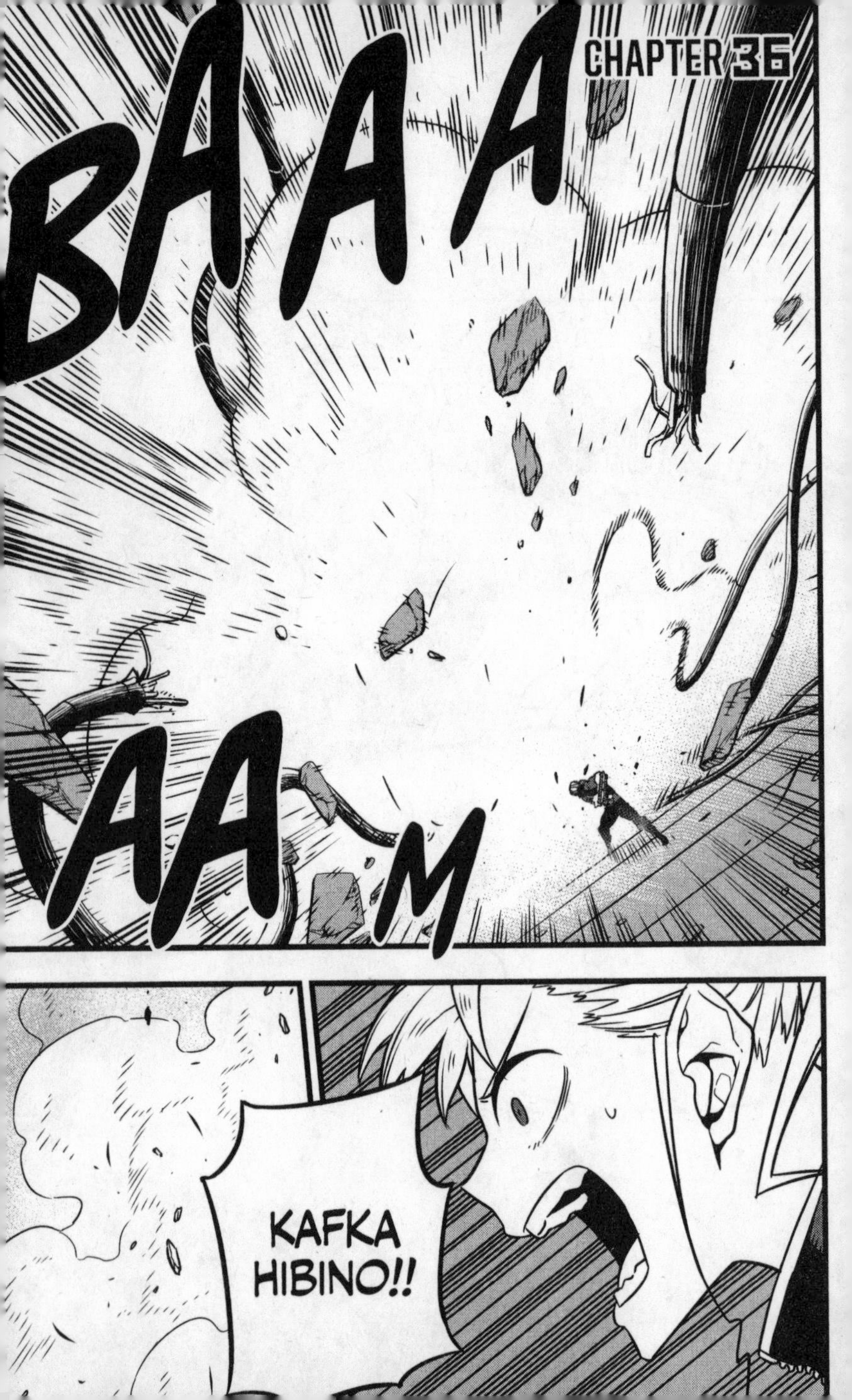
CHAPTER 36
BAAAAAAM
KAFKA HIBINO!!

CNTS CONTENTS CONTENTS CON

KAIJU NO. 8

5

NTS CONTENTS CONTENTS CON

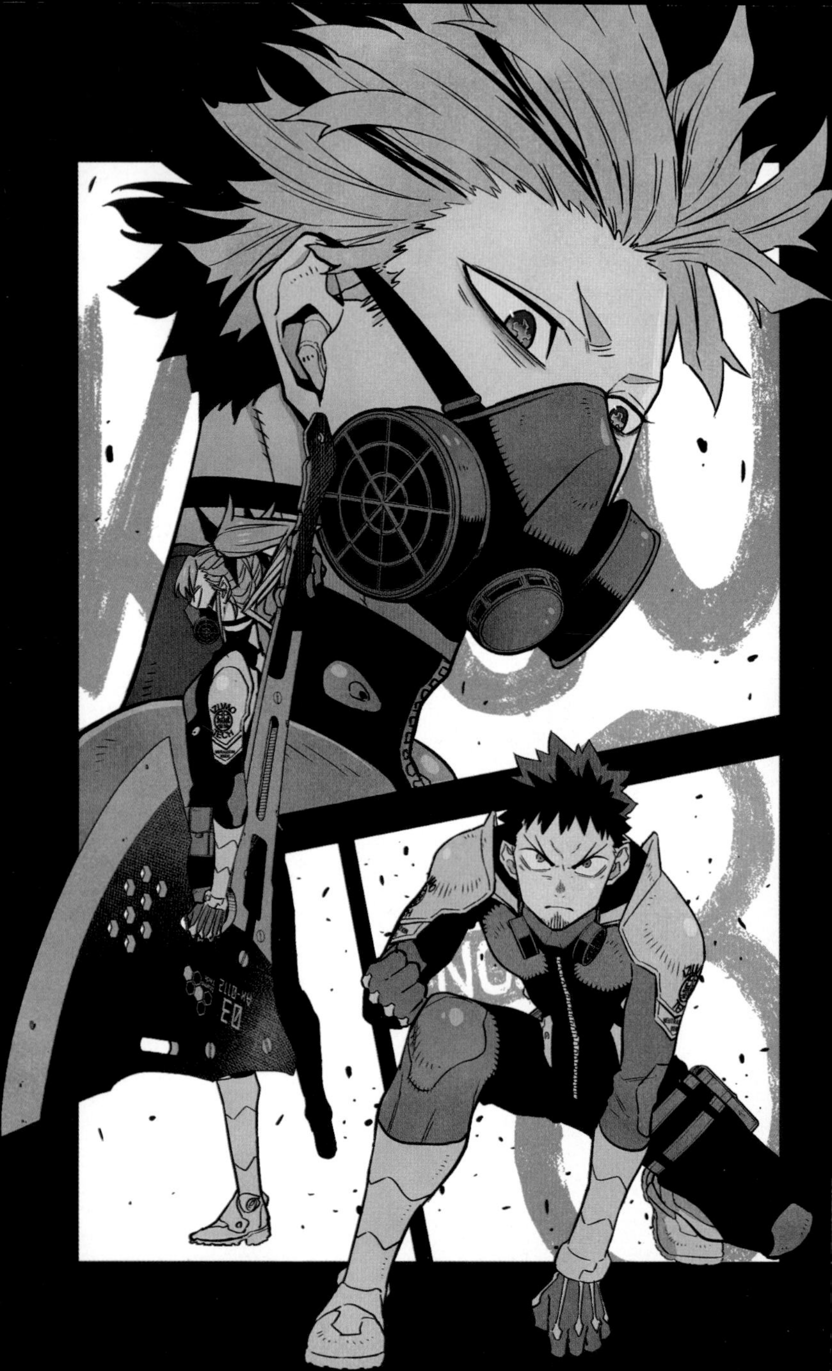

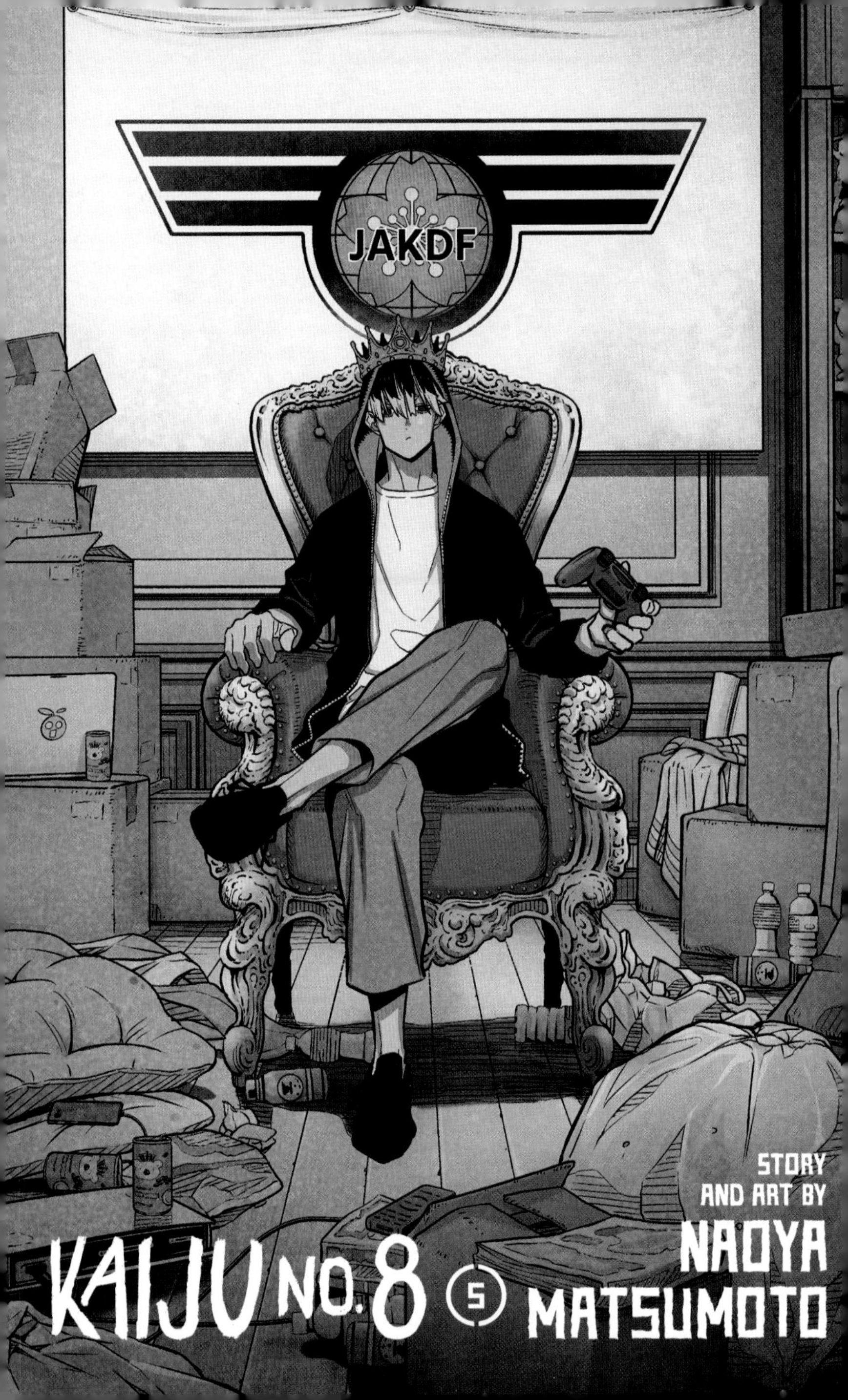
JAKDF
STORY
AND ART BY
NAOYA
MATSUMOTO
KAIJU NO.8
5

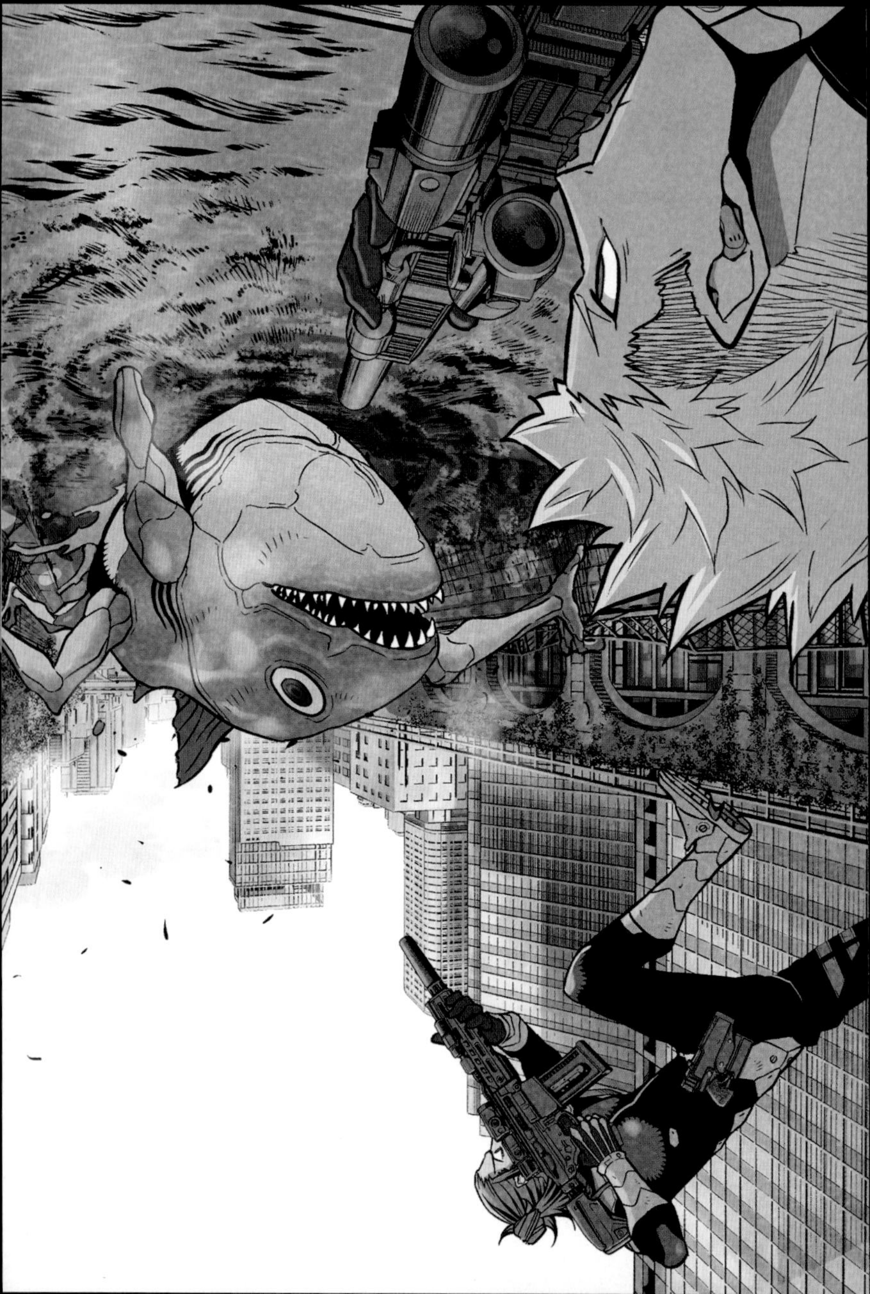